Readings in Marketing Management

Readings in Marketing Management

From the *European Journal of Marketing*

Edited by

Gordon E. Greenley
University of Birmingham

David Shipley
University of Bradford
Management Centre

McGRAW-HILL BOOK COMPANY

London · New York · St Louis · San Francisco · Auckland · Bogotá
Guatemala · Hamburg · Lisbon · Madrid · Mexico · Montreal
New Delhi · Panama · Paris · San Juan · São Paulo · Singapore
Sydney · Tokyo · Toronto

Published by
McGRAW-HILL Book Company (UK) Limited
MAIDENHEAD · BERKSHIRE · ENGLAND

British Library Cataloguing in Publication Data

Readings in marketing management from the European Journal of Marketing.
1. Marketing
I. Greenley, Gordon E.   II. Shipley, David D.   III. European Journal of Marketing
658.8   HF5415

ISBN 0-07-084183-7

Library of Congress Cataloging-in-Publication Data

Readings in marketing management from the European Journal of Marketing/edited by Gordon E. Greenley, David Shipley.
  p. cm.
  Half title: Readings in marketing management.
  Bibliography: p.
  ISBN 0-07-084183-7
1. Marketing-Management. I. Greenley, Gordon E. II. Shipley, David. III. European Journal of Marketing. IV. Title: Readings in marketing management.
HF5415.13.R3634 1988
658.8-dc19   87-26847

1 2 3 MAT 8 9 8

Printed and bound in Great Britain by M&A Thompson Ltd, Glasgow.

iv

Contents

Preface

This collection was assembled to provide a balanced complement and supplement to the commonly used marketing textbooks. Our objectives in formulating this recent (1980s) mix of articles were twofold.

First, we wanted to include readings which expand the typical textbook treatment of important topics or which approach them in an unconventional but revealing way. Among the contributions in this category are those of Foxall, Arndt, Yorke, and Espey.

Our second objective was to provide, within a single cover, a selection of articles concerned with important marketing topics which considerations of space-economy enable textbook writers to treat only skimpily or not at all. The range of these papers includes those by Avlonitis and James, Holstius, Buttle, Kasulis and Spekman, Piercy, and Carson.

There are twenty-four readings, presented in five parts. The papers in Part 1 are concerned with the underlying concepts, philosophies, and the scope of marketing. Part 2 consists of articles that address vital issues in understanding consumer and industrial customers and relevant modes of market segmentation. Part 3 addresses elements of the marketing mix. In keeping with most textbooks, it is the largest section. Unlike most textbooks, however, it gives considerable space to important topics such as product elimination, credit strategy, attitudes to advertising copy, merchandising, and channel power. Part 4 focuses on a selection of the key issues in the management of marketing: strategic and marketing planning, objectives, organisation and the recently-popularised marketing asset accounting. Finally, Part 5 addresses the selected marketing applications of services, non-profit making, small firms, and exporting.

The book will be of value to undergraduate students of business studies, management or other relevant subjects, and to graduates studying on CAM, Institute of Marketing, MBA and DMS courses. Equally, the book provides interest and instruction for managers, including marketing specialists and others.

We offer our sincere thanks to MCB University Press Ltd, the publishers of the *European Journal of Marketing,* from which this anthology was selected.

We also wish to thank the authors of the articles. Without their generous efforts and talents this collection would not have been possible.

Gordon E. Greenley
David Shipley

Part 1   Marketing Concepts

1. Marketing's Domain

by Gordon Foxall

Introduction

The development and refinement of teaching syllabi and research programmes in mature disciplines is seldom the result of the autonomous selection and decision-making of individual teachers and investigators. In marketing, as is the case in other developing sciences, both the content of educational programmes and the scope of research projects reflects the consensus of opinion within the "scientific community" of the nature of their subject matter, the most appropriate ways of examining it and the canons of judgement which should be applied in the appraisal of empirical findings. Such a consensus is similar to what Kuhn [1] calls a scientific paradigm, a shared network of research priorities, approved methodologies, terminology and perspectives. It resembles also what Thelen and Withal [2] nominate a "frame of reference" by means of which the educator or researcher "perceives and interprets events by means of a conceptual structure of generalisations or contexts, postulates about what is essential, assumptions as to what is valuable, attitudes about what is possible, and ideas about what will work effectively".

Paradigms, perspectives or frames of reference are not static except in the most moribund of disciplines: indeed, scientific progress depends significantly upon the refinement or even replacement of prevailing paradigms by viewpoints and assumptions which more accurately portray the aims and methods of members of the scientific community [3]. As such progress occurs so the consensus upon which teaching and research are established opens up innovative approaches to education and training and makes possible the extension of general research efforts into new areas of concern. The relationship between the formation of this consensus of opinion and the shape of teaching and research programmes tends to corroborate the "trickle-down hypothesis" which postulates that ideas and practices which originate in or are initially adopted by an élite group are passed on over time to less avant-garde, more imitative sections of the population [4]. The outcomes of academic debates reported in leading journals of ten or fifteen years ago frequently find an uncontested place in the syllabi and research horizons of the present. All too often, however, the contentions and arguments upon which those debates were founded are lost as the conclusions reached by their observers are enshrined in contemporary texts and reflected in the prevailing view of what constitutes acceptable, "mainstream" research.

Marketing is in the middle of such a process. During the last fifteen years, the academic journals have ceased to define marketing simply in terms of a business function which is the concern of corporate managers and to represent its scope in terms of a much wider domain of applicability. In particular, marketing management has been actively projected as relevant and applicable to non-business organisations such as churches and private colleges and to social programmes such as anti-smoking campaigns. The new thinking developed by exponents of this view has, moreover, found a place in basic and advanced marketing texts; the journal papers authored by advocates of the extended concept of marketing have appeared in anthologies; and research projects and programmes have been conceptualised and undertaken firmly within the context of the much more comprehensive domain of applicability now widely attributed to marketing [5]. In the last five years, many undergraduates and postgraduate students of marketing have begun to be taught within a much wider framework of conceptualisation and analysis than existed in the early 1970s. Such terms as "metamarketing", "social marketing", "non-business marketing" have found a place within the language of academic marketing, reflecting the new scope attributed to marketing by members of its educational and research communities.

The purpose of this article is to examine critically the extension of marketing thought suggested by these phenomena. While the so-called extended concept of marketing has impinged upon the consciousness of marketing educators and researchers, the other side of the debate has generally been ignored. Papers by those who have not embraced the broader view of marketing's domain have been published by the academic journals but have tended not to be reproduced in the anthologies aimed at the majority of teachers and students; nor has their content been reflected in the majority of texts. Furthermore, while the trend towards the broader application of marketing thought and practice has not been strongly and effectively challenged, many marketing researchers, teachers and managers confess themselves perplexed at the attempt to make marketing universally relevant by equating it with "human exchange relationships" at large. This article challenges the emerging exchange paradigm of marketing and concludes that the concept of marketing as a process of *matching* — of aligning the relationships between organisations and/or individuals — may provide a more coherent framework for any extended concept of the marketing function and marketing oriented management.

The Broadened Concept of Marketing

If critical self-assessment and a desire to contribute more effectively to the solution of human problems are evidence of a maturing discipline, then marketing shows signs of coming of age. For many people engaged in marketing education, research and management, their discipline's current phase of maturity began with the publication of the paper, "Broadening the Concept of Marketing" by Kotler and Levy [6] in 1969. Since then, the belief that perspectives and techniques which once were thought to apply only to the commercial sphere actually have much wider significance has gained ground. So pervasive are the extensions of marketing's domain based upon this broadened concept — to "social marketing" and "non-business marketing", for example — that some advocates of the reconceptualised marketing claim that its scope and relevance now include such themes as political administration, law enforcement and birth control programmes. So acceptable has the extended concept proved in the academic context of marketing (and so ineffectual the attempts of critics to re-establish marketing's traditional, narrower concerns as the legitimate domain of their subject) that social and non-business marketing are now covered by several texts and evaluative status reports and have found a place in the marketing curriculum. Administrators of social programmes, health campaigns and other non-business projects have also shown a clear willingness to conceptualise their objectives and endeavours in terms derived from the marketing philosophy and to use its derivative techniques [7]. The extended concept of marketing has clearly emerged over the last 15 years as an idea whose time has come.

The Basis of the Extended Concept

The broadening of an academic discipline which was, until recently, generally understood to be exclusively concerned with the advancement of corporate objectives, to include such activities and causes as furthering the arts in society, encouraging abstinence from tobacco and the elimination of refined sugar from the national diet, requires sound redefinition of the nature and scope of that discipline. Parallel with the development of social and non-business marketing, there has been an attempt by some marketing academics to rationalise the extension of marketing's domain by offering a "generic" account of the marketing perspective. In particular, this intellectual process has resulted in the belief that marketing is concerned essentially with human exchange relationships, that its subject matter is found wherever such exchanges occur, in short that "marketing=exchange" and "exchange=marketing" [8]. A measure of their success in establishing this definition of the nature and scope of marketing lies in its acceptance by many authors of standard, managerially-oriented textbooks of marketing. Kotler [9] writes, for instance, that "marketing is human activity directed at satisfying needs and wants through exchange processes". Two other American authors, Kerin and Peterson [10] also exemplify this trend by opening their text/case-book with the observation that: "It is generally accepted that marketing is the process of facilitating mutually-beneficial exchange relationships between entities". In a recent British text, Oliver [11] states that: "Marketing concerns market exchange processes, and organisations' marketing efforts are designed to facilitate these exchanges". Finally, Baker [12], writes that, in essence "the marketing concept is concerned with exchange relationships" and states that in his opinion, "this is the essence of marketing — a mutually-satisfying exchange relationship . . . Marketing is a process of exchange between individuals and/or organisations which is concluded to the mutual benefit and satisfaction of the parties".

There can be no argument with the proposition that marketing involves exchange: its traditional and undisputed domain certainly includes mutually-acceptable exchanges which are effected by means of pecuniary markets. A problem may arise, however, in response to the assertion that marketing is not concerned with pecuniary exchange alone but embraces a whole range of human exchange relationships which are unrelated to marketing's traditional concerns. Yet the thinking upon which the extended concept is based and by which it has been justified in the marketing literature leads one to the conclusion that exchange, whenever it occurs, is marketing and is, therefore, part of the subject matter of a discipline whose domain has been conventionally limited to the concerns of business managers and the consumers of their economic products and services.

Universal Application
This conclusion has, moreover, been explicitly drawn by advocates of the broadened concept of marketing. Kotler and Levy's seminal definition of the marketing function transcends corporate concerns by suggesting that marketing management is a central requirement of publicly-exposed organisations generally: marketing, they write, "is that part of the organisation that can keep in constant touch with the organisation's consumers, read their needs, develop 'products' that meet these needs, and build a programme of communication to express the organisation's purposes" [13]. In his "generic concept of Marketing" Kotler [14] casts marketing as "specifically concerned with how transactions are created, stimulated, facilitated and valued" and defines a transaction as an "exchange of values between two parties". So crucial is this idea of transaction that he refers to it as marketing's "core concept". This generic understanding of marketing's domain does much more than simply free marketing studies from an exclusive preoccupation with the world of business management: it broadens its scope well beyond the corporate sphere to include virtually all facets of human activity within their remit. Bagozzi [15] refers to marketing in this vein as "a general function of universal applicability. It is the discipline of exchange behaviour, and it deals with problems related to this behaviour." This sentiment is echoed and reinforced by Levy [16] who goes to some lengths to stress that limited definitions of marketing cannot do justice to its natural relevance and capacity.

"It seems important to insist on the issue of universal applicability, mainly because there seems no adequately consistent way to define marketing that limits it short of universality. What is a marketing exchange as different from any other exchange? Some try to restrict marketing to the exchange of money for products, a distinction which fails immediately with consideration of markets in which money is exchanged for money, products for products, and money or products are exchanged for services. Then is there any way to limit which moneys, products or services will be considered elements of marketing exchange, and which will not? . . . In a world in which there is no truly free air . . . in which all exchanges are economic choices and all are exchanges of satisfactions, there can be no nonmarketing exchanges. What is being exchanged may sometimes be hard to analyse, but marketing cannot be limited to being the science of *simple* exchanges."

There is need to appraise the quality of the argument which has been advanced in favour of the universally-applicable concept of marketing and to judge its alleged justification as the basis of marketing education, research and managerial practice. If this novel concept is of broader relevance than to corporate marketing alone, then its intellectual underpinnings must be well-established, for the teaching, investigation and practice based upon it will founder should it prove unreliable. If marketing is genuinely of universal application, failure to appreciate its true domain represents a new and dangerous form of marketing myopia. In any case, it is important that marketing academics and practitioners in general take part in the debate which is underway rather than allow any new thinking merely to enter the consensus of marketing opinion unquestioned and unevaluated. Later sections of this article examine in some detail (i) the case for including the furtherance of ideas and causes ("social marketing") and the client-oriented management of non-business organisations as components of marketing's domain, and (ii) whether *exchange* comprises a logical conceptual foundation for the definition of marketing. Before these themes are addressed, however, the nature of the marketing function and of marketing-oriented management require clarification.

Marketing: Function and Orientation

While it is difficult to formulate an accurate definition of marketing which is both complete and concise, it clearly has to do with relationships between producers and consumers. Members of a subsistence economy hardly need such relationships but economic and social systems based on exchange develop, of necessity, formal arrangements for the transfer of information among buyers and suppliers and for the geographical distribution of goods and services. The more complex the relationships involved in such exchange, the greater is the need for formal arrangements for physical distribution, marketing communications, pricing and product development. Exchange based on simple barter may require only very basic formalisation of marketing relationships but, with the complexities introduced by increasing numbers of participants and products, even this system requires the establishment of a commonly-accepted medium of exchange; and further complexity facilitates the development of exchange relationships based on pecuniary markets. Societies in which the division of labour is thoroughly developed, be they characterised by centralised or decentralised decision-making, tend to rely extensively on the exchanges made possible by such markets.

The impetus for the systematic study of the functional, marketing relationships derives also from their tendency towards complexity in advanced economies and societies. In order that the network of market-based inter-relationships, expectations, provisions, reactions and valuations which is a feature of marketing exchange may be made more effective, its contents and mode of functioning must be more accurately perceived and understood. Analysis of the marketing functions which link producers and consumers — i.e., of the creation and operation of the marketing mix and buyers' reactions to it — has thriven in all types of economic system. Despite their obvious differences of form and intent, even the most contrasting "capitalist" and "socialised" societies possess a large stake in encouraging the precise and valid comprehension of the marketing functions which derive from the four Ps: product, price, promotion and place.

Within more decentralised systems, however, the analysis of marketing behaviour has an additional dimension which stems from the greater frequency of marketing-oriented management encountered in such economies. Marketing-oriented management is not only the dominant approach to corporate management in decentralised economies, it is clearly the approach which is prescribed by the majority of marketing thinkers and practitioners. But, while marketing-orientation may be the predominant philosophy underlying the fulfilment of basic marketing functions in such economies, it is to be distinguished from the management of the marketing *functions* themselves. The history of marketing thought and practice, as elucidated by such writers as Bartels [17] and King [18], lend support to this distinction between *marketing*, which embraces a set of managerial functions which are in all but the most primitive economic systems, and *marketing-oriented management* which is the way in which these functions are discharged in many societies where economic decision-making is decentralised, notably Western industrial societies. Many definitions of marketing and of the concept of marketing-oriented management bring out this distinction. For example, Converse, *et al.*[19] speak of *marketing* as "the performance of business activities that direct the flow of goods and services from producer to consumer . . . Marketing moves goods from place to place, stores them, and effects changes in ownership by buying and selling them . . . Marketing consists of the activities of buying, selling, transporting and storing goods." Bartels [20] writes that: "Marketing is the process whereby society, to supply its consumption needs, evolves distributive systems composed of participants, who . . . create the transactions or flows which resolve market separations and result in exchange and consumption."

While centralised and decentralised economies must both make arrangements for the fulfilment of these functions, the latter tend to employ a style of marketing management founded upon consumer-orientation. The marketing concept which guides this managerial style assumes an approach which is quite distinct from the fulfilment of marketing functions in most centralised societies. The marketing concept is that "managerial philosophy is concerned with the mobilisation, utilisation, and control of total corporate effort for the purpose of helping consumers solve selected problems in a way compatible with planned enhancement of the profit position of the firm" [21]. Marketing and marketing-orientation are so intertwined in the managerial thought and action of Western industrial economies that their marketing authors often make the prescribed managerial style implicit in their definitons of marketing itself. The Institute of Marketing [22] defines marketing as "the management process which identifies, anticipates and supplies customer requirements efficiently, and profitably", a statement which presupposes customer-orientation in the fulfilment of marketing functions. Chisnall [23] notes that "marketing as a separate, identifiable function of management has evolved from the business philosophy which recognises the importance of the customer to the success of the business". However, the author who most closely integrates marketing and consumer-oriented management is Drucker [24] who writes that:

> "*True* marketing starts . . . with the customers, their demographics, realities, needs and values. It does not ask, 'What do we want to sell?' It asks, 'What does the customer want to buy?' It does not say, 'This is what our product or service does.' It says, 'These are the satisfactions the customer looks for.'"

Marketing-Oriented Management
That definitions of marketing are culture-bound is hardly surprising but the distinc-

tion between *marketing* as a common, human, economic activity and *marketing-oriented management* as an approach to marketing under particular circumstances is important to the correct identification of marketing's domain. Marketing-orientation is the latest in a series of business perspectives: production-orientation, sales-management-orientation and marketing-orientation have provided a sequence of managerial styles, each suited to, and appropriate for, a given set of environmental conditions. Thus, *production-orientation* is a valid and predictable response to conditions of scarcity, where demand exceeds supply either throughout an economy or in a discrete product-market; consumers' discretionary income is likely, under such circumstances, to be small. Although it is common to find that production-orientation is strongly criticised in the marketing literature, it *may* be a legitimate response to prevailing conditions. While it deserves censure when it represents no more than the marketing myopia described by Levitt [25], it is a predictable response among those companies which are temporarily sheltered from the vicissitudes of the marketplace by, for example, patent rights, monopoly positions or similarly myopic competitors. As Baker [26] points out, "the much-despised production orientation with its emphasis upon manufacturing and volume of output may be the most appropriate to conditions of chronic under-supply" or, it may be added to *any* conditions which do not compel a more customer-oriented marketing outlook.

Similarly, *sales-oriented management* is the requisite response to rather more affluent circumstances, in which there are fewer constraints on production and an understanding that high levels of sales volume are likely to contribute effectively to the attainment of corporate financial objectives. *Marketing-orientation* is itself no more than an appropriate response to a given market structure: high levels of intra-industrial competition, the capacity for supply to exceed demand and consumer affluence as manifested in a large measure of discretionary spending. The adoption and implementation of the marketing concept are by no means the altruistic acts implied by some marketing textbooks: they derive from the recognition that, under appropriate conditions, a particular form of attention to customer requirements is essential if the goals of the producer are to be achieved. Decentralised economies evince marketing-orientation as their characteristic managerial mode simply because they provide the structural conditions which compel this managerial mode. Such conditions do not characterise centralised economic systems and nor does customer-oriented marketing. But, even within privatised, decentralised economies, the conditions which make marketing-orientation an appropriate response are far from universally encountered. This observation, fundamental as it is to the study of marketing, raises a number of issues in connection with delineation of the legitimate domain of marketing-oriented management.

Business and Non-Business Marketing
Figure 1 presents a typology of organisations, all of which are assumed by Kotler [27] to be capable of adopting a marketing-oriented approach to their management and thus of implementing fully integrated marketing mix strategies. The dimensions on which institutions are categorised are:

(1) ownership and control, which may be private or public; and
(2) organisational purpose, which may be for profit or not-for-profit.

Figure 1. The Scope of Marketing (after Kotler)

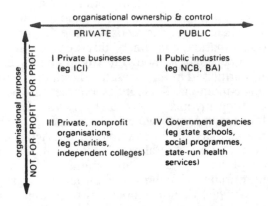

Marketing management has traditionally been a concern of type I organisations, namely private businesses, and of certain type II bodies such as nationalised industries. Organisations of types III and IV may be involved in straightforward, business marketing in so far as they operate within pecuniary markets and within the structural constraints which correspond to a marketing-oriented style of administration. Independent colleges which are in competition with other education institutions for scarce students are capable of implementing fully-consumer-oriented management modes, for instance, as are state-run hospitals which also cater for private patients who might choose other independent medical facilities.

But the advocates of the "exchange = marketing" paradigm go further than this. Non-business organisations, they argue, are capable of planning and implementing a comprehensively marketing-oriented approach to the primary sphere of their activities: police departments, private universities, charities and public hospitals are organisations which are commonly cited as able to pursue marketing-oriented management in spite of being non-business and in spite of not operating through pecuniary markets. The first question which those who would broaden the marketing concept to make it relevant to non-business activities must face is: *Can non-business organisations be predicted to show consistent marketing-oriented management in the absence of the structural conditions which, in the business sphere, compel and legitimise long-term consumer-orientation?*

For many organisations of type II a large degree of marketing-orientation is both possible and predictable. Nationalised undertakings, public utilities, and the like are often subject to severe competition in the markets they serve; their customers frequently enjoy the opportunity to select other suppliers; and their political supervisors usually impose upon them economic constraints. They do not differ from type I organisations in that both face the structural economic conditions with which a marketing-oriented approach is associated. Their consumer-centred outlook stems not from managerial philanthropy or political fashion but from the need to react to the nature of the markets in which they operate by emphasising consumer-oriented management. Even in the case of type II organisations, however, the capacity to implement this philosophy to the full may be questioned. Nationalised industries do not face the rigours of the marketplace to the same extent as many private firms and their ability to allow the business they are in to be determined by buyers rather than by politicians is often severely constrained. Marketing-orientation is far less predictable in the case of organisations of types III and IV, however. The analysis presented earlier in this article leads to the conclusion that genuine and lasting marketing-orientation is unlikely in these cases simply because such organisations rarely encounter the conditions which normally compel it. Naturally, the officers of such organisations may display consumer-orientation for many reasons — altruism, the pleasure of being of service, and so on. But sustained consumer-orientation is not at all predictable in these circumstances as it is in the case of competitive businesses.

Social Marketing

Nor is consistent consumer-orientation the logical expectation suggested by the structural environment in which much so-called social marketing occurs. Social marketing — "the design, implementation, and control of programmes seeking to increase the acceptability of a social idea, cause, or practice in a target group" [28] — may be undertaken by any of the four types of organisations depicted in Figure 1: private airlines may encourage flying as a mode of transportation, a nationalised coal industry may exhort householders to use open fires in their homes, public hospitals may support anti-smoking campaigns and private colleges may disseminate the value of higher education. Generic advertising is a well-known means by which commercial organisations, often acting collectively, attempt to increase the demand for their product class or, in terms derived from the theory of social marketing, for the general service offered by that product class.

Most social marketing projects discussed and documented in the marketing literature in the years since the emergence of the broadened concept concern organisations of types III and IV, however; typically they invoke state-run health or family planning campaigns, educational programmes and environmental preservation projects. Social marketing emerges from the accounts provided by this literature as an activity which is more likely than not to be undertaken by organisations which face radically different market conditions from those usually encountered by type I and type II organisations. Notably, almost all social marketing agencies (and many organisations which are described as engaging in non-business marketing) face either unlimited demand for their services (e.g., social work agencies) or a considerable excess of demand over supply (e.g., anti-smoking campaigns). They are not usually in competition with one another and their clients are thus prevented from exercising sovereignty by turning to alternative sources of supply. Such organisations are unlikely to pursue the integrative, co-ordinated style of marketing management which is a feature of the typical marketing-oriented business firm. Rather, judged according to the market conditions in which they operate, they are likely to embrace a production-oriented approach. This is not to argue that organisations are not or cannot be accommodated to their clients to any degree for the term "production orientation" itself suggests a managerial style which corresponds to customers' requirements and discretion while implying that these requirements and their freedom to exercise choice are rather limited. Baker [29], as noted, points out that the derogatory use of the term "production orientation" is not always justified: Henry Ford's restriction of his customers' choice to *black* Model Ts is often cited as evidence of his heinous production-orientation but it would surely have been both unnecessary and unreasonable of him to adopt a more diversified product policy. Similarly, it is unreasonable to expect social agencies such as those which are typically described as undertaking social marketing to adopt a managerial mode which is more appropriate for private firms operating under competitive market conditions. The former certainly need to be accommodated to their clients in ways suggested by the professional code of their personnel but to describe their work in terms of the managerial approach known as marketing-orientation is not necessarily consistent with this.

Social Marketing or Social Communication?
While many organisations of type III and IV are unlikely to pursue *marketing-orientation*, they may nevertheless undertake one or more of the *marketing functions* pursued by conventional commercial organisations. Indeed, a major contribution of those who have augmented the concept of marketing has been the recognition that the techniques involved in customer research, strategic planning, marketing mix management and marketing control are applicable to a wider range of organisations than has been traditionally assumed. However, a second question for advocates of the broadened marketing concept stems from the foregoing analysis of the types of organisations for which marketing is a suitable managerial perspective: *Are type III and type IV organisations able to employ the entire marketing mix and the full repertoire of associated managerial techniques in the same customer-oriented manner as other organisations?*

It is not feasible to review in this article all of the reports of social and non-business marketing available. However, the cases cited by Fox and Kotler [30] in a recent status report of social marketing's first decade support the view that the answer to this question must be in the negative. These authors claim that social marketing is especially appropriate in three situations: (i) when there is a need to disseminate new information and practices, such as novel dietary habits; (ii) when *countermarketing* is required, for instance, to inform third-world mothers of the advantages of breastfeeding as opposed to the use of strongly-advertised branded baby foods; and (iii) when it is necessary to "move people from intention to action", e.g., in the case of a local food shortage. These situations appear to require standard marketing communication or social communication rather than the comprehensively integrated and co-ordinated use of the whole marketing mix. This impression is, moreover, strengthened by consideration of the particular instances of social marketing described by Fox and Kotler.

In one instance, the cause of family planning was advanced in a third-world country by what can only be described as selected marketing techniques. Massively-subsidised contraceptives appear to have been marketed much as any other product would be promoted among potential users who were ignorant or suspicious of its effects. In another case, Fox and Kotler describe a health campaign directed towards the prevention of heart disease as "fundamentally a sophisticated use of social communication". Although this was skilfully accomplished — notably by means of the establishment of sound objectives, segmentation analysis and campaign evaluation —it could be more accurately described as extremely effective social advertising rather than integrated marketing management. Finally, of the six health improvement programmes which these authors describe only briefly, five are, in essence, social communications exercises and the other is the extension of a medical screening programme which is described as the use of "new [distribution] channels".

The third question posed by this article is: *May some of the activities which are described as social marketing actually comprise no more than the stimulation of generic demand?* A bicycle manufacturer who co-sponsors a generic advertising campaign which extols the merits of pollution-free travel might be said by advocates of the broadened marketing concept to be engaged in social marketing. Is it clear, however, that he is doing anything other than conventionally increasing the demand for his highly-tangible product? In the example of family planning which has been briefly noted, so-called social marketing appears to represent no more than traditional commercial marketing in peculiar circumstances. The product happened to be highly valued by the authorities who subsidised it on a grand scale but the campaign involved, predominantly, the use of mass communications and local promotions in support of a virtually free good. Can this be genuinely considered an example of *social marketing*, given all that is implied by that terminology?

The fourth question is closely related: *Does not so-called social marketing tend to employ in most cases a single element of the marketing mix, usually advertising?* The use of marketing communications techniques in an effective manner, based on sound research, segmentation analysis, the setting of feasible, measurable objectives and subject to appropriate appraisal and control, is to be welcomed. It is certainly preferable by far to the often all-too-crude social advertising which is still widely-encountered. But the impression given by Fox and Kotler's examples is not one of comprehensive, integrated marketing mix management nor of complete client-orientation. Rather, it is entirely consistent with the fundamental thesis advanced in this article to the effect that the domain of marketing-oriented management is limited by its responsive nature and is considerably narrower than the marketing literature has, of late, come to claim. Far from being a universally-applicable managerial style, marketing-orientation is an appropriate response to conditions which are encountered only *comparatively* infrequently.

Marketing and Exchange Revisited

In view of this reasoning, it is appropriate that the exchange paradigm introduced earlier be critically reconsidered. There can be no doubt that the conventional domain of marketing involves exchange. As has been pointed out, pecuniary markets rely directly upon exchange processes. Perhaps organisations which operate in such markets can be found in every category delineated in Figure 1. There are many aspects of non-business and social marketing, however, which not only involve no pecuniary exchange but, given the common definition of the word, no exchange at all. Charity fund-raising, for example involves financial transfer but hardly exchange in the dictionary sense of "giving one thing and receiving another in its place". The donor may experience psychological relief or reward but the notion of exchange has no place in this. Similarly, in an anti-smoking campaign, what is exchanged and for what? Who is the consumer and of what? To ascribe exchange to these situations, other than in terms of the straightforward purchase of a service if a price or fee is charged, is to distort the meaning of "exchange". Even the components of an exchange listed by Kotler [31] as (i) two parties, each of whom (ii) has something valued by the other, (iii) which can be communicated and delivered, (iv) under conditions of voluntary acceptance, do not appear to be entirely present in many non-business and social marketing contexts.

In an attempt to rationalise their acceptance of the exchange = marketing paradigm, some writers have offered more elaborate definitions of exchange. Bagozzi [32], for example, puts forward a typology of exchange relationships which relegates the commonplace dictionary definition quoted above to the status of "restricted" exchange. Marketing, he argues, is concerned with "generalised" and "complex" exchanges such as those which putatively link an advertising agency with a member of a television programme's audience (see Figure 2). It is difficult to imagine how this line of marketing thought can be reconciled with the fundamental principle upon which customer-oriented management rests, namely consumer sovereignty. Try as one might, however, it is impossible to find room for this principle in examples of social marketing provided by even the ablest exponents of the new paradigm. Consider the following, which Bagozzi [33] reports as a "typical social marketing exchange".

> "Society authorises government — through its votes and tax payments — to provide needed social services such as welfare. In return, the members of society receive social insurance against common human maladies. Government, in turn, pays the salaries of social workers, giving them the authority to provide social services, and so on. It also distributes welfare payments directly to the needy."

The relationships here rule out all of the principles upon which marketing-oriented management is founded: the "customer" has no discretion because he has no choice of supply; he cannot withdraw his taxes; nor is he able to resist the legally-enforced ministrations of social workers. It is difficult to perceive *exchange* relationships in the example described here, let alone identify the freely-entered, invariably mutually-beneficial transactions which are the essence of modern marketing.

If relationships such as these give little if any indication of a recognisable role for consumers, they fail also to suggest solutions to fundamental managerial questions about the basic issues which any economic system must resolve and, according to Samuelson [34], what to produce, how much to produce and for whom to produce. The firm is also faced with these choices. However, in the absence of a recognisable market exchange process, its managers cannot formulate objectives and control

Figure 2. Bagozzi's Example of Complex, Circulate Exchange

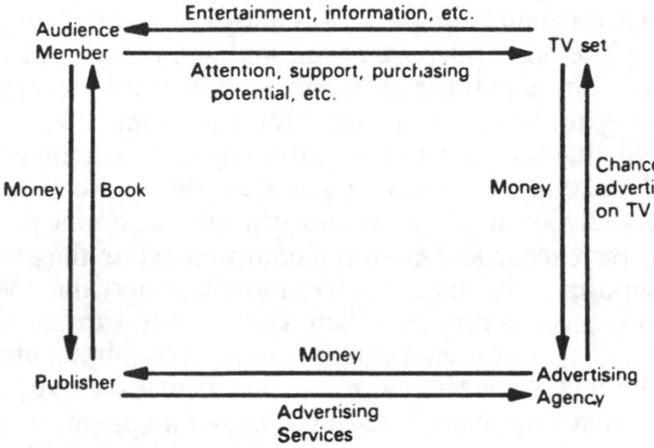

Source: Adapted from Bagozzi, R., "Marketing as Exchange", *Journal of Marketing*, Vol. 39 No. 4, 1975, pp. 32-9.

criteria by reference to the demand for their services. If governments rather than consumers determine the amount which will be spent on particular services, the market ceases to have a legitimate role in signalling opportunities or guiding the allocation of limited resources among competing projects. Social marketing, which confuses relationships with exchanges, renders the marketplace redundant; it has no place for consumers' choice or for the functions of a market mechanism. In spite of the considerable virtues of employing relevant marketing managerial techniques in the improvement of the efficiency and effectiveness of extra-business organisations — and this article is by no means an attempt to argue against those virtues — there are significant conceptual difficulties in the attempt to rationalise this trend by incorporating it in a perspective which purports to represent a broadened concept of the marketing-oriented management encountered in competitive industries. Nor is it easy to follow the logic of arguments which attempt to justify this perspective on the basis of the universal relevance and applicability of exchange relationships.

The Domain of Marketing
Perhaps it is no accident that standard marketing texts, though they open with definitions of marketing which portray it as a universally-pervasive activity, concentrate nevertheless upon the traditional sphere of business marketing. However, there has emerged a strong desire to use the proven tools of business marketing more widely. More than this, the possibility of so doing has been demonstrated and, whatever the conceptual difficulties inherent in the exchange paradigm, it remains necessary to find a common thread which logically connects the various components of the extended marketing domain. The final question for those who have argued for a reconceptualised marketing is: *Can an alternative concept to that of exchange be found in order to provide a link between business and extra-business marketing?*

It may be that the required concept is that of matching. The view that matching is the appropriate synonym for marketing has been developed within the functional study of distribution. Thus, McAmmon and Little [35] state that "the concept that marketing is essentially a 'matching' process is a logical point of origin for channel decision-making ... The basic purpose of marketing, in this context, is to 'match' supply and demand." These authors go on to demonstrate, through the work of such classic marketing authors as Alderson [36], Clark and Clark [37] and Vaile, Grether and Cox [38], that the equation of marketing with matching has a long and consistent history. Marketing as matching also harmonises well with the view expressed by Newman [39] that "marketing as a social and economic process becomes significant as one which intervenes between and *synchronises* the processes of production and consumption". Matching involves the integrated and co-ordinated use of the entire marketing mix in a process which is directed towards achieving the correspondence between corporate offerings and consumer requirements which is at the heart of marketing-oriented management, as several recent texts have pointed out [40].

An advantage of "matching" over "exchange" is that it appears not to require the same intellectual contortions in order that it may be generalised from business to extra-business activities. The meaning of "matching" is straightforward; for instance, its dictionary definition renders it as "showing proper similarity or correspondence", while *well-matched* refers to "being equal or fit to be pitted against each other or united, corresponding". Matching properly expresses the intentions of both functional marketing and marketing-oriented management, though these remain conceptually distinct.

Summary and Conclusions
The nature of extra-business marketing is such that it is likely to involve the use of elements of the marketing mix rather than comprehensive and integrated marketing-oriented management necessary for the effective pursuit of business marketing in competitive industries. This fact has implications for the extension of the marketing concept. The concept of "exchange" has severe defects as a means of describing marketing's new domain — especially in view of its apparent extension of marketing to encompass all human exchange relationships. As yet there is nothing to suggest that marketing scientists are capable of making a contribution to the study of, say, family relationships or crime prevention. Yet these are among the facets of human behaviour which *some* prominent marketing theorists have declared to constitute marketing's domain. The concept of exchange is, moreover, seriously distorted when applied to many of the managerial problems described as social or non-business marketing. "Matching", circumscribed by the observations governing the effective domain of marketing-oriented management which have been re-emphasised in this article, may not justify so wide a conceptual framework as the adherents of the exchange paradigm would like. But matching, or another concept which better expresses and delineates marketing's domain, must surely help resolve the confusion of those marketing educators who have been driven to ask: "What brand of marketing should we market?" [41].

References

1. Kuhn, T. S., *The Structure of Scientific Revolutions*, Chicago, Chicago University Press, 1970.

2. Thelen, H. and Withal, J., "Three Frames of Reference", *Human Relations*, April, 1949.

3. Kuhn, T. S., "The Function of Dogma in Scientific Research", in *Scientific Change*, A. C. Crombie, (ed.), London, Heinemann, 1963, pp. 347-69.

4. For example, Barber, B. and Lobel, L. S., "Fashions in Women's Clothes and the American Social System", *Social Forces*, Vol. 31, No. 4, 1952, pp. 124-31; Fallers, L. A., "A Note on the Trickle Effect", *Public Opinion Quarterly*, Vol. 18, No. 4, 1954, pp. 314-21; Simmel, G., "Fashion", *American Journal of Sociology*, Vol. 62, No. 3, 1957, pp. 541-58. As a general approach to the stratified diffusion of innovations, the trickle down theory has been criticised by King, C. W., "Fashion Adoption: A Rebuttal to the 'Trickle Down' Theory", *Proceedings of the American Marketing Association*, Chicago, AMA, 1963, pp. 108-25.

5. For example, Enis, B. M. and Cox, K. K. (eds.), *Marketing Classics: A Selection of Influential Articles*, Boston, Mass., Allyn and Bacon, 1981 — see Part 1, "Marketing Philosophy". See also [7] and [8] below.

6. Kotler, P. and Levy, S. J., "Broadening the Concept of Marketing", *Journal of Marketing*, Vol. 33, No. 1, 1969, pp. 10-15.

7. Kotler, P., *Marketing for Nonprofit Organisations*, Englewood Cliffs, NJ, Prentice-Hall, 1975; "Strategies for introducing marketing in nonprofit organisations", *Journal of Marketing*, Vol. 43, No. 1, 1979, pp. 37-44; Montana, P. J., (ed.), *Marketing in Nonprofit Organisations*, New York, Amcom, 1979; Fox, K., and Kotler, P., "The Marketing of Social Causes: the first 10 years", *Journal of Marketing*, Vol. 44, No. 3, 1980, pp. 24-33; Bloom, P. N., and Novelli, W. D., "Problems and Challenges in Social Marketing", *Journal of Marketing*, Vol. 45, No. 2, 1981, pp. 79-88, *JMRS* special issue.

8. Dawson, L. M., "Marketing Science in the Age of Aquarius", *Journal of Marketing*, Vol. 35, No. 3, 1971, pp. 66-72; Kaldor, A. G., "Imbricative Marketing", *Journal of Marketing*, Vol. 35, No. 2, 1971, pp. 19-25; Hunt, S. D., "The Morphology of Theory and the General Theory of Marketing", *Journal of Marketing*, Vol. 35, No. 3, 1971, pp. 65-8; "The Nature and Scope of Marketing", *Journal of Marketing*, Vol. 40, No. 3, 1976, pp. 17-28; Kotler, P., "Metamarketing: The Furthering of Organisations, Persons, Places and Causes", *Marketing Forum*, July-August, 1970, pp. 13-23; "A Generic Concept of Marketing", *Journal of Marketing*, Vol. 36, No. 2, 1972, pp. 46-54; Kotler, P., and Zaltman, G., "Social Marketing", *Journal of Marketing*, Vol. 35, No. 3, 1972, pp. 3-12; Bagozzi, R. P., "Marketing as an Organised Behavioural System of Exchange", *Journal of Marketing*, Vol. 38, No. 4, 1974, pp. 77-81; "Marketing as Exchange", *Journal of Marketing*, Vol. 39, No. 4, 1975, pp. 32-9; Bartels, R., "The Identity Crisis in Marketing", *Journal of Marketing*, Vol. 38, No. 4, 1974, pp. 74-80; Arndt, J., "How Broad Should the Marketing Concept Be?", *Journal of Marketing*, Vol. 42, No. 1, 1978, pp. 101-3; Levy, S. J., "Marcology 101 or the Domain of Marketing", in *Marketing Management and Administrative Action*, Britt, S. H. and Boyd, H. W., (eds.), New York, McGraw-Hill, 1978.

9. Kotler, P., *Marketing Management: Analysis, Planning and Control*, Englewood Cliffs, NJ, Prentice-Hall, 1980, p. 19.

10. Kerin, R. A. and Peterson, R. A., *Strategic Marketing Problems*, Boston, Mass., Allyn and Bacon, 1981, p. 1.

11. Oliver, G., *Marketing Today*, London, Prentice-Hall, 1980, p. 10.

12. Baker, M. J., *Marketing: An Introductory Text*, London, Macmillan, 1979, pp. 336-7; see also Baker, M. J. (ed.), *Marketing : Theory and Practice*, London, Macmillan, 1976, Chapter 1.

13. Kotler, P., and Levy, S. J., *op. cit.*

14. Kotler, P., *op. cit.*

15. Bagozzi, R. P., "Marketing as Exchange", *op. cit.*, p. 39.

16. Levy, S. J., "Marcology 101", *op. cit.*

17. Bartels, R., *The Development of Marketing Thought*, New York, Irwin, 1962.

18. King, R. L., "The Marketing Concept", in Schwartz, G. (ed.), *Science in Marketing*, New York,

Wiley, 1965, pp. 70-97.

19. Converse, P., *et al., Elements of Marketing,* Englewood Cliffs, NJ, Prentice-Hall, 1965.

20. Bartels, R., "The General Theory of Marketing", *Journal of Marketing,* Vol. 32, No. 1, 1968, pp. 29-33.

21. King, R. L., "The Marketing Concept", *op. cit.,* p. 85.

22. Institute of Marketing, *Quarterly Review of Marketing,* any issue.

23. Chisnall, P., *Marketing: A Behavioural Analysis,* London, McGraw-Hill, 1975, p. 1.

24. Drucker, P. F., *Management,* London, Pan, 1979, p. 59.

25. Levitt, T., "Marketing Myopia", *Harvard Business Review,* July-August, 1960.

26. Baker, M. J., *Marketing: Theory and Practice, op. cit.,* pp. 4-9.

27. Kotler, P., *Marketing Management, op. cit.,* p. 682.

28. *Ibid.,* p. 20.

29. Baker, M. J., *Marketing: Theory and Practice, op. cit.,* p.9.

30. Fox, K., and Kotler, P., *passim.*

31. Kotler, P., *Marketing Management, op. cit.,* p. 20.

32. Bagozzi, R. P., "Marketing as Exchange", *op. cit.,* pp. 38-9.

33. *Ibid.*

34. Samuelson, P. A., *Economics, op. cit.*

35. McAmmon, B. O., and Little, R. W., "Marketing Channels", in Schwartz, (ed.), *op. cit.,* pp. 356-8.

36. Alderson, W., *Marketing Behaviour and Executive Action,* Homewood, Illinois, Irwin, 1957.

37. Clark, F. E., and Clark, C. P., *Principles of Marketing,* New York, Macmillan, 1942.

38. Vaile, R. S., *et al., Marketing in the American Economy,* New York, Ronald Press, 1944.

39. Newman, J. W., "Marketing Science and the Marketing Professor", in Schwartz (ed.), *op. cit.,* p. 34.

40. For example, Christopher, M., *et al., Effective Marketing Management,* Aldershot, Gower, 1981; Foxall, G. R., *Strategic Marketing Management,* London, Croom Helm, and New York, Wiley, 1981.

41. Mason, J., "What Brand of Marketing Should We Market?", *Proceedings of the Annual Conference of the Marketing Education Group,* 1978, pp. 407-22. See also: Arndt, J., "The Conceptual Domain of Marketing", *European Journal of Marketing,* Vol. 16, No. 1, 1982, pp. 27-35. A more radical approach to paradigm change which appears to harmonise generally with that presented in this article has been put forward by Gordon Wills in the monograph "Customer Policy as an Alternative Orientation to Marketing Simple", (*European Journal of Marketing,* Vol. 16, No. 4, 1982, pp. 1-26.) Professor Wills's paper raises interesting empirical questions whose resolution will determine the extent to which the idea that marketing is synonymous with *matching* can be accommodated within the customer policy paradigm.

2. Delineating the Boundaries of Marketing

by Charles L. Martin

Much has been written during the past two decades in an attempt to develop a conceptual framework of marketing. Academicians have searched for a *single* theory of marketing, contemplated the proper scope of marketing, and have struggled to define marketing. Marketing practitioners have assumed a greater number of responsibilities in the organisation and have demonstrated that there is more to marketing than selling and physical distribution. Despite the evolution of marketing thought, there is still no clear consensus as to marketing's definition nor to marketing's boundaries — although both academicians and practitioners recognise the pervasiveness of marketing phenomena.

Therefore, the purpose of this article is threefold. First, a brief review of the scope of marketing will be presented, making the distinction between the definition of marketing and the domain of marketing. Second, the popular notion of exchange as the core concept of marketing will be discussed and shown to be inadequate. Finally, an alternative perspective of the core of marketing will be presented and will be shown to be a useful guide for the delineation of marketing's boundaries.

Review of the Scope of Marketing

One of the difficulties involved in defining marketing and delineating the scope of marketing is rooted in the basic question of ontology. That is, does marketing have an inherent definition and domain that must be discovered, or does one assign a meaning and domain to marketing? Apparently, practitioners and academicians have taken the latter route. Enis, for example, points out that marketing's label, like that of other disciplines, is arbitrary and subject to change[1]. Robin concurs[2]. Leonard seems to take a stronger stance suggesting that marketing *has* to evolve due to widespread changes throughout society[3].

Tracing the scope of marketing suggests a definite evolution toward broadening. During the first half of this century, commodity, institutional and functional approaches focused primarily on distribution, channel members and activities, respectively. In 1954 Nystrom noted: "In its broadest sense, marketing includes not only dealings in goods, but in services as well"[4]. Today, of course, services are routinely found under the marketing umbrella.

During the past two decades the scope-of-marketing issue has accelerated. A 1965 position paper by the Marketing Faculty at Ohio State University recognised marketing as a social process inherent in any society, detached from technologies employed to facilitate the process[5]. Since 1965, numerous authors have addressed the social and societal aspects of marketing[e.g., 6, 7, 8, 9, 10, 11, 12].

The broadening issue was further sparked by the 1969 Kotler and Levy article which pointed to the use of marketing by politicians, fund raisers, universities and other non-business entities who routinely market themselves, their ideas, and their organisations[13]. According to Kotler and Levy, the choice for all organisations is not whether to engage in marketing; rather, the choice is how well marketing is performed. Although Luck challenged Kotler and Levy, advocating the restriction of marketing's scope to "those processes or activities whose ultimate result is a market transaction"[14], a survey of marketing academicians by Nichols in 1974 showed overwhelming support for a broadened concept of marketing[15]. Consequently, the marketing discipline continues to grow and continues to embrace an ever growing number of issues, phenomena and applications.

Marketing's Definition Differs from Marketing's Domain

The definition of marketing differs from the domain, scope or boundaries of marketing. The fact that "marketing" ends in "ing" suggests that marketing is something that is done and refers to the definition of marketing. The definition of marketing must be behaviourally anchored in the marketing efforts of marketers. As Law and Wensley point out, "marketing is, first of all, something that people practise"[16].

However, the domain of marketing includes not only what marketers do, but also phenomena and issues which are related to marketing. For example, the thought process of the consumer as it relates to choice, and the numerous exogenous, endogenous, and situational variables which impact on marketing efforts and consumer choice are included within the scope of marketing. Consequently, the domain of marketing is much broader than the definition of marketing.

Several academicians have alluded to possible distinctions between the domain of marketing and the definition of marketing. Nickels suggests the study of marketing (domain-oriented) be termed "marketology" while the practice of marketing (definition-oriented) be termed "marketing"[17]. Bagozzi describes marketing as "the discipline of exchange behaviour" (definition-oriented) which "deals with problems related to this behaviour" (domain-oriented)[18]. Lastly, according to Hunt, marketers should not worry about a precise definition of marketing as long as there is a developing consensus as to marketing's total scope[19].

Exchange as the Core of Marketing

One method for delineating the boundaries of a discipline is to identify the core concept central to the discipline. The presence (absence) of the core helps to delineate which issues and phenomena should (should not) be included within the boundaries of the discipline.

Alderson proposed the "Law of Exchange" in an attempt to describe marketing phenomena[20]. The discipline quickly recognised the intuitively appealing concept of exchange as the core of marketing. However, the notion of exchange began to collapse as exchange blossomed into a concept as nebulous and ambiguous as the concept of marketing. In 1972, for example, Kotler maintained that an individual who watches television is engaged in an exchange, and therefore is engaged in marketing[21]. Bagozzi concurred[22] and also suggested that social interactions are also a form of exchange relationships[23], but was challenged to delineate which social exchanges are marketing[24]. Although Bagozzi attempted "to give practitioners and consumers a model serving as a guide for influence and control of exchanges" in response to the challenge[25], his efforts were considered unsuccessful[26]. In 1979, Bagozzi himself lamented that marketing still lacked a coherent conceptualisation of exchange[27].

The notion of exchange has lost much of its momentum in the marketing literature during the last four to six years. The promise exchange once held as marketing's core has been seriously questioned. Exchange abstractions have become too ambiguous and too complex to be considered useful[28], and it has become increasingly clear that not all exchanges are marketing exchanges[29, 30]. As Ferrell and Perrachione note: "Equating marketing exchange with all exchange (social or otherwise) can only be self-defeating"[31].

Given the failure of the discipline to clarify adequately the notion of exchange in a useful manner, perhaps it is now time to explore an alternative perspective of the core of marketing which will lead to a clearer, more useful, delineation of marketing's boundaries.

Behaviour as the Core of Marketing

In an apparent search for profundity and esotericism, most marketing theorists of the last decade seem to have overlooked the analytical truism that marketing is what marketers do. Notable exceptions include Nickels[32], Law and Wensley[33] who suggest that the crux of marketing is a behavioural orientation; marketing is something that is done. Therefore, marketing behaviour is a key component in the core of marketing. However, not all behaviours of marketers are marketing behaviours. To qualify as a marketing behaviour, the behaviour must be deliberately designed to influence the thought process of the marketee with the intention of eliciting a specific response. Behaviour can be one act or a series of acts. The marketer is any party who actively initiates the behaviour, while the marketee is the party to whom the behaviour is directed. The specific response may be an economic exchange, but it might also be the acceptance of an idea, a change in the marketee's behaviour, or whatever other response the marketer might intend. In order to be deliberate, the behaviour must be preceded by a strategy formulation process and fuelled by the presence of one or more underlying motives.

Consequently, we propose that the Core of Marketing Model (Figure 1) represents the four essential components of marketing. Should any phenomenon under consideration lack any one of these four components, the phenomenon cannot be considered a marketing one. In contrast to exchange theory, note that the marketee's response is irrelevant in discerning whether or not marketing has taken place. Even if the marketee ignores marketing behaviours, marketing has still occurred.

Although the notion of using marketee-directed behaviour rooted in motives, intentions and strategy formulation may be a "new" perspective from which to view marketing, the literature does lend some support to the proposed core. For example,

Arndt describes marketing as a social process consisting of "conception" (intention), "planning" (strategy formulation), and "implementation" (behaviour directed toward marketee)[34]. Similarly, Luck suggests that marketing behaviours must be qualified by intentions when he notes, "a particular *act* must be related to an eventual or *intended* offer to buy and/or sell" (emphasis added)[35]. Robin highlights the critical role of strategy, intentions and motives when he points out that "the essence of marketing today involves the creation of marketing *strategy* to achieve organisational or individual *objectives*" (emphasis added)[36]. Last, Meyer suggests that marketing includes both "influential procedures" (directed behaviour) and the "concomitant research" (strategy formulation)[37].

Figure 1. The Core of Marketing Model

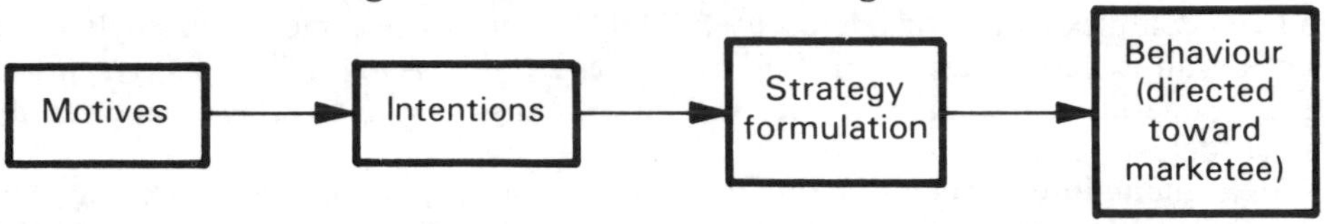

Motives → Intentions → Strategy formulation → Behaviour (directed toward marketee)

The Boundaries of Marketing Model

Using the Core of Marketing Model as a guide, both academicians and practitioners are in a better position to determine whether or not an issue or phenomenon should be included within the boundaries of marketing. When faced with such a decision one should first ask whether the particular phenomenon or issue in question is marketing *per se?* That is, is behaviour involved, and if so, are the requirements outlined in the Core of Marketing Model satisfied? If so, the issue or phenomenon is a marketing one and obviously falls within the boundaries of marketing. If not, the issue or phenomenon is not marketing *per se,* but may qualify for inclusion within the boundaries of marketing *if* it can be shown to be marketing-related. There are two basic ways an issue or phenomenon might be marketing-related, as shown in Figure 2 by the Boundaries of Marketing Model.

First, *consequences* of marketing are directly related to marketer behaviours. Consequences are usually short-term and involve only two parties — the marketer and the marketee. Issues and phenomena which focus upon the effectiveness and efficiency of marketer behaviours, the thought process of the marketee, and the responses of the marketee would be classified as marketing consequences. Examples of marketing consequences include profitability analysis, market analysis, sales response, efficiency of marketing systems, sales forecasting, and consumer choice, to name a few. Implicitly included are the numerous endogenous and exogenous variables that influence both the marketer and the marketee.

The second way an issue or phenomenon may be marketing-related is by being an implication of marketing. Marketing *implications* are similar to marketing consequences in that both stem from marketer behaviours and both affect the core of marketing, as well as each other. The distinction is that implications are less direct than consequences, are usually longer-term, and may involve parties other than the marketer and the marketee. In addition, while consequences of marketing behaviour are usually explicitly stated as marketing intentions or motives, implications may be only implicitly rooted in intentions and motives. Issues and phenomena which focus upon the impact of marketing on society and the environment, and upon the long-term well-being of the marketer and the marketee would be classified as marketing implications.

Figure 2. The Boundaries of Marketing Model

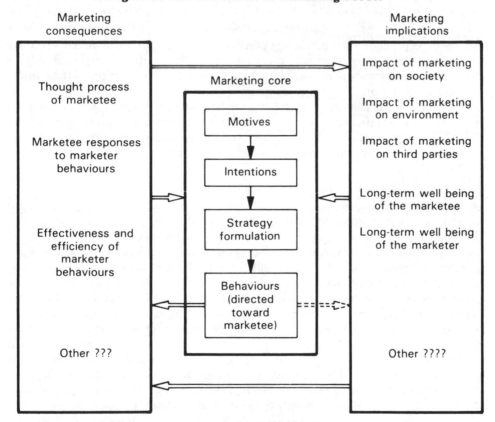

So What?

Although marketing and marketing-related phenomena are pervasive throughout society, no one would argue that *everything* is marketing; fuzzy or not, boundaries of marketing must exist. There are several reasons why both academicians and practitioners should be concerned with the delineation of marketing's boundaries.

Reasons for the Academician

Without a clear delineation of marketing's boundaries, the discipline will develop without direction and without guidance. Such aimless wandering is likely to result in the discipline becoming extremely fragmented and preoccupied with fringe topics which have questionable marketing relevance. The discipline cannot be all things to all people; a clear focus is essential toward the development of professionalism in any discipline, and marketing is no exception.

In the role of teacher, the academician's chief concern is (should be?) to help prepare students for marketing careers. With a clear focus of the core of marketing, marketing instructors are in a strong position to link topics together by demonstrating their marketing relevance. Students exposed to a series of seemingly unrelated and fragmented topics may learn something *about* marketing, and will probably develop a fuzzy perception of what marketing practitioners do. In contrast, students who are constantly shown the marketing relevance of the materials they are expected to learn develop an *understanding* of marketing and a crystallised perception of their future role as marketing practitioners.

This is not to say that there is no place for basic research and exploratory inquiry in marketing academe; certainly there is. However, we maintain that research findings should not be included within the boundaries of marketing until they are shown to be relevant to the core of marketing — what marketers do.

Reasons for the Practitioner
In addition to the obvious stake the practitioner has in what marketing academicians do, there are at least two more reasons why the practitioner should be concerned with the delineation of marketing's boundaries. First, a clear focus of marketing's boundaries leads to efficient and effective deployment of the practitioner's time and energies. The core of marketing is most controllable and, as such, the return on the practitioner's time and energy invested in the core is greatest. Marketing implications and consequences should be monitored to provide feedback for the core; however, they are less controllable and therefore demand less emphasis than the core itself.

Another reason for concern relates to the role marketing practitioners play in the context of the organisation. As Walker and Child note, "the establishment of a clear identity is a critical stage in the emergence of an occupation"[38]. Without a clear understanding of marketing's domain, how can marketing activities be effectively coordinated? Similarly, how can resources be deployed without a clear delineation of the Marketing Department's responsibilities? And, without an adequate understanding of marketing's distinctive competencies, how does one determine whether or not the Marketing Department should become involved with a particular problem or issue the organisation may face?

Concluding Note
Practitioners and academicians have long argued that marketing is something more than selling. A convincing argument, however, must articulate exactly what that "something more" is. The Boundaries of Marketing Model is offered as a guide toward that articulation — enabling practitioners, academicians, and students to reconsider what is within the scope of marketing and what is not.

References

1. Enis, B., "Deepening the Concept of Marketing", *Journal of Marketing,* Vol. 37, October 1973, p. 58.
2. Robin, D. P., "Useful Boundaries for Marketing", in *Conceptual and Theoretical Developments in Marketing,* O. C. Ferrell, S. W. Brown and C. W. Lamb, Jr. (Eds.), Chicago, American Marketing Association, 1979, p. 605.
3. Leonard, F., "The Attraction of Marketing, Today and Tomorrow", *European Journal of Marketing,* Vol. 14 No. 9, 1980, p. 20.
4. Nystrom, P. H., *Marketing Handbook,* New York, New York Press Company, 1954, p. 9.
5. Hunt, S. D., *Marketing Theory: The Philosophy of Marketing Science,* Homewood, Illinois, Richard D. Irwin, 1983, p. 6.
6. Corlett, T. and Barnes, M., "Publicity on Social Issues: The Need for Research", *Journal of the Market Research Society,* Vol. 13 No. 3, 1971, pp. 131-145.
7. Sweeney, D. J., "Marketing: Management Technology or Social Process?", *Journal of Marketing,* Vol. 36, October, 1972, pp. 3-10.
8. Dawson, L. M., "Marketing Science in the Age of Aquarius", *Journal of Marketing,* Vol. 35, July 1971, pp. 66-72.
9. Dixon, D. F., "The Poverty of Social Marketing", *MSU Business Topics,* Vol. 26, Summer 1978, pp. 50-56.
10. Hunt, S. D., "The Nature and Scope of Marketing", *Journal of Marketing,* Vol. 40, July 1976, pp. 17-28.
11. Crosier, K., "How Effective is the Contribution of Market Research to Social Marketing?", *Journal of the Market Research Society,* Vol. 21 No. 1, 1979, pp. 3-16.
12. Jones, S., "Social Marketing: Dimensions of Power and Politics", *European Journal of Marketing,* Vol. 16 No. 6, 1982, pp. 46-53.
13. Kotler, P. and Levy, S. J., "Broadening the Concept of Marketing", *Journal of Marketing,* Vol. 33, January 1969, pp. 10-15.
14. Luck, D. J., "Broadening the Concept of Marketing Too Far", *Journal of Marketing,* Vol. 33, July 1969, p. 54.
15. Hunt, S. D., *op. cit.,* p. 19.
16. Law, P. and Wensley, R., "Marketing Teaching", *European Journal of Marketing,* Vol. 13 No. 1, 1979, p. 17.
17. Nickels, W. G., "Theory Development and the Broadened Concept of Marketing" in *Conceptual and Theoretical Developments in Marketing,* O. C. Ferrell, S. W. Brown and C. W. Lamb, Jr. (Eds.), Chicago, American Marketing Association, 1979, pp. 614-615.
18. Bagozzi, R., "Marketing As Exchange", *Journal of Marketing,* Vol. 39, October 1975, p. 39.
19. Hunt, S. D., *op. cit.,* p. 24.
20. Alderson, W., *Dynamic Marketing Behaviour,* Homewood, Illinois, Richard D. Irwin, 1965, p. 84.
21. Kotler, P., "A Generic Concept of Marketing", *Journal of Marketing,* Vol. 36, April, 1972, pp. 46-54.
22. Bagozzi, R., *op. cit.,* p. 34.
23. Bagozzi, R., "Marketing as an Organized Behavioural System of Exchange", *Journal of Marketing,* Vol. 38, October 1974, pp. 77-81.
24. Ferrell, O. C. and Zey-Ferrell, M., "Is All Social Exchange Marketing?", *Journal of the Academy of Marketing Science,* Vol. 5, Fall 1977, pp. 306-314.
25. Bagozzi, R., "Is All Social Exchange Marketing? A Reply", *Journal of the Academy of Marketing Science,* Vol. 5, Fall, 1977, p. 316.
26. Ferrell, O. C. and Perrachione, J., "An Inquiry into Bagozzi's Formal Theory of Marketing Exchange", in *Marketing Theory: The Philosophy of Marketing Science,* Hunt, S. D., Homewood, Illinois, Richard D. Irwin, 1980, pp. 336-341.
27. Bagozzi, R., "Toward a Formal Theory of Marketing Exchanges", in *Conceptual and Theoretical Developments in Marketing,* O. C. Ferrell, W. Brown and C. W. Lamb, Jr. (Eds.), *op. cit.,* pp. 431-447.
28. Robin, D. P., "Useful Boundaries for Marketing", in *Conceptual and Theoretical Developments in Marketing, op. cit.,* p. 610.

29. Arndt, J., "Perspectives for a Theory of Marketing", *Journal of Business Research,* September 1980, p. 393.

30. Arndt, J., "How Broad Should the Marketing Concept Be?", *Journal of Marketing,* Vol. 42, January 1978, p. 101.

31. Ferrell, O. C. and Perrachione, J., *op. cit.,* p. 337.

32. Nickels, W. G., *op. cit.,* pp. 614-615.

33. Law, P. and Wensley, R., *op. cit.,* pp. 15-26.

34. Arndt, J., *op. cit.,* p. 101.

35. Luck, D. J., *op. cit.,* p. 54.

36. Robin, D. P., *op. cit.,* p. 609.

37. Meyer, P. W., "Proposals for a New Approach to Marketing in Economic Science", *European Journal of Marketing,* Vol. 12 No. 6, p. 448.

38. Walker, D. S. and Child, J., "The Development of Professionalism as an Issue in British Marketing", *European Journal of Marketing,* Vol. 13 No. 1, 1979, p. 30.

3. Modelling in Marketing: Explicating Subjective Knowledge

by Sue Jones and Colin Eden

"The big problem with management science models is that managers practically never use them." This statement made by Little [1] reflects a theme which has repeatedly exercised those involved in the development and application of management science models to assist decision making in organisations [2-6]. It is a theme found in marketing, as in other fields [7-12], where the problems of implementation have tended to be seen as coming from two main sources: firstly, from the difficulty of modelling the complex marketing process itself, and, secondly because of conflicts that arise from the different perspectives and backgrounds of marketing managers and management scientists.

Concentrating on the latter, Crawford [7] proposed that there exists both a lack of realism among model builders and a lack of understanding and involvement by marketing executives. He cited problems such as the inability of quantitative models to handle intangibles such as intuitive creativity and the idiosyncratic and political beliefs and concerns of the people involved. He criticised the inappropriateness of the mathematical techniques used. He also suggested that models are often badly presented and communicated by model builders, with excessively technical language and insensitivity to the potentially threatening nature of these sophisticated models.

The picture he presents is one that is all too familiar over a decade later. The management scientist invariably constructs models dominated by highly objectivated, rational-analytic, quantifiable content. If then the marketing manager does not use the models, the consultant can blame this upon all or one of several factors. He can blame the client's ignorance of quantitative analysis including his lack of awareness about the fact that the simplification accompanying any modelling activity does not invalidate its usefulness. He can ascribe to the client fear of being exposed as in some way incompetent, or simply berate the client's stubborn refusal to think rationally and analytically (and therefore sensibly) rather than by gut-feel and intuition.

The client, on the other hand, may feel that the consultant has clearly not understood the real complexity of the problem. He may feel that the consultant is totally unaware of how important creativity and judgement are in marketing. More sympathetically, he may feel that the consultant has done his best in trying to involve him and explain "how it all works", but has been somewhat naive in the way, for example, he seems to have forgotten that policy formulation also needs to take account of the politics of its presentation to, and implementation by, other people in the organisation.

In our view the majority of implementation problems with management science marketing models derive from a concern by the management scientist with science and rationality. Thus he wishes to direct the client to a discovery of the "right" problem which will then be solved rationally and "objectively" — such a problem being free of the muddying confusion of subjectivity, irrationality and organisational politics. Yet we would argue that to fail to pay attention to the particular images of the world *defined by the client,* who works within an organisational context including power, negotiation and internal political games, and to ignore the particular knowledge, experience and wisdom the client has about his own situation, significantly increases the likelihood of the consultant being ignored [see also 13, 14, 15].

Concepts and Implications

The stance taken in this paper comes from considering definitions of issues as deriving the schemata of beliefs, values and attitudes with which a person construes events [see 16, 17]. From this stance comes our concern with the body of *subjective* knowledge and experience which an individual develops about his world as he makes sense of, and acts within it [see also 18].

The problem of finding ways of capturing and representing meaningfully to an individual the rich complexity and individuality of his thinking is clearly not trivial. Indeed, it is unlikely that any model produced by a management scientist will succeed in doing so, except in some part. Furthermore, there will be other not insignificant difficulties that derive from the expectations and norms surrounding the client-consultant relationship [19]. For example, our experience suggests that data about organisational politics, while often a crucial aspect of an individual's thinking about an issue, is usually seen as too "illegitimate" to reveal to a consultant.

Yet we believe that the management science consultant who wishes to find ways of assisting a client with systematic and relevant analysis to which the client is committed must find some way of learning about and explicating his client's particular and complicated reality and the "intuitive" judgements and beliefs he uses in his decision making. What is made explicit becomes a model through which an individual can "dialogue" with his own thinking in a way that can give him a new awareness with which to evaluate and use it.

Modelling Subjective Knowledge

The method which we have developed of listening to and formally representing the definition of a situation by our clients involves the coding of the articulated scenarios given by the client or client group to produce a "cognitive map". A cognitive map is intended to capture the stucture and content of an individual's beliefs about his world expressed as theories about "what is" and "what causes what is" within that world and thus as a description of events, explanations of the occurrence of those events and enactments of the consequences of those events for others. We shall attempt below to describe some of the salient features and basic "building blocks" for constructing a cognitive map. (For further details, with examples, [see also 18, Chapter 4].) The coding sets out deliberately to *capture the language of the client and depict concepts in his terms.* Concepts, descriptions, ideas and beliefs may be:

(1) *Assertions or attributions:* such as "central buying is now a fact of life", "the managing director is totally inflexible", "we have suffered a severe depression in this market during the past two years". These are a part of a map if they offer an explanation for a circumstance or are believed to cause an event. They are attributions made in an assertive manner as if they were a matter of fact. Quite often they represent historical facts.

(2) *Alternative circumstances:* most descriptions which contribute to a problem definition tend to be statements about current circumstances with either an implicitly or explicitly stated alternative circumstance representing a psychological, rather than a logical, opposite. Thus "working by guesswork rather than knowing what senior management is up to", "concentration on upmarket segments rather than covering stock business", "no up-to-date research information".

(3) *Increasing or decreasing conceptualisations:* a conceptualisation of this sort normally implies the possibility of a monotonic change in a circumstance rather than discrete alternatives. Thus "an increase or decrease in the amount of advertising", or "product attractiveness", or "level of commitment".

(4) *Causality:* each concept may be linked by a belief in causality. The link is by arrow, as with directed graphs, or influence diagrams in System Dynamics [20].

Thus a statement such as "One of the factors affecting the editorial standards of the journal is that we are always late, because of the current printer's timing. We need a better timing so that we can produce immediate news" could become:

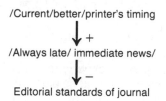

Figure 1, taken from a consulting project in which we were involved is an example of how a small network of beliefs can thus be coded to produce an explicit model in the form of a cognitive map.

The clients for this project were the editor and advertising manager of a trade and technical journal. Over the past seven years, the journal has suffered a slow but continuous decline in both circulation and profitability, despite several attempts to revive its fortunes. The decision to involve ourselves in the problems the journal team were facing was seen to be a last resort. All of the members of the journal team apparently believed that without their making some new and significantly different proposals to their directors, their own future within the organisation was at an end.

The first stage of working with the journal team was deliberately designed to be with small groups and to allow us to listen to their ramblings, worries and understandings about the nature of the current situation and its possible implications for any preferred futures. The purpose here was not only to learn about some

Figure 1. Early stages of Problem Definition Represented by a Cognitive Map

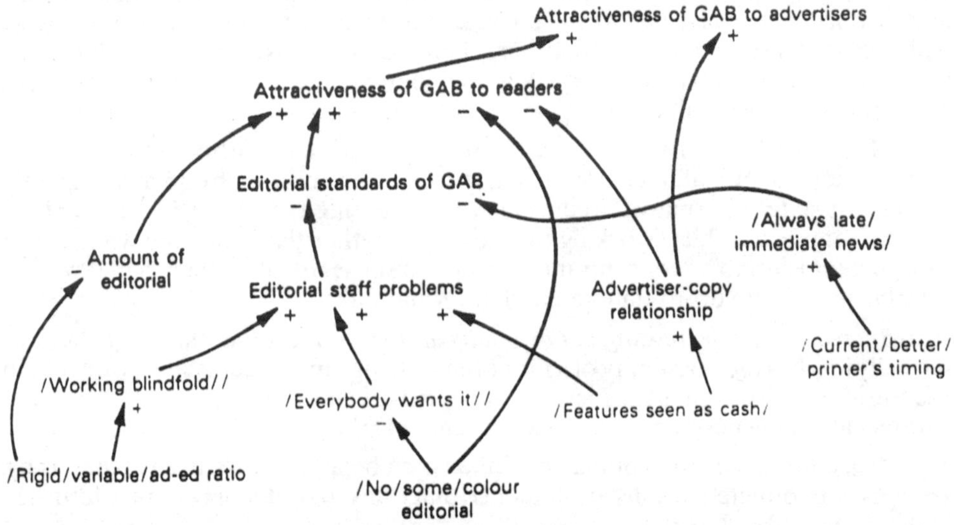

Slashes are used to separate discrete opposite poles of a concept. Where no opposite pole has been articulated the double slash indicates a void pole. Concepts without slashes are seen as monotonic where the positive pole is taken to be an increase while the negative is a decrease. A + ve attached to an arrow indicates a relationship between similar poles, a − ve sign indicates a relationship across poles. Thus here "an increase in editorial standards of GAB" is explained by "immediate news" which is explained by "better printer's timing".

of the most important elements of the situation defined by the client team but also to begin the process of building a trusting relationship with them. Individuals in organisations have, not infrequently, experiences which lead them to be suspicious about the political consequences of revealing particular kinds of data to consultants. Through a deliberately empathetic stance on the part of the consultant, however, it is usually possible for individuals or groups to discuss freely many of the things that seem to them to characterise the situation they find themselves in. To this end the team was broken into manageable groups, with all of the advertisement staff in one group and two other groups comprising a mixture of editorial and production staff. At this stage the processes of listening varied with each group — with one group we tape-recorded the meeting, with the others we took notes and used "on-the-spot" rough coding which we have found to be a particularly helpful way of introducing the client to the purpose and methods of cognitive mapping.

From the tape-recordings, notes and rough coding from these initial meetings, we were then involved in coding the descriptions of the members of the journal team to produce a cognitive map, as an aggregated model of the theories and hypotheses about the nature of their situation. Not surprisingly there were at this stage a significant number of contradictory and conflicting views expressed within the model and we saw the next stage of feeding back this model as an opportunity to begin addressing and analysing these differences. The process of constructing a model which reflects the richness and complexity of the understandings the members of the team had about their issues also inevitably resulted in a large and complex body of data. Although it is not always necessary to use a computer, we have developed a suite of computer programmes called COPE (COgnitive Policy Evaluation) which assist with the management and analysis of complex qualitative data. The programmes take the coded maps and allow for an analysis of the maps through tracing the sequence of relationships between concepts and exploring the complex ramifications of inter-related often contradictory beliefs and values about an issue. The software is designed to be used primarily by decision makers and thus is written in a form which enables a decision maker to respond to simple prompts via a visual display unit and seek answers to the following questions: If we can describe an event in the following way, what beliefs do we bring to bear to explain the occurrence of the event? What beliefs do we use that enable us to predict the consequences of an event occurring? Can a particular event be explained through a sequence of theories by another event? Does the occurrence of an event have consequences for this other event? [See also 18, Chapter 5.]

It was this COPE model which formed the basis for the next stage of meetings, for which we transported the computer (a PDP 11/03) to the clients' offices, during which we expected to begin the process of a more focused evaluation and analysis and the negotiation of a "group" issue. There is a facility within the COPE programmes for grouping concepts related to each other within a particular field of interest, and which, on a prompt, lists those concepts contained within each "group". From the list of concepts within each of the fields of interest discussed at the previous meeting, one or other of the members of the team would then select one concept which they would like to explore in more depth by asking for the explanations or consequences linked to it. This would in turn reveal other concepts of interest to explore further, and so on. Figure 2 gives an example of the use of the computer in this way for analysis of a cognitive map.

During this time the team were inevitably involved in a further process of model elaboration and modification as new knowledge was added and other views expressed within the model were discussed and deleted through consensual agreement. As the conflicting views contained within the model were revealed they were also addressed and debated. The process of negotiation within teams has often been noted to be a problematic and stressful experience for their members. Here the model was presenting conflicting views in a depersonalised manner which allowed them to be addressed by all members of the group without the need for ascribing particular views to particular people while nevertheless considering them to be worthy of evaluation. This process of *negotiating a problem definition* we see as critical to the commitment of members of a team to working on a problem and helping devise a solution which they can implement effectively together [see also 21].

The emphasis so far has been on the crucial importance of paying attention to the issue as it is defined by the client, and finding ways of capturing his idiosyncratic, qualitative and subjective theories and hypotheses in an explicit model. It would, however, be inappropriate to ignore the way in which an individual's picture of his world includes quantitative aspects, and to suggest that there is not a need for the mathematical and technical expertise of much typical management science. Better

```
COPE > E - 21
   - 21    A decrease in ATTRACTIVENESS OF GAB TO READERS
           can be explained by
   - 30    ..a decrease in EDITORIAL STANDARDS OF GAB

           and/or can be explained by
     36    NO COLOUR EDITORIAL...

           and/or can be explained by
   - 43    a decrease in AMOUNT OF EDITORIAL
           which can be explained by
     42    RIGID AD-ED RATIO...

   - 21    A decrease in ATTRACTIVENESS OF GAB TO READERS
           can be explained by
     46    an increase in ADVERTISER-COPY RELATIONSHIP
           which can be explained by
     45    FEATURES SEEN AS CASH..

•••••••••••••••••••••••••••••••••••••••••••••••••••••••••••••••••

COPE > E - 30
   - 30    A decrease in EDITORIAL STANDARDS OF GAB
           can be explained by
     34    an increase in EDITORIAL STAFF PROBLEMS

           and/or can be explained by
     60    ALWAYS LATE
           which can be explained by
     61    CURRENT PRINTERS TIMING

•••••••••••••••••••••••••••••••••••••••••••••••••••••••••••••••••

COPE > E - 34.
     34    An increase in EDITORIAL STAFF PROBLEMS
           can be explained by
     36    EVERYBODY WANTS IT
           which can be explained by
   - 36    SOME COLOUR EDITORIAL...

     34    An increase in EDITORIAL STAFF PROBLEMS
           can be explained by
     45    FEATURES SEEN AS CASH...

           and/or can be explained by
     41    WORKING BLINDFOLD
           which can be explained by
     42    RIGID AD-ED RATIO...

•••••••••••••••••••••••••••••••••••••••••••••••••••••••••••••••••

COPE > C - 36
   - 36    SOME COLOUR EDITORIAL
           can lead to
     21    ..an increase in ATTRACTIVENESS OF GAB TO READERS
           which can lead to
     10    ..an increase in ATTRACTIVENESS OF GAB TO ADVERTISERS

   - 36    SOME COLOUR EDITORIAL
           can lead to
     36    EVERYBODY WANTS IT
           which can lead to
     34    ..an increase in EDITORIAL STAFF PROBLEMS
           which can lead to
   - 30    ..a decrease in EDITORIAL STANDARDS OF GAB
           which can lead to
   - 21    ..a decrease in ATTRACTIVENESS OF GAB TO READERS
           which can lead to
   - 10    ..a decrease in ATTRACTIVENESS OF GAB TO ADVERTISERS

•••••••••••••••••••••••••••••••••••••••••••••••••••••••••••••••••
```

Here a group member has chosen to explore the concept "Attractiveness of GAB to readers". (Numbers are identification codes). Each set of statements, separated by rows of asterisks, represents a chain of explanations or consequences until a choice point, between two or more further explanations/consequences is reached. The arrows here indicate the progressive search made by the decision-maker using the instruction E for explanations (or C for consequences) with the number of the concept, and the appropriate sign for the pole of the concept of interest (positive pole + ve, negative pole − ve). Dots before or after a concept indicate that further concepts as explanations or consequences, respectively, are linked to it. There is also a facility, not shown here, for exploring whether routes between two particular concepts exist using the instruction X: for example X + 45, 21 would print out the routes between "Features seen as cash" and "Attractiveness of GAB to readers".

that this should be *grounded in the world of the client.* A model in the form of a cognitive map leads naturally, and transparently, to the client investing in help from technical mathematical analysis, particularly that of computer simulation. During this stage in the project we took some of the more easily operationalised concepts within the COPE model and attributed to them some of the numerical implications that had been broadly specified during the previous meetings. These formed the basis for the construction of a computer simulation model which would be used to demonstrate to the client group how their qualitative and subjective model could be the basis for exploring quantitative implications. The two models were then used iteratively, as exploring the content and ramifications of one led to a reassessment and re-evaluation of the content of the other.

This phase lasted over several sessions as the team moved towards the negotiation of a mutually owned problem definition. Between each session we were involved in elaborating and rebuilding the two models. The changes made were substantial and a reflection of the growth in ideas and awareness of complexity about the nature of the issue. All the members of the team have mentioned the extent to which there was considerable learning about the nature of the journal, the market place, their own organisation and the working of their own group. They became committed to a considerable amount of "knowledge-gathering" research themselves within the organisation as they sought to fill gaps in their knowledge revealed through interacting with the models which they regarded as significant, or to find evidence to help resolve certain contradictory beliefs or to validate others that seemed to be crucial to understanding the situation and the devising of satisfactory policies. Again, however, this research came from and was relevant to their problem which *they* had defined. Above all, during this stage the members of the team were beginning to see "as legitimate knowledge their own subjective understanding of their organisational life and then to self-consciously reflect upon this knowledge so that they may learn to know what they know, and learn from its implications, and thus learn by enquiring in a relevant way" [18, p.5].

The final stage of the project was characterised by the way in which a mutually owned problem definition could be examined in order to devise, pre-enact and evaluate a final set of policies. The last four meetings with the team were then devoted to finding the most powerful way of presenting their ideas to senior management for the negotiation of mutually acceptable outcomes which could ensure that the team participated in "designing" their own future within the organisation.

Concluding remarks

It has been the argument of this paper that the apparent failure of much management science analysis in marketing is the result of the failure to pay adequate attention to the qualitative as well as quantitative images of the world as the client sees it. It is also argued that this is not a trivial and obvious point but rather one which requires a significantly different orientation from that adopted in much typical management science consultancy in marketing. This orientation involves a commitment to finding ways of providing the facility for the client not only to articulate his qualitative, idiosyncratic and subjective views about his world but also to be able formally and systematically to analyse and evaluate them. It involves paying attention to qualitative and personal values in terms of the outcomes desired from any strategy. Thus personal needs, for example, to work on a journal which is enjoyable to work on, can be seen explicitly as valid and to be traded off, if necessary, against other more obvious "organisational" outcomes such as highest profitability.

Currently there exists an acute lack of processes and techniques for paying attention to and explicating an individual's subjective knowledge and definition of his organisational world and this article has described one attempt to develop a method for so doing. In using this method perhaps one of the most striking aspects of our experience has been the degree to which those individuals and groups with whom we have worked have not only learned a great deal about their own organisational world, through coming to "learn what they know", but also have developed a new self confidence in the validity and legitimacy of their own subjective knowledge.

We believe our involvement with the client team in the project we have described to have been highly successful. This is not necessarily because the journal will be more profitable but primarily because the client team believe that the contribution we made was "invaluable" both in terms of the learning that they developed and because it resulted in support for a set of policies designed to create their own future, previously at risk. Whether solving the problem defined and owned by the client team will be "good" for senior management is a question which depends upon the ethics, and the choices, of the consultant.

References
1. Little, J. D. C., "Models and Managers: The Concept of a Decision Calculus", *Management Science,* Vol. 16 No. 8, B446-B485, 1971.
2. Miller, E. C., *Advanced Techniques for Strategic Planning,* New York, American Management Association, 1971.
3. Brewer, G. D., *Politicians, Bureaucrats and the Consultants,* New York, Basic Books, 1973.
4. Barton, R. F., "Models with more than one criterion — or why not build implementation into the model?", *Interfaces,* Vol. 7 No. 4, 1977, pp. 71-75.
5. Roberts, E. B., "Strategies for effective implementation of complex corporate models", *Interfaces,* Vol. 8 No. 1, 1977, pp. 26-33.
6. Ackoff, B. L., "The future of operational research is past", *Journal of the Operational Research Society,* Vol. 30, 1979, pp. 93-104.
7. Crawford, C. M., "A shotgun marriage of mathematics and marketing?" *Business Horizons,* Vol. 9 No. 2, 1966, pp. 37-48.
8. Cardwell, J. T., "Marketing and management science — a marriage on the rocks?", *California Management Review,* Summer 1968, pp. 3-11.
9. Montgomery, D. B. and Urban, G. L., *Management Science in Marketing,* Englewood Cliffs, NJ., Prentice-Hall, 1968.
10. Kotler, P., *Marketing Decision-making: A Model Building Approach,* New York, Holt, Rinehart and Winston, 1971.
11. Fisher, K. and Hirst, M., "Model building in marketing: problems, developments and state of the art", *European Journal of Marketing,* Vol. 6, No. 2, 1972, pp. 80-86.
12. Leeflang, P. S. H. and Koerts, J., "Modelling and marketing: two important concepts and the connection between them", *European Journal of Marketing,* Vol. 7, No. 3, 1973, pp. 203-217.
13. Allison, G. T., *Essence of Decision: explaining the Cuban Missile Crisis,* Waltham, Little, Brown, 1971.
14. Pettigrew, A., *The Politics of Organizational Decision-Making,* London, Macmillan, 1973.

15. Jones, S., Eden, C. and Sims, D., "Subjectivity and Organizational Politics in Policy Analysis", *Policy and Politics,* Vol. 7, No. 2, 1979, pp. 145-163.
16. Thomas, W. I. and Thomas, D. S., *The Child in America: behaviour, problems and progress,* New York, Knopf, 1928.
17. Kelly, G. A., *The Psychology of Personal Constructs,* New York, Norton, 1958.
18. Eden, C., Jones, S. and Sims, D., *Thinking in Organizations,* London, Macmillan, 1979.
19. Eden, C. and Sims, D., "On the nature of problems in consulting practice", *Omega,* Vol. 7, No. 2, 1979, pp. 119-127.
20. Coyle, R. G., *Management System Dynamics,* London, Wiley, 1977.
21. Sims, D., Eden, C. and Jones, S., "Facilitating Problem Definition in Teams", *European Journal of Operational Research,* forthcoming.

Part 2 Market Analysis

4. Paradigms in Consumer Research: A Review of Perspectives and Approaches
by Johan Arndt

Introduction
The purpose of this article is to conduct a comprehensive state-of-the-art review of existing paradigms — accepted examples of actual scientific practice — in consumer behaviour. The organising principle for the various perspectives has been borrowed from the area of organisation theory. Such a stock-taking endeavour is hoped to contribute a systematisation of knowledge and to stimulate creative thinking about future directions in theory development and research.

Since the consumer behaviour area was established in its own right in the early 1960s, thousands of publications have appeared reporting theoretical schemes and empirical findings. During the last two decades the consumer behaviour field has become both multinational and multidisciplinary. Consumer behaviour studies have been conducted in many countries of the world. In marketing, consumer behaviour has become the most important sub-field. In addition, important contributions to the understanding of consumer behaviour have been made by economists, psychologists, sociologists and political scientists. There are prestigious professional organisations in many countries, and there are several specialised scholarly journals.

A cost of the proliferation of research and the diversity thereof is fragmentation and lack of unity. The attempts to integrate the field into comprehensive models have so far not been very successful. This article makes a different tack. By classifying the different approaches and traditions in a fairly simple typology, the review inventories the knowledge and suggests areas deserving more or less emphasis.

The article is organised as follows: the first section presents a short historical review of consumer behaviour discipline. Next, a typology for classifying the different perspectives on consumer behaviour is outlined. The following six sections review characteristic studies in each of the six cells given by the typology. Finally, the further development of consumer theory and research is addressed.

Phases in the Development of the Consumer Behaviour Field
The domain of consumer behaviour will be fairly broadly conceived in this review article. The definition used was originally proposed several years ago (Arndt, 1977) and has much in common with the view of Jacoby (1978). In this view, consumer behaviour is defined as (1) the mental and physical acts of (2) individuals, households

or other decision-making units concerned with ultimate consumption involving (3) the acquisition, own production, use and, in some cases, the dispossession of products and services.

The cumulative research effort over time is both diverse and quantitatively impressive as can be judged from various reviews of theoretical and empirical findings, such as Guest (1962), Howard (1965), Twedt (1965), Burk (1968), Perloff (1968), Sheth (1967, 1974(b), 1979), Sandell (1969), and Robertson and Ward (1973). These reviews suggest that it is meaningful to distinguish among five fairly distinct phases of differential thoughts and research priorities in the discipline.

Early Empiricist Phase

This phase, which covered the years between 1930 and the late 1940s was dominated by empirical, commercial research having a pronounced applied focus. As observed by Sheth (1974, p. 392), this era was characterised by attempts in industry to identify the effects of distribution, advertising, and promotion decisions. The theoretical underpinnings came mainly from the economic theory of the firm.

The Motivation Research Phase

The 1950s brought the entry of clinical psychologists armed with Freudian concepts on the marketplace. The tools of the trade included depth interviews, focus groups, thematic apperception tests and other projective techniques, which were used to dredge consumers' real motives out from the inner recesses of the mind (Ferber and Wales, 1958). Perhaps the most widely quoted motivation study was Haire's (1950) "shopping list" investigation of the reasons for the early resistance to instant coffee.

Later on this tradition became tainted by criticism of non-representative samples and subjective interpretation of the findings resulting in unreproducible conclusions.

The Formative Phase

The period from 1960 to 1965 can be regarded as the formative phase for consumer behaviour. These years saw the arrival of the first generation of marketing consumer behaviour specialists, including pioneers such as Alan Andreasen, Richard Cardozo, James Carman, Donald Cox, James Engel, and Francesco Nicosia. To a considerable extent, the early contributions built on the work of Lazarsfeld and his colleagues at Columbia University's Bureau of Applied Social Research (Katz and Lazarsfeld, 1955), the writings of the Katona group at University of Michigan (Katona, 1960) and the thoughts of Raymond Bauer at Harvard (Bauer, 1960). Important European contributions came from Karl-Erik Wärneryd (Sweden) and Hans Raffée (West-Germany).

Typical of the efforts in this phase were the many attempts to "explain" some aspect of consumer purchase behaviour by single constructs such as perceived risk (Cox and Rich, 1964), cognitive dissonance (Engel, 1963), personality (Evans, 1959), social character (Kassarjian, 1965), or social class (Carman, 1965).

The Utopian Grand Theories Phase

It is a common phenomenon in science that over-emphasis and bias in one direction leads to a compensation in the form of similar error in the opposite direction.

The many single-shot bivariate analyses caused the field to be fragmented and unorganised, thereby instigating attempts to build integrative, comprehensive theories.

Among these conceptualizing attempts, Nicosia (1966) can safely be characterised as the first one, Engel, Kollat, and Blackwell (1968) and the subsequent three additional editions of their works the most widely read, Howard and Sheth (1969) the most rigorous, and Hansen (1972) perhaps the most creative and idea-generating formulation.

As in the case of the notion of total management information systems, the idea of very comprehensive theories was too much before its time, even though the goals and ambitions were admirable. In retrospect, the conceptualisations are somewhat limited and culture-bound as they mainly address prepurchase decision processes for consumers in the Western world. Though some attempts have been made critically to evaluate the theories (Zaltman, Pinson and Angelmar, 1973, pp. 103-122; Engel and Blackwell, 1982, pp. 677-690), the early grand theories apparently have had little impact on empirical research (Kollat, Blackwell, and Engel, 1973, p. 577).

The Information-Processing Phase

Disappointments resulting from the limitations of the grand theories brought about a search for action-worthy, middle-range theories, following the suggestion by Robertson and Ward (1973, pp. 20-22). In addition, the pragmatic concerns of advertisers and planners of consumer information programmes have resulted in an enhanced interest in how consumers search for, receive, interpret, store, and utilise information in the short-term and long-term memory. A perusal of the *Journal of Consumer Research* and the *Proceedings of the Association for Consumer Research* since the early 1970s will underscore the present importance of consumer information processing. Central concepts include cognitive complexity, memory organisation and function, low-involvement learning, brand categorisation strategies, evoked set, and encoding processes (Hughes and Ray, 1974; Bettman, 1978; and Monroe, 1981).

Problems in Consumer Research

In the midst of the proliferation of consumer studies, there are critical voices regarding the quality of the research effort. Some years ago, Kollat and his associates (Kollat, Blackwell and Engel, 1973, p. 577) argued that it would not be surprising if 90 per cent of the findings and lack of findings in consumer research would ultimately prove to be wrong (because of inadequate conceptualisation). Later on it has become almost a tradition for chief officers of the Association for Consumer Research to use the annual presidential address to castigate their field for lack of rigour (Jacoby, 1978) or for producing trivial results (Cohen, 1973). For several years the ACR has failed to make the JCR/ACR award in recognition of a doctoral dissertation article's contribution to knowledge in consumer behaviour (Wilkie, 1981). Reviewers such as Jacoby (1978) and Kollat and his colleagues (Kollat, Blackwell and Engel, 1973) have made a strong case for developing better field methodologies and more accurate measures. It is not difficult to agree.

However, this article takes issue with another contention — that the main route to scientific progress lies through developing large-scale integrative models and theories organising the field. Such has not happened in sociology, psychology and other behavioural sciences where many different orientations and traditions co-exist.

Similarly, at its present state of development, it appears that a synthesising, "melting pot" effort would still be premature. Instead, it would seem more meaningful to sharpen methods for revealing the diversity of the field. This leads to the problem of developing taxonomies.

A Typology for Paradigms in Consumer Behaviour

As was earlier pointed out, typologies or classification systems are devices for organising a field. By partitioning the inventory of paradigms or research traditions in the field into homogeneous sub-groups, the contents, priorities and also limitations of the research effort may be revealed.

So far, published reviews of consumer behaviour have failed to use explicit typologies. One early exception is the comprehensive review undertaken by Sheth (1967) who used a classificational scheme borrowed from Coan (1964) based on the observational status of central concepts. Later, Arndt (1976) developed a matrix based on the two dimensions stage in decision process and level of process (brand choices up to acquisition of strategic items). None of these typologies, however, addressed paradigms or the fundamental perspective used.

The organising principle selected for the present review was proposed by organisation theorist Pfeffer (1982). Pfeffer distinguishes among the main theoretical approaches (paradigms) by using two dimensions. The first is level of analysis or level of aggregation (individuals or sub-units of the organisation versus the whole organisation). The second is perspective on action taken, identifying three such perspectives. The first is the rational or quasi-rational approach. The second is the situationist or external control approach. The third and more complex social constructionist notion views behaviour as almost a random process, arguing for the importance of intrapsychic processes, but maintaining that behaviour can only be understood by analysing how these processes unfold over time.

This typology appears relevant also for consumer behaviour for several reasons. Like organisation theory, consumer behaviour addresses actual human choice behaviour and its consequences, both at the individual and at aggregate levels. Both areas are multidisciplinary and may roughly have reached the same maturity stage (for instance, the key journal, the *Administrative Science Quarterly,* began publication in 1956).

In adapting the Pfeffer scheme to consumer behaviour, a problem relates to the unit of analysis dimension. In this case, the dimension could well be treated as a continuum ranging from individual behaviour to large national aggregates. For reasons of simplicity, this continuum is here forced into the dichotomy of individual versus group behaviour. The resulting 3 x 2 matrix shown in Table I then isolates the following six different paradigm groups:

— individual-level rational action,
— group-level rational action,
— external control of individual behaviour,
— external control of consumer group behaviour,
— social constructionist views of individual consumer behaviour,
— social constructionist approaches to consumer group behaviour.

Table 1. Categorisation of Theoretical Perspectives in Consumer Behaviour Perspectives on Action

		Purposive, intentional goal-directed, rational	Externally constrained and controlled	Emergent, almost-random, dependent on process and social construction
Level of analysis	Individual	Cognitive consistency paradigm	Behaviour modification paradigm	Attribution theory perspective
		Multi-attribute attitude models	Situationist paradigm	Low-involvement learning perspective
		Information-processing paradigm	Consumer socialisation paradigm	Structuralist approach
		Consumer satisfaction/ dissatisfaction and complaining studies		
	Group	Household decision-making paradigm	Comparative research tradition	Compensatory consumption formulation
		Household economics paradigm	Structurally determined consumer behaviour	Deviant consumption view
		Household management perspective		
		Diffusion of innovations paradigm		

The typology is adapted from Pfeffer (1982, p. 13).

Individual-Level Rational Action

A dominating part of consumer research has adopted a focus on the individual consumer as the unit of analysis and has assumed that behaviour can be viewed as conscious, foresightful action being goal-directed and boundedly rational. Hence, a central premise for this perspective is the assumption that consumer behaviour is the consequence of intent and choice. The choice processes are directed to maximising value or utility. A common feature of the studies in this group is their heavy reliance on cognitive, information-processing assumptions about the causes of human activity (Pfeffer, 1982, p. 42).

Four important paradigms in this category have been identified: the cognitive consistency paradigm, multi-attribute attitude models, the information-processing paradigm and the consumer satisfaction/dissatisfaction and complaining traditions. Examples of studies in each group will be given.

The Cognitive Consistency Paradigm

The theoretical underpinnings of this paradigm can be found in the various logical consistency theories such as cognitive dissonance (Festinger, 1957), balance theory

(Heider, 1958), and congruity theory (Osgood and Tannenbaum, 1955). In short, the cognitive consistency theorists proceed from the premise that human beings strive to achieve and maintain harmony among beliefs, attitudes and behaviours. Hence, inconsistencies arouse psychological tension and become a motivational force. In this way they build on the field-theoretic framework of Lewin (Kassarjian, 1973). The paradigm was one of the first behavioural science traditions to be adapted to marketing settings (Venkatesan, 1973) perhaps due to its simplicity and intuitive appeal.

Consumer behaviour studies of this type include the efforts of Engel (1963) and Bell (1967) to produce evidence that car buyers tend to avoid discrepancies while seeking supporting information justifying their choice. Kassarjian and Cohen (1965) examined the case of the cigarette smoker and the surgeon-general's finding linking cigarette smoking with lung cancer.

It appears that this approach to consumer behaviour peaked in the mid-1960s.

Multi-Attribute Attitude Models
The compositional multi-attribute attitude formulations share an ill-acknowledged origin in the work of economist, Lancaster (1966), who asserts that the utility of a given product or brand is derived from the attributes (properties of characteristics) of the product rather than from the product itself (Ratchford, 1975). Common to all the multi-attribute models, whether they are based on the formulation of Rosenberg (1956) or Fishbein (1963), is that they view attitudes as a function of consumers' beliefs about the attributes (expectancies or perceived instrumentalities) of each competing brand and the evaluative criteria (importance weights or saliences) regarding the attributes (Wilkie and Pessemier, 1973).

The pioneering studies using this paradigm, such as Sheth and Talarzyk (1972), applied a simple affective measure to "validate" additive models with and without importance weights. Hence, this paradigm is to some extent related to the cognitive consistency work. A recurring finding in this and subsequent studies is that importance weights do not significantly improve predictions (Wilkie and Pessemier, 1973). Later work in the area has revolved around other forms of cognitive algebra than the simple compensatory (additive) model, such as conjunctive, disjunctive and lexicographic formulations. Another issue has been the use of cross-sectional analyses (across individuals) versus individual-level analysis (making separate predictions for each individual (Bass and Wilkie, 1973). Finally, the formulation has been further refined in substituting attitudes towards performing the behaviour-buying (A_{act}) for attitudes toward the brand (A_b), (see Engel and Blackwell, 1982, pp. 444-451).

After the culmination of research interest in the multi-attribute models in the 1970s, there has been a levelling off in the number of studies. This is partly due to the incorporation of this paradigm in the more comprehensive information-processing formulation. Another reason may be the tautological nature of the paradigm, demonstrating in some cases no more than that Attitudes $= f$ (Attitudes).

The Information-Processing Paradigm
As earlier pointed out, this has been a dominant research tradition in the last decade. For a summary, the reader is referred to Engel and Blackwell (1982). Rather than quoting individual studies, the following central institutions should be pointed out: Purdue University (Jacoby and his Ph.D. students), University of California at Los

Angeles (Kassarjian, Bettman), and Pennsylvania State University (Bither, Olson). This tradition is characterised by many rigorous and inventive laboratory experiments. While the early work tended to concentrate on high-involvement decision processes, later studies have also addressed low-involvement situations; see, for instance, papers in Monroe (1981, pp. 15-34), building on and extending Krugman's (1965) provocative ideas.

Consumer Satisfaction/Dissatisfaction and Complaining Studies
Unlike the preceding paradigms, the consumer satisfaction paradigm places the consumer in a proactive role focusing on consumer reaction to disconfirmations of expectations in the marketplace.

This paradigm gathered momentum in the mid-1970s. For instance, recently, Hunt (1983, p. 262) noted that by 1972, there were published only seven papers on consumer satisfaction. However, just for the 1982 Consumer Satisfaction Conference, more than 600 papers were submitted.

Central persons in the development of this paradigm are Ralph Day (Indiana University) and H. Keith Hunt (Brigham Young University) who have organised a series of research conferences on the subject matter (Hunt, 1977; Day, 1977; Day and Hunt, 1979, 1982). While the earliest studies such as Andreasen and Best (1977) tended to be descriptive, newer work has grown in theoretical sophistication (Oliver, 1980). Another trend is the increasing use of laboratory experimentation as contrasted with the early survey studies. Olander (1977) has seriously questioned the use of objective indicators of consumer satisfaction. Though an even stream of consumer satisfaction studies still reach the scholarly journals, few new conceptual or methodological advances are appearing. For the time being it seems as if this tradition has reached the region of diminishing returns.

Group-Level Rational Action
Most studies on consumer behaviour have approached the subject matter at the individual rather than at the group level. This would not present any problem either if all consumer decision processes were an individual affair only or if individual behaviour could be aggregated in a meaningful way. However, neither assumption seems to be realistic. Sociological consumer studies are few in number despite well-argued calls to arms from Nicosia and his associates (Glock and Nicosia, 1964; Nicosia and Mayer, 1976; and Zaltman and Wallendorf, 1977).

The following four paradigms have been assigned to this group: the household decision-making paradigm, the household economics paradigm, the household management perspective and the diffusion of innovations paradigm.

The Household Decision-Making Paradigm
The nuclear family or the household is the appropriate unit of analysis for many product and service categories. Hence, it is not surprising that the household decision-making paradigm has been the most actively researched tradition in this group, as documented in Sheths' (1974(a)) comprehensive literature review. More than many other parts of consumer behaviour, the research effort inspired by this paradigm has been truly interdisciplinary. For instance, as early as in 1958, Foote (1961) chaired a conference on intra-familial decision-making in Ann Arbor, with participants from several social science fields.

Some of the studies, such as that by Arndt and Crane (1975), have used observational methods to examine patterns of interaction. Other studies have addressed the issue of the relative influence of the spouses (Wolgast, 1958). A frequent finding is that the husband often plays the instrumental role while the wife acts in an expressive capacity (Kenkel, 1961). Relative influence clearly varies with type of decision (Davis and Rigaux, 1974).

Important methodological problems remain in this area. Observational studies using contrived settings suffer from questionable external validity. The survey approach using key informants presents problems of low reliability and lack of consistency between the responses of the spouses (Ferber, 1955). Perhaps unobtrusive methods may prove useful (Webb, 1978).

The Household Economics Paradigm

While the paradigms so far have mainly addressed prepurchase decision processes, the household economics paradigm also includes actual consumption behaviour. Moreover, the tradition covers fundamental decision areas such as allocation of time to work versus leisure and allocation of budget into savings and various spending categories (Ferber, 1973).

Applications of this paradigm can be found in the reports of the Scandinavian consumer policy commissions (Konsumentutredningen, 1969; Forbrukerrådsutvalget, 1971) developing proposals for consumer legislation and new institutions. A related approach is Odhnoff's (1969) attempt to describe household economics by systems analysis. In Germany, Fegebank (1975) has studied how households use information.

Many of the studies in this group have very descriptive orientation. However, a promising attempt to apply and extend microeconomic concepts is reported by Etgar (1978) who advocates treating household economic behaviour as production processes drawing on Becker's (1965) formulations about the role of time. Other studies in the "new home economics" tradition have been reviewed by Ferber and Birnbaum (1977).

The Household Management Perspective

This tradition, which is still in its infancy, views the household as a small firm having limited information and using informal routines in its exchanges with the environment. Applying a systems approach, Billgren (1975) has developed a model of the impact of critical incidents on the household, using concepts such as goals, resources, activity and management system. Building on work in the management area, Arndt and Holmer (1978) distinguished between household management problems at three different levels: the strategic, the administrative and the operating. A factor analytic study isolated key dimensions of administrative level routines.

The Diffusion of Innovations Paradigm

For the last four decades, researchers in a variety of fields including rural sociology, medical sociology, education and marketing have published some 2,000 studies of the diffusion of new ideas, customs, fashions, and products through social networks. As meticulously chronicled by Rogers and his associates (Rogers, 1963; Rogers and Shoemaker, 1971) a commonly accepted conceptual framework has gradually emerged. Important components of this framework are: (1) characteristics of the innovation; (2) different adopter categories; (3) role of opinion leadership; (4) stages in the individual decision processes; and (5) existing social norms and values.

Though this tradition also considers "irrational" resistance to innovation, the adopters are, on the whole, viewed as being active problem solvers.

External Control of Individual Behaviour
A basic premise for the paradigms in this group is the idea that individual consumers adapt to their environment. Environmental factors are viewed as both necessary and sufficient causes of consumer behaviour. This means less emphasis on utilities, preferences and motives. Instead, the focus is on observable and measurable behaviour and the situational factors controlling it.

Three paradigms belong to this group: the behaviour modification, the situationist and the socialisation paradigms.

The Behaviour Modification Paradigm
To a substantial extent, this paradigm builds directly on the theories of the noted Harvard behaviourist-psychologist, Skinner (1972), who argues forcefully that human behaviour is shaped by external influences. Therefore the notions of consumer sovereignty and free will are illusions. Markin and Narayana (1977) are to be commended for introducing this paradigm into marketing.

In a subsequent contribution Nord and Peter (1980) identified four ways of externally modifying behaviour: respondent conditioning, operant conditioning, vicarious learning (influence by using models which are observed), and ecological design (design of physical situations). Rothschild and Gaidis (1981) have extended these ideas further. However, while the behaviour modification paradigm has had some few advocates, there is an absence in consumer behaviour of empirical research making explicit use of the paradigm. The resistance to the paradigm may be explained by its deviation from the currently dominating paradigms in the area assuming reasonably rational decision making.

The Situationist Paradigm
The essence of this position is that much consumer behaviour can be traced back to circumstances, contexts or use-situations. Hence, the paradigm parallels contingency theories in organisational behaviour.

A pioneering consumer behaviour contribution is Sandell's (1968) experiment on the role of hypothetical use situations on brand choice. This work has later been substantially extended by Belk (1974, 1975) and has further been incorporated into multi-attribute attitude formulations (Arndt and Grønhaug, 1976).

From the recent comprehensive review of the situationist literature by Leigh and Martin (1981), it appears that this paradigm has become quite popular in consumer research. A reason may be that it is more compatible with existing theories than is the behaviour modification perspective.

The Consumer Socialisation Paradigm
This tradition addresses the process of how consumers absorb or learn the culture in which they are raised. In contrast to the behaviour modification perspective which essentially uses the mechanism of *exchange* for social influence, this paradigm assumes

informational social influence effects on individuals. People learn the perception of products and services, how to make sense of things, and even what their preferences should be from other persons in their social environment (Pfeffer, 1982, pp. 117-118).

The research problems posed by this paradigm lend themselves perhaps mostly to longitudinal, case-oriented studies. The many unsolved methodological problems have caused this area to be mostly ignored so far in contemporary consumer research, in spite of the importance of the subject matter (Ward, 1974; Kuhlmann, 1983).

In consumer behaviour, the few studies available have addressed advertising (Robertson and Rossiter, 1974.; Myers, 1978) and parental influences on adolescent consumer learning (Ward and Wackman, 1971).

External Control of Consumer Group Behaviour
This paradigm differs from the preceding one in centring on the behaviour of aggregates of consumers rather than individuals. The two paradigms classified into a group are the comparative research tradition and the notion of structurally determined consumer behaviour.

The Comparative Research Tradition
The studies in this group attempt to explain consumer group behaviour by comparing observations of samples of consumers selected from different cultures, sub-cultures or special locations or nations.

One stream of research has focused on the different nationality groups in the United States (Engel and Blackwell, 1982, pp. 79-81) or in Canada (Tigert, 1973). The socalled "black market" has been very actively researched (Sexton, 1972). A long list of studies have addressed the plight of the disadvantaged consumer segments who are captives of the inner-city decay (Caplovitz, 1963; Andreasen, 1978).

Many behavioural science disciplines such as sociology and political science have active cross-national research traditions. As demonstrated in van Raaij's (1978) and Boddewyn's (1981) review articles, such a tradition is yet to come of age in marketing. Many of the studies, such as Green and Langeard (1975) and Barksdale *et al.* (1982), seem to be of the "safari" type with local questionners or head researchers imported from the United States. Other studies (Thorelli, Becker and Engledow, 1975) have a descriptive focus, though digging up many interesting facts.

Research in this area is not only costly but also presents difficult problems of comparability of samples and measurement instruments. Nevertheless, such comparative studies should, and are likely to, grow in importance and to be improved methodologically.

Structurally Determined Consumer Behaviour
In essence this tradition attempts to link fundamental patterns of consumer behaviour (such as allocation of budgets among major expenditure categories) to environmental factors.

Critics such as Helenius (1974) and the Dholakias (1983) charge that much consumer behaviour is determined by structural conditions and norms and the lack of true alternatives in the marketplace, making individual choice irrelevant. Uusitalo (1979) has reported promising results relating to the identification of consumption style and its antecedent correlates.

Social Constructionist Views of Individual Consumer Behaviour
As underscored by Pfeffer (1982, p. 208) both perspectives on action considered so far — rational and external control — are, in a way, stimulus-response theories. In each case, there is some (internal and external) stimulus that elicits some (individual or group) response.

By contrast, the paradigms classified as social constructionist formulations do not lead to theories which may be expressed in terms of causal models. Instead they focus on processes, how action and interaction unfold in consumer units over time, and how meanings and interpretations are constructed around such events (Pfeffer, 1982, p. 209). Consumers' activities, accordingly, are often expressive behaviour and a search for meaning. Other aspects of consumer action are relatively mindless, in that many habits are instituted and cemented over time without much conscious evaluation of how sensible they are.

Three paradigms have, with some doubt, been classified into the social constructionist, individual group: the attribution theory perspective, the low-involvement learning formulation, and the structuralist approach.

Attribution Theory Perspective
This view opens up for both internal and external loci of control. As developed by Kelley (1971) the attribution approach involves trying to capture the "naive psychology" of consumers to understand the cognitive processes through which an individual infers the cause of an actor's behaviour (Calder and Burnkrant, 1977, p. 29). Covariation of effect and presumed cause is a dominating criterion.

In consumer behaviour, hypotheses have been derived from this theory to explain consumer confidence in advertising claims (Settle and Golden, 1974) and interpersonal influence (Calder and Burnkrant, 1977). It seems as if the potentials of this paradigm have not really been fully tapped in marketing. While the attribution notion is dynamic, the consumer studies so far have been single-shot experiments. Outside the area of advertising content, the attribution theory formulation offers an alternative explanation to cognitive consistency phenomena and to social-stereotyping (Mizerski, Golden and Kernan, 1979). As with the other formulations in this class, attribution theory suffers from the absence of unified hypotheses and propositions.

Low-Involvement Learning Formulation
It may be that no other paradigm has aroused so much controversy in marketing and consumer behaviour as the low-involvement learning notion. For instance, Engel and his associates rewrote their popular textbook so as, in the 1982 version, to emphasise low-involvement behaviour (Engel and Blackwell, 1982).

This paradigm dates back to a pioneering article by Krugman (1965) who argued that the content of television advertising for trivial products tends to be learned like meaningless material. Such advertising has little impact on attitudes or on immediate behaviour. Instead, if repeated frequently over time, advertising results in significant changes in the structures of perceptions, thereby building up a preparedness to act. Such latent learning can then be activated by situational cues at the point of purchase. This means that the traditional hierarchy-of-effects (cognition-attitude change-behaviour) does not apply. Instead, the consumer is believed to pass from cognition to behaviour, followed later by attitude change (Ray, 1973). It seems as if the degree of involvement is related to brain lateralisation. Hansen (1981) has presented evidence suggesting that low-involvement learning is dominated by right brain processes.

This tradition was reviewed by Robertson (1976) who spelled out some of its implications for marketing. Several empirical studies have appeared during the last few years, as evident in a review paper by Finn (1983). As of now it is easy to agree with Kassarjian (1981, p. 33) that the low-involvement learning paradigm may turn out to alter many if not most of our conceptions of consumer behaviour models and middle range theories. Hence, it is a healthy challenge to the supreme role of cognitive theories.

The Structuralist Approach
The only entrant is this class is Levy's (1981) prize-winning article advocating more sophisticated use of qualitative approaches to consumer behaviour. Drawing directly on the structuralist notions of anthropologist Lévi-Strauss (1963), Levy proposed that verbal materials elicited from people in the marketplace can be interpreted for meaning in the same way as myths, fairy tales, and novels. Such myths and anecdotes can be viewed as ways of organising and expressing perceptions of realities. While this view is still only at the idea stage, Levy's proposal is so provocative and mined with implications, that it warrants further development and explication.

Social Constructionist Approaches to Consumer Group Behaviour
Two paradigms have tentatively been identified in this group: the compensatory consumption formulation and the deviant consumption view.

The Compensatory Consumption Formulation
The essence of this position is that many consumer purchase "decisions" are compensatory activities, undertaken because more meaningful goal-fulfillment alternatives (such as occupational or educational achievements) are blocked. Hence, the paradigm provides an explanation for why poor minority consumers and other disadvantaged consumer segments establish "irrational" consumption patterns in flashy cars and expensive foods (Caplovitz, 1964, pp. 180-181; Firat, 1978; Grønmo, 1984). Such a view is also a central part of the neo-Marxist critique of the alleged spiritually empty consumptionist society (Marcuse, 1964; Helenius, 1974). Though this paradigm is conceptually intriguing it is difficult to harness into methodologically adequate research designs.

The Deviant Consumption View
This perspective parallels the preceding one by trying to interpret apparently irrational behaviour. None of the existing paradigms can adequately explain why people engage in excessive consumption of food, alcohol and drugs. Conceptual and methodological

tools may possibly be borrowed from sociological studies of deviance and crime (such as prostitution and gambling) including marketing exchanges violating societal norms enforced by law (Zaltman and Wallendorf, 1977).

Because of the lack of research attention to this topic, this paradigm only exists in a most tentative, rough form. Creative developmental work is clearly needed to build up a tradition.

Developing Theories in Consumer Behaviour

This view of consumer behaviour research underscores that some themes and some paradigms have been overworked at the same time as many critical questions remain unexplored. In view of the low coefficients of determination often found, it is difficult to understand the massive testing and retesting of hypotheses relating to consumer information processing. The popularity of this research area can hardly be explained by the strengths of the results. A more likely explanation is the dominance in the consumer behaviour area of researchers with a marketing orientation. This orientation has perhaps led to a search for determinants of consumer behaviour which may be controlled by advertising and other elements of the marketing mix.

It is therefore easy to agree with Sheth (1979) that the perspective on action should to some degree be shifted from the rational model of choice to other perspectives. Similarly, more attention should be directed at group behaviour contrasted with individual behaviour.

The review has also revealed that the great majority of the studies have been conducted in North America or by Americans abroad. This means that there is a surplus knowledge about some aspects of consumer behaviour, while there are shortages of knowledge about areas. If consumer behaviour is to become a full-fledged science, there have to be truly international participation and research priorities. The field would benefit particularly from rigorous studies from the less developed countries which could provide a basis for consumer policies for the Third World, as shown by Thorelli (1981).

Finally, as pointed out by Pfeffer (1982, p. 294) the null hypothesis as routinely practised is useless as a test for the strength of an idea. A better test would be to compare the ability of one paradigm to produce intriguing hypotheses and to test them against a competing perspective. Such a procedure may enable us to break out from the treadmill of normal science in contemporary consumer research.

Concluding Comments

The field of organisational behaviour has been characterised by using the metaphor of "lay preaching" (Pfeffer, 1982, p. 291). This metaphor is clearly applicable also for consumer behaviour. The gospel preached is that of individual, proactive, foresightful choice. This notion is very compatible with our rationalistic culture stressing volition and personal responsibility. The preaching is "lay" because its practitioners do not acknowledge the extent to which their research is strongly flavoured with their ideals, values and predjudices. There is also a growing group of philosophy of science "Pharisees", rigorously on guard against conceptual and methodological heretics.

Zaltman and his colleagues have argued persuasively for broadening the field of consumer behaviour by expanding application areas (Zaltman and Sternthal, 1975). This review leads to the conclusion that there is as much need for a paradigmatic broadening.

References

Anderson, P.F., "Marketing, Scientific Progress, and Scientific Method", *Journal of Marketing,* Vol. 47, Fall, 1982, pp. 18-31.

Andreasen, A.R., "The Ghetto Marketing Life Cycle: A Case of Underachievement", *Journal of Marketing Research,* Vol. 15, February, 1978, pp. 20-8.

Andreasen, A.R. and Best, A., "Consumers Complain — Does Business Respond?", *Harvard Business Review,* Vol. 55, July-August, 1977, pp. 93-101.

Arndt, J., "Reflections on Research in Consumer Behavior", in *Advances in Consumer Research,* Vol. III, Anderson, B.B., (Ed.), Ann Arbor, Association for Consumer Research, 1976, pp. 213-21.

Arndt, J. and Crane, E., "Observing Stages in Consumer Decision Processes", in *Advances in Consumer Research,* Vol. II, Schlinger, M.J., (Ed.), Ann Arbor, Association for Consumer Research, 1975, pp. 63-70.

Arndt, J. and Grønhaug, K., "Predictive Power of Multi-Attribute Attitude Models", in *Proceedings of the Fifth Annual Workshop on Research in Marketing,* Chevalier, M. (Ed.), Fontainebleau, France, 1976.

Arndt, J. and Holmer, O., "Dimensions of Household Economic Management", *Journal of Consumer Studies and Home Economics,* Vol. 2, March, 1978, pp. 27-34.

Barksdale, H.G. et al., "A Cross-National Survey of Consumer Attitudes Towards Marketing Practices, Consumerism and Government Regulations", *Columbia Journal of World Business,* Vol. 17, Summer, 1982, pp. 71-85.

Bass, F.M. and Wilkie, W.L., "A Comparative Analysis of Attitudinal Predictions of Brand Preference", *Journal of Marketing Research,* Vol. 10, August, 1973, pp. 262-9.

Bauer, R.A., "Consumer Behavior as Risk Taking", in *Dynamic Marketing for a Changing World,* Proceedings of the 43rd Conference of the American Association, Hancock, R.S., (Ed.) Chicago, Illinois, American Marketing Association, 1960, pp. 389-98.

Becker, G.S., "A Theory of the Allocation of Time", *Economic Journal,* Vol. 75, 1965, pp. 493-517.

Belk, R.W., "An Exploratory Assessment of Situational Effects in Buyer Behaviour", *Journal of Marketing Research,* Vol. 11, May, 1974, pp. 156-63.

Belk, R.W., "Situational Variables and Consumer Behavior", *Journal of Consumer Research,* Vol. 2, December, 1975, pp. 157-64.

Bell, G.D., "The Automobile Buyer After the Purchase", *Journal of Marketing,* Vol. 31, July, 1976, pp. 12-16.

Bettman, J., *An Information Processing Theory of Consumer Choice,* Reading, Massachusetts, Addison-Wesley, 1978.

Billgren, J., *Hushållsekonomiska beskrivningsmodeller: Kritiska händelsers inverkan på hushållet,* Lund, Sweden, University of Lund, 1975.

Boddewyn, J.J., "Comparative Marketing: The First Twenty-Five Years", *Journal of International Business Studies,* Vol. 12, Spring-Summer, 1981, pp. 61-79.

Burk, M.C., *Consumption Economics: A Multidisciplinary Approach,* New York, John Wiley and Sons, 1968.

Calder, B.J. and Burnkrant, R.S., "Interpersonal Influence on Consumer Behavior: An Attribution Theory Approach", *Journal of Consumer Research,* Vol. 4, June, 1977, pp. 29-38.

Carman, J.M., *The Application of Social Class in Market Segmentation,* Berkeley, California, Graduate School of Business Administration, University of California, 1965.

Caplovitz, D., *The Poor Pay More,* New York, The Free Press, 1963.

Coan, R.W., "Theoretical Concepts in Psychology", *British Journal of Statistical Psychology,* Vol. 17, November, 1964, pp. 161-76.

Cohen, J., "Presidential Address: Untitled", *Association for Consumer Research Newsletter,* No. 3, January, 1973, pp. 3-5.

Cox, D.F. and Rich, S.U., "Perceived Risk and Consumer Decision-Making — The Case of Telephone Shopping", *Journal of Marketing Research,* Vol. 1, November, 1964, pp. 32-9.

Davis, H.L. and Rigaux, B.B., "Perception of Marital Roles in Decision Processes", *Journal of Consumer Research,* Vol. 1, June, 1974, pp. 51-62.

Day, R.L., (Ed.), *Consumer Satisfaction, Dissatisfaction and Complaining Behavior,* Bloomington, Indiana, School of Business, Indiana University, 1977.

Day, R.L. and Hunt, H.K. (Eds.), *New Dimensions of Consumer Satisfaction and Complaining Behavior,* Bloomington, Indiana School of Business, Indiana University, 1979.

Day, R.L. and Hunt, H.K., *New Findings on Consumer Satisfaction and Complaining,* Bloomington, Indiana School of Business, Indiana University, 1982.

Dholakia, N. and Dholakia, R.R., "Choice and Choicelessness in the Paradigm of Marketing", paper presented at the Workshop on Alternative Paradigms in Marketing, Kingston, Rhode Island, University of Rhode Island, 13-14 May, 1983.

Engel, J.F., "Are Automobile Purchasers Dissonant Consumers?", *Journal of Marketing,* Vol. 27, April, 1963, pp. 55-8.

Engel, J.F. and Blackwell, R.D., *Consumer Behavior,* fourth edition, New York, Dryden Press, 1982.

Engel, J.F., Kollat, D.T. and Blackwell, R.D., *Consumer Behavior,* New York, Holt, Rinehart and Winston, 1968.

Etgar, M., "The Household as a Production Unit", in *Research in Marketing,* Sheth, J.N., (Ed.), Greenwich, Connecticut, JAI Press, 1978, pp. 79-98.

Evans, F.B., "Psychological and Objective Factors in the Prediction of Brand Choice: Ford vs. Chevrolet", *Journal of Business,* Vol. 32, 1959, pp. 340-69.

Fegebank, B., *Die Informationslage des Privathaushalts bei Güterbeschaffung,* Berlin, Duncker & Humblot, 1975.

Ferber, R., "On the Reliability of Purchase Influence Studies", *Journal of Marketing,* Vol. 19, January, 1955, pp. 225-32.

Ferber, R., "Family Decision Making and Economic Behavior: A Review", in *Family Economic Behavior: Problems and Prospects,* Sheldon, E.B., (Ed.), Philadelphia, J.B. Lippincott Company, 1973, pp. 29-61.

Ferber, R. and Wales, H.G. (Eds.), *Motivation and Market Behavior,* Homewood, Illinois, Richard D. Irwin, 1958.

Ferber, M.A. and Birnbaum, B.G., "The 'New Home Economics': Retrospects and Prospects", *Journal of Consumer Research,* Vol. 4, June, 1977, pp. 19-28.

Festinger, L., *A Theory of Cognitive Dissonance,* Evanston, Illinois, Harper & Row, 1957.

Finn, D.W., "Low Involvement Isn't Low Involving", in *Advances in Consumer Research,* Vol. X, Bagozzi, R.P., (Ed.), Ann Arbor, Association for Consumer Research, 1983, pp. 419-27.

Firat, A.F., "Social Construction of Consumption Patterns", unpublished Doctoral dissertation, Evanston, Illinois, Northwestern University, 1978.

Fishbein, M., "An Investigation of the Relationships between Beliefs about and Object and the Attitude toward that Object", *Human Relations,* Vol. 16, 1963, pp. 233-40.

Foote, N.N., (Ed.), "Household Decision-Making", in *Consumer Behavior,* Vol. IV, New York, New York University, 1961.

Forbrukerrådsutvalget, *Innstilling om Fortbrukerrådets arbeidsoppgaver, sammensetning og organisasjon m.m.,* Oslo, Departementet for familie- og forbrukersaker, 1971.

Glock, C. and Nicosia, F.M., "Uses of Sociology in Studying 'Consumption' Behavior", *Journal of Marketing,* Vol. 28, July, 1964, pp. 51-4.

Green, R.T. and Langeard, E., "A Cross-National Comparison of Consumer Habits and Innovation Characteristics", *Journal of Marketing,* Vol. 39, July, 1975, pp. 34-41.

Grønmo, S., "Compensatory Consumer Behavior: Conceptual Foundations and Theoretical Perspectives", paper presented at the Theory Conference of the American Marketing Association, Fort Lauderdale, 19-22 February, 1984.

Guest, L., "Consumer Analysis", *Annual Review of Psychology,* Vol. 13, 1972, pp. 315-44.

Haire, M., "Projective Techniques in Marketing Research", *Journal of Marketing,* Vol. 14, April, 1950, pp. 649-56.

Hansen, F., *Consumer Choice Behavior: A Cognitive Theory,* New York, The Free Press, 1972.

Hansen, F., "Hemispheral Lateralization: Implications for Understanding Consumer Behavior", *Journal of Consumer Research*, Vol. 8, June, 1981, pp. 23-36.

Heider, F., *The Psychology of Interpersonal Relations*, New York, John Wiley & Sons, 1958.

Helenius, R., *Konsumera allt och alla*, Stockholm, Rabén & Sjögren, 1974.

Howard, J., *Marketing Theory*, Boston, Allyn & Bacon, 1965.

Howard, J. and Sheth, J.N., *The Theory of Buyer Behavior*, New York, John Wiley & Sons, 1969.

Hughes, G.D. and Ray, M.L., (Eds.), *Buyer/Consumer Information Processing*, Chapel Hill, North Carolina, University of North Carolina, 1976.

Hunt, H.K. (Ed.), *Conceptualization and Measurement of Consumer Satisfaction and Dissatisfaction*, Cambridge, Massachusetts, Marketing Science Institute, 1977.

Hunt, H.K., "Consumer Satisfaction: Discussant Comments", in *Advances in Consumer Research*, Vol. X, Bagozzi, R.P. and Tybout, A.M., (Eds.), Ann Arbor, Association for Consumer Research, 1983, pp. 262.

Jacoby, J., "Consumer Research: A State of the Art Review", *Journal of Marketing*, Vol. 42, April, 1978, pp. 87-96.

Kassarjian, H.H., "Riesman Revisited", *Journal of Marketing*, Vol. 30, April, 1965, pp. 54-6.

Kassarjian, H.H., "Field Theory in Consumer Behavior", in *Consumer Behavior: Theoretical Sources*, Ward, S. and Robertson, T.S., (Eds.), Englewood Cliffs, New Jersey, Prentice-Hall, 1973, pp. 118-140.

Kassarjian, H.H., "Low Involvement: A Second Look", in *Advances in Consumer Research*, Vol. VIII, Monroe, K.B., (Eds.), Ann Arbor, Association for Consumer Research, 1981, pp. 31-4.

Kassarjian, H.H. and Choen, J.B., "Cognitive Dissonance and Consumer Behavior", *California Management Review*, Vol. 8, Fall, 1965, pp. 55-64.

Katona, G., *The Powerful Consumer*, New York, McGraw-Hill, 1960.

Katz, E. and Lazarsfeld, P.F., *Personal Influence*, Glencoe, Illinois, The Free Press, 1955.

Kelley, H., *Attribution in Social Interaction*, Morristown, New Jersey, General Learning Press, 1971.

Kenkel, W.F., "Husband-Wife Interaction in Decision Making and Decision Choices", *Journal of Social Psychology*, Vol. 54, August, 1961, pp. 255-62.

Kollat, D.R., Blackwell, R.D. and Engel, J.F., "The Current Status of Consumer Behavior Research: Developments During the 1968-1972 Period", in *Proceedings of the Third Annual Conference*, Venkatesan, M., (Ed.), Chicago, Association for Consumer Research, 1973, pp. 576-85.

Konsumentutredningen, *Synpunkter på den framtida konsumentpolitiken*, Stockholm, 1969.

Krugman, H.E., "The Impact of Television Advertising: Learning without Involvement", *Public Opinion Quarterly*, Vol. 29, 1965, pp. 349-56.

Kuhlmann, E., "Consumer Socialization of Children and Adolescents: A Review of Current Approaches", *Journal of Consumer Policy*, Vol. 6, 1983, pp. 397-418.

Lancaster, K., "A New Approach to Consumer Theory", *Journal of Political Economy*, Vol. 74, April, 1966, pp. 132-57.

Leigh, J.H. and Martin, C.R. Jr., "A Review of Situational Influence Paradigms and Research", in *Review of Marketing 1981*, Enis, B.M. and Roering, K.J., (Eds.), Chicago, American Marketing Association, 1981, pp. 57-74.

Lévi-Strauss, C., *Structural Anthropology*, Book 1, New York, Basic Books, 1963.

Levy, S.J., "Interpreting Consumer Mythology: A Structural Approach to Consumer Behavior", *Journal of Marketing*, Vol. 45, Summer, 1981, pp. 49-61.

Marcuse, H., *One-Dimensional Man*, Boston, Beacon Press, 1964.

Markin, R.J. and Narayana, C.L., "Behavior Control: Are Consumers Beyond Freedom and Dignity?", in *Advances in Consumer Research*, Vol. III, Anderson, B.B., (Ed.), Cincinnati, Association for Consumer Research, 1976, pp. 222-8.

Mizerski, R.W., Golden, L.L. and Kernan, J.B., "The Attribution Process in Consumer Decision Making", *Journal of Consumer Research*, Vol. 6, September, 1979, pp. 123-40.

Monroe, K.B., (Ed.), *Advances in Consumer Research*, Vol. VIII, Ann Arbor, Association for Consumer Research, 1981.

Myers, J.G., "Advertising and Socialization", in *Research in Marketing,* Vol. 1, Sheth, J.N., (Ed.), Greenwich, Connecticut, JAI Press, 1978, pp. 169-91.

Nicosia, F., *Consumer Decision Processes: Marketing and Advertising Implications,* Englewood Cliffs, New Jersey, Prentice-Hall, 1966.

Nicosia, F. and Mayer, R.N., "Toward a Sociology of Consumption", *Journal of Consumer Research,* Vol. 3, September, 1976, pp. 65-75.

Nord, W. and Peter, J.P., "A Behavior Modification Perspective on Marketing", *Journal of Marketing,* Vol. 44, Spring, 1980, pp. 36-47.

Odhnoff, J., "Systemanalys av hushållsbeteende", in *Konsumenten och Samhället,* Lundvall, L., (Ed.), Stockholm, Rabén & Sjögren, 1969, pp. 135-47.

Olander, F., "Consumer Satisfaction — A Skeptic's View", in *Conceptualization and Measurement of Consumer Satisfaction and Dissatisfaction,* Hunt, H.K., (Ed.), Cambridge, Massachusetts, Marketing Science Institute, 1977, pp. 409-52.

Oliver, R.L., "Theoretical Bases of Consumer Satisfaction Research: Review, Critique and Future Direction," in *Theoretical Developments in Marketing,* Lamb, C.W. Jr. and Dunne, P.M., (Eds.), Chicago, American Marketing Association, 1980, pp. 206-10.

Osgood, C.E. and Tannenbaum, P.H., "The Principle of Congruity in the Prediction of Attitude Change", *Psychological Review,* Vol. 62, 1955, pp. 42-55.

Perloff, R., "Consumer Analysis", *Annual Review of Psychology,* Vol. 19, 1968, pp. 437-66.

Pfeffer, J., *Organizations and Organization Theory,* Boston, Pitman, 1982.

Ratchford, B.T., "The New Economic Theory of Consumer Behavior: An Interpretive Essay", *Journal of Consumer Research,* Vol. 2, September, 1975, pp. 65-75.

Ray, M.L., "Marketing Communication and the Hierarchy of Effects", Working Paper, Palo Alto, Stanford University, 1973.

Robertson, T.S., "Low-Commitment Consumer Behavior", *Journal of Advertising Research,* Vol. 16, April, 1976, pp. 19-24.

Robertson, T.S. and Rossiter, J.R., "Children and Commercial Persuasion: An Attribution Theory Analysis", *Journal of Consumer Research,* Vol. 1, June, pp. 13-20.

Robertson, T.S. and Ward, S., "Consumer Behavior: Promise and Prospects", in *Consumer Behavior: Theoretical Sources,* Ward, S. and Robertson, T.S., (Eds.), Englewood Cliffs, New Jersey, Prentice-Hall, 1973, pp. 3-42.

Rogers, E.M., *Diffusion of Innovations,* New York, The Free Press, 1962.

Rogers, E.M. and Shoemaker, F.F., *Communication of Innovations: A Cross-Cultural Approach,* New York, The Free Press, 1971.

Rosenberg, M.J., "Cognitive Structure and Attitudinal Effect", *Journal of Abnormal and Social Psychology,* Vol. 53, November, 1956, pp. 367-72.

Sandell, R.G., "Effects of Attitudinal and Situational Factors on Reported Choice Behavior", *Journal of Marketing Research,* Vol. 5, November, 1968, pp. 405-8.

Sandell, R.G., *Att förstå konsumenten,* Stockholm, Norstedts, 1969.

Settle, R.B. and Golden, L., "Attribution Theory and Advertiser Credibility", *Journal of Marketing Research,* Vol. 11, May, 1974, pp. 181-5.

Sexton, D.E., Jr., "Black Buyer Behavior", *Journal of Marketing,* Vol. 36, October, 1972, pp. 36-9.

Sheth, J.N., "A Review of Buyer Behavior", *Management Science,* Vol. 13, August, 1967, pp. 718-56.

Sheth, J.N. (a), "A Theory of Family Buying Decisions", in *Models of Buyers Behavior: Conceptual, Quantitative, and Empirical,* Sheth, J.N., (Ed.), New York, Harper & Row, 1974, pp. 17-33.

Sheth, J.N. (b), "The Next Decade of Buyer Behavior Theory and Research", in *Models of Buyer Behavior: Conceptual, Quantitative and Empirical,* Sheth, J.N., (Ed.), New York, Harper & Row, 1974, pp. 391-406.

Sheth, J.N., "The Surpluses and Shortages in Consumer Behavior Theory and Research", *Journal of the Academy of Marketing Science,* Vol. 7, Fall, 1979, pp. 414-27.

Sheth, J.N. and Talarzyk, W.W., "Perceived Instrumentality and Value Importance as Determinants of Attitudes", *Journal of Marketing Research,* Vol. 9, February, 1972, pp. 6-9.

Skinner, B.F., *Beyond Freedom and Dignity,* New York, Alfred E. Knopf, 1972.

Thorelli, H.B., "Consumer Policy for the Third World", *Journal of Consumer Policy,* Vol. 5, Summer, 1981, pp. 197-211.

Thorelli, H.B., Becker, H. and Engledow, J., *The Information-Seekers: An International Study of Consumer Information and Advertising Image,* Cambridge, Massachusetts, Ballinger, 1975.

Tigert, D.J., "Can a Separate Marketing Strategy for French Canada be Justified? Profiling English-French Markets through Life-style Analysis", in *Canadian Marketing: Problems and Prospects,* Thompson, D. and Leighton, D. (Eds.), Toronto, John Wiley and Sons, 1973, pp. 113-42.

Twedt, D.W., "Consumer Psychology", *Annual Review of Psychology,* Vol. 16, 1965, pp. 265-94.

Uusitalo, L., *Consumption Style and Way of Life: An Empirical Identification and Explanation of Consumption Style Dimensions,* Helsinki, Helsinki School of Economics, 1979.

van Raaij, W.F., "Cross-Cultural Research Methodology as a Case of Construct Validity", in *Advances in Consumer Research,* Vol. V, Hunt, H.K., (Ed.), Ann Arbor, Association for Consumer Research, 1978, pp. 693-701.

Venkatesan, M., "Cognitive Consistency and Novelty Seeking", in *Consumer Behavior: Theoretical Sources,* Ward, S. and Robertson, T.S., (Eds.), Englewood Cliffs, New Jersey, Prentice-Hall, 1973, pp. 354-84.

Ward, S., "Consumer Socialization", *Journal of Consumer Research,* Vol. 1, September, 1974, pp. 1-14.

Ward. S. and Wackman, D., "Family and Media Influences on Adolescent Consumer Learning", *American Behavioral Scientist,* Vol. 14, January-February, 1971, pp. 415-27.

Webb, P.H., "Creative Scanner: A New Method for Studying Family Decision-Making", *Journal of Marketing,* Vol. 42, January, 1978, pp. 12, 126.

Wilkie, L., "Presidential Address: 1980", in *Advances in Consumer Research,* Vol. VIII, Monroe, K.B., (Ed.), Ann Arbor, Association for Consumer Research, 1981, pp. 1-5.

Wilkie, W.L. and Pessemier, E.A., "Issues in Marketing's Use of Multi-Attribute Attitude Models", *Journal of Marketing Research,* Vol. 10, November, 1973, pp. 428-41.

Zaltman, G. and Sternthal, B., (Eds.), *Broadening the Concept of Consumer Behavior,* Chicago, Association for Consumer Research, 1975.

Zaltman, G., Pinson, C.R.A. and Angelmar, R., *Metatheory and Consumer Research,* New York, Holt, Rinehart and Winston, 1973.

Zaltman, G. and Wallendorf, M., "Sociology: The Missing Chunk or How We've Missed the Boat", in *Contemporary Marketing Thought,* Proceedings of the 1977 Educators' Conference, Greenberg, B.A. and Bellenger, D.N. (Eds.), Chicago, American Marketing Association, 1977, pp. 235-8.

5. Conceptual and Methodological Issues in Buying Centre Research*

by Robert E. Spekman and Kjell Gronhaug

Introduction

Marketing scholars have long acknowledged the multiperson nature of the industrial/business buying process. Early work by Robinson, Faris and Wind (1968) and Webster and Wind (1972) was instrumental in developing the notion of the buying centre as the "proper" unit of analysis for business/organisational buying behaviour. Indeed, Zaltman, LeMasters and Heffering (1982) point to the buying centre as a core concept in the study of organisational buying. Sixteen years have passed and, despite a growing tradition of research, marketing scholars (e.g., Bonoma, Zaltman and Johnston, 1978; Thomas and Wind, 1980) have been critical of our progress to date and have questioned the overall contribution to this burgeoning field of inquiry. Much of the frustration and inability to move forward our knowledge of the buying centre can be attributed both to a difficulty in conceptualisation and to methodological problems inherent in capturing the multi-person nature of the buying centre.

The purpose of this article is to bring some convergence to this rather diffuse area of scholarly inquiry. By organizing a common point of reference it is hoped that this article can serve as a catalyst for others to look constructively towards future buying centre research opportunities and problems. As part of our development of the buying centre construct we address implicitly two major themes:

- conceptual issues and alternative views,
- methodological dilemma.

We begin our discussion by developing the concept of the buying centre. Next, we discuss structural properties and process considerations of the buying centre. Finally, research opportunities are outlined.

Towards a Definition of the Buying Centre

Our approach to the buying centre construct grows from an organisational perspective; for, as noted by Zaltman (1975) the study of industrial marketing, in general, and organisational buying, in particular, is the study of the behaviour of formal

---

*An earlier version of this article was presented at the workshop on Organisational Buying Behaviour held at the European Academy for Advanced Research in Management, Brussels 1982.

organisations. Not only does such an approach provide a better appreciation for, and understanding of, buying centre properties and its response to environmental exigencies; it furnishes a relevant body of literature from which conceptual clarity and methodological rigour can be adapted and utilised. To begin, buying centres possess properties similar to those ascribed by Aldrich (1979) to define organisations. Specifically, buying centres are purposeful (Spekman and Stern, 1979); distinguish among members and non-members (Wind, 1978); and possess a "technology" (i.e., mechanism) for accomplishing their goals. Nonetheless, it might be better to conceive of the buying centre as "organisation-like" as it is often not a formal organisation, or sub-unit, in the strict Weberian sense. To facilitate our conceptual development our focus will shift to the concepts of *boundary* and *domain* as both are fundamental to a buying centre definition and embrace basic theoretical and methodological issues.

Buying Centre Boundaries

Given the adoption of a systems perspective in buying centre inquiry (Johnston and Bonoma, 1981), it is crucial that the buying centre be distinguished from its environment. For organisational theorists (e.g., Starbuck, 1976; Weick, 1969) the distinction between an organisation and its environment is less than clear and the boundary is seen often as a subjectively determined barrier. For the buying centre researcher this problem is no less real and is exacerbated by the fact that it is not uncommon to find extra-organisational members serving as buying centre members (see, Lilien and Choffray, 1980). To compare the buying centre, and its boundary, to a cloud is to capture two important properties of the construct. First, boundaries are not fixed and are subject to change depending on which criteria are used to delimit inclusion in (or exclusion from) the buying centre. Second, one must consider the notion of periphery, for as one moves out from the "core" of the buying centre one's ability to determine boundaries fades since the distinction between the environment and the buying centre becomes less clear.

Early research suggests that the buying centre boundary was often set arbitrarily at the "edge" of the organisation. Such a demarcation was an outgrowth of the tendency to separate empirically buyers and sellers. As researchers developed a more dyadic view of the buyer-seller relationship (see, Bagozzi, Bonoma and Zaltman, 1978), buying centre research began slowly to consider a boundary that could, in fact, transcend the organisation and encompass an "inter-organisational dyad" (Johnston and McQuistan, 1985). Clearly, organisational membership is not necessarily the primary criterion for deciding buying centre membership and, in a number of contexts, it may be inappropriate. Perhaps a better criterion is decision relevance which links a person to the buying centre by virtue of that person's ability to contribute, in a purposive fashion, to the buying centre's decision-making activities. Such a rule for inclusion is very consistent with methods for determining organisational membership (Aldrich, 1979; Thompson, 1968).

The relevance criterion lends itself very well to a sociometric methodology for examining buying centre membership. Marketing researchers (e.g., Johnston, 1981; Moriarty, 1980; and Spekman, 1977) have, after locating a "central" buying centre member, relied on a snowballing technique to ascertain purposive involvement in a particular procurement decision. Such an approach satisfies part of the buying centre boundary problem and permits a reasonably accurate portrayal of the communications network dedicated to that particular buying decision. In addition, this methodology is not subject to criticisms evolving from the respondent versus key informant debate. Also, the snowballing methodology is less likely to fall prey to the partial systems fallacy whereby erroneous data result from a failure to include all members of the sociometric network (Laumann, Marsden and Prensky, 1983).

Despite these benefits, the unfolding technique is limited by the cross-sectional nature of most research approaches. Given that the procurement decision consists of a number of phases, a static framework will miss the dynamics of the process. That is, one is likely to find that the buying centre composition (and, hence, its boundary) changes as members enter and leave depending on their perceived relevance to the buying decision at hand. Marketers have not captured this "ebb and flow" of the procurement decision process. Recent protocol (Crow, Olshavsky and Summers, 1980) and observational (Vyas and Woodside, 1982) are steps in that direction. We are, then, faced with the trade-offs inherent in the case study versus more quantitative approaches. Rather than view these methodologies as mutually exclusive it would be advantageous to recognise strengths in each that can be heightened through an integration of both in our research designs.

Buying Centre Domain

Domain embodies the specific goals of an organisation and the functions required to achieve these goals. Thus, domain not only defines organisational boundaries (i.e., sets the criteria for membership) it focuses the organisation's energy. Warren (1967) argues that domain gives the organisation purpose and legitimacy. To be sure, marketers have emphasised implicitly the notion of domain in their attempts to define and delimit the activities of a particular buying centre. Extant research converges on the precepts that buying centres are decision-making units and their decision-making activities are tied to the procurement of a particular commodity, product or service (Spekman, 1977; Wind, 1978).

Although we benefit from an improved understanding of buying centre purpose, we do not gain an appreciation of buying centre fit — i.e., the nature of the relationships and linkages with other department/units and extra-organisational units. More precisely, marketers have focused mainly on information needs and choice criteria and have not examined information flows between and among other organisational units and the buying centre. For example, researchers have sought typically to determine differences in information sources utilised by buying centre members (e.g., Cardozo and Cagley, 1971; Ozanne and Churchill, 1971). With the exception of Calder (1977) and Johnston (1981) there has been little attempt to investigate information flows and communications networks between the buying centre and other organisational units.

Defining the Buying Centre

The buying centre takes on life as a purposeful, decision-making unit (see Grashof and Thomas, 1976; Johnston and Bonoma, 1981; Nicosia and Wind, 1978; Wind, 1978). Its domain consists of information acquisition, search processes, developing choice criteria and actually deciding among alternatives. Its boundaries are drawn around those individuals contributing relevant purchasing-related information to the procurement decision process, regardless of the phase in the overall decision process. While similar to Duncan's (1972) decision-making unit, the buying centre construct is not a formally defined entity which can be found on an organisation chart. (It is acknowledged, however, that standing buying committees are an exception.) Buying centres are seen as emerging, quasi-organisational units whose derivation, composition and behaviour are controlled less by formal organisational linkages and more by informal, cross-functional, lateral ties that are likely to take shape during the procurement decision process. Decision participants enter the decision process as their stake in the decision outcome increases (e.g., Patchen, 1975; Pettigrew, 1975); their expertise/opinion is deemed relevant (e.g., Bonoma, Zaltman and Johnston, 1977); their formal role in the organisation mandates involvement (e.g., Robinson, Faris and Wind, 1968); and/or as a number of non-task related factors become operative (Webster and Wind, 1972). The problem for the researcher is to capture the composition of the buying centre as it changes over time as well as to articulate the nature of the ties that bind the various buying centre members. Certainly, the complexity of the evolving "role set" comprising the buying centre adds to the methodological challenges confronting the researcher.

Dimensions of Buying Centres
Any attempt to gain insight into, and an appreciation for, the dynamics of the buying centre must consider two dimensions along which organisation behaviour can be explained: structure and process. Structure is the arrangement of components and sub-systems within a system and refers to the pattern of relationships among the individuals and units (Rogers and Agarwalla-Rogers, 1976). In this fashion, structural variables tend to prescribe formal role requirements while process variables deal, instead, with power and conflict relationships, communications flows and decision making (Hall, 1978). Thus, structure helps us understand *how* an organisation is and process tells us *why* it is the way it is.

Buying Centre Structure
Structural variables become important to marketing researchers as organisational theorists have shown that structure is a critical variable in determining the effectiveness of a decision unit's (here, the buying centre) information-processing potential (see, Aiken and Hage, 1968; Duncan, 1972; Hall, 1978; Lawrence and Lorsch, 1967; Pugh, Hickson and Hinnings, 1969). Building on these earlier studies marketers have utilised structural measures to explain buying centre influence patterns (Spekman, 1979; Thomas, 1980); the diffusion of marketing information (Deshpande, 1982); communications flows within buying centres (Johnston and Bonoma, 1981); market planning models (Martin, 1979); and buyer-seller dyadic relationships (e.g., Hakansson, 1982).

While these results are less than univocal, several general conclusions can be gleaned. First, these results suggest that structural variables are viable constructs for measuring aspects of the buying centre's influence and communication networks. Second, the results tend to be consistent with work by organisational contingency theorists in that it appears that buying centre composition, structure and information-processing capabilities will vary depending on certain contextual factors and external exigencies. Third, the research is fraught with a number of methodological problems including the use of objective versus subjective measures (Johnston, 1981), the use of respondents versus informants (Phillips and Bagozzi, 1980), issues related to the aggregation of buying centre data (Wind, 1978), and the question of formal versus informal structure within the buying centre (Spekman, 1977).

In addition, recent organisational research suggests that these earlier studies may be flawed due to methodological and conceptual shortcomings that may have predetermined the outcomes of the research and that the contingency model of organisational performance (e.g., environment → structure → performance) may be inadequate. As Child (1972) and others have shown, the strong empirical link between environment/structure and performance has not been forged. In its place, others have suggested a more integrative paradigm that combines strategy as part of the antecedents to organisational performance (Chandler, 1962; Rumelt, 1974). For the buying centre researcher it is clear that dependence on a particular conceptualisation may not be wise and that a more multi-disciplinary approach to buying centre research is warranted.

Contributions can be made by developing research projects that attempt to rectify some of these problems. Research must demonstrate: (1) a greater sensitivity to the importance of hypothesis testing; (2) a better appreciation for theories that explain empirical observations that are falsifiable; and (3) a devotion to improved operationalisation and methodological rigour. For instance, greater attention should be given to the structure-environment nexus. It is important to understand how organisational structure may differ from or may shape the structure of the buying centre. Similarly, it is useful to examine how a particular buying strategy may serve to mediate the effects of environmental uncertainty on the structure of the buying centre. Both approaches converge on the need to improve our understanding of how buying centre structure facilitates/impedes a decision participant's ability to gather, process and act on relevant procurement-related information. However, it would be inappropriate to suggest that we can focus only on organisational structure and neglect process concerns. The two are far from being independent.

Process Considerations in Buying Centres

Over the years marketing scholars have tended to focus primarily on process-related variables as evidenced by a convergence on the following kinds of research issues:

● defining the locus and power of buying responsibility;

● mapping the decision processes utilised by buying centre members;

● understanding the patterns of authority and communication within the buying centre (see, Thomas and Wind (1980) for a review).

Despite the energy devoted to these areas of inquiry our present ability to understand the dynamics and complexity of buying centre processes is limited. To structure our discussion we follow a typology by Hall (1978) who defines organisational process as consisting of three primary components: power and conflict, decision making and communications.

Power and Conflict. The importance of power and conflict to the study of buying centre decision processes evolves from the observation that organisational decision making is a group process involving some kind of accommodation among units and/or individuals (Patchen, 1975) that lead to satisficing rather than an optimising problem solution (Cyert, Simon and Trow, 1956; Strauss, 1962). Power can either be embedded within the formal hierarchy (i.e., authority) or can evolve as a result of interactions among organisational actors. It is the latter concern that has been the focus of buying centre research. Power is viewed as relational, a function of dependence and is defined in terms of the resources available to the more influential participant in the decision process (Dahl, 1963; Emerson, 1962; French and Raven, 1959).

Buying centre research has examined the perceived influence of purchasing managers (Spekman, 1979); various functional areas (Cooley, Jackson and Ostrom, 1977); gatekeepers, users and other buying centre roles (Pettigrew, 1975). Findings have been reported also for both individual phases as well as for the overall procurement decision (an excellent review is found in Silk and Kalwani (1982)). Furthermore, Johnston and Bonoma (1981) have furnished some exploratory results comparing hierarchical and horizontal influence patterns. What becomes evident is that greater rigour is needed in the construction of scales used to measure influence and that multiple respondent, rather than single informant, approaches are preferable.

It is interesting to note that the typical research paradigm builds on an Emersonian definition of power that is based implicitly on a dyadic interpretation of power dependence. Recently, Cook (1982), Emerson (1962) and others have abandoned the dyadic model as inappropriate and have developed an exchange network approach to accommodate the complexity of multi-person structures. Building on concepts drawn from social network analysis (see, for example, Freeman, 1978) power is measured by network centrality and one's ability to control information flows. Simply, centrality embodies the convergence of communications activities that suggest relative power differences among organisational members. As buying centre definition and measurement has been linked to sociometric techniques, the exchange network methodology might be a useful tool for future buying centre research. In addition, this approach is based on the distribution of valued resources among network members which implies that buying centre power studies could benefit from organisational studies that consider resource dependency as the key to power dependence relationships (e.g., Aldrich, 1979; Pfeffer and Salancik, 1978; Provan, Beyer and Kruytbosch, 1980). Furthermore, these studies recognise ties between power and conflict which are not captured presently in "power in the buying centre" studies. While some of the problem can be traced to the cross-sectional nature of present buying centre research, little if any research has attempted to assess the manner in which power/influence affects decision conflict, impacts on the number and kind of decision alternatives, and/or shapes the final decision outcome.

Conflict not only is the handmaiden of organisational influence attempts, it is the natural occurrence of the differences in personal and organisational goals among decision participants (March and Simon, 1958; Thomas, 1976). It is important to note that conflict should not be viewed as dysfunctional and that Hall (1978) and others have demonstrated that some confrontation (i.e., conflict) may produce a better decision. Despite the centrality of the conflict construct to present models of organisational buying behaviour (Sheth, 1973; Webster and Wind, 1972) empirical examination of conflict within a buying centre context is, at best, scant. Typically, research has inferred conflict from differences in attribute importances among buying centre members (Gronhaug, 1976) or has posed potential conflict situations to examine the salience of supplier characteristics and product attributes (Lehmann and O'Shaughnessy, 1974). For the most part, however, empirical evidence has been limited to anecdotal, qualitative examinations of buying decisions (e.g., Cyert *et al.*, 1956).

Although descriptive research has done much to further our appreciation of the power/conflict dynamics inherent during the procurement process, it has not encouraged the quantitative investigations that are needed for theory testing, validation of results and the interpretation of statistical relationships (Jick, 1979; Sieber, 1973). This void in the empirical buying centre literature is difficult to understand given both the amount of organisational literature devoted to the construct's (i.e., conflict) scale construction and psychometric properties as well as to the importance accorded conflict in models of organisational buying. Certainly, our knowledge of buying centre processes is limited to the extent that conflict within the buying centre — its antecedents and its consequences — remains a neglected area of scholarly inquiry.

Decision Making. Consistent with other organisational decision theorists the procurement decision process has been defined broadly as the set of actions and dynamic factors that begins with the identification of a stimulus for action and ends with the specific commitment to action (Mentzberg *et al.*, 1976). Furthermore, the procurement decision process is governed by both task and non-task-related factors (March and Simon, 1958) and is subject to the same limitations/constraints that are imposed by the concept of bounded rationality (Simon, 1956). Within the extant research one finds two implicit streams of research. One stream focuses on the number of decision phases and their timing and the other emphasises the type of decision-making model (or choice routine) utilised.

There appears to be some debate regarding the number of phases comprising the buying decision and whether these phases are iterative or sequential (see Johnston, 1981). While one can vacillate between a desire to mirror exactly a specific buying decision and a need to present a more general, pedagogically sound (and, for that matter, a more managerially useful) decision model, it becomes clear that the debate regarding the precise number of phases is, at best, academic. Nonetheless, there must be recognition that the actual number of phases cannot be fixed and that the "true" (i.e., observable) number of phases is ruled by the decision context and those idiosyncratic factors (i.e., individual, organisational and environmental) that help shape organisational buying behaviour (see Lilien and Choffray, 1980). Based on work by Cyert, March and Simon, and others it is apparent that in spite of the potential for a seemingly infinite number of decision phases one can distill three major sub-processes that comprise organisational decision making — problem recognition, the screening of alternatives and the selection phase.

Our position regarding the iterative/sequential controversy is bolstered by research that views organisational decision making as "muddling through" (Lindblom, 1956) whereby a decision may ebb and flow towards a solution and notes that a strictly sequential progression may not be indicative of many procurement decisions. Indeed, the iterative nature of the decision process becomes more representative as the buying centre members approach their bounds of rationality. Of central importance here is the observation that problems at one phase of the decision process are likely to lead to a re-cycling until a "solution" at that phase has been crystallised (Witte, 1972). To concentrate effort searching for the unique characteristics of each buying centre decision is to ignore the importance of research devoted to developing paradigms that improve our ability to understand and measure buying centre decision behaviour. Such an endeavour will bring to organisational buying behaviour research a sense of purpose and direction. Paradigms afford a foundation for scientific inquiry as they define what should be studied, what questions should be asked, and what rules should be followed in interpreting the answer obtained (Kuhn, 1970).

The second major research theme converges on the decision model utilised during the procurement process and has focused mainly on the selection phase (see above) of the buying process. Mentzberg *et al.* (1976) discuss three models of choice which can be used to categorise organisational buying research: judgement, bargaining and analysis. *Judgement* refers to individual decision making whereby one acts either autonomously without the input of others or jointly (i.e., information is gathered from others but the ultimate decision is made unilaterally). A flaw in early organisational buying behaviour research was its focus on only one member of the buying centre (see, for example, Wilson, 1971; Feldman and Cardozo, 1969). In buying situations where a buying centre member acts unilaterally based on information supplied by others, marketers would benefit from organisational research that examines the potential power of subordinates (Mechanic, 1968), boundary spanners and gatekeepers (e.g., Adams, 1976).

Bargaining describes group decision making in which conflicting goal systems exist. Although this model is at the core of Sheth's (1972) model of organisational buying behaviour marketers have failed to test empirically this decision mode. The trade-offs, concessions and attempts at gamesmanship that were described by Strauss (1962) have recently been captured in elaborate descriptions of buying episodes (see work by Moller, 1981) but have escaped the scrutiny of explicit quantitative examination. The *analytical* mode is stressed in the normative organisational buying literature where alternatives can be elucidated and preferences among decision participants can be known. For example, both Lilien and Choffray's (1980) market response model and Wind and Cardozo's (1974) micro-segmentation heuristic capture this form of decision making. While the extent to which each of the above decision models is used in a buying centre context is not known, other organisational researchers suggest that analytical approaches are in the minority. Part of the problem is that our ability to understand and address such concerns is limited, to a very large extent, by our research methods. While a fairly robust literature dedicated to models of multiperson choice exist (see, Lilien and Choffray (1980) for a brief review) marketers have been less than eager to bring these multi-disciplinary approaches to buying centre research.

Communications Flows. This area of research best reflects the informal interactions that emerge during the buying process. While organisational structure lends predictability and stability to buying activities, it cannot solely control nor can it account for a good deal of buying centre interactions. Network analysis and, concurrently, the need to understand better the communications patterns within the buying centre can be traced to research by Bavelas (1951) and Leavitt (1951) who examined information flows within small groups. Network analysis provides a framework for describing processes by which resources are gained and mobilised and the resultant social system. Through such research we can appreciate better the complexity of the buying process and can gain insight into the potential ability of buying centre members to filter, control and/or distort relevant procurement-related information by virtue of one's position in the network. We gain also from the benefits of an established methodology. However, network analysis is not without its critics (e.g., Wellman, 1982; Blau, 1982) who charge that the approach is descriptive only and does not relate the emergent network to its antecedent factors nor does one gain a sense of what the consequences of a particular network hold. With the exception of Bonoma and Zaltman (1978), Calder (1977), and Johnston (1979) there has been little effort given to incorporating formally network analysis in research dedicated to the informal communications flows that are at the heart of the buying centre concept.

Concluding Comments

Our primary concern here has been twofold. First, we have attempted to present an organising framework to the study of the buying centre. Second, we have pointed to a number of competing paradigms from which buying centre research and, for that matter, the whole of organisational buying behaviour might benefit. Present research suffers from two major flaws that serve to inhibit the scholarly development of this field of inquiry. The first weakness is that buying centre research tends to be very descriptive, relying heavily on anecdotal information. As a consequence, much buying centre research is devoid of any theoretical foundation. The second flaw is that many of the existing findings have grown from research that, while acknowledging the multi-person nature of the buying process, reflects individual level methodologies. Indeed, the void in current research can be attributed to a lack of conceptual and methodological rigour that is the direct result of the fragmented and idiosyncratic nature of the field of industrial/business marketing.

For this field to prosper researchers must develop and nurture a tradition of research that searches for foundations upon which paradigms can be presented and tested. In short, buying centre research must be a theory-driven, programmatic attempt to gain an understanding of the complex array of factors that comprise the organisational buying process. It is not enough to reach consensus that the buying centre is the proper unit of analysis for delving into organisational buying problems and issues. We must strive to gain a better appreciation of the complex set of issues that are embedded in the study of an emergent, informal (yet purposeful) organisational decision unit. Domain and boundary were offered as providing a framework for improving our ability to understand conceptually and to delimit methodologically the purpose, scope and composition of the buying centre. Nonetheless, additional research is needed if we are to understand more fully how and to what extent contextual, temporal and environmental factors affect the decision-making capability (i.e., performance) of the buying centre membership.

We have proposed structure and process-related variables as the major determinants of buying centre behaviour. Not only do structure and process-related variables determine the buying centre's ability to search, acquire and filter procurement-related information, but these constructs also serve to explain the decision participants' (i.e., buying centre members) decision-making behaviour. In addition, both have served as vehicles to present and categorise a number of potentially appropriate paradigms for testing empirically buying centre problems. Rather than present solutions, we have chosen, instead, to raise a number of yet unresolved conceptual and methodological problem areas. Part of our objective here is to challenge conventional industrial/ business marketing wisdom by questioning established methods of inquiry.

The Fall 1983 edition of the *Journal of Marketing* presented a number of papers that posed the need for marketing to develop paradigms as possible foundations for theory building in marketing. Such an appeal is even more critical for research focusing on organisational buying behaviour, in general, and the buying centre, in particular. While some of the papers spoke about the scientific method and scientific practice in marketing (e.g., Anderson, 1983), others became advocates for the adoption of a particular paradigm. The latter article symbolises the political aspects of theory building whereby one paradigm gains hegemony within a discipline because supporters have more power (Bagozzi, 1980). As buying centre research has developed without the benefit of a strong theoretical base our goal has not been to challenge an existing paradigm. Furthermore, we have not championed an emerging paradigm by arguing that our paradigm is "better". Too often such attacks focus only on discrediting extant approaches and fail to understand competing paradigms. Instead, we have argued implicitly that buying centre research warrants a multi-paradigm approach. The field of inquiry is too young to be guided by a singular, dominant paradigm. To prosper, buying centre research will benefit from debate that centres on arguing the relative "scientific" merits of competing paradigms. We have helped to begin that debate.

It is important to note that we have not attempted to offer a buying centre theory. Our contribution is limited to providing a framework for further inquiry. That is, we have presented a number of competing paradigms from a number of disciplines that are intended to stimulate a cross-fertilisation of research approaches and guiding concepts. Our hope is that others will journey down the research paths we have outlined and begin the scientific inquiry from which a set of theory-driven buying centre hypotheses can be developed and tested.

References

Adams, J., "The Structure and Dynamics of Boundary Roles", in Dunnette, M., (Ed.), *Handbook of Industrial and Organizational Psychology*, Chicago, Rand McNally, 1976.

Agular, F., *Scanning the Business Environment*, New York, Macmillan, 1967.

Aiken, M. and Hage J., "Organizational Interdependence and Intraorganizational Structure", *American Sociological Review*, Vol. 33, 1968.

Aldrich H., *Organizations and Environments*, Englewood Cliffs, New Jersey, Prentice Hall, 1979.

Anderson, P.F., "Marketing, Scientific Progress, and Scientific Method", *Journal of Marketing*, Vol. 47, 1983, pp. 18-31.

Bagozzi, R.P., *Causal Models in Marketing*, New York, John Wiley, 1980.

Bagozzi, R., Bonoma, T.V. and Zaltman, G., "The Dyadic Paradigm with Specific Application toward Industrial Marketing", in Bonoma, T.V. and Zaltman, G., (Eds.), *Organizational Buying Behavior*, Chicago, American Marketing Association, 1978, pp. 49-66.

Bavelas, A., "Communication Patterns in Task-Oriented Groups", *Journal of Acoustical Society of America*, Vol. 22, 1951, pp. 725-730.

Blau, P., "Structural Sociology and Network Analysis", in Marsden, P. and Lin, N., (Eds.), *Social Structure and Network Analysis*, Los Angeles, Sage Publications, 1982.

Bonoma, T., Zaltman, J. and Johnston, W. J., *Industrial Buying Behaviour*, Cambridge, Massachusetts, Marketing Science Institute, 1977.

Bonoma, T. and Zaltman, J. (Eds.), *Organizational Buying Behaviour*, Chicago, Illinois, American Marketing Association, 1978.

Calder, B., "Structural Role Analysis in Organizational Buying", in Woodside, A., Sheth, J. and Bennett, P., (Eds.), *Consumer and Industrial Buying Behaviour*, New York, North Holland, 1977.

Cardozo, R. and Cagley, J., "Experimental Study of Industrial Buyer Behaviour", *Journal of Marketing Research*, Vol. 8, 1971, pp. 329-334.

Child, J., "Organizational Structure, Environment and Performance: The Role of Strategic Choice", *Sociology*, Vol. 6, 1972, pp. 2-22.

Chandler, A., *Strategy and Structure: Chapters in the History of American Industrial Enterprise*, Cambridge, Massachusetts, MIT Press, 1962.

Cook, K.S., "Network Structures from an Exchange Perspective", in P. Marsden and N. Lin, (Eds.), *op. cit.*, 1982.

Cooley, J., Jackson, D. and Ostrom, L., "Analyzing the Relative Power of Participants in Industrial Buying Decisions", in Greenberg, B., *et al.*, (Eds.), *Contemporary Marketing Thought*, Chicago, American Marketing Association, 1977.

Crow, L., Olshavsky, R. and Summers, J., "Industrial Buyers' Choice Models: A Rotocal Analysis", *Journal of Marketing Research*, Vol. 17, 1980, pp. 34-44.

Cyert, R., Simon, H. and Trow, D., "Observation of a Business Decision", *Journal of Business*, Vol. 29, October, 1956, pp. 237-248.

Cyert, R. and March, J., *A Behavioural Theory of the Firm*, Englewood Cliffs, New Jersey, Prentice Hall, 1963.

Dahl, R., *A Modern Political Analysis*, Englewood Cliffs, New Jersey, Prentice Hall, 1963.

Deshpande, R., "The Organizational Context of Market Research Use", *Journal of Marketing*, Vol. 46, 1982, pp. 91-101.

Duncan, R., "Characteristics of Organizational Environments and Perceived Environmental Uncertainty", *Administrative Science Quarterly*, Vol. 17, 1972, pp. 313-327.

Emerson, R., "Power Dependence Relations", *American Sociological Review*, Vol. 27, 1962, pp. 31-41.

Emerson, R., "Social Exchange Theory", in Rosenberg, M. and Turner, R., (Eds.), *Social Psychology: Sociological Perspectives*, New York, Basic Books, 1981.

Feldman, W. and Cardozo, R., "The Industrial Revolution and Models of Buyer Behavior", *Journal of Purchasing*, Vol. 5, 1969, pp. 77-88.

Freeman, L., "Centrality in Social Networks Conceptual Clarification", *Social Networks,* Vol. 1, 1978, pp. 215-239.

French, J.R.P. and Raven, B., "The Bases of Social Power", in Cartwright, D. (Ed.), *Studies in Social Power*, Ann Arbor, Michigan, Institute for Social Research, 1959.

Grashof, J. and Thomas, G., "Industrial Buying Center Responsibilities: Self versus Other Member Evaluation of Importance", *Educators' Proceedings*, Chicago, American Marketing Association, 1976, pp. 344-347.

Gronhaug, K., "Exploring Environmental Influences in Organizational Buying", *Journal of Marketing Research*, Vol. 13, 1976, pp. 225-229.

Gronhaug, K., "Autonomous vs. Joint Decisions in Organizational Buying", *Industrial Marketing Management*, Vol. 4, 1975, pp. 265-271.

Hakansson, H., *International Marketing and Purchasing of Industrial Goods*; An Interaction Approach, Chichester, John Wiley & Sons, 1982.

Hall, R., *Organizations: Structure and Process*, Englewood Cliffs, New Jersey, Prentice Hall, 1978.

Jick, T., "Mixing Qualitative and Quantitative Methods: Triangulation in Action", *Administrative Science Quarterly*, Vol. 24, 1979, pp. 602-11.

Johnston, W., "Communication Networks and Influence Patterns in Industrial Buying Behavior", unpublished doctoral dissertation, University of Pittsburgh, Pittsburgh, Pennsylvania, 1979.

Johnston, W., "Industrial Buyer Behavior: A State of the Art Review", in Roering, K. (Ed.), *Review of Marketing*, Chicago, American Marketing Association, 1981.

Johnston, W. and Bonoma, T., "The Buying Center: Structure and Interaction Patterns", *Journal of Marketing*, Vol. 45, 1981, pp. 143-156.

Johnston, W. and McQuistan, D., "Managing Interorganizational Marketing", in Spekman, R. and Wilson, D. (Eds.), *A Strategic Approach to Business Marketing*, Chicago, American Marketing Association, 1985. 1985.

Klebba, J., "The Structure of the Purchasing Function as Determined by Environmental Uncertainty", unpublished Ph.D. dissertation, University of Minnesota, 1978.

Kuhn, T.S., *The Structure of Scientific Revolutions*, second edition, Chicago, University of Chicago Press, 1970.

Lauman, E., Marsden, P. and Prensky, D., "Boundary Specification Problems in Network Analysis", in Burt, R. and Minor, M., (Eds.), *Applied Network Analysis,* Los Angeles, Sage Publications, 1983.

Lawrence, P.R. and Lorsch, J., *Organizations and Their Environment*, Cambridge, Massachusetts, Harvard University Division of Research, 1967.

Leavitt, H., "Some Effects of Certain Communication Patterns on Group Performance", *Journal of Abnormal and Social Psychology*, Vol. 46, 1951, pp. 38-40.

Lehmann, D. and O'Shaughnessy, J., "Differences in Attribute Importance for Different Industrial Products", *Journal of Marketing*, Vol. 38, 1974, pp. 36-42.

Lilien, G. and Choffray, J.M., *Market Planning for New Industrial Products*, New York, John Wiley and Sons, 1980.

Lindblom, C., "The Science of Muddling Through", *Public Administration Review,* Vol. 19, 1956, pp. 79-88.

March, J., "An Introduction to the Theory and Measurement of Influence", *American Political Science Review*, Vol. 49, 1955, pp. 433-51.

March, J. and Simon, H., *Organizations*, New York, J. Wiley and Sons, 1958.

Martin, J., "The Effects of Organizational Structure on Marketing Planning", *unpublished doctoral dissertation,* Northwestern University, 1979.

Mechanic, D., "Sources of Power in Lower Participants in Complex Organizations", *Administrative Science Quarterly,* Vol. 7, 1968, pp. 349-369.

Mentzberg, H., Raisirghani, D. and Theoret, A., "The Structure of 'Unstructured' Decision Processes", *Administrative Science Quarterly*, Vol. 21, 1976, pp. 246-275.

Merton, R., *Social Theory and Social Structure*, New York, Free Press, 1957.

Moller, K., *"Industrial Buying Behaviour of Production Materials: A Conceptual Analysis*, Helsinki, Helsinki School of Economics, 1981.

Moriarty, R., "The Use of Organizational Buying Behavior in Assessing Industrial Markets", unpublished DBA dissertation, Graduate School of Business, Harvard University, 1980.

Moriarty, R. and Bateson, J., "Explaining Complex Decision Making Units", *Journal of Marketing Research*, Vol. 19, pp. 182-192.

Nicosia, F. and Wind, Y., *Behavioral Models for Market Analysis*, New York, Holt, Rinehart and Winston, 1978.

Ozanne, U. and Churchill, G., "Five Dimensions of the Industrial Adoption Process", *Journal of Marketing Research*, Vol. 8, 1971, pp. 322-328.

Patchen, M., "The Locus and Bases of Influence on Organizational Decisions", *Organizational Behaviour and Human Performance*, Vol. 11, 1975, pp. 195-221.

Pettigrew, A., "The Industrial Purchasing Decision as a Political Process", *European Journal of Marketing*, Vol. 9, 1975, pp. 4-19.

Pfeffer, J. and Salancek, G., *The External Control of Organizations: A Resource Dependence Perspective*, New York, Harper & Row, 1978.

Phillips, L. and Bagozzi, R., "On Measuring Organizational Properties: Methodological Issues in the Use of Key Informants", Working Paper, Sloan School of Management, 1980.

Provan, K., Beyer, J. and Kruytbosch, C., "Environmental Linkages and Power in Resource Dependence Relations in Complex Organizations", *Administrative Science Quarterly*, Vol. 25, 1980, pp. 200-225.

Pugh, D., Hickson, D. and Hinings, C.R., "An Empirical Taxonomy of Work Organizations", *Administrative Science Quarterly*, Vol. 14, 1969, pp. 123-139.

Robinson, P., Faris, C.W. and Wind, Y., *Industrial Buying and Creative Marketing*, Boston, Allyn and Bacon, 1968.

Rogers, E. and Rogers, R.A., *Communication in Organizations*, New York, The Free Press, 1976.

Rumelt, R., *Strategy, Structure and Economic Performance*, Cambridge, Massachusetts, Harvard University Press, 1974.

Sheth, J., "A Model of Industrial Buyer Behavior", *Journal of Marketing*, Vol. 37, 1973, pp. 50-56.

Sieber, S., "The Integration of Fieldwork and Survey Methods", *American Journal of Sociology*, Vol. 78, 1973, pp. 1335-1359.

Silk, A. and Kalwani, M., "Measuring Influence in Organizational Purchase Decisions", *Journal of Marketing Research*, Vol. 19, 1982, pp. 165-181.

Simon, H., *Models of Man*, New York, John Wiley, 1956.

Simon, H., and Nowell, A., *Human Problem Solving*, Englewood Cliffs, New Jersey, Prentice Hall, 1972.

Spekman, R.E., "A Contingency Approach to Power Relationships Within the Organizational Buying Task Group", unpublished Ph.D. dissertation, Northwestern University, 1977.

Spekman, R.E., "Information and Influence: An Exploratory Investigation of the Boundary Role Person's Basis of Power", *Academy of Management Journal*, Vol. 22, 1979, pp. 104-117.

Spekman, R. and Stern, L.W., "Environmental Uncertainty and Buying Group Structure: An Empirical Investigation", *Journal of Marketing*, Vol. 43, 1979, pp. 54-64.

Starbuck, W., "Organizations and Their Environment", in Dunnette, W. (Ed.), *Handbook of Industrial and Organizational Psychology*, Chicago, Rand McNally, 1976.

Strauss, G., "Tactics of Lateral Relationships: The Purchasing Agent", *Administrative Science Quarterly*, Vol. 7, 1962, pp. 161-186.

Thomas, K., "Conflict and Conflict Management", in Dunnette, W., (Ed.), *op. cit.*

Thomas, R., "Correlates of Interpersonal Purchase Influence in Organizations", unpublished doctoral dissertation, University of Pennsylvania, 1980.

Thomas, R. and Wind, Y., "Conceptual and Methodological Issues in Organizational Buying Behaviour", *European Journal of Marketing*, Vol. 14, 1980, pp. 239-263.

Thompson, J., *Organizations in Action*, New York, McGraw Hill, 1968.

Vyas, N. and Woodside, A., "Micro-Analysis of Supplier Choice Strategies", a paper presented at the European Institute for Advanced Studies in Management, Brussels, on Organizational Buying Behaviour, 1982.

Warren, R., "The Interorganizational Field as a Focus for Investigation", *Administrative Science Quarterly*, Vol. 12, 1967, pp. 396-419.

Weber, M., *The Theory of Social and Economic Organization*, New York, The Free Press, 1947.

Webster, F. and Wind, Y., *Organizational Buying Behavior*, Englewood Cliffs, New Jersey, Prentice Hall, 1972.

Weick, K., *The Social Psychology of Organizing*, Reading, Massachusetts, Addison Wesley, 1969.

Wellman, B., "Studying Personal Communities", in Marsden, P. and Lin, N. (Eds.), *op. cit.*

Wilson, D.T., "Industrial Buyers' Decision Making Styles", *Journal of Marketing Research*, Vol. 7, 1971, pp. 433-436.

Wind, Y., "The Boundaries of Buying Decision Centers", *Journal of Purchasing and Materials Management*, Vol. 14, 1978, pp. 23-29.

Wind, Y., "Research Agenda in Organizational Buying Behavior", in Zaltman, J. and Bonoma, T. (Eds.), *Organizational Buyer Behavior*, Chicago, American Marketing Association, 1978.

Wind, Y. and Cardozo, R., "Industrial Marketing Segmentation", *Industrial Marketing Management,* Vol. 3, 1974, pp. 28-36.

Wind, Y., Robertson, T. and Fraser, C., "Industrial Product Diffusion by Market Segment", *Industrial Marketing Management*, Vol. 11, pp. 1-8.

Witte, E., "Field Research on Complex, Decision-Making Processes — The Phase Theorem", *International Studies of Management and Organization*, 1972, pp. 156-182.

Zaltman, J., "The Frontiers of Marketing", Albert W. Frey Lecture, University of Pittsburgh, 1975.

Zaltman, J., LeMasters, K. and Heffering, M., *Theory Construction in Marketing*, New York, John Wiley, 1982.

6. The Definition of Market Segments for Banking Services

by D. A. Yorke

Market Segmentation Theory

In a highly competitive market situation, the inability to identify and to develop market segments will in most cases lead to a failure to achieve organisational objectives, or, at best, result in a less effective performance than that of more alert competitors. Many organisations, however, seemingly still do not understand the practical significance of market segmentation, preferring either to try to be all things to all people, or in other cases, attempting to sell to so-called "market segments", which are in reality based on a definition of the products or service being offered.

According to Kotler [1] market segments should satisfy three criteria. They should, first of all, be measurable. Thus, market segments based on traditional geographic, demographic or socio-economic variables are relatively cheap and easy to measure from published data sources, albeit that such sources do become out of date. Market segments based on "personality" or user behavioural variables are less easy to quantify and are relatively expensive to identify, given the necessity to carry out the requisite field surveys. The second criterion is that each segment should be accessible. Such accessibility implies cost-effectiveness. Mass media advertising may well reach a chosen market segment, but at what cost? Many of the "audience" may well have no interest whatsoever in the product or service, and consideration should be given to finding other methods of communicating with the target group at a lower cost. Again, the more qualitative, the less quantitative the segment, the more difficult it becomes to adopt such a cost-effective approach. Thirdly, each segment should be substantial, i.e., large enough to be worthy of consideration. Perhaps a better term might be "viable" because certain segments may only display viability at some future date, e.g., students.

The advantages to be gained by adopting a strategy of market segmentation or target marketing are said by Engel, Fiorillo and Cayley [2] to be many. For example, the organisation is committing its limited resources efficiently, i.e., it is attempting to maximise its income for a given outlay. Secondly, such a strategy will enable an organisation to spot opportunities in the market place or to be able to capitalise on them more quickly. Thirdly, the whole ethos of the organisation will become outward looking, attempting to achieve its own objectives by giving customer satisfaction and developing customer loyalty. The customer is central to the adoption of a strategy based on market segmentation and too many organisations still attempt to fit the customer to the existing product or service — i.e., they remain inward looking, basing their approach on a definition of a product or products, rather than on market needs. One example which may be used to illustrate this rather myopic approach is that of manufacturers of slide rules who, it is argued, would have identified

71

themselves more favourably with market needs and spotted relevant opportunities had they defined themselves as being in the "problem solving" business rather than that of "slide rules". The market need is to solve a problem, a slide rule is only one type of product which can satisfy such a need.

The Banks and Their Business

Traditionally, it would seem that UK banks have been guilty of following a rather similar approach to that outlined immediately above. Before the legislation of the early seventies competition had been rather limited, partly as a result of the necessity to observe "the rules" with respect to their asset structures. Nevertheless, at the extreme, it might be said that the banks were acting merely as "cloakrooms" into which deposits were paid, some of which were eventually drawn out again.

The Competition and Credit Control Act 1971 had some effect in stirring the banks into some form of action and the term "marketing" began to be mentioned, albeit in a rather imprecise way. It was described by Derek Vander Weyer as "that part of management activity which seeks to direct the flow of banking services profitably to select customers" [3]. This was a start, but such a definition did not include any reference to customer needs in detail. What do existing (and potential) customers need in the way of financial services from an institution such as a bank? Any answers to this question would be most helpful in framing a definition of what "business" or "businesses" a bank was operating in.

Reekie [4] made such an attempt. He saw a bank as operating in the "business" of cash security, cash accessibility, monetary transfers and time. This was sound thinking because each of the above attempts to define an activity in terms of what the customer actually needs. The author's own preference is for slight modifications and an addition to such a definition, resulting in the following:

A bank may be said to be operating in five "businesses":

— cash accessibility
— asset security
— money transfer
— deferred payment
— financial advice.

Each of these terms is an identification of needs from the customer's point of view. Thus, customers (both corporate and private) need to have access to cash at frequent intervals in order to buy products and services and to repay debts for which cash is the specified medium of exchange, and such access is not necessarily limited to the hours at which shops and other services are open.

Secondly, customers need to find security for their accumulated assets, (not only those in liquid form — cash savings — but also other more tangible items such as property deeds or objets d'art) and, furthermore, in most cases, customers wish to receive a reasonable rate of return on their liquid assets but do not wish to see the value of such assets depreciate in real terms.

Thirdly, customers need to be able to transfer money from one account to another in settlement of a debt, and where the physical transfer of cash is not specified. In the interests of safety, this "business" is bound to increase rather rapidly in the future.

Fourthly, and also growing at a rapid rate as post-war attitudes have changed, is the need to defer the payment of a debt for as long as possible at a reasonable cost. Whereas it was considered almost a crime to run into debt before the Second World War and sufficient savings had to be accumulated before any substantial purchase was undertaken, nowadays almost anything can be bought and paid for at a later date. Indeed, in times of high inflation and equivalent increases in income, if the cost of such borrowing is low enough, the purchaser would be foolish not to repay later.

Finally, the modern world is becoming financially increasingly complex and many customers have a genuine need for financial advice of one form or another, not only in the form of guidance on the day-to-day management of financial affairs, but also with respect to investment of surplus funds, the avoidance of tax and similar problems.

The banks have responded to these needs in a variety of ways. Cash accessibility has been improved by the development and installation of machines which dispense cash at all hours of the day and by the use of cash cards, giving customer access to a limited amount of cash at any branch.

The need for asset security has been met by a variety of savings and deposit schemes, although the degree of success achieved has been limited when compared with other competing organisations such as the building societies. Money transfer has seen a multitude of developments in the past 20 years. The humble cheque has grown in importance and reduced the need to transfer large quantities of cash between contracting parties but it too has seen the increasing popularity of other forms of payment, in particular the credit card. Indeed, the credit card is a "product" which can satisfy two market needs — that of money transfer and deferred payment and, as will be described later, different market segments perceive and use the credit card in entirely different ways. Various forms of loan and overdraft facilities try to meet the needs of the deferred payment business and financial advice has been dispensed in many ways, from straight advice on investments to more indirect advice on financial management by the introduction of budget schemes to control more evenly the outflow of household money.

What would seem to be required is an ability on the part of the banks not only to recognise more fully the business in which they are operating, but also at which segments of the "market" each service should be developed and aimed in order to achieve optimum yields.

Bases for Market Segmentation of Banking Services
Reference has been made earlier to "traditional" and "more recent" bases for segmentation. Let us now examine in more detail such bases and relate them to a bank's activities.

A primary basis for segmentation would be the "type" of customer, i.e., personal or corporate. Almost all "organisations" whether a major joint stock company or a local Parent-Teachers Association, will maintain a current bank account of some kind. However, only 20 million private individuals in Britain have a bank account — less than half of the total number of adults, (a low figure when compared with North America, Australia, West Germany, and France, where the figures are over 95 per cent).

Traditionally, corporate customers have been segmented on the basis of type of industry, size of organisation or geographical location. Size of organisation may still be defined in terms of annual turnover, number of employees, capital employed, etc., and geographical location will still be relevant, but "type" of industry may be given a new dimension to include those organisations established for industrial, commercial, charitable or social purposes. More interestingly, perhaps, a basis for segmentation may reflect the "management" structure of an organisation, i.e., whether the demand for financial services is the responsibility of one person (the "Treasurer") or of a number of interested parties (the Decision Making Unit) some of whom may adopt a positive and others a negative attitude towards such services.

The above analysis may be illustrated three-dimensionally (as in Figure 1) although, of course, there is a much greater number of dimensions possible.

Figure 1. Market Segmentation for Corporate Markets

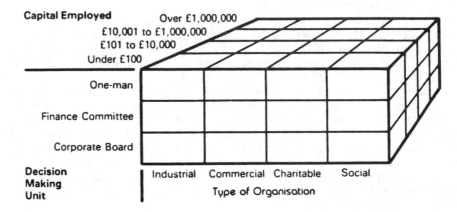

It is stressed that the labels used are purely hypothetical and in reality the bases for segmentation are the responsibility and judgement of the supplier organisation. However, it can be seen from the above diagram, that even with only three major bases, and three or four subdivisions of each, there are a total of 48 possible market segments. Some may not physically exist, e.g., an industrial organisation with capital of less than £100 and where financial decisions are made by the corporate board, or a social organisation with capital of over £1 million and where financial decisions are the responsibility of one man. Nevertheless, a substantial number of segments will exist for consideration later with respect to viability and accessibility.

Personal customers may be segmented in many ways. Traditionally, age has been used, together with social class (based on a classification by occupation of the head of the household). However, other possibilities present themselves, e.g., sex, stage in family life-cycle, working/not working, single or multiple-person households, etc. The combination of such variables, as with corporate customers, could result in the following segments being identified (Figure 2).

Figure 2. Market Segmentation for Consumer Markets

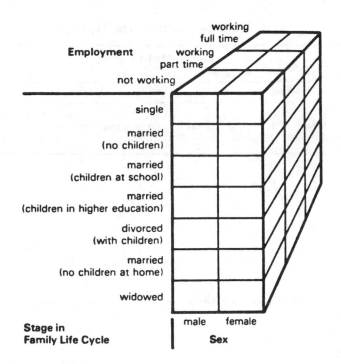

Here there are 42 theoretical segments, each with possibly different financial needs. In this case, there may be some degree of overlap, e.g., both male and female may be part of the same household (with or without children) and both may be working.

Business Strategies

The basic task is to link the concept of "What business we are in" to the structure of the total market in order that the banks can develop a suitable range of products and services to meet specific market needs. There is no magic formula for deciding *how* to segment a market, i.e., what bases to use. The approach may well need to be empirical, i.e., preliminary research may uncover possible broad bases for segmentation (for example, "working women") and then further, more detailed research may discover that, within this broad segment, there are fundamentally different sub-segments with different needs.

The discovery of such needs will enable a matrix to be drawn up setting "needs" against "business" (see Table I). An examination of each possible segment can then be made in terms of its viability; a particular service (or product) can be developed to meet each viable segment; and a communications strategy chosen which will convey the necessary information to that segment and hopefully motivate customers to buy.

Table I. Market Segmentation Typology

"Business"	Market Segment									
	Personal				Div'd	Organisational				
	Working		Married			Industrial			Social	
	M	F	(i)	(ii)	(ii)	One-man	Corp board	Cap. over £1m	Cap. Under £100	(iii)
Cash Accessibility	✓	✓			✓				✓	
Asset Security			✓				✓	✓	✓	✓
Money Transfer	✓	✓			✓			–		
Deferred Payment			✓			✓	✓			✓
Financial Advice			✓	✓	✓	✓			✓	✓

(i)   No children.

(ii) Children at home.

(iii) Finance committee.

Again, such a matrix is shown hypothetically, although the segment entitled "working women" together with the sub-segments identified, will be more fully discussed in a following article. Nevertheless, how may such a chart be interpreted?

Taking the "deferred payment business" as an example, it has been a feature of the last decades that the banks have not lent money to the personal sector in the same proportion that they have borrowed from it. The banks have argued that the average Briton will not borrow as much as his North American counterpart, but that does not explain why much of the borrowing which does take place does so outside the banking system altogether. Historically, the banks have seen their task as that of collecting private deposits through the branch system and using the proceeds to "finance trade and industry". From Table I above, using a segmented approach to the market, one can see that there are different groups of customers in this "deferred payment" market, namely a variety of organisations and, more particularly, specific types of individuals.

Until recently, the bulk of personal bank lending has taken the form of overdrafts, and it has been stated in *The Economist* [5] that direct personal lending through the branch system (excluding overdrafts and credit cards) only amounts to about £50 per existing captive customer, let alone current non-customers. It can be argued that lending through subsidiaries does help to redress the balance, but many of the existing retail outlets (the branches) are still not making a profit. Who may then be customers for personal loans? From Table I it would appear that the young marrieds with no children are a prime target for mortgage finance and for loans to establish a household. Similarly, divorced persons, perhaps with no children, could be a profitable segment to attack for similar reasons — and the number of divorced people is growing.

Secondly, the other half of a bank's business has traditionally been in attracting deposits of one sort or another — part of the "asset security business". Again, arguably, the banks have been less than successful in recognising the change in personal habits with respect to future security, particularly where cash savings are concerned. Savings, as a percentage of disposable income, have risen, but whereas just over a decade ago the building societies were second to the banks in the total sterling deposit market, the position is now reversed, and building societies attract almost all of their deposits from private individuals. Thus, it seems that the banks have failed substantially to attract the savings of individuals, even though many are already existing customers for other services. Taking a segmented approach would mean identifying which customers save, and for what purposes. Few people nowadays are prepared to hold large idle balances of cash, recognising its constant depreciation in real terms. Therefore, the banks must consider a move away from their traditional seven-day deposit account towards newer, higher interest savings facilities which meet the needs of specific customer groups. For example, the elderly (again a growing market, at least for the next twenty years) may need a form of term share with a deposit commitment of some years but with a higher rate of interest. Indeed, the building societies' deposits now contain over 10 per cent of such savings. Secondly, non-commercial organisations, even of a local nature, may represent a potentially viable segment for deposits, holding as they do idle balances for periods of time, until they have decided what to do with them.

The same sort of analysis could be applied to the other "businesses". Credit cards, for example, to the higher income groups are a means of convenience and of assisting money transfer, and not, as they are to the lower income groups, a form of deferred payment.

Marketing Strategy

Having analysed a "market" and segmented it, what action can be taken to utilise the data in the pursuit of organisational objectives? What is required is a marketing strategy for each viable segment identified.

Figure 3 illustrates how this might be achieved from the point of view of the company as a whole. (A further stage might be to identify the appropriate product/market segments for each geographical area, and/or an individual branch and to develop a detailed strategy for each).) Taking three hypothetical services and four target market segments, the first "tier" shows, from an analysis of existing records, the current "value" of each service/market segment for the company.

The second takes one of the twelve segments (that of mortgages for young marrieds) and shows the company's current market share of the total segment, together with the forecast change in the segment for the ensuing year and the company's objectives. Thus the total market segment is forecast to grow from £100 million to

£150 million (or by 50 per cent) but the company is setting, as its objective, a growth of 66 per cent, which, as a result, will increase its market share from 15 per cent to 16 per cent.

Figure 3. Marketing Strategy Financial Plan

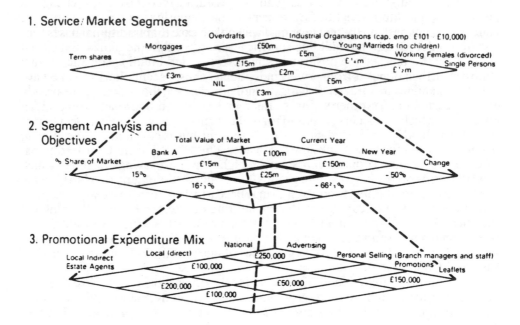

The third tier is, in essence, a budget, i.e., what promotional and selling resources the company is to apply in this segment. It recognises that there are three so-called "channels of communication" — national, local (direct to the "customer") or finally, indirect (via estate agents). Thus, national advertising will claim £250,000 of the budget, leaflets £150,000 and, perhaps, personal selling of the service to estate agents by branch managers and their staff, £200,000. The allocation of these recources is, of course, a top management responsibility.

A similar exercise should be carried out for each market segment which is considered viable. It is possible that the same promotional expenditure could be used for two or more segments at the same time, but the essence of this approach is not to treat the total market for a particular service as a homogeneous entity, but to recognise that different market segments have different needs and consequently invite a different marketing attack.

Conclusions

This article has attempted to show how a more "market" or "customer" oriented approach by a banking company can yield possible benefits both to the organisation (in terms of meeting its objectives) and to the customer (in generating satisfaction). An essential first step is to define "what business or businesses we are in". However, a "business" should not be viewed as a homogeneous entity, but rather as a collection of heterogeneous market segments comprising groups of customers with different needs, each of which may be better satisfied by the introduction of marginally or wholly different services. With a few notable exceptions (e.g., the "student" segment) the banks have not pursued an in-depth strategy of identifying particular market segments and, furthermore, it may well be the case that traditional bases for segmentation, e.g., age, income, geographical location, are unsuitable for the operations of a bank. Life-style, status, organisational buying structure, etc., may well be more suitable bases for segmentation, although it is recognised that there are fundamental problems of measurement. Nevertheless, these problems should not deter banks from setting out to collect market information, particularly at a local branch level where even basic information, hitherto, has not always been readily found.

References

1. Kotler, P., *Marketing Management*, 4th edition, Prentice-Hall, 1980, pp. 205-206.
2. Engel, J. F., Fiarillo, H.F. and Cayley, M. A., *Market Segmentation*, Holt Rinehart and Winston, 1972, pp. 2-3.
3. Wcycr, D. V., *Ernest Sykes Memorial Lecture*, Institute of Bankers, 1969.
4. Reekie, W. D., "Marketing in Banking: II", *Bankers' Magazine*, September 1972, p. 99.
5. *The Economist*, "Retail Banking in Britain", 8-14 December, 1979, pp. 22-25.

7. Identifying and Qualifying Industrial Market Segments

by James D. Hlavacek and N. Mohan Reddy

A producer of electrical motors captured the number one market position by developing different strategies for five market segments. The remaining competitors continued to treat all five segments as one homogeneous marketplace. A successful producer of large off-highway trucks focused on the distinctly different requirements of fleet owners and the owner/operator customer segments. The competition continued to view and treat these two customer groups as one.

The success of the above electric motor manufacturer and heavy equipment producer was possible by identifying distinct requirements of specific industrial market segments. However, many industrial firms are largely product-driven and, as a result, view and treat many customers alike. A successful market-driven industrial firm will first identify customers with similar requirements and then gear its operation to serve more effectively the needs of each specific customer group or market segment.

The identification and then selection of market segments to focus upon is the most important decision facing the industrial firm. The failure properly to segment an industrial market can result in missed opportunities, surprise competition, and even business failure. The strategic importance of industrial market segmentation is captured by Corey[8]:

> All else follows. Choice of market is a choice of the customer and of the competitive, technical, political, and social environments in which one elects to compete. It is not an easily reversed decision; having made the choice, the company develops skills and resources around the markets it has elected to serve. It builds a set of relationships with customers that are at once a major source of strength and a major commitment. The commitment carries with it the responsibility to serve customers well, to stay in the technical and product-development race, and to grow in pace with growing market demand.
>
> Such choices are not made in a vacuum. They are influenced by the company's background; by its marketing, manufacturing, and technical strengths; by the fabric of its relations with existing customers, the scientific community, and competitors; and by other considerations.

Pitfalls in Practice

Technical, engineering, or manufacturing-driven industrial firms frequently have a product emphasis and little or no real market segment identification and selection in practice. Still other industrial firms do not think as clearly as they should about the

requirements of market segments before launching into the development of marketing plans, manufacturing capabilities and products.

Many industrial companies tend to think of a market as one large marketplace that buys and uses like products. At best, they might list their current customers by amount of annual purchases for an item. Grouping customers by annual purchases is even more common in industries characterised by products that are essentially commodities where the buying decision turns primarily on price and delivery. Such sales "segmentation" rather than market segmentation can easily happen in industrial firms where any one customer is very important or where there is a narrow customer base. For example, one medium-sized plastic closure company that makes containers for consumer product goods manufacturers had 26 per cent of its business coming from one large customer. This heavy dependency kept the company from thinking in terms of applying its capabilities to different sets or groups of customers that had similar container closure problems. However, one of its most successful competitors focused on child-resistant and tamper-proof pharmaceutical packaging applications.

Many industrial firms do not distinguish between an industry and market segments within an industry. For example, one component manufacturer stated, "We serve the computer market with solid state connectors", but there are many kinds of computer market segments within the computer industry and each identified segment has specific customer requirements. After studying the solid state connector requirements of the computer industry, it might have been more useful for the firm to state, "We primarily serve the connector requirements of main frame computer builders and some micro processor computer builders". An *industry* is a wide group of manufacturers producing a wide range of products. A *market* segment is a much more distinct group of customers who have similar requirements that may be served by alternative products and technologies.

A factor that further complicates the definition of industrial market segments is environmental turbulence. Due to competitive activity and technological advances, industrial market segmentation is a dynamic activity. Kodak is the largest supplier of photographic film to most market segments. DuPont, however, concentrated on and achieved a large market share in the X-ray film market. Recently, developments in nuclear magnetic resonance (NMR) technology may replace a portion of the need for X-rays because the "picture" is developed electrically and shown on a computer screen. NMR scanners produce images similar to those made by CT scanners, but instead of using X-rays, the NMR machines use large powerful magnets. There is thus a need periodically to evaluate existing segments and consider new or different segmentation approaches. Business history is replete with cases in which an existing competitor saw market segment boundaries as static and did not identify new or emerging market segments.

Previous Research

Though most of the literature on industrial market segmentation has been developed in the last ten years, Fredrick[12], as early as 1934, suggested the need to define industrial markets and listed factors including product use, geographic location, industry and common buying habits. Though not explicitly stated to be such, these factors are a causal and descriptive basis for segmentation. Hummel[15, 16] discusses the use of SIC codes to measure market and sales potentials, and thus contributes to an understanding of industry (SIC) as a segment descriptor. Yankelovitch[29], in evaluating three industrial markets, argues in favour of benefits and customer's determination of value as appropriate bases for segmentation.

Cardozo[4] developed a model of industrial buyer behaviour directed at the development of industrial market segments and strategies. However, Cardozo's primary focus was on purchasing strategies, information search and personal characteristics. This work, coupled with that of Kernan and Sommers[18] and Robinson, Faris and Wind[23], forms more of a theoretical base in industrial buyer behaviour than a contribution to industrial market segmentation theory. Their primary thrust is on how the procurement process takes place and no attention is paid to grouping customers with common requirements into market segments. Wilson, Mathews and Sweeney[27] in a study show how a market can be segmented based on decision styles of purchasing agents. Their focus also is on the procurement process and personal characteristics.

Wind and Cardozo[28] in an attempt to provide a more comprehensive framework, present a two-step conceptual model of industrial market segmentation. They term the first step a macro-stage and suggest that one identify segments based on an appropriate set of organisational characteristics from among such factors as size of customer, usage, application of product, SIC code and geography. They then suggest further segmentation (micro-stage) based on key decision-making unit (DMU) characteristics. DMU characteristics include position in authority and communications networks of the firm, personality characteristics, demographic characteristics, personality and social status. Wind and Cardozo clearly provide the first major step towards a normative theory of industrial market segmentation. However, their two-step model, termed macro and micro, is simply an extensive listing of factors that they believe play a role in segmenting industrial markets. From a user or managerial standpoint, they do not provide specific guidance on the ordering or the use of these factors.

Unger[26] discusses a case study of industrial market segmentation based on the application or end use of the product. He notes the centrality of end use in the segmentation process and takes exception to the Wind and Cardozo model for its minimal attention to it. Assael and Ellis[1] later present empirical evidence to Unger's argument by defining segments in the industrial telecommunications market based on the end use of the product.

Choffray and Lillien[6] build on Wind and Cardozo's micro-stage using a "decision matrix". The decision matrix measures buying centre influence at various stages of the purchase process. The result is the identification of the structure of the purchasing process for a given product. Choffray and Lillien[7] demonstrate the value of their decision matrix in determining at whom (in the DMU) to target the marketing communications and what needs to be said to them. Choffray and Lillien's decision matrix is an attempt to operationalise Wind and Cardozo's micro-stage. The decision matrix, by providing an understanding of the structure of the purchasing process, enables determination of the communications mix, content and targets for a given product form. By focusing on *how* procurement takes place to define market segments, they proceed under the assumption that market segmentation, based on *why* these organisations buy and *what* they buy has already been determined. This is not a criticism of the matrix *per se*, but rather a note of its limitation in *identifying* industrial market segments.

Cardozo[5] uses four situational dimensions — familiarity with the buying task, product type and product use, importance of the purchase, and type of risk to classify organisational buying situations. These factors are then used separately or in combination to form market segments. Cardozo's focus again is on the buying process, coupled with situation-specific variables. Spekman[25] studied purchasing agents and managers from various types of organisations and found that they vary by type and the degree of information they seek in their purchasing decisions. Spekman concludes that organisational type may be an adequate macro-segmentation variable. Spekman's finding may have implications in designing the communication strategy. The finding, however, does not aid one in deriving market segments.

Forbis and Mehta[11] introduce the notion of economic value to the customer (EVC) defined along the same lines as value-in-use[19] as a means to segment industrial markets. The focus of their approach is to isolate segments based on the relative value of a given product to a specific customer in a particular application. The segmentation is based upon variables that underlie significant variations in the relative value. The variables they identify include application, growth potential in the customer business and geographical coverage.

Garda[13] introduces the notion of strategic market segmentation (SMS), highlighting the problems encountered when segmentation is viewed as a technique. His concept (SMS) stresses the need to look at the attractiveness criteria as well when defining market segments. Similar sentiments, i.e., the need to view segmentation as a means to achieve more efficient allocation of resources rather than an end to itself, have been expressed by Mahajan and Jain[20] and Johnson and Flodhamer[17].

Moriarty[21] used a combination of individual and decision-making characteristics with organisational variables to arrive at 33 selection criteria. These criteria were reduced to seven benefits: speed, ease of use, aesthetics, system compatibility, service, delivery, and price. The benefits were then used to profile 319 buying groups from five different industries in the market for dumb computer terminals, into benefit segments. Moriarty found evidence that benefits do differ by traditional grouping (industry, size) of segments. Moriarty's major contribution is the illustration that benefits do differ among market segments for the *same* product based on the customer application it performs. His work, short of suggesting an exhaustive survey of all organisations who may have the need for a given product, provides little guidance to those attempting to perform segmentation.

Bonoma and Shapiro[2] in the most comprehensive work to date on the subject, propose a nested approach to industrial market segmentation, with the user of this model moving from the outer nest to the inner nests. The five nests — demographics, operating variables, purchasing approaches, situational factors, and personal characteristics — are arranged in terms of the relative ease of observance, the outer nest being the most easily observable. Demographics, the most easily identified nest, includes industry, geographic location and size of the organisation. Operating variables which are detailed as less easily observable include technology, user/non-user status, customer operating technical and financial capability. The middle nest, referred to as purchasing approaches, lists five variables. These are formal organisation of the purchasing function, power structure in purchasing situation, organisational relationship in a dyadic concept, general purchasing policies, and purchasing criteria. The fourth nest, titled situational factors, includes urgency, specific application, type of purchase, environmental situation, order size, and buying risk specific to the situation. The innermost nest, which they type as the most difficult to observe, is personal characteristics. The factors listed are buyer/seller similarity, motivation, perception, and risk management strategies. Bonoma and Shapiro conclude with a recommendation of the need to achieve a balance between seller-oriented (traditional) and buyer-oriented (benefits) approaches.

Bonoma and Shapiro, in introducing their nested approach, make known their deep belief that the segmentation process cannot be separated from how the customer buys. They then go on to provide an extensive review of industrial buyer behaviour literature organised along their five nests. The nested approach is basically a multi-step version of what Wind and Cardozo had proposed. Bonoma and Shapiro's primary contribution is in their recognition and treatment of the importance of market segmentation, and the cost-benefit considerations of segmentation. In terms of operational relevance or implementation of the segmentation process their contribution is not marked. Their arrangement of nests along the dimension of ease of identification is suspect as well. For example, it is difficult to envision identification of the power structure for purchasing (purchasing approach nest) to be easier than the application of the product (situational factors nest). Corey[9], in discussing industrial segmentation research, cites product use or application as a very visible and meaningful attribute, and coupled with industry as an obvious starting point to segment industrial markets.

Overall Weakness of Past Research
This brief review clearly illustrates that scholarly industrial segmentation research has primarily been concerned with the buying process in organisations. The grouping of customers with similar requirements is assumed away. In segmenting industrial markets it is the definition of this broad marketplace for a given product concept that is a crucial and often frustrating first step. This definition, in turn, provides the ground work for effective segmentation[3].

Starting with a focus of "what" and "why" and not "how" of industrial markets highlights the importance of first segmenting by product application and benefits. The practitioner-oriented published literature[29, 26, 1, 24, 11, 13] clearly illustrates this point. An application- and benefits-oriented approach to segmentation enables derivation of segments with causal variables. In the literature on industrial segmentation the use of product application and benefits as a segmentation base is mentioned only in passing. For example, Bonoma and Shapiro note that literature on application as a segmentation base is virtually absent, at the same time stating that it remains one of the most useful and powerful bases of segmentation.

Though benefit segmentation is clearly stated as the most meaningful one, problems exist in identification and access to relevant data[22]. End uses for industrial products are not always easily identified and multiple market uses are often possible. The same product often provides *different* benefits based on its *application*. Moriarity's[21] study supports this. The benefits thus are derived from the specific application of the product. Therefore, the starting point of any customer-based (benefit) segmentation approach should be the identification of this customer function or application. As Bonoma and Shapiro[2] state, academics, however, have not extended their research in this direction.

Most academic research, has, unfortunately, attempted to transpose literature on the industrial buying process to explain industrial market segmentation. The issue of industrial segmentation must be addressed in terms of the operational value it has to industrial marketers. Only then will the segmentation models take on managerial significance.

The Process of Industrial Market Segmentation
This article proposes a model where product application is the primary focus of industrial segmentation. It focuses on the derivation of segments that have common problems to be solved or a common application to perform. This "application" orientation coupled with descriptive factors enables the identification of segments that have well defined causal links (benefits) as well as readily understood market descriptors to make the segments operational for resource allocation. By using product application as the core building block it becomes possible to introduce the important notion of segment stability. The literature to date has totally ignored the dynamic and changing nature of industrial market segments over time. By keying in on application requirements of the segments it is possible to monitor the impact of competitive activity and technological change on industrial market segment boundaries.

Figure 1. The Process of Industrial Market Segmentation

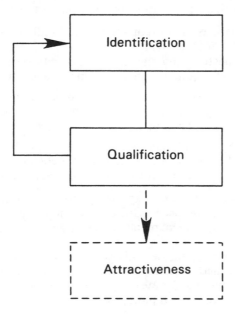

The process of identifying and qualifying industrial market segments is outlined in Figure 1.

The first stage is that of identifying segments by the function the customers seek, i.e., identification based on a common problem to be solved or common requirements to be satisfied. The second stage attempts to qualify these tentative segments. The identification-qualification stages often go through a few iterations before a segment is clearly defined. The qualified segments are then evaluated for relative attractiveness within each competitive segment and between segments to prioritise resource allocation. However, the primary purpose of this article is in the identification and qualification stages of industrial segmentation. Stage 3, the attractiveness linkage, is described simply to illustrate the nature of its interdependency with the segmentation process.

Identifying Specific Segments

The focus of the proposed model is to show how to segment a general industrial marketplace, given a proposed product or product concept. With the product concept as the starting point, this model does not presuppose a predetermined or fixed product form, but rather views the product as a variable that results from understanding and identifying customer requirements. Figure 2 details the identification process.

Step 1 is of crucial importance, as it details the core benefit or the generic function the product concept is capable of providing to a broadly defined group of customers. This definition, whether "provide means to move material", or "enable metal working", is the foundation for the industrial segment identification process.

Step 2 matches the product concept with one of the industrial marketing goods classifications of (a) components (b) machinery and equipment, and (c) materials, as described below. Cardozo[5], conducting 30 interviews with various types of companies, found this classification helpful in describing market segments.

(a) *Components:* parts or items that are used to build and repair machinery and equipment, which include items such as switches, integrated circuits, machine tools parts, connectors, and pistons. Components are often required for both the OEM (original equipment manufacturers) and aftermarkets.

(b) *Machinery and equipment:* end-products used by industrial users, such as machine tools, bulldozers, computers, laboratory instruments and trucks. They require repair parts (components) as aftermarket items.

(c) *Materials:* these are consumed in the end-user's production process or components and include items such as chemicals, coolants, metals, herbicides, and adhesives. Materials do not usually have an aftermarket.

Steps 3 and 4 require a creative and judgemental listing of organisations which have a need for the function or end use by SIC codes. The components users are further broken down by original equipment manufacturers (OEMs) and maintenance, replacement and overhaul.

Each of the SIC groupings in Step 4 is evaluated in terms of the exact function or end use to be performed, forming *Step 5*. Taking the organisation that defined its product idea as "providing the means to move material", the essential function in construction would be to move rapidly a lot of earth; in strip mining, however, the

Figure 2. Identifying Specific Segments

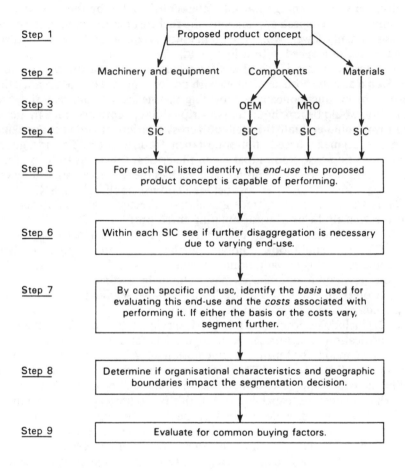

Step 1 — Proposed product concept

Step 2 — Machinery and equipment   Components   Materials

Step 3 — OEM   MRO

Step 4 — SIC   SIC   SIC   SIC

Step 5 — For each SIC listed identify the *end-use* the proposed product concept is capable of performing.

Step 6 — Within each SIC see if further disaggregation is necessary due to varying end-use.

Step 7 — By each specific end use, identify the *basis* used for evaluating this end-use and the *costs* associated with performing it. If either the basis or the costs vary, segment further.

Step 8 — Determine if organisational characteristics and geographic boundaries impact the segmentation decision.

Step 9 — Evaluate for common buying factors.

function could be moving earth with controlled precision. Much of this information is available from secondary sources [10, 14, 15, 16]. In addition, many trade association directories provide detailed product information by individual companies.

Industrial products frequently provide different economic value for different customer applications. The different economic value is caused by the way the customer uses the product. As a result, distinct market segments can emerge from different applications or uses of the same product. For example, a grading device may have greater economic value to a customer who uses it in a strip mining operation than to a customer who uses it for occasional road maintenance work.

Step 6 looks at end use within each SIC code to see if further disaggregation is necessary. It is possible for multiple end-users to be found within each four-digit SIC code. For example, a manufacturer of off-highway vehicles found that, on the average, his product had a purchase price and life-cycle cost disadvantage against a powerful competitor. This disadvantage was alleviated considerably by the discovery that, in higher-tonnage, slower-speed applications, the fuel cost per ton mile of the company's vehicle was actually lower, while the competitor's vehicle had the advantage when operating at cruising speed with a light load.

Step 7 attempts to identify the *basis* for evaluating the end-use or function identified in *Step 6* and the costs associated with performing it. For the organisation that had defined its product concept as providing the means to move material, the basis for excavation would be ton/hour, and in strip mining, depth accuracy in inches. The supplier firm should evaluate the user cost across a variety of end uses and tentatively define market segments based on user cost/benefit differences. This is a good point at which to develop case studies that detail the critical functions to be performed in each of the segments identified thus far. This enables the firm to identify those variables that underlie differences in user cost between end use applications. SIC-related data from county business patterns, trade association directories and input-output tables can prove extremely helpful in formulating these profiles.

Step 8 looks at organisational characteristics to see if further disaggregation is necessary. This step could look at annual purchases, size and number of plants, age of plants, and technology as additional considerations in the identification decision. In addition, geographic boundaries may at times be a consideration.

Step 9 involves an evaluation to see if the tentative segments identified are likely to exhibit homogeneity along important buying factors. These termed benefits by Moriarty[21] include performance, reliability, service, delivery, price and appearance.

The identification model presented in Figure 2 is for a product idea. It is possible to use the same model for business segmentation as well by replacing the "proposed product idea" in *Step 1* with the "customer functions a firm is capable of providing". This will enable the supplier to achieve the best "match" possible between customer needs and its resources, i.e., capabilities, or distinctive competences. Segmentation based on capabilities will also provide feedback or the type of change a supplier firm should consider in its capabilities to improve their competitive posture.

It is quite possible that not all of the above steps will be necessary for many industrial products. Cycling through the steps, however, may uncover segmentation issues that were previously not considered.

Finally, the segments identified at the end of Step 9 are still tentative and need to be qualified before they may be declared operational. Operational segments are those which can be served and whose reaction is expected to be similar to a specific marketing mix. In the process of qualification, further disaggregation may occur.

Qualification of Segments
The qualification stage evaluates the identified segments from Figure 2 for operational relevance, as shown in Figure 3.

After identifying a segment there are a number of criteria to consider before it may be declared operational. The qualification criteria are:

Figure 3. Qualification of Industrial Segments

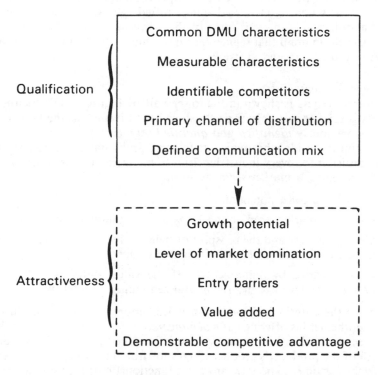

(a) each target segment should be characterised by a *distinct* set of user requirements or needs (e.g., four-digit SIC, end-use application, after-sales service, OEM/MRO, annual purchases);

(b) each segment should be identifiable by *measurable characteristics* (e.g., number of customers, yearly growth rate, competitive market shares, substitute products or technologies);

(c) each target segment should have *identifiable external competitors* who supply similar or functionally substitute products;

(d) each target segment should be served by a *common* or *primary* sales or channel of distribution;

(e) each segment should lend itself to be targeted by a distinct combination of *personal selling* and *advertising*;

(f) there may be instances where further segmentation based on DMU characteristics is needed. Choffray and Lillien's[6] decision matrix may prove helpful at this stage to determine who in the buying organisation should be targeted.

Qualification, in addition to further disaggregation and regrouping, enables the researcher to test whether the segments are truly operational. At the end of the qualification stage, all the segments identified and qualified against the above criteria should be looked at collectively to see if some of these can be collapsed or regrouped. It is important to bear in mind that segmentation is a means for more effective allocation of resources and not an end in itself.

Attractiveness of Segments

Segment attractiveness is shown in the lower half of Figure 3. The treatment of attractiveness is brief as our objective is to show attractiveness as the final stage in the *selection* of previously *identified* and *qualified* segment(s).

The decision to decide what segments to serve and what segments not to serve is a strategic decision for every industrial firm. Some attractiveness criteria to be considered in evaluating a market segment are [8]:

— the market growth potential,

— the level of market domination by large and powerful competitors,

— the entry barriers and the prospect of being able to attain and maintain a certain "critical mass" to be an efficient producer,

— the value added by manufacturer. If the value added is high, it gives the manufacturer leverage in pricing and remaining competitive.

In addition to the criteria mentioned above, it is imperative that a producer be able to determine whether his offering has a *demonstrable competitive advantage* in a defined market segment. The best measure of this is value-in-use analysis. Value-in-use is the worth of the producer's product when substituted for the product presently being used by the customer to perform any given function[19]. If the value-in-use is greater than the price of the producer's product then his product has a demonstrable competitive advantage. The greater the difference between value-in-use and price, the greater the incentive to switch to the producer's product. Value-in-use calculations should be done for competing products both in the same technology and different technologies. This analysis should form the critical GO/NO GO decision. If the product does not offer something new or better to the customer, going ahead and targeting the segment will result in inefficient allocation of resources that could have been better used in a different segment.

Industrial Segment Boundaries Change

All segments identified and qualified should be monitored for changes in competitive position and environmental changes that may shift market boundaries. This monitoring should encompass the identification, qualification and attractiveness stages, as shown in Figure 4. Competitive activity and technological change can dramatically change the boundaries and attractiveness of segments. Deere, the large farm equipment manufacturer, identified a market trend to fewer but larger farms that required large-horsepower tractors and equipment. Deere designed and manufactured large-horsepower machinery and subsequently captured a market opportunity. The existing

Figure 4. Monitoring of Industrial Market Segments

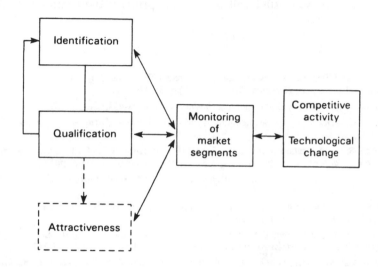

market leader, International Harvester, was late to recognise and pursue the new and growing market segment and lost substantial market share as a result. Xerox, the pioneer of photocopy machines, emphasised the high-speed segment for very large customers. The Japanese competitors were the first to identify and develop a desktop plain paper copier for the low-speed needs of businesses. It rapidly became the fastest-growing copier market segment. Xerox failed to monitor changes in "its" marketplace and by so doing allowed Canon and other Japanese competitors to gain competitive positions. In markets where there is rapid technological change, there is a need to re-segment more frequently because new technologies often blur segment boundaries.

Segmenting industrial markets is a creative process; managment should not allow ties to the way in which markets were previously segmented to strangle new ways to segment. An open-minded approach to periodic re-segmentation of industrial markets helps to protect and improve competitive positioning.

Conclusion

Successful industrial market segmentation is central to identifying and choosing the strategic direction of a business unit. If segmentation is properly done and monitored for changes, it can reduce threats and uncover innovative product, price, distribution, and service strategies.

The approach we present in this article has two important dimensions. First, product application (and hence benefits) is the key building block for the segmentation process, and managers and scholars have consistently stressed the need for such an approach. Second, and an equally important point, is the article's heavy reliance on secondary data. Few organisations have the resources or the capability to carry out the primary data analysis called for in studies such as Choffray and Lillien[6] and

Moriarty[21]. Even for those organisations that do, defining and evaluating segments along the approach suggested will make their primary data analysis much more meaningful.

References
1. Assael, H. and Ellis, R., "A Research Design to Predict Telephone Usage among Bell System Business Customers", *European Research*, Vol. 1, 1976, pp. 38-42.
2. Bonoma, T. and Shapiro, B., *Segmenting the Industrial Market*, Lexington, D.C. Heath & Co., 1983.
3. Brandt, S.C., "Dissecting the Segmentation Syndrome", *Journal of Marketing*, Vol. 30, October 1966, pp. 22-27.
4. Cardozo, R.N., "Segmenting the Industrial Market" in King, R.L. (Ed.), *Marketing and The New Science of Planning*, Chicago, American Marketing Association, 1968, pp. 433-440.
5. Cardozo, R.N., "Situational Segmentation of Industrial Markets", *European Journal of Marketing*, Vol. 14 No. 5/6, pp. 264-276.
6. Choffray, J-M. and Lillien, G.L., "A New Approach to Industrial Market Segmentation", *Sloan Management Review*, Vol. 19, Spring, 1978, pp. 17-29.
7. Choffray, J-M. and Lillien, G.L., "Industrial Market Segmentation by the Structure of the Purchasing Process", *Industrial Marketing Management*, Vol. 9, 1980, pp. 331-342.
8. Corey, R.E., "Key Options in Market Selection and Product Planning", *Harvard Business Review*, Vol. 53, September/October, 1975, pp. 119-128.
9. Corey, R.E., "Frontiers in Research", Address to the AMA Faculty Consortium on Industrial Marketing, Ohio State University, 1982.
10. Cox, W.E., *Industrial Marketing Research*, New York, Wiley, 1979.
11. Forbis, J. and Mehta, N., "Value-Based Strategies for Industrial Products", *Business Horizons*, Vol. 24, 1981, pp. 32-42.
12. Frederick, J., *Industrial Marketing*, New York, Prentice Hall, 1934.
13. Garda, R.A., "Strategic Segmentation: How to Carve Niches for Growth in Industrial Markets", *Management Review*, August, 1981, pp. 15-22.
14. Haas, R.W., "SIC System and Related Data for More Effective Market Research", *Industrial Marketing Management*, Vol. 6 No. 6, 1977, pp. 429-435.
15. Hummel, F., "Market Potentials in the Machine Tool Industry", *Journal of Marketing*, Vol. 19, July, 1954, pp. 34-41.
16. Hummel, F., "Pinpointing Prospects for Industrial Sales", *Journal of Marketing*, Vol. 25, July, 1960, pp. 64-68.
17. Johnson, H. and Flodhammer, A., "Some Factors in Industrial Market Segmentation", *Industrial Marketing Management*, Vol. 9, 1980, pp. 201-205.
18. Kernan, J. and Sommers, M., "The Behavioral Matrix — A Closer Look at the Industrial Buyer", *Business Horizons*, Summer, 1966, pp. 59-72.
19. Lee, D.E., *Industrial Marketing Research*, Westport, Connecticut, Technomic, 1978.
20. Mahajan, V. and Jain, A., "An Approach to Normative Segmentation", *Journal of Marketing Research*, Vol. 15, August, 1978, pp. 338-345.
21. Moriarty, R.T., 1983, *Industrial Buyer Behavior*, Lexington, Massachusetts, Lexington Books, 1983.
22. Moriarty, R.T. and Reibstein, D.J., *Benefit Segmentation: An Industrial Application*, Cambridge, Massachusetts, Marketing Science Institute, 1982.
23. Robinson, P., Faris, C. and Wind, Y., *Industrial Buying and Creative Marketing*, Boston, Allyn and Bacon, 1967.

24. *Scientific American*, Inc., *How Industry Buys/1970*, New York, *Scientific American*, 1970.

25. Spekman, R.E., "Segmenting Buyers in Different Types of Organizations", *Industrial Marketing Management*, Vol. 10, February, 1981, pp. 43-48.

26. Unger, L., "Market Segmentation in the Chemical Fragrance Market", *Industrial Marketing Management*, Vol. 3, 1974, pp. 341-347.

27. Wilson, D., Mathews, H. and Sweeney, T., "Industrial Buyer Segmentation: A Psychographic Approach", in Alvine, F.C. (Ed.), *Marketing in Motion*, Chicago, American Marketing Association, 1971, pp. 433-436.

28. Wind, Y. and Cardozo, R.N., "Industrial Market Segmentation", *Industrial Marketing Management*, Vol. 3, March 1974, pp. 153-166.

29. Yankelovich, D., "New Criteria for Market Segmentation", *Harvard Business Review*, Vol. 42, March/April 1964, pp. 83-90.

Part 3 Marketing Mix

8. Project NewProd: Factors in New Product Success

by Robert G. Cooper

What the manager can glean from recent studies into the new product process is the topic of this article. The article is based largely on the findings of Project NewProd, an investigation of almost 200 actual new product cases to probe what separates the "winners" from the "losers". Results are presented from a managerial perspective, and in particular help in the selection of appropriate new products and improve the prospects of launching a "winner". The key factors that underlie new product projects, and that can be used to characterise ventures, are outlined. In particular, the influence of each on product success is demonstrated. The merits of emphasising certain new product activities, seeking particular information, and stressing specific elements of the launch are examined, with a focus on the expected impact on product success.

New Product Development

New product development stands out as one of the most crucial yet deficient functions of the modern corporation. Thousands of new products are developed and introduced by firms each year. But only a minority bring home the profits needed to justify their development in the first place. Faced with staggering R&D expenses and no shortage of product failures, more and more firms are taking a critical look at their new product efforts.

What makes a new product a success is the topic of this article. In it, the results of Project NewProd, an extensive investigation into industrial new product success and failure, are reviewed with a focus on the managerial implications. The results of NewProd are instrumental in shedding light on the age-old quest for routes to improve new product success rates.

Just how important the key to new product success is can be gauged by the financial impact of product development on industrialised economies. For example, in the US in 1979, an estimated 51 billion dollars, or 2.2 per cent of GNP, was spent on industrial R&D, most of this on the development of new products. But this R&D expenditure is only part of the total cost of new products. It does not include commercialisation costs, which recent studies have indicated may be even greater than development costs [10].

Product development, besides being very costly, is also critical to the firm in a strategic sense. One investigation of corporate strategy revealed product development to be among the most important routes to corporate growth [13]. Product development, successfully undertaken, is also very profitable: a median payback period of 1.5 years was found for successful Canadian industrial products [4]. Finally the PIMS study found product development, measured by R&D expenditures, to play a strategically positive role, particularly in the case of firms with a dominant market position [20].

In spite of its strategic importance, product development is plagued by an unacceptably high failure rate. For every six man hours spent on industrial R&D, five of these are spent on products that fail or are cancelled [1]. Further, of every 58 product ideas that enter the process, only two reach the commercialisation stage, and only one is commercially successful. New product failure rates are estimated to range between 30 per cent and 60 per cent [7]. Finally, Project NewProd data reveal that for every 100 industrial products developed, 21.9 are killed prior to launch, 18.7 fail commercially and 59.4 are successes. And NewProd's data do not include truncated new product projects, terminated prior to completion of development, but nonetheless having had considerable resources spent on them.

The strategic importance of product development coupled with the high failure rate point to two areas that need greater managerial attention:

(1) *screening:* improved methods for selecting new product projects, so that scarce resources can be efficiently allocated to the probable "winners".

(2) *execution:* improved design and execution of the various stages and activities of the new product process to enhance the odds of success of the selected projects.

These two issues — selecting projects, and undertaking more proficiently the new product process — logically lead to the research question addressed in Project NewProd: "what makes a new product a success?"

The Keys to New Product Success

The route to success in product innovation is not a new research topic. Beginning in the mid-1960s, a number of studies investigated new product *successes* with the hope of uncovering the common ingredients of success. Concurrently, probes of new product *failures* sought the reasons for failure as a first step towards curing future ailments. Finally, recent research has focused on comparing and contrasting successes with failures as the key to identifying factors that separate the two.

New Product Successes

An extensive descriptive investigation of 567 successful *incremental innovations* found that the great majority of these innovations (three-quarters) were market derived, or *market pull* ventures, and only 21 per cent were *technology push* [11]. An existing demand or need was the most common single ingredient in comparing these successes. Sources of information outside the company also were found to play a critical role. A study of *radical innovations* revealed a different set of important characteristics for success: a recognition of a technical opportunity; a need (market) recognition; proficient internal R&D management; well-executed venture decisions; ample development funds; a technical entrepreneur. External factors were found to be the least important, while technological and internal variables appeared to dominate the list.

Another study into product successes at the GE Laboratories identified the following key characteristics [14]:

— market needs were recognised and R&D was targeted at satisfying these needs;
— when a technical success did not have a specific market need, the product was adapted to suit the identified need;
— research managers communicated the possibility of a technical breakthrough clearly to other departments, which facilitated the identification of a market need;
— communication existed between engineers and scientists in the operating departments.

Once again the call is for better communication and, most important, the matching of technological possibilities with market needs.

New Product Failures

Studies of new product failures are premised on the argument that it is easier to diagnose "what went wrong" than it is to identify "what went right"; and that a critical analysis of past failures is the first step towards prescriptive solutions. A study of 87 industrial products identified the following reasons for failure [12]: inadequate market analysis (33 per cent of cases); product defects (25 per cent); and higher costs than anticipated (15 per cent). Other reasons were identified, including: bad timing, heavy competition, insufficient marketing effort, inadequate sales force, and distribution weaknesses. A sequel study, that overcame problems of the previous research, yielded surprisingly similar results [8]. The most frequent cited reasons for product failure were: inadequate market analysis (45 per cent); product technical problems or defects (29 per cent); lack of effective marketing effort (25 per cent); higher than expected costs (19 per cent); competitive strength or reaction (17 per cent); poor timing (14 per cent); and technical/production problems (12 per cent).

In a recent study by the author, the causes of industrial new products failure were investigated for a sample of 114 actual product failures [3]. The major reason for financial failure was that sales fell below expectations (63.2 per cent of cases). The causes of this poor sales performance were: under-estimated competitive strength and/or competitive position in market (36.4 per cent); overestimated number of potential users (20.5 per cent); product's price set too high (18.2 per cent) and technical difficulties/deficiencies with product (20.5 per cent). The sample of products was later subdivided into clusters on a six-dimensional map, and scenarios of product failure were identified: The Better Mouse Trap No One Wanted (28 per cent of cases); The Me-Too Product Meeting a Competitive Brick Wall (24 per cent of cases); Competitive One-Up-Manship (13 per cent of cases); Environmental Ignorance (7 per cent of cases); The Technical Dog Product (15 per cent of cases); and The Price Crunch (13 per cent of cases) [2].

The study also pinpointed areas of weakness with the firm and the new product process [3]. In almost two-thirds of the cases, a lack of marketing research skills or personnel was thought to have contributed significantly to the failure, while the detailed market study phase was the most poorly undertaken activity of the new product process. Again, this research points to a lack of a market and marketing orientation as the culprit in industrial new products.

Success Versus Failure

Studies into success and studies into failures have provided provocative and insightful results. But there is a fundamental flaw in these investigations: they looked at only one side of the coin, at *only* successes or *only* failures, but not both in the same study. Simply because a characteristic is found to be common to a group of successes *does not necessarily* mean that this characteristic is a factor in success. Had a group of failure products been studied as well, this characteristic might have been equally true of them.

Recent research, beginning with the British Project SAPPHO in 1972, has taken the stance that only through a direct comparison of successes and failures will the keys to success be uncovered. SAPPHO sought a pattern of differences between a sample of 43 pairs of successful and unsuccessful innovations [15, 17]. Of the 122 variables measured, 41 were found to discriminate between successes and failures, while five underlying factors were identified:

(1) understanding of users' needs;
(2) efficiency of development;
(3) characteristics of management and managers;
(4) effectiveness of communications (internal and external);
(5) magnitude of marketing efforts.

Other conclusions were that many variables leading to product outcomes were amenable to better management control, particularly in the area of marketing.

A similar but smaller scale study was undertaken in the Hungarian electronics industry [16]. In spite of the differences in research design and setting, the Hungarian results were strikingly similar to the British SAPPHO. A Finnish success/failure study also yielded results very similar to the two studies mentioned above, even though the methodology was different [9]. In addition, successful innovations: utilise company potentials better (good product-company fit); exploit market opportunities better; and utilise the technical "know how" of the company. Familiarity with technology and markets were both determinants of success, with market familiarity having a more pronounced effect. Failures were often the result of a few critical factors, but in order to succeed, competence must be demonstrated in a wide range of tasks.

A similar study undertaken on European and Japanese firms measured the impact of the external environment and industry maturity on the innovation process [21]. Successful innovations, when compared to failures: had no initial difficulties in marketing; had a real product advantage; had market needs recognised prior to a solution; had more customer contact; and involved top management initiation. Also, advance planning, the use of outside consultants, the absence of patent protection, and responses to government actions were all positively related to success. A major US study compared a large sample of successes and failures, but used a method quite different from the SAPPHO-type research [18, 19]. Managerial opinion was used to identify facilitators and barriers, rather than contrasting the characteristics of successful and unsuccessful ventures. Overall, 54 significant facilitators for success were identified, but no single characteristic of success or failure was found. One person's facilitator could be someone else's barrier. Some of the important facilitators included: existence of a strong product champion; marketing factors, such as need recognition; strong internal communication; superior techniques for data gathering, analysis and decision making; and planned approaches to venture management.

What Previous Research Shows
The quest for the secret to new product success appears more difficult than anticipated. One fact that is clear from the research is that there is no direct answer to the question: "what makes a new product a success?". Rather, the relationships and variables involved in determining product outcomes constitute a complex network of effects.

A second fact is that the nature of the venture moderates the answer to the question. Different types of ventures appear to have different variables as the critical determinants of success.

The role of a strong market and marketing orientation was prevalent throughout much of the research. Having a market-derived product idea and recognising a market need were familiar themes. The existence of a strong need, understanding user needs and matching technology to user needs appeared to be vital ingredients in success. Market information and the need to do market research also stood out. Relatively few studies looked directly at the marketing activities surrounding the launch, but the few that did found these to be important too.

The nature of the new product process, besides being market-orientated also impacted on outcomes. Effective communication, both inside and outside the firm, was identified as a significant factor in several studies. The existence of key personnel, the involvement of senior management and the characteristics of managers were similarly cited. The nature of decisions made, the techniques used for decision making and data analysis, management effectiveness, the way activities were executed and other *management processes* were found to influence new product outcomes.

Project NewProd Results
Project NewProd is a major investigation into what separates successful new products from the failures. NewProd data are based on almost 200 new product cases — half failures, the other half successes. A large number of characteristics were measured for each project, the objective being to see which characteristics or properties differentiate the "winners" from the "losers". The 77 characteristics (variables), measured fall into six categories, the first three being controllable for a given project, the last three being environmental or non-controllable.

(a) *The Commercial Entity:* what the firm entered the marketplace with. Includes the attributes and advantages of the product and the nature of the launch effort.

(b) *Information acquired:* the nature and quality of information acquired (or known) during the new product process.

(c) *Proficiency of process activities:* how well certain activities were undertaken during the new product process (if at all), from idea generation to launch.

(d) *Nature of the marketplace:* the characteristics of the new product's market.

(e) *Resource base of the firm:* the compatibility of the resource base of the firm with the requirements of the project (the company-project fit).

(f) *Nature of the project:* the characteristics of the venture or project*.

Results of the relationships between these properties and the outcomes of the 195 products have been presented elsewhere [5, 6]; only a review is provided here. The specific properties that best separated the successes from the failures, in descending order, were:

(1) proficiently executing the launch — selling, promoting and distributing;

(2) having a new product that more clearly meets customers' needs than do competitor products;

(3) having a higher quality new product than competitors in terms of tighter specifications, greater durability and reliability, and so on;

(4) undertaking a good prototype test of the product with the customer;

(5) having the sales force and/or distribution effort well targeted — at the right customers;

(6) undertaking a proficient test market or trial sell;

(7) proficiently starting up full-scale production;

(8) knowing customers' price sensitivities;

(9) executing product development well;

(10) understanding buyer behaviour and the customer's purchase decision process;

(11) having a product that permits the customer to reduce his costs;

(12) having a good "company-product fit" in terms of sales force and/or distribution;

---

*The Research Method

A sample of 177 firms was randomly selected from a government listing of firms known to be active in industrial product development. Firms were initially contacted by telephone to solicit co-operation, identify the appropriate respondent and provide direction. A detailed questionnaire that had been extensively pre-tested, was mailed to each respondent. He was asked to select two product projects for discussion: one a commercial failure, the other a commercial success. Projects were to be recent (five years); typical to the firm; and undertaken solely by that division or firm. Success and failure were defined from the firm's viewpoint and in terms of profitability: the degree to which a product's profitability exceeded (or fell short of) the minimum acceptable profitability for this project or investment, regardless of the way the firm measured profitability.

The respondent characterised each venture on each of the 77 variables that made up the six major blocks. He was presented with a short description of a particular characteristic, and indicated whether this described the particular project (agree/disagree: 0 to 10 scale). A success/failure scaled rating was also requested for each project.

The eventual sample numbered 102 successes and 93 failures, a total of 195 projects from 103 firms. This represents an effective response rate of 69 per cent after correction for inappropriate or non-existent firms.

(13) having a good "company-product fit" in terms of marketing research skills and needs;

(14) doing a good job on idea screening;

(15) understanding customers' needs, wants, and specifications for the product.

On a group by group basis, the way in which the activities of the new product process were undertaken had the strongest impact on product outcomes. Of the 12 activities measured, the three most important were:

- market launch;
- prototype test with customer;
- test-marketing/trial sell.

The market-oriented activities were particularly strong correlates of success. The least important activities, although still related to positive outcomes, were: trial production; preliminary technical assessment; and financial analysis.

Almost as important as activities were the elements of the commercial entity — the extended product and the launch strategy. The product itself was the *core* of critical strategy:

- having a product that met customers' needs better than competitors' products;
- having a high quality product — more reliable, tighter specifications, lasted longer, etc.

Proper targeting of the sales force and distribution effort was also a deciding variable. Other product advantages (but not price) and the remaining elements of the marketing mix were all correlated with success.

The final set of controllable variables — information acquired — also impacted strongly on product outcomes. The most important types of information to acquire included:

- knowledge of customer price sensitivity;
- an understanding of buyer behaviour;
- a knowledge of the customers' needs, wants and specifications for the product.

All three were closely related, and together represent "customer knowledge".

Of the non-controllable variables, only the measures of synergy — company-product fit — had a major influence on product outcomes. A compatibility between the needs of the new product and the firm's existing resource base was important to success for almost every resource. The most critical areas in separating successes from failures were:

- compatible sales force and/or distribution system;
- marketing research skills;
- management talent;
- advertising and promotion skills and resources.

Characteristics of the marketplace for the most part did not determine success or failure. The exceptions were: degree of customer need for this type of product;

market growth rate; and degree of customer satisfaction. Many properties describing the stage of product life cycle had minimal impact on product outcome.

The characteristics of the venture itself also had a weak relationship to product results. How new the product class and customer need were to the firm were both negatively correlated with success. But other measures of project newness or innovativeness, the level and complexity of technology employed and the source of this idea had little impact on eventual outcomes.

Because so many of the properties measured were themselves highly inter-related, it proved difficult to isolate the impact of any one variable or set of variables on product success. As a result, the data were re-organised to generate underlying dimensions or factors.* The 18 resulting dimensions captured the original 77 variables, each dimension being a composite factor comprised of a number of the original variables, (Table I).

Table I. Dimensions that Characterise New Product Projects

Factor name	% Variance explained†
(1) Technical/Production synergy and proficiency	28.8
(2) Market knowledge and marketing proficiency	11.7
(3) Newness to the firm	10.1
(4) Product uniqueness/superiority	9.0
(5) Market competitiveness and customer satisfaction	6.7
(6) Marketing and managerial synergy	5.1
(7) Product technical complexity and magnitude (big ticket item)	4.4
(8) Market need, growth and size	3.5
(9) Strength of marketing communications and launch effort	3.1
(10) Product determinateness (needs and solution pre-determined)	2.8
(11) Production start-up proficiency	2.5
(12) Product uniqueness (first to market)	2.2
(13) Existence of dominant competitor; customer satisfaction	2.1
(14) Market dynamism (frequency of new product introductions)	1.8
(15) Relative price of product	1.7
(16) Proficiency of pre-commercialisation activities	1.6
(17) Product custom-ness	1.6
(18) Source of idea/investment magnitude	1.4

†*After rotation, add to 100 per cent.*

When product outcomes were related to these 18 factors, 11 factors entered the "success equation" as determinants of product success, 9 in a fairly strong way. The three dominant dimensions were, (see Table I):

(1)   product uniqueness and superiority;

(2)   market knowledge and marketing proficiency;

(3)   technical and production synergy and proficiency.

The dramatic impact of each of these three factors on product success is shown in Figure 1. Here projects are split into three groups: the bottom 20 per cent, the top 20

*Using the data reduction technique, factor analysis, varimax rotation.

Figure 1. The Impact of Three Dominant Factors on New Product Success Rates

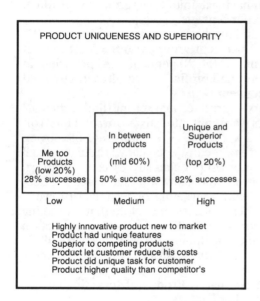

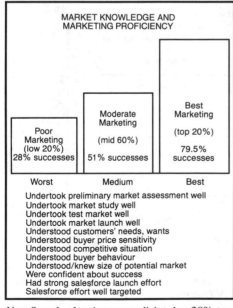

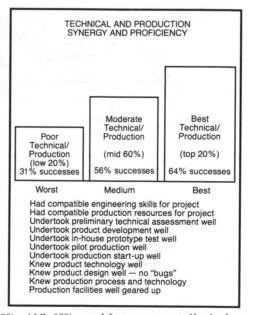

Note: Sample of projects was split into low 20%, top 20%, middle 60% on each factor, represented by the three columns. The sample contains 52.3% successes.

per cent and the middle 60 per cent for each factor. The proportion of successes jumped from 28 per cent for "me too" products to 82 per cent for unique, superior products, demonstrating the importance of having a unique, superior new product. Note that the entire sample contained 52.3 per cent successes.

Similarly, improving market knowledge and marketing proficiency increased the success rate from 28 per cent (for the 20 per cent group with the least market knowledge and proficiency) to 79.5 per cent (for the 20 per cent most proficient in marketing). Technical and production synergy and proficiency resulted in a twofold gain in successes, from 31 per cent to 64 per cent.

The multiple impact of these three factors — product, market(ing) and technical/production — is shown in Figure 2. Projects were split into halves (low and high) on each dimension, and the results — a "2 x 2 x 2 cube" — demonstrate the strong influence of the three factors. The one-eighth of the projects that were "high" on all three factors exhibited a dramatic success rate: 90 per cent successes. In contrast, only seven per cent of products "low" on all three dimensions were successes. Product remains the critical variable: even lacking both marketing or technical prowess, unique superior products scored a 62 per cent success rate. Note that marketing and technical strength *must both be present* in order to have a strong impact on unique superior product outcomes. The marketing dimension becomes particularly crucial when the product is a weak "me too" effort: here the success

Figure 2. New Product Success as determined by Product, Marketing and Technical/Production Factors

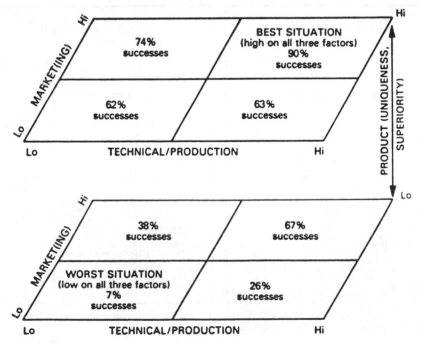

rate moves from 15 per cent for "me too" products "low" on the market factor to 59 per cent for those "high" on marketing. Similarly technological/production variables play a greater role when the product lacks uniqueness and superiority. But the overriding conclusion from the 2 x 2 x 2 cube analysis is the essential presence of all three factors — product, market(ing) and technical/production — as the key to success (90 per cent); and that deficiency in any one area drops the success rate dramatically.

Guides to Management Action
Project NewProd has identified the specific properties and dimensions that differentiate industrial new product successes and failures.* A review of the important variables — for example, the 15 that most decide the fate of new products — helps pinpoint areas for special attention. Armed with this list, the new product manager can set priorities and allocate resources to critical activities, essential information gathering, and key elements of the commercial entity. Moreover, this understanding of what makes for a successful product helps in the selection of new product projects.

Besides these direct insights, Project NewProd yields more general conclusions, each with its own managerial implications.

The outcome of a new product project — success or failure — lies more in the hands of managers and implementors than was otherwise assumed.

We are the *captains of our ship* in the new product game. Evidence from Project NewProd shows clearly that the immediate correlates of success/failure were the controllable variables, while only a handful of environmental properties had an impact. The commercial entity (the product offering and launch strategy), the activities undertaken during the new product process and the information acquired were all closely related to product outcomes. Certain activities, information areas, and elements of the commercial entity were so strongly linked to new product success that they were, on their own, able to account for a considerable proportion of variability in outcomes. The eventual outcome of the new product venture thus lies in the hands of the company people involved. The product fatalists have been proven wrong. The message clearly is that "it matters not what situation you face; it matters more what you do about it!".

There is no one key to success. Success depends on many characteristics and variables.

A subsequent and related conclusion from the analysis of individual variables and their impact on outcomes concerns the *large number* and *variety* of controllable variables linked to success. There was no one variable that stood out as *the key* to success. Success does not hinge on doing one thing in a spectacular fashion; rather success depends on doing many things well. But failure could result from a single miscue.

The usefulness of checklist new product screening models is disputed.

The relative lack of impact of controllable variables challenges the validity of currently used checklist (or rating scale) screening models. Such qualitative models are

---

* A detailed listing of these is found in [5, 6].

usually based on a list of characteristics of the venture, the market and other properties known at the time of the idea screening decision. Clearly such environmental variables are simply not that useful as predictors of product outcomes. Moreover, controllable variables that do impact on success are often not known at the time of screening, and hence are usually omitted from screening models.

If screening models are to be effective, the types of qualitative variables they consider should change. There should be less emphasis on environmental variables — for example, nature of the marketplace and the venture. Instead, screening models must measure the firm's likely performance on the controllable variables: that is, the firm's capacity for proficiently executing the key process activities; the firm's skill at gathering the needed market and technical information; and the firm's competence in designing and executing the product and launch strategies for the project in question.

There is much to be gained from focusing more on the new product process activities, and perhaps a little less on project selection issues.

NewProd results also suggest a current over-emphasis on the "front end" of the new product process. Recent years have witnessed the development of scores of new product screening models, some of which are quantitative, probabalistic and quite intricate. In contrast, little attention has been devoted to improving the various steps or activities that comprise the new product process. Yet it is precisely here that modifications and improvements are likely to have their greatest effects on product success rates. New product managers must meet the challenge of the design of an effective, complete and balanced scheme for developing and commercialising new products; the necessary skills and resources to execute the process activities and information gathering must be acquired; and the process must be managed and monitored to ensure that the process activities are indeed proficiently executed.

Certain types of new product projects are more likely to be successful. Screening criteria should reflect these attributes of success.

Even though NewProd's results suggest that more attention should be paid to the new project process, the screening decision logically remains an important step. The research yields several rules of thumb that are useful in the selection of new product projects (from Table I). In order of importance, these are:

(1)   Pick projects where the resulting product is likely to yield significant and unique benefits to the user. Avoid "me too" products unless a differential advantage can be found.

(2)   Seek projects where you already know the market well (or are prepared to acquire the information) and where you are likely to execute the marketing activities competently.

(3)   Score projects high when technical and production synergy exists between the product and company, and where these technical and production activities are likely to be skilfully undertaken.

(4)   Avoid dynamic markets, where users' needs change often and new product introductions are frequent.

(5)   Look for products aimed at large and growing markets, and where a high

level of need exists for this type of product.

(6)   Seek products with an economic advantage to the user: products that permit the customer to reduce his costs, or whose price is more competitive. Be especially wary of high-priced products with no economic payoffs to the user.

(7)   Favour projects where a high degree of marketing and managerial synergy exists between the project and the company: financial; market research; managerial; sales force/distribution; and advertising/promotion.

(8)   Avoid highly competitive markets (many competitors; intense price and other forms of competition) where customers are well satisfied by competitors' products.

(9)   Stay clear of projects new to the firm: new customers, new product class; new need served; new production process; new technology; new distribution/sales force; new advertising/promotion; and new competitors.

Three important dimensions dominate the results, and appear to be critical to new product success.

The three composite factors or dimensions that dominated the "success equation" were:

PRODUCT: Having a product with a differential advantage in the eyes of the customer.

MARKET: Obtaining a sound knowledge of the marketplace and customer together with proficiently carrying out the market research and launch activities.

TECHNICAL/   Having synergy between project and firm in terms of production
PRODUCTION: and technical resources, and well-executed technical and production activities.

These three were consistently dominant, *regardless of the type of venture or type of firm.** Each factor is comprised of a number of specific characteristics, and when closely investigated, has important implications to new product management.

(1) *Product Strategy*

Having a unique and superior product was critical to success. Such products should incorporate the following features (in descending order of importance):

(a) meet customers' needs better than competitors' products;
(b) offer unique features or attributes to the customer, relative to competing products;
(c) be of higher quality (tighter specifications, stronger, more reliable, last longer) than competing products;
(d) do a unique task or job for the customer;
(e) be a highly innovative product, totally new to the market;
(f) permit the customer to reduce his costs.

*Further analysis showed that the impact of the three main dimensions on success was independent of the nature of the firm and type of new product project.

Note that the newness alone was *not* the answer. Project NewProd identified three dimensions of newness, all independent of each other. A product can be "new" in the sense that:

— it is new to *the firm*, taking it into new markets, new technologies, new production processes, etc;
— it is new *to the market,* the first of its kind, a radical innovation;
— it is new because it does something better, more reliably, faster, more economically, etc. *for the customer* than what he is now using.

Only the last factor had a positive impact on success. Simply being new or unique or different is not enough. Newness is not an end in itself, nor is brilliant technology or a clever design. Rather the product must be unique and superior in the *eyes of the customer:* the product's uniqueness and innovativeness must yield a net benefit to the customer. Thus the technical side of product design and engineering must somehow be married to the intricacies of the marketplace — customer needs, preferences, use patterns, etc. — to ensure that the resulting new product delivers unique benefits to the customer.

(2) *Market Orientation*

The second key to new product success lies in a strong market and marketing orientation. Operationally this means (in descending order of importance):

(a) proficiently undertaking a detailed market study or marketing research: a detailed study of market potential, customer preferences, purchase process, etc;
(b) having a well-targeted salesforce and/or distribution effort at launch;
(c) performing a good preliminary market assessment early in the product project;
(d) proficiently executing the market launch;
(e) undertaking well a test market or trial sell prior to launch;
(f) having a strong salesforce and/or distribution effort at launch.

Not only are the above activities and efforts important to a strong market orientation, but this dimension also involved acquiring information on (or having a sound knowledge of) the following areas (in descending order of importance):

(a) the customers' purchase decision: the "who, what, when, where and how" of his purchase behaviour;
(b) the size of the potential market for the product;
(c) the competitive situation: competitors' products, pricing, strategy and strengths;
(d) how much the customer would pay for the product: his price sensitivity;
(e) potential customers' needs, wants and specifications for the product.

This requirement for a strong market orientation — market knowledge and proficient marketing activities — parallels closely the first dimension, namely the need for a unique, superior product in the eyes of the customer. These complementary dimensions stand out as the two keys to new product success; together they point to the need for a conscious and determined effort to include the marketplace and marketing activities throughout the innovation process. Technical research must be integrated with market research if a consistently successful new product programme is the goal.

(3) *Technical Strength*

The final dominant dimension in the success equation is a technical one, namely technical and production synergy and proficiency. In practice, this means carrying out certain activities particularly well (all five of almost equal importance):

   (a) preliminary technical assessment;
   (b) product development;
   (c) in-house prototype testing;
   (d) pilot production;
   (e) production start-up

The following resources, information and efforts were also critical to this dimension:

   (f) engineering skills;
   (g) product technology;
   (h) product design;
   (i) production resources;
   (j) "geared-up" production facilities at launch;
   (k) production process technology.

That technical and production resources, skills and knowledge are important to new product success has been known for years. The emphasis placed on R & D spending by individual firms and by policy-makers bears witness to the importance of the technical dimension in the success formula. What is noteworthy is that the technical dimension *does not* stand alone, nor does it stand first, as the key to the product success.

New product development is one of the most complex and least understood of business endeavours. Yet product innovation remains an important function, both for society and for the individual firm. Project NewProd began as an attempt to understand what makes for successful new products. Many of the vital ingredients of successful product innovation were identified, and most were found to be within the control of management. Other identified factors in success prove useful in selecting new product projects for exploration. Translating these keys to success into managerial action may prove to be a challenge, but certainly a worthwhile one if new product performance is the goal.

References
   1. Booz, Allen & Hamilton, *Management of New Products,* Booz, Allen and Hamilton, Inc., New York, 1986.
   2. Calantone, R. and Cooper, R. G., "A Discriminant Model for Investigating Scenarios of Industrial New Product Failure", *Journal of the Academy of Marketing Science,* Summer, 1979.
   3. Cooper, R. G., "Why New Industrial Products Fail", *Industrial Marketing Management,* Vol. 4, pp. 315-26.

4. Cooper, R. G. and Little, B., "Determinants of Market Research Expenditures for New Industrial Products", *Industrial Marketing Management,* Vol. 6 No. 2, 1977.

5. Cooper, R. G. and Little, B., "The Dimensions of Industrial New Product Success and Failure", *Journal of Marketing,* Vol. 43 No. 3, July 1979, pp. 93-103.

6. Cooper, R. G. and Little, B., "Identifying Industrial New Product Success: Project NewProd", *Industrial Marketing Management,* Vol. 8, 1979, pp. 136-44.

7. Crawford, C. M., "Marketing Research and the New Product Failure Rate", *Research Management,* March, 1977, pp. 29-31.

8. Hopkins, D. S. and Bailey, E. L., "New Product Pressures", *The Conference Board Record,* 1971, pp. 16-24.

9. Kulvik, H., "Factors Underlying the Success or Failure or New Products", Helsinki, University of Technology, Report No. 29, 1977.

10. Mansfield, E. and Rapoport, J., "The Costs of Industrial Product Innovation", *Management Science,* August, 1975, pp. 1380-6.

11. Myers, S. and Marquis, D. A., "Successful Industrial Innovations: A Study of Factors Underlying Innovation in Selected Firms", *National Science Foundation,* NSF, 1969, pp. 69-71.

12. National Industrial Conference Board, "Why New Products Fail", *The Conference Board Record,* New York, NICB, 1964.

13. National Industrial Conference Board, "The Marketing Executive Looks Ahead", *Experience in Marketing Management,* No. 13, New York, NICB, 1967.

14. Roberts, R. W. and Burke, J. E., "Six New Products — What Makes Them Successful", *Research Management,* May, 1974, pp. 21-4.

15. Rothwell, R., "Factors for Success in Industrial Innovation", from *Projects SAPPHO — A Comparative Study of Success and Failure in Industrial Innovation,* Science Policy Research Unit, University of Sussex, Brighton, 1972.

16. Rothwell, R., "The Hungarian Sappho — Some Comments and Comparison", *Research Policy,* Vol. 3, 1974, pp. 30-8.

17. Rothwell, R., Freeman, C., Horsley, A., Jervis, V. I. P., Robertson, A. B. and Townsend, J., "SAPPHO Updated — Project SAPPHO Phase II", *Research Policy,* Vol. 3, 1974, pp. 258-91.

18. Rubenstein, A. H., Chakrabarti, A. K. and O'Keefe, R. D., "Field Studies of the Technological Innovation Process", in Clauser, H. R. (ed.), *Process in Assessing Technical Innovations,* Technomic Publication, Westport, Conn., 1974.

19. Rubenstein, A. H., Chakrabarti, A. K., O'Keefe, R. D., Souder, W. E. and Young, H. C. "Factors Influencing Innovation Success at the Project Level", *Research Management,* May, 1976, pp. 15-20.

20. Schoeffler, S., Buzzell, R. D. and Heary, D. F., "Impact of Strategic Planning on Profit Performance", *Harvard Business Review,* March-April, 1974, p. 137.

21. Utterback, J. M., "Innovation in Industry and the Diffusion of Technology", *Science,* Vol. 183, February, 1974, pp. 620-6.

9. Some Dangerous Axioms of Product Elimination Decision-Making

by George J. Avlonitis* and Bert G. S. James

Historically, major consideration given to product-line management by practitioners and scholars has focused on the development of new products. The problems of idea generation, the development and testing of new products and the commercialisation process, for example, have received extensive attention in the literature [1].

It is the problem of eliminating products from the line which is becoming increasingly recognised as being the most neglected. As Bell has recently pointed out: "Product deletion as a strategy for mature products is a neglected topic in marketing. Some attention has been directed to it in recent years, but interest in the subject lags far behind interest in the development of new products" [2].

However, despite the generalised aversion to product elimination decisions, the inflationary pressure and the economic stagnation of the 1970s have forced many companies to stick to their guns, especially with their decisions to discontinue products [3]. Questions related to which, when and how products should be eliminated have naturally caused managers numerous headaches.

To remedy this situation, *prescriptions* have been offered in the literature. Naturally, the nature of the remedy varies with the primary interests of the person dispensing it, ranging from statements about alternative methods to identify "weak" products, through comprehensive and systematic computer-aided techniques for the evaluation of weak products and decision-making, to hopeful statements about the importance of formalised product elimination programmes. It might be said that these general prescriptions which seem theoretically appropriate to the problem are axiomatic to product elimination decisions. However, one cannot be confident of their merit without discovering the practical procedures being used by industrial companies in eliminating their products.

With this in mind, a study was devised whose primary purpose was to begin to form an empirically-based body of descriptive knowledge about product elimination decision-making in the industrial field which can be used to build a stronger theory and better practice in the area of product elimination.

The research evidence collected during the study led us seriously to challenge most of the axioms upon which much of the product elimination literature is established.

In this article, the tendency to associate the product elimination decision only with "weak" products is questioned, as is the desirability and relevance of comprehensive and systematic product elimination procedures and the necessity for formal product elimination programmes.

It should be pointed out, however, that the objective of this article is not to pour

*The financial support provided by the Alexandres S. Onassis Foundation to the senior author during the course of the study is gratefully acknowledged.

113

critical scorn upon basically useful guidelines and valuable work, nor is it to propose a new theory. The primary attempt here is to put forward some empirical evidence which is both illustrative of the inadequacy of the existing knowledge and theory on product elimination to provide an understanding of company behaviour in this area, and suggestive of directions for future research efforts to which academic scholars should turn their interests if a useful body of product elimination theory is to be developed. Basically, we seek to demonstrate that academic scholars must approach the area of product elimination with a research-oriented view as opposed to an ends-oriented view directed towards the provision of normative product elimination decision-making models.

The Study
This article reports evidence from a wider ranging examination of all aspects of the product elimination decision-making process in the UK engineering industry. The population subject to investigation in this study was restricted to the engineering companies employing more than 100 people and engaged in the manufacture of mechanical, instrument and/or electrical engineering products. The study was focused on the rational, formal, ethical and dynamic aspects of the product elimination process. An extensive set of variables describing the company's environment (internal/external) was investigated to detect possible relationships between characteristics of product elimination decision-making behaviour and characteristics of the company's environment.

The study involved three stages: (a) a pilot study; (b) an interview survey which involved twenty in-depth company interviews ranging from two days to one week duration each; and (c) a mail survey which resulted in 94 completed mail questionnaires constituting a 31 per cent response rate from the sample contacted.

The companies which participated during the interview and mail survey stages of the study were selected using a stratified sampling procedure with three size strata (small 100-499; medium 500-999; large 1000 and over employees) and five industry/SIC strata (machine tools — SIC332; pumps, valves, compressors — SIC333; other machinery — SIC339; scientific and industrial instruments and systems — SIC354; electrical machinery — SIC361). Their sizes ranged from 100 to 6000 employees and from an annual turnover of less than £5 million to over £50 million; and they exhibited substantial variations in certain contextual environmental and organisational factors of interest in this study including organisational technology, degree of market competition and rate of technological change [4].

Areas of Concern — Some Findings
In the ensuing sections we put forward some findings of our study which call into question three fundamental beliefs that most of the writers in this field adhered to explicitly or implicitly:

   (a) the elimination decision arises only when a product is not performing satisfactorily with respect to the company's sales, profit and/or market share objectives;

   (b) comprehensive and systematic procedures are central to the product elimination process;

(c) the product elimination decision should be formalised.

The findings also raise issues which are suggestive of directions for future research efforts in this largely unexplored area.

The Scope of the Product Elimination Problem

Much of the literature on product elimination either explicitly or implicitly assumes that product elimination is a strategy for mature products, i.e., for those products that have been moved through the various stages of the conventional life cycle and have reached the maturity or decline stage. In other words, much of the literature assumes that the basic problem situation that evokes the elimination of a product is its weak performance, measured usually in terms of sales and profits. This becomes obvious if one considers the fact that a large number of the contributions that have been made in the literature on product elimination deal exclusively with the problem of identifying "weak" products, and prescribe alternative ways to tackle this problem [5].

However, the findings of the study clearly indicate that not all weak products are ready for elimination, nor are elimination candidates only those with low profitability and declining sales. The various factors which should result in the elimination decision are not always easy to detect, and in a number of cases a company can be dependent on outside forces to form the "lead" in its elimination decisions.

In the course of this study, eight basic problem situations were identified under which a product may be eliminated:

(1) government policies and regulations;
(2) changes in the third party specifications;
(3) decline in market potential;
(4) parent organisation decisions and policies;
(5) poor product performance (despite a generally viable market);
(6) development of new products;
(7) rationalisation brought by mergers and acquisitions;
(8) development of an active variety reduction policy.

The problem situations identified are indicative of the character and mix of the conditions under which a product may be eliminated and highlight the fact that management of a company is not always "independent" in making the elimination decision. There are situations under which management has little or no control of the subject matter or the scheduling of the elimination process. The aforementioned problem situations (1), (2) and (4), for instance, present problems which are unanticipated by management in terms of content (the type of products affected) and time of arrival. These problems are often accompanied by severe limitations with respect to time in which management has to define and choose its action. In contrast, the problem situations (6), (7) and (8) are created to a large extent by management itself as part of the company's product planning process; require a lower level of urgency with which they must be resolved; and lead to the elimination of products which are usually of the management's choosing.

However, the existence of different kinds of problem situations evoking the elimination of products implies that there are different types of product elimination decisions, each necessitating a different kind of approach. Indeed, we found evidence in our study suggesting that the decision variables (criteria, evaluation factors) and procedures utilised in the product elimination process tend to vary even within companies, depending, among other things, on the problem situation that evoked such a process.

It seems, therefore, that what is needed is the development of a classification scheme able to define the different types of product elimination decisions and identify their associated decision processes.

The different problem situations evoking the elimination decision provide a useful starting base for the development of such a scheme. Consequently, in-depth field studies are required to uncover the decision variables and procedures utilised under specific product elimination situations. Pletcher's [6] research effort to determine the decision variables utilised by the American small-appliance companies in their elimination processes initiated by the "poor product performance" problem situation, may be seen as a step in the right direction.

It should be stated, however, that the classification of the product elimination decisions by the problem situation that evoked them is not a straightforward task, mainly for two reasons.

(a) There might be an overlap between the problem situations under which a product may be eliminated. For instance, the development of a new product leading to the elimination of the existing one may be the natural consequence of the poor performance of the existing product. Similarly, the development of a variety reduction policy leading to the discontinuation of certain products from the range may be the natural consequence of the decline in market potential of these particular products.

(b) More than one problem situation may evoke the elimination decision at the same time. This becomes apparent in the following example. The management of a large manufacturer of industrial valves was considering for a long period of time the elimination of certain types of valves whose performance, in terms of sales and profitability, did not meet the company's expectations. However, no apparent time constraint on the resolution of the problem existed. The matter was frequently discussed inside the management meetings, and outside, but with no fruitful results. Elimination was viewed as something that should be done but can "wait until tomorrow". It was in fact a change in the British Standards concerning these particular valves which set a time constraint and forced management to drop these products. It is obvious that two problem situations, namely "poor product performance" and "changes in the third party specifications" evoked the elimination decision in this particular case.

However, despite these difficulties of assigning a product elimination decision to a particular problem situation, the latter remains an important base for the development of a useful typology of the product elimination decisions made by a business organisation. Such a typology could undoubtedly stimulate research aimed at the discovery of the elimination decision processes followed under specific product elimination situations.

The Comprehensive and Systematic Nature of the Product Elimination Process
Much of the literature on product elimination is based upon a variety of theoretical and normative views of the product elimination process [7]. Each author takes a somewhat different view of the product elimination process, in that the approach each advocates contains a different number of procedural steps and varies in complexity from "qualitative-factor listing" that deals only with the evaluation factors pertinent to the elimination decision [8], to "quantitative" product evaluation and decision-making, via the utilisation of computer-aided techniques [9].

However, basic to these approaches is the proposition that the product elimination decision is a sequential multiple-stage process (i.e., detection of weak products to analysis and evaluation of weak products to elimination decision to implementation of the decision); and that management should make and implement such a decision only after a comprehensive and systematic investigation of all the decision variables (criteria, evaluation factors) that bear on each specific step of the process.

There would certainly seem to be *a priori* grounds for believing that adoption of such comprehensive and systematic procedures would improve the effectiveness of the product elimination process. Yet, in practice, the product elimination process is a much more complex business.

(1) To start with, it is not comprehensive but "eclectic", involving informed managerial judgement and discretion. Analysis of the data suggests that managers tend to focus their attention on a few key decision variables which appear to cover the critical areas of consideration as they perceive the product's situation within the company's environment. More specifically, elimination decision variables tend to be logically selected by management depending on whether or not a new product is available to replace the one under consideration, as well as the importance of the role played by the product within the company's environment.

The importance of the product refers to the percentage of company's resources and sales for which it accounts. It may also refer to the uncertainty with respect to the outcome of the product elimination decision in the company's overall activities. Generally, the larger the percentage of the company's resources and sales that the product accounts for, the greater its importance, and the higher the uncertainty regarding the effects of its elimination on the company's overall activities. However, as our findings indicate, the greater the importance of the product involved (and in this case the higher the uncertainty associated with its elimination) the larger the number of decision variables considered by management, and more detailed the analysis of the product's past and future performance, and the effects of the elimination decision on the company's activities. For instance, when a product of minor importance to the company's activities in considered for possible elimination, then the elimination process is found to be rather simple and straightforward, involving an assessment of (a) the marketing implications of the product's removal through the subjective opinions of the sales force, and (b) the product's current inventory level with the objective to clear out before the product's discontinuation. On the other hand, when a product which forms an important part of the company's product range is to be dropped, without being replaced, then the elimination process involves detailed investigations regarding the marketing, financial, managerial and social implications of the product's elimination, and extensive discussions and consultations among the departmental members of the company. These findings are more consistent with the behaviour theory of the firms as revised by Carter [10] who hypothesised that the greater the uncertainty of a decision outcome in the total environment of the organisation, the greater the number of criteria which will be sought to guide the decision.

However, besides the product's particular situation, the choice of decision variables is also conditioned by the market structure within which the company operates. Evidence in our study clearly indicates that while the companies which operate in highly competitive markets tend to emphasise (as the normative literature does) the decision variables related to the financial aspects of the product and the company (perhaps due to financial contingencies posed by competition in general and price competition in particular), the companies which face monopsonistic or oligopsonistic situations tend to place much less emphasis on these variables. This is so because, for the companies which operate in monopsonistic or oligopsonistic markets, the retention/elimination decision is based more on customer considerations than financial considerations. These companies tend to have little control over their marketing policy, and as a result they are often obliged to produce a product which, despite the fact that it makes insufficient contribution to the company's sales and profits, does, nevertheless, satisfy their large customer(s) requirements; failure to satisfy such customer requests could lead to severe disruption of their business [11]. It is obvious from the foregoing discussion that, in contrast to normative views, it makes little sense for the companies to conduct comprehensive and detailed analysis and evaluations of every product considered for elimination, and to attempt to quantify a rather exhaustive number of decision variables generally considered as being germane to the product elimination decision.

(2) Furthermore, while the most basic product elimination process, as presented in the literature, involves simply the detection of a weak product and then the analysis and evaluation of it which logically leads to a decision point, we found no case quite that simple. The problem situation that triggers the elimination consideration initially is usually more influential towards forming management decisions than the analysis and evaluation process itself. Also, entire sections of the more general approaches to be found in the literature may be left out in practice. For instance, as our findings indicate, in the companies which operate in an innovative environment, the product elimination process is an integral part of the new product development process; and as a consequence the acceptability of the new product to the customer and the determination of the most opportune time and method of the existing product's withdrawal, to minimise the elimination's effect upon customers and the company's profit structure, are the management's primary concern in these companies.

Similarly, in the cases where elimination of a product is seriously considered due to coercion by external forces (i.e., government policies and regulations, changes in the third party specifications), the decision process is abbreviated and efforts, if any, are devoted either to modification to meet the standards of the external forces or to orderly withdrawal of the product from the market.

(3) Finally, the apparent self-evident attractions of a systematic and sometimes inflexible approach are less clear in the light of practical difficulties. This is true because the product elimination process is conducted by management in a dynamic, highly political environment. As elimination decisions affect the balance of resources, the practices of several functional areas within the organisation, and sometimes the individuals and groups in the organisation, the product elimination process naturally involves conflict and bargaining among interested groups inside and even outside the organisation. We found cases where political activity and bargaining occurred early in the decision process, when the company's senior management disputed the need to recognise the "weaknesses" of the product. We also found cases where political impasses took place late in the decision process, when members of the organisation and/or the customers blocked the elimination proposals. In these cases the political impasses led either to an intensive bargaining to confront the resistance directly and remove it, or to cycling back to an earlier stage for the modification of the unacceptable elimination proposals in line with the objections. Thus, we found logic in delineating distinct stages of the product elimination process, but not in postulating a simple sequential relationship between them. There is a frequent reversion to earlier stages, caused mainly by political activities which represent a distinguishing characteristic of the product elimination process, particularly when a product that forms an important part of the company's product line is involved [12].

Thus, whereas the intellectual appeal of the approaches prescribed in the literature on product elimination is substantial, it seems to bear little resemblance in practice. In other words, the axiomatic assumption that comprehensive and systematic sequential procedures are central to the product elimination process cannot be accepted without qualifications. Consequently, new, broader and more flexible approaches which recognise that the product elimination process is dynamic and political, and is fine-tuner to the unique product and company circumstance, should be developed. While it is reasonable to assume that the new approaches can be developed from systematic studies of product elimination decision-making within organisations, it is also reasonable to assume that these approaches will be highly qualitative (as opposed to sophisticated quantitative approaches), deterministic and of relatively simple structure with limited generality over products and companies; their basic aim would be to spell out the conceptualisation of the product elimination process that prevails under given conditions by explicating otherwise obscure assumptions and/or relationships. Such conditions would include three levels of factors that affect the product elimination process. The first level is the immediate characteristics of the product elimination process itself: the problem situation that evokes the elimination process and the importance of the product involved. The second level is the organisation (size, structure, technology, management style, susceptibility to political influence) within which the product elimination process takes place, while the third level is the techno-economic environment (market structure, rate of technological change) within which the organisation operates.

The Value of Formal Product Elimination Programmes
It is perhaps axiomatic to product elimination that the use of formal product elimination programmes is associated with higher financial performance. This is implicitly assumed, or explicitly stated in the published work of the outstanding authorities on the subject [13]. Yet, there is a lack of research-oriented evidence on this very fundamental issue. In fact, only a longitudinal study designed to analyse and evaluate companies' experiences before and after the adoption of formal elimination programmes could produce definitive evidence on this issue, and this is still to be done.

However, one of the major findings that emerged from our study was the lack of formal elimination procedures in many companies, including some of the largest and the most advanced in the UK engineering industry. In fact, of the 94 companies in the mail survey sample, only seven appeared to have formal elimination programmes in writing, while less than one third tended to carry out a regular review of the product-line and assign specific responsibilities for product elimination. Likewise, the work done by Hise and McGinnis [14] in the US has clearly indicated the lack of formal product elimination programmes in America's largest manufacturing companies.

Is it conceivable, that the vast majority of companies, including some of the most progressive ones in industry, have not constituted formal product elimination programmes?

Are these believable findings in the face of the widespread axiomatic assumption that formal product elimination programmes pay handsome returns in terms of increased sales volume and profitability? Yes, they are believable and there are, in fact, a number of reasons which account for this slow adoption of formal product elimination programmes.

Firstly, it may be due to an inherent conservatism of management and/or the absence of adequate information to constitute the input of such formal programmes. It is obvious from the study that while some top management do recognise the need for, or the value of, a more professional and "formal" approach to product elimination, they simply do not have the knowledge, the "management style" and/or comprehensive information that is required for the development of a formal product elimination programme; indeed, the lack of accurate and factual information was found to be the biggest problem encountered by the companies contacted in their product elimination decision-making process.

Secondly, it may be due to the fact that management do not feel that product elimination is an important part of the company's product planning process. In fact, we found evidence in our study suggesting that the degree of formal development of the product elimination decision is associated with the degree of importance of the product elimination activities to the company's operations as it is perceived by its top management.

Finally, this slow adoption of formal product elimination programmes indicates, in some cases at least, recognition of the fact that a formal product elimination programme is not appropriate to the specific circumstances of the company concerned; thus reflecting an intuitive management grasp of a contingency theory of product elimination. In the smaller companies, which generally have relatively fewer product-lines, the need for formal product elimination programmes is found to be less pressing. The same applies to the companies which operate in relatively non-competitive markets; as long as there is a lack of competition, the pressures on the company's management for more detailed formal approaches to product elimination are minimised. Another condition which, according to our findings, allows management to handle product elimination on an informal basis is the rapid rate of product oriented technological change experienced by the company. In fact, companies operating in environments characterised by rapid technological change were found to treat the product elimination process informally as an integral part of their new product development process. The validity of this is strongly supported by the frequently expressed views that successful companies in dynamic environments are less formalised and tend to adopt management practices and procedures which are "organic" rather than "mechanistic" [15]. Indeed, to the extent that formal product elimination programmes exhibit characteristics of "mechanistic organisation", they are not particularly suited to dynamic situations.

It is obvious from the foregoing discussion that the fundamental belief that the product elimination process should be formalised cannot be accepted without qualifications. There is clearly a case for determining the *appropriate* degree of formality or informality of the product elimination decision for specific company conditions, or alternatively the conditions in which formal product elimination programmes will pay or not pay. Indeed, one of the problems may well be the difficulty of defining formality in elimination programmes.

In our study, the "structuring of activities" dimension of organisation structure was adopted as a frame of reference for defining, exploring, and measuring the degree of formality in elimination programmes [16]. Accordingly, the following components of the formality dimension (conceptualised as "structuring of activities") of the product elimination process were investigated: (a) the existence and/or degree of regular systematic procedures and rules governing the product elimination process (standard routines/systematic behaviour); (b) the presence and/or degree of defined and specialised roles and assigned responsibilities regarding product elimination decision-making (task specialisation/assignment of responsibilities); and (c) the extent and intensity of documentation pertaining to product elimination (formal paperwork/documentation). Our study showed that while formalised product elimination programmes are generally more common in large, multi-product companies employing primarily large batch and mass production technologies and operating in a stable environment, the emphasis that is placed on each of the components of the formality dimension (i.e., systematic behaviour, assignment of responsibilities, and documentation) tends to vary from company to company.

Thus, there is clearly a case for examining in greater detail the *appropriate* degree of formality or informality for specific company conditions, and for determining the extent to which each of the components of formality is appropriate or inappropriate to these specific conditions. Such conditions would include the size of the company, its product/market diversity, manufacturing technology, style of top management, rate of technological change related to its product and processes and market competition. Others could, of course, be added.

Conclusions

The experiences recorded in this paper have clearly indicated that there is a need for much deeper analysis into product elimination theory and company practices. Clearly, there is a gap between theory and practice in the area of product elimination. The existing knowledge and theory about the product elimination function is woefully inadequate to provide an understanding of company behaviour in this area. This may be attributed to both the paucity of empirical contributions to the understanding of the product elimination function [17], and the shortcomings of the normative approaches developed to provide some evidence in this area. In fact, the normative approaches proposed in the literature being distilled from somewhat limited experience, common sense and logic, have distinct overtones of evangelical fervour and draw no boundary as to the specific product and company conditions to which they apply.

However, as the findings of our study indicate, the process through which elimination decisions are made and implemented in a particular company is related to the problem situation that evoked such a process; the importance of the role played by the product within the company and *vis-à-vis* its users; and the nature of the company, its business, its management, and its environment. Put another way: the product's past, present and future role within the company's environment on the one hand, and the relationships between management, the organisation and the environment on the other, will always determine the product elimination process adopted by a particular company.

This does not necessarily mean that normative models will have no place in the area of product elimination decision-making. The point here is that the search for the "golden", "general purpose" product elimination model should be replaced with a search designed to uncover the product elimination process as it is being conducted by management in particular organisational settings and for particular product circumstances.

Indeed, there is a need for a "micro" rather than "macro" approach to the problem; and as a consequence in-depth field studies are required to explore and describe fully the behaviour of each important aspect of the product elimination process, from the recognition of a product's elimination candidacy to its eventual removal from the company's product-line, under specific product and company circumstances. These studies, which are absolutely essential since we need to establish knowledge as to what exists before making recommendations for improvement, should be designed with theory construction in mind, and should adopt specific theoretical constructs for recording observed behaviour. We strongly believe that the literature on organisational and decision-making theory is, beside the literature on product elimination, a fruitful source of theoretical constructs for the study of the product elimination decision. For instance, it would be very interesting to examine and analyse the product elimination decisions being made by management in particular organisational settings within the framework of the behavioural theory of the firm as proposed by Cyert and March [18], and revised by Carter [19].

However, once a useful body of theory that describes in a realistic manner the distinct variations in behaviour patterns *vis-à-vis* the product elimination process and the factors that lead to such variations begins to take shape, more rigorous research methodologies may be employed which are normative in character. Such research efforts should be carefully designed in terms of testing hypotheses derived from the theory, and should include performance measures to allow normative conclusions to be drawn about the appropriate content, frequency, decision-making entity, and degree of formality or informality, to name a few aspects, of the product elimination process for given idiosyncratic product, managerial, organisation and environmental conditions. The end product of research of this kind would be the development of a contingency theory of product elimination decision with significant normative implications for better management practice in this area. In other words, the ultimate objective of research of this kind is better product elimination practice which, given the current harsh economic environment, is more crucial than ever before.

It is, therefore, in the practitioners' and academic scholars' best interests to work together to develop a body of knowledge and theory on the product elimination decision to facilitate practice, teaching and research. Indeed, future advances in our knowledge of product elimination decision-making depend on the close co-operation between the academic scholars who will, hopefully, be involved in research along the lines suggested in this article, and the practising managers who have access to all pertinent information that would be needed by the scholars. This article is written in the spirit of wishing to see this field advance from infancy to adolescence.

References
1. An extensive discussion of these problems may be found in the following references: Crawford, C. M., "The Trajectory Theory of Goal Setting for New Products", *Journal of Marketing Research,* May 1966; Goslin, L. N., *The Product Planning System,* R. D. Irwin Inc. 1967; Urban, G. L., "A New Product Analysis and Decision Model", *Management Science,* April 1968; Toll, A. P., "New Techniques in Product Planning", in *New Ideas in Industrial Marketing,* Coram, T. C. and R. W. Hill, (eds), London, Staple Press, 1970, pp. 44-51; Spitz, A. E., (ed), *Product Planning,* Auerbach Publishers, 1972; Mathey, C. J., "New Approaches to the Management of Product Planning", *Research Management,* November 1976; Stone, M., *Product Planning: An Integrated Approach,* Macmillan, 1976; Baker, M. J., *Marketing New Industrial Products,* Macmillan, 1975; Baker, M. J., and McTavish, R., *Product Policy and Management,* Macmillan, 1976; Pessemier, E. A., *Product Management: Strategy and Organisation,* Wiley, 1977; Parkinson, S. T., "Successful New Product Development — An International Comparative Study", *R & D Management,* April 1981.

2. Bell, M., *Marketing: Concepts and Strategy,* third edition, Boston, Houghton Mifflin, 1979, p. 264.

3. This trend is well documented in the following references: "Galloping Trend: Profit Shape-Up via Product Shake-Out", *Grey Matter,* May 1972; "The Squeeze on Product-Mix", *Business Week,* January 5, 1974; *Sales Management,* January 21, 1974; Johnson, M. L., "End of the Line for Weak Products?", *Industry Week,* September 15, 1975; Shama, A., "Management and Consumers in an Era of Stagflation", *Journal of Marketing,* July 1978.

4. A fuller account of choice of sample frame, selection of the sample, and company characteristics at each stage of the study, as well as details of the research methodology may be found in Avlonitis, G. J., *Exploratory Investigation of the Product Elimination Decision-Making Process in the UK Engineering Industry,* unpublished PhD thesis, University of Strathclyde, 1980, Vol. 1, pp. 242-316.

5. See for instance: Houfek, L. J., "How to Decide which Products to Junk", *Printers Ink,* August 1952; Sonnecken, E.H. and Hurst, D'O., "How to Audit your Existing Products for Profit", *Management Methods,* April 1960; Drucker, P., "Care and Feeding of the Profitable Product", *Fortune,* March 1964; Henderson, B. D., *The Product Portfolio,* a pamphlet by the Boston Consulting Group, 1970; Kratchman, S. H., Hise, R. T. and Ulrich, T. A., "Management's Decision to Discontinue a Product", *The Journal of Accountancy,* June 1975; Wind, Y. and Claycamp, H. T., "Planning Product Line Strategy: A Matrix Approach", *Journal of Marketing,* January 1976.

6. Pletcher, B. A., *The Product Elimination Process in the Small Home Appliance Industry: An Empirical Study,* unpublished DBA Dissertation, Kent State University, 1973.

7. See: Berenson, C., "Pruning the Product-Line", *Business Horizons,* Summer 1963; Alexander, R. S.,"The Death and Burial of Sick Products", *Journal of Marketing,* April 1964; Kotler, P., "Phasing-Out Weak Products", *Harvard Business Review,* March-April 1965; Eckles, R. W., "Product Line Deletion and Simplification", *Business Horizons,* October 1971; Worthing P. M., "The Assessment of Product Deletion Decision Indicators", in *Fortran Applications in Business Administration,* (eds) Schriber, T. J. and Madeo, L. A., Ann Arbor, Graduate School of Business Administration, The University of Michigan, 1971; Hamelman, P. H., and Mazze, E. M., "Improving Product Abandonment Decisions", *Journal of Marketing,* April 1972; Winkler, J., *Marketing Planning,* Cassell Associated Business Programmes, 1972, pp. 159-167; Browne, W. G., and Kemp, P. S., "A Three-Stage Product Review Process", *Industrial Marketing Management,* Vol. 5, 1976.

8. See, for example: Alexander, R. S., *op. cit;* Eckles, R. W., *op. cit.*

9. See for instance: Kotler, P., *op. cit;* Hamelman, P. H. and Mazze, E. M., *op. cit.*

10. Carter, E. E., "The Behavioural Theory of the Firm and Top Level Corporate Decisions", *Administrative Science Quarterly,* December 1971.

11. For an interesting discussion on the importance of individual orders and "customer orientation" in the industrial field see James, B. G. S., *Integrated Marketing,* Penguin Books, 1972, pp. 349-352.

12. The impact of political activities on organisational decision-making has also been demonstrated by studies on the capital investment, resource allocation, divestment and acquisition decision processes of organisations. See for example: Berg, N. A., "Strategic Planning in Conglomerate Companies". *Harvard Business Review,* May-June 1965; Bower, J. L., *Managing the Resource Allocation Process,* Harvard University Press, 1970; Carter, E. E., "The Behavioural Theory of the Firm and Top Level Corporate Decisions", *op. cit;* Gilmour, S. C., *The Divestment Decision Processes,* unpublished DBA dissertation, Harvard Business School, 1973.

13. Berenson, C., "Product Abandonment: A Forgotten Step in Innovation", in *Innovation — Key to Marketing Progress,* American Marketing Association, 1963; Alexander, R. S., *op. cit;* Kotler, P., *op. cit.*

14. Hise, R. T. and McGinnis, M. A.. "Product Elimination: Practices, Policies, Ethics", *Business Horizons,* June 1975.

15. See, for instance: Burns, T. and Stalker, G. M., *The Management of Innovation,* London, Tavistock Publications, 1961; Child, J., "Managerial and Organisational Factors Associated with Company Performance — Part II: Contingency Analysis", *Journal of Management Studies,* February 1975.

16. The "structuring of activities" dimension which has been derived from the Weberian archetype of formal organisation and the subsequent multi-dimensional analysis of the structural variables of the organisation by the Aston group, represents the degree to which the behaviour of employees is overtly defined by task specification, standard routines and formal paperwork. See by Pugh, D. S., *et. al,* "Dimensions of Organisation Structure", *Administrative Science Quarterly,* Vol. 13, 1968; "The Context of Organisational Structures", *Administrative Science Quarterly,* Vol. 14, 1969, pp. 91-117; "An Empirical Taxonomy of Structures of Work Organisations", *Administrative Science Quarterly,* Vol. 14, 1969, pp. 115-126.

17. Very few empirical studies on the product elimination decision have been undertaken and reported to date including those conducted by (a) Rothe, J. T., "The Product Elimination Decision", *MSU Business Topics,* Autumn 1970; (b) Eckles, R. W., "Product Line Deletion and Simplification", *op. cit;* (c) Banville, G. B. and Pletcher, B. A., "The Product Elimination Function", *Journal of*

the Academy of Marketing Science, Summer 1974; and (d) Hise, R. T. and McGinnis, M. A., "Product Elimination: Practices, Policies, Ethics", *op. cit.* These studies, however, by (a) focusing almost exclusively on the decision variables (criteria, evaluation factors) most commonly used to recognise and evaluate weak products in selected American consumer-goods industries, and (b) failing to identify and evaluate those contextual organisational and environmental factors that might be expected to have significant impact on the nature of the product elimination process adopted, have done little to enhance our understanding of product elimination decision-making.

18. Cyert, R. M. and March, J. G., *A Behavioural Theory of the Firm,* Prentice-Hall, 1963.

19. Carter, E. E., "The Behavioural Theory of the Firm and Top Level Corporation Decisions", *op. cit.*

10. Value-In-Use Pricing

by Martin Christopher

The pricing decision is one of the most important issues that the marketing executive has to face. Its impact will usually be reflected in the quantity of the product sold, the contribution to profits that the product will make and, even more crucially, the strategic position of the product in the market place. In addition, in a multi-product company it is frequently the case that a decision taken on the price of one product will have implications for other products in the range. It is not surprising, therefore, that much has been written and spoken on the subject of pricing and that it has created considerable controversy as to how the price decision should be made.

Frequently this controversy has centred around the role that costs should play in determining price. Traditionally the price of a product was based upon the identification of the costs associated with manufacturing, marketing and distributing the product with the subsequent addition of a mark-up to reflect the desired profitability. Such an approach has been criticised on a number of counts. Firstly it can prove to be extremely difficult in practice to identify the true costs of a product. In so many cases the company will have joint costs and fixed costs which can only be allocated to a specific product on an arbitrary basis. Secondly such a cost-plus approach to pricing ignores the demand sensitivity of the market place. It may be that a price determined on a cost-plus basis is higher than the market place will accept or perhaps it may even be lower than the price that the market would bear. Attempts have been made to overcome these problems by using a *marginal cost* approach rather than a *full cost* approach so that the pricing decision becomes one of attempting to maximise the contribution that the product will make, i.e., the difference between the price and the direct and attribute costs.

The basic problem with any cost-based approach to pricing is that it implicitly assumes that the customer is interested in our costs whereas in reality the customer is only concerned with his own costs. This can be expressed another way — the customer seeks to acquire benefits and it is for those benefits that the customer is prepared to pay a certain price in order to acquire them. Seen from this perspective the company making the price decision is faced with the need to identify the value — in the customer's eyes — of the benefits inherent in their product. The costs of that product thus become irrelevant to the pricing decision even though they are highly pertinent to the profitability of that decision. In other words costs determine profits not price.

The Concept of Benefits

In any purchase it can be argued that the customer is seeking to acquire "benefits". A product must bring with it the promise of performing certain tasks, of solving identified problems, or even of providing specific gratifications. Thus the product is not bought for the particular components or materials that go into its manufacture *per se* but it is bought for what, as an entity, it can do. It was Theodore Levitt [1] who once said: "People don't buy $\frac{1}{4}''$ drill bits, what they buy are $\frac{1}{4}''$ holes". In other words the drill bit has no value of itself and would never be purchased if it did not offer the benefit of making the hole. This is a vitally important concept and is more than mere semantics.

The implication of the benefit concept from a pricing point of view is that the company must first identify the benefits that the customer perceives the product to offer and then attempt to ascertain the value that the customer places upon them. The key issue here is that it is the customer *perception* that is important. It may be, for example, that two competing companies offer products which are technically identical to all intents and purposes and yet one company can command a premium price. Why should this be? It may be that additional benefits in the way of technical advice or after-sales service are perceived to be superior from one company to another. Or it may just be that the "image" of one company is seen as superior. Whatever the reason there are many cases of this type of "differential advantage" which cannot be explained simply in technical or quality terms. One study looked at the price advantage that IBM have traditionally had in computers and reported:

"This study has found that IBM machines are priced substantially above competing machines of equal performance and that this price differential appears to be independent of machine size. Since a substantial percentage of users are still willing to employ IBM machines even though their relative price is very high, the implication is that IBM offers customers something to induce them to pay a substantial premium for an IBM machine. Apparently, IBM offers substantially more (or higher quality) non-hardware services than do its competitors. Possible examples of these non-hardware services are superior after-sales service, more product reliability, better software, and more assistance in developing applications of the machine. The fact that the large price differential between IBM and its competitors persisted over the period of this study (1964-71) suggests that other manufacturers have not been able to make their non-hardware offerings as attractive as IBM's." [2]

Another way to look at this price advantage is to think of the maximum price at which the product could be sold as being the sum of two elements. Firstly there is the "commodity price" element. This is the base price for the generic product which would be determined by supply and demand in the market place. On top of this should then be added the "premium price differential" which reflects the totality of the benefits that the customer perceives will be acquired through purchase of that product. Figure 1 presents this concept diagrammatically.

The existence of this "premium price differential" can only be explained in terms of perceived benefits. The task of the pricing decision maker therefore becomes one of identifying these benefits and placing a customer value upon them. It is in reality a "bundle" of benefits and so the first step in this suggested approach to pricing is to "unbundle" the product and identify the individual benefit components which together constitute the totality. We shall return to this issue later in more detail.

Figure 1. The Components of Price

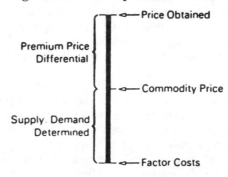

Price and Value

Every purchase by a customer is a "trade-off". The trade-off is between the value that the customer places on the acquisition of the product versus the costs that are involved in that acquisition plus any subsequent costs that might be involved, e.g., maintenance or up-grading costs.

There is nothing new in this idea. Economists have long talked about the concept of "utility". Whilst some of their ideas on the relationship between price and demand may seem naive there nevertheless is an important message for the pricing decision maker in the recognition that price must be seen in terms of *value*.

The Victorian economist, Alfred Marshall, was the first really to articulate the idea of price as a reflection of the value placed on a good or service by the consumer. He developed the concept of the demand curve which simply stated that the higher the price charged for a product the lower will be the demand for it as potential consumers see the price exceed the product's perceived value to them. It is interesting to note that this concept suggests that the price charged for a product may be lower than the value placed upon it by some customers. This is the notion of a "consumer surplus". In Figure 2 a demand curve for a particular product is represented and the

Figure 2. The Demand Curve

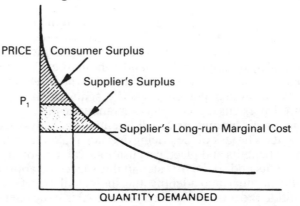

price currently prevailing in the market place is P_1. Now it can be seen from the diagram that there are some consumers, albeit fewer in number, who would actually be prepared to pay a higher price. The numbers of such consumers obviously decline the higher the price that is charged. The consumers who fall into this category are actually paying a price less than the value they perceive they are gaining through purchasing the product. They are enjoying a "consumer surplus". Now at the same time it can be seen from the same diagram that the price P_1 is actually higher than the supplier's long-run marginal cost. In other words in this case there is a "surplus" accruing to the supplier as well. This analysis is an over-simplification of the real world but it might be a useful focus for the price decision maker to think of this problem along the lines suggested by Figure 3.

Figure 3. Consumer and Supplier Surplus

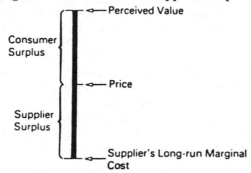

The pricing problem can be seen in this way as an attempt by the supplier to achieve the greatest possible "surplus" over long-run marginal cost but still pricing no higher than the perceived value placed on the product by potential customers.

An alternative way of looking at this is to see the problem in terms of the need to identify what value the target market places upon the product and then to convert that value into a market price. The first step to solving this problem is to recognise that there will be different groupings of customers with different perceptions of a product's value. These groupings are in effect *market segments*. Thus we might identify a specific segment of the market that seeks certain benefits from a product and who value them at a particular level. The concept of "benefit segmentation" is not new [3] and has been well tried and tested. What is not so well advanced though is the executive's ability to quantify these benefits in a way which will be of positive assistance in the pricing decision. The technology required to quantify identified benefits does, however, exist and we shall turn shortly to this particular topic.

However, it is not sufficient just to identify the perceived value of a product to the customers and then set price equal to that value. Frequently there will be costs other than price that face the customer in acquiring that product. In a pioneering article Shapiro and Jackson [4] pointed out that:

"The costs a customer perceives are . . . . . diverse. They include clearly defined acquisition costs: seller's price, incoming freight, installation, and order handling costs. They also include less clearly defined costs such as the risk to the customer of a product failure (which can include the personal risk of making a poor decision, as well as the risk to the company of shutting down a production line or repairing a piece of equipment), fear of late or inaccurate delivery, custom modification after receipt of the item and so forth."

From the customer's point of view, therefore, it can be argued that the decision to purchase is a trade-off between all the costs involved on the one hand and the perceived benefits resulting from acquisition on the other. Shapiro and Jackson [5] expressed this relationship as follows:

Highest price the customer will pay =
Perceived benefits − Costs other than price.

Thus it can be seen that in the pricing decision it is as important to understand the cost structure of our potential customer as it is to know our own! It is essential to the pricing decision to recognise the total cost impact on the customer of the acquisition of our product. Even though the customer may not himself have fully evaluated the implication of the acquisition the supplier will be better positioned to sell to the customer if these costs are known. The appropriate concept here is that of "Life Cycle Costs" which refers to all the customer costs that will be incurred by the customer from the acquisition of the product through to the end of its useful life. For example, in pricing a piece of numerical control equipment the manufacturer should identify the effects that the equipment will have on the customer's manufacturing economies, the machine's estimated life, any maintenance and upgrading costs and its disposal value, if any.

Given a full analysis of the life-cycle cost implications of the product the pricing decision maker can now focus attention upon the identification and quantification of the product's perceived benefits.

Benefit Evaluation
One of the first attempts to break loose from the constraints of cost-oriented pricing and to seek instead to incorporate some recognition of perceived value was the technique developed by the Glacier Metal Company which they termed "product analysis pricing" [6]. Product analysis pricing attempts to build up a final price by identifying the physical features that go into the product and then to value these features in customer terms. The method is based upon a statistical analysis of previous prices obtained for similar products to provide quantified estimates of the relative contribution of each physical component to the final price. The analysis is limited as such to the physical attributes of the product and does not quantify non-physical benefits other than by talking loosely about the "product surround". Because of these limitations it does not provide the pricing decision maker with the crucial information on customer evaluation of perceived product benefits — both physical and intangible. To do this we need to seek an alternative approach to benefit evaluation.

In recent years a number of developments have taken place in the fields of mathematical psychology and psychometrics which have great value in quantifying the relative importance that potential customers place upon the various attributes of a product. These techniques are based upon a type of trade-off analysis called "conjoint measurement" [7]; a powerful device for quantifying the intangible as well as the physical benefits present in a product.

To demonstrate the techniques in action in a pricing decision let us go through the process step-by-step.

The Trade-Off Method
Step (1): Identification of benefit components. It is important to recognise that the potential customer for a product will have his/her own perceptions of the benefits contained within that product. To identify these perceived benefits it is necessary to conduct a limited, small-scale survey of potential and/or actual customers. The purpose of this study is to elicit the key features or benefits that are expected to be acquired as a result of using the product. Direct questioning can be used such as: "What is it that makes Brand X different from Brand Y?" or "why do you use this product rather than that product?" More sophisticated procedures for elicitation of benefits exist but essentially they all have the same purpose: to draw from consumers their own perceptions of product features rather than those of the manufacturers. So in a study of customers for a new chemical compound the following attributes might emerge:

quality,

availability,

impact on production economics,

storage conditions necessary,

technical assistance.

The question is then: What relative value is placed upon each of these components?

Step (2): Quantifying benefit values. Because a product is in effect the totality of its component attributes a way must be found of separating these and measuring their individual value to the customer. It is here that conjoint analysis becomes particularly useful. Using the attributes identified in Step (1) the researcher then presents to the sample of customers a variety of hypothetical products which contain different configurations of the previously identified attributes, each configuration having a different price. Thus, for the example of the chemical compound the hypothetical product configurations as shown in Table I might be constructed.

Clearly there are many different combinations of attribute levels and only two examples are given here but it will be sufficient to demonstrate the concept of trade-off. The question put to the survey respondents is: "Given that the two alternative products above are available from competing suppliers at the prices shown which would you prefer?" Both products have their advantages and their disadvantages and the final choice will be based upon the trade-off of the pluses and minuses. By extending the questioning to include other configurations of the same attributes it is

Table I.

Attribute	Product 1	Product 2
Quality	Impurities less than one part per million	Impurities less than ten parts per million
Availability	Make to order	Available from stock
Impact on production economics	No impact	Improves usable output by 10 per cent
Storage conditions	Stable product, long shelf life	Requires high level storage environment
Technical assistance	Manufacturer provides high level technical advice	Weak
Price	£5 a pound	£5.50 a pound

possible, using conjoint analysis, to produce a numerical "weight" for each attribute which reflects the relative importance attached to each of the attributes in question. More specifically it enables the researcher to identify for each attribute the weight given to different *levels* of that attribute. Thus on "Quality" it will be possible to determine the extent by which "Impurities less than one part per million" is preferred over "Impurities less than ten parts per million" or any level of impurity in the range under consideration.

However, the greatest advantage of using conjoint analysis in this context is that it also provides the researcher with *the relative utility of different price levels.* Thus we have a means of interpreting the price equivalence of differences in the perceived values of different combinations of product attributes. Step (3) illustrates the procedure.

Step (3): Determining the price equivalence of value. The output of the conjoint analysis of the data collected in Step (2) might typically appear as in Figure 4.

For each level of each attribute a "utility" is computed and this can be graphed to give a visual indication of the importance of that attribute. More importantly, though, it enables the value of this arbitrary "utility" measure to be given a price equivalence. It will be seen from Figure 4 that the difference in utility between a price of £5 and £5.50 is 0.25 (i.e., 1.00 − 0.75) thus the price equivalence of one unit of "utility" is (£5.50 − £5)/0.25, that is £2.

Taking this knowledge we can say, for example, that a 10 per cent improvement in saleable output is worth a price difference of £1 a pound (£2 (1.00 − 0.5)). Again we can say that the benefit of a stable product with a long shelf life is worth an additional £0.5 a pound (£2 (0.75 − 0.5)) over a product requiring a high-level storage environment.

Given this information it is clear that the price decision maker has a very powerful insight into the components of value in the customer's mind. The decision maker also can now identify which product attributes have the biggest influence on value perception. In the case examined here, for example, availability and quality are seen as the two major components of value. A change from Level 2 to Level 1 in availability brings an increase in utility of 1 and a change in quality from Level 2 to

Level 1 brings an increase in utility of 0.75 (worth £2 and £1.50 a pound respectively).

Figure 4. Graphical Output of Conjoint Analysis

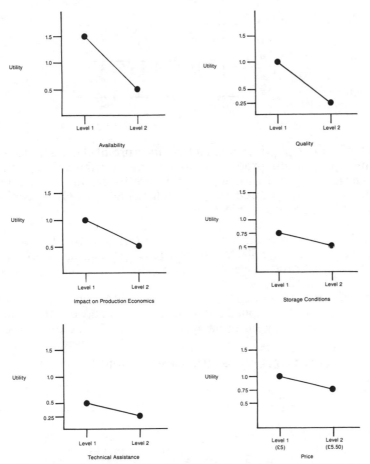

N.B Level 1 corresponds to the lowest level identified in the study for each attribute, Level 2 corresponds to the highest level.

Step (4): Rating competitive and alternative products. To provide a benchmark for price determination a comparison must be made of the product under consideration against competitive or alternative products. This comparison is made in terms of the same attributes that are identified in Step (1). A series of simple rating scales are constructed for each of the identified attributes and the customer sample is asked to rate each of the competitive or alternative products against those attributes. A simple 5-point scale, as in the following example, will suffice:

	Poor				Excellent
Quality					
	1	2	3	4	5
Availability					
	1	2	3	4	5
Impact on Production Economics					
	1	2	3	4	5
Storage conditions					
	1	2	3	4	5
Technical assistance					
	1	2	3	4	5

This step in the analysis provides a numerical measure of the extent to which potential customers perceive our product to contain a given attribute compared with competitive products. In the case of a new product where there is no prior experience then the rating must be performed internally on a judgmental basis. Obviously in this case there is a need for the greatest objectivity.

Step (5): Quantifying value-in-use. All the data necessary for quantifying value-in-use to the customer has now been collected. It only remains·to compare the ratings achieved in Step (4) by our product against the ratings for the product that we see as providing the main competition.

We can use the differences in ratings for our product and the competitor's on each attribute as an indication of the implied differences in utility between the products. Thus if our product scored 4, say, on availability compared with a score of 2 for the

Figure 5. Identifying Differences in Utility

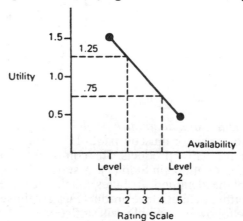

main competitive product this could be interpreted as meaning that our product offers greater "utility" on this attribute than the competitive product. Just how much more can be easily calculated from the information contained in the output of the conjoint analysis (as shown in Figure 4). To illustrate let us take the graphical representation of the utility of availability and match the scores on the rating scale (4 and 2 respectively) to the existing horizontal axis as in Figure 5.

Thus in this case it can be seen that our product is seen as having an advantage in "utility" terms of 0.5 (i.e, $1.25 - 0.75$) which translates into a price advantage of £1 a pound on that attribute. Needless to say there is no need to perform this exercise graphically. All that is required is to identify the range of utility for each attribute, e.g., in the case of "availability" from 0.5 to 1.5 and to calculate the "utility equivalent" of a one-point difference on the rating scale for that attribute. So in this case a one-point difference on a five-point rating scale for availability converts to 0.25 in terms of utility (i.e., $(1.5 - 0.5)/(5 - 1)$).

This exercise needs to be repeated for each attribute and the total summated utility equivalent calculated as in the example in Table II.

Table II.

Attribute	Ratings		Utility equivalent	(A) − (B)	(C)x(D)
	Our product	Competitors product			
	(A)	(B)	(C)	(D)	(E)
Availability	3	4	.25	−1	−0.25
Quality	4	2	.1875	+2	+0.375
Impact on production economics	3	3	.125	0	0
Storage conditions	1	3	.0625	−2	−0.125
Technical assistance	4	1	.0625	+3	+0.1875
Total					+0.1875

This total utility equivalent converts to a potential value-in-use advantage of £0.375 a pound (i.e., £2 x 0.1875) given the value of a unit of utility being seen in this case to be £2.

To complete the identification of value-in-use to the customer, however, it will be remembered that life cycle costs to the customer must also be incorporated into the offer price. Step (6) shows the way.

Step (6): Fixing the price: It will be recalled that it was earlier stated that the highest price the customer will pay is the difference between the perceived benefits and the costs to the customer other than price. We can now operationalise this concept by using the competitive or alternative product utilised in the preceding analysis as the price benchmark:

Price $(A - B)$ = Benefits $(A - B)$ − Costs $(A - B)$
   where Price $(A - B)$ is the achievable price differential of Product A over Product B
      Benefits $(A - B)$ is the value-in-use advantage identified in Step (5)

and Costs $(A - B)$ is our estimate of any difference in the life-cycle costs of the two products.

In the example we have used so far it was calculated that the "benefit differential" was £0.375 per pound weight. If we were to identify no significant life-cycle cost differences between our price and the competition then our product should be capable of supporting a price differential in the market place of £0.375 per pound weight. Whilst in the case we have used here, a chemical compound, it is unlikely that there would be major life cycle costs it is worth remembering that for other products, e.g., machinery and technical equipment, life-cycle cost differences may well outweigh benefit differences.

The Strategic Implications of Value-in-Use
Perhaps one of the most important features of the value-in-use approach that has been advocated here is that it focuses our attention upon customer perceptions of product attributes and away from the more narrow production-orientation of supplier's costs. In this sense it is very much a market-directed approach to pricing.

Whilst this article has gone into some detail on the techniques for operationalising the concept, this is rather less important than the impact that value-in-use, as an idea, can have upon the firm's strategic thinking.

From the point of view of value-in-use there are two strategic dimensions that the firm can operate on if it wishes to enhance profitability. These are:

— *Perception:* To what extent does the customer/potential customer perceive that our product embodies certain attributes?

— *Value/Utility:* To what extent does the customer/potential customer consider these attributes to be important in the purchase decision?

In the first case if the perception of product performance falls below that of competitive products what can be done? It may be that the problem is largely one of communication. Perhaps we have not been forceful enough in our attempts to inform the market about the strengths of our product or, if we have, the message still has not come across. Alternatively, it may be that our product is deficient in these attributes and it may thus be desirable to institute a programme of product improvement.

If, on the other hand, we identify that our product scores highly, but on attributes that are perhaps given less weight by the customer, i.e., their value/utility is lower, then we could downgrade the product on those attributes to improve overall profitability, or indeed reduce the price if appropriate. Likewise recognising the value/utility placed upon the various product attributes should be of great help in designing and introducing new products or in re-formulating old ones.

From the point of view of marketing strategy value-in-use can become the basis of a more effective segmentation strategy. Because different customers will have different perceptions of a product's attributes and also will differ in the value/utility that they place upon those attributes it will often be possible to target products to specific groups, or segments in the market. Price is one of the simplest ways of segmenting markets but price segmentation can become far more effective when based upon value-in-use.

Clearly the ideas that we have discussed require that the pricing decision maker go out into the market and develop a detailed understanding of the customer. This understanding must look at the benefits sought by the market as well as the costs to the customer of using our product. This combination of benefit and cost evaluation will then provide a much surer base for pricing decisions than the traditional alternatives.

References
1. Levitt, T., *The Marketing Mode,* McGraw-Hill, 1969.
2. Patchford, B. T. and Ford, G. T., "A Study of Prices and Market Shares in the Computer Mainframe Industry", *Journal of Business,* April 1976.
3. Haley, R., "Benefit Segmentation: A Decision-Oriented Research Tool", *Journal of Marketing,* July 1968.
4. Shapiro, B. P. and Jackson, B. B., "Industrial Pricing to Meet Customer Needs", *Harvard Business Review,* November-December 1978.
5. Shapiro, B. P. and Jackson, B. B., *op. cit.*
6. Brown, W. and Jaques, E., *Product Analysis Pricing,* Heinemann, 1964.
7. For a clear description of the techniques see: Green, P. E. and Wind, Y., "New Way to Measure Consumer's Judgements", *Harvard Business Review,* July/August, 1975.

11. An International Comparative Study of Credit Strategy*

by C. W. Neale and David D. Shipley

Introduction

Empirical findings such as those of Michell[1], Pass[2] and Udell[3] suggest that many marketing executives do not perceive the provision of credit as a substantial influence on their firms' success. Moreover, it appears that some marketing pedagogues hold the same view, as indicated by the frequent tendency, when seeking the opinions of practitioners about the importance of mix elements, to omit credit from the lists of possible variables from which respondents are asked to choose. The studies by Banting and Ross[4], Greenley[5, 6] and Saimee[7], for example, fit into this mould. This tendency is in sharp contrast to findings about the vendor selection criteria applied by executives who make or influence purchasing decisions reported by Kiser, Rao and Rao[8], Lehmann and O'Shaughnessy[9] and Shipley[10]. These reveal that, although few purchasers rate sellers' credit packages among the two or three most important patronage determinants, many buyers *do* regard the credit terms offered as an important selection criterion.

Viewed in this light, it would appear that sellers can only ignore credit conditions at the risk of losing sales and profit opportunities. It has been pointed out by writers including Dempsey[11] and Shipley[10] that the *ultimate* determinants in source selection need not be the most highly rated factors such as product, delivery and price. Rather, when rival sellers offer an equally attractive mix of these attributes, other criteria like breadth of product range, efficiency of sales quotation procedures and credit offerings may become decisive. In particular, these factors are likely to become most significant influences on marginal patronage decisions in some oligopolistic markets as, for example, Sheth[12] and Willets[13] have noted.

These arguments suggest that many firms may be able to achieve a position of competitive advantage through the development of an effective credit strategy. Accordingly, manufacturers might be expected to offer credit packages differentiated from those of competitors by, say, duration of payment period or by interest charges.

A strategy based on credit competitiveness might be objected to on the grounds that costs may be prohibitive. However, this would seem a myopic argument reflecting

*The findings reported here were extracted from a broader study of international competitiveness being conducted by one of the authors. The broader study has received generous support from Shell UK Limited, the Foundation for Management Education, North Staffordshire Polytechnic, Hallmark International Inc. and Western Litho Plate Company.

ignorance of customer requirements and lack of financial acumen. The costs of credit granting are always ultimately borne in some form or another by the final customer. Indeed, large numbers of the executives who participated in this study indicated that many of their customers were content to provide compensation for the convenience and other benefits of receiving credit, such as the favourable impact on cash flow.

It might also be argued that manufacturers cannot always risk the possibility of costly late payment or even of non-payment. However, for many classes of customer, risks can be quantified according to historical frequencies. This enables the effects of such risks to be overcome by adjustment of interest charges or product prices. Hence, sellers can shift credit risks on a self-insurance basis. That is, by accepting liabilities and charging risk premia via the credit package, with the size of the premium varying directly with the sellers' perception of the risks involved. Alternatively, manufacturers can gain the benefits of credit provision without incurring credit risks by buying the services of credit agencies or factors, as recommended by Dewdney[14] for example.

It appears that, if suitably insured, sellers could have much to gain and little or nothing to lose from providing credit. Optimal credit terms from the sellers' perspective depend crucially on the opportunity cost of capital. Juskow[15] observes: "If funds could have been invested for a higher return in other directions, the logical charge is not the interest rate, but the expected return on the most profitable alternative forgone", — and, we would add, the expected rate of inflation. For exporters, an expected adverse or favourable exchange rate movement would be a further consideration. The interaction of these factors under different conditions has been modelled in depth in the financial management literature by, for example, Ben-Horim and Levy[16, 17], Hill and Riener[18] and Halloran[19]. However, what seems to be absent from the literature is evidence concerning the components of firms' credit packages and the extent to which these vary among sellers in different countries, among buyers in different countries and among buyers in different product markets.

The purpose of this article is to provide more insight into the credit offerings of manufacturers via an analysis of data which are unique in several ways. Specifically, the article focuses on the dimensions of the credit package supplied to customers for consumer and industrial goods in both domestic and export markets by US and UK companies. The findings are presented in the third section and discussed in the fourth section, where a tentative analytical model for use in improving credit policy is also offered.

Methodology and Sample Characteristics

Data were gathered in two interview surveys carried out by one of the authors. The first involved the senior marketing executives of 108 UK manufacturing enterprises in 1979 and the second involved 105 of their equivalents in the US during 1980. The UK sample was selected from a larger sample of businessmen who had previously co-operated in a different study.* Efforts were made to match the US sample to the UK interview sample, firstly by broad product type and secondly by size of workforce, although some imperfections in the match were inevitable. The disparities were most

---

*Information about the larger sample and its associated research methodology is presented in Shipley[20] and other articles referred to therein.

marked among the two sets of exporters extracted as subsets from the original interview samples (only firms which export more than five per cent of output were included). In general, the samples were reasonably similar, as shown in Table I. The UK firms were well dispersed nationally and the US companies were located in the region bounded by Omaha, Houston, Atlanta and Chicago. Additional information about the present samples has been presented elsewhere[21].

The questionnaire, which was concerned with marketing strategy, comprised a total of 66 questions. The final UK version of this was drafted after a ten-firm pilot study and, prior to its being taken to the US, it was altered slightly to account for small language differences pointed out by four American expatriates. Technical terminology was generally absent from the questions and the interview character of the surveys enabled any respondents' queries to be clarified.

Table I. Characteristics of the Firms

	Domestic		Export	
	UK firms N=108 %	US firms N=105 %	UK firms N=85 %	US firms N=45 %
Broad product type				
consumer non-durable	19 } 38	22 } 36	15 } 36	16 } 29
consumer durable	19	14	21	13
manufactured materials	12	12	12	4
components	26 } 63	30 } 64	26 } 64	31 } 71
machinery	25	22	26	36
Number of employees				
fewer than 201	20	27	16	20
201-1000	53	42	59	47
more than 1000	27	31	25	33
Manufacturing experience				
less than 11 years	5	3	2	0
11-20 years	10	8	12	9
21-50 years	32	39	34	40
more than 50 years	54	51	52	51
Product concentration				
single product type	27	17	28	11
multiple product range	73	83	72	89
Ownership				
independent	44	56	41	53
subsidiary	56	44	59	47

The findings discussed in this article are confined to manufacturers' credit offerings. Specifically, attention is directed to four important dimensions of credit strategy:

(1) incidence of credit provision;
(2) rates of interest charged to credit recipients;
(3) maximum duration of credit;
(4) relationship between credit provision and price discounts.

The determinants of whether and in what form to offer a credit package are complex and are likely to vary according to business circumstances. Besides allowing a comparison between US and UK firms, the presentation of the findings offers a contrast between two further important pairs of influences. On the one hand, behaviour in domestic and export markets is compared and, on the other, consumer and industrial products. This categorisation requires further discussion.

Formulation of credit strategy can be highly complex for domestic marketers but the special circumstances of international marketing make this procedure potentially far more hazardous for exporters. This is because, for overseas sales, there are forces which simultaneously create pressures both for more generous and also for more stringent credit offerings.

Coherent marketing principles urge firms to be customer-oriented with regard to all aspects of their product offerings (see, for example, Kotler[22]) — a package which obviously includes credit terms. Hence, exporters must recognise that the credit requirements of customers can vary across countries so that credit strategy may be tailored to market needs and thereby become an important dimension of competitive advantage. Terpstra[23] suggests that sellers of industrial equipment, for example, often find that the credit package offered is the decisive factor among customers' patronage criteria and that very liberal credit can also be a crucial factor in selling consumer durables in countries where distribution intermediaries are small and financially weak and consequently reluctant to expand their own working capital commitments. Hence, in many cases, export credit should be more generous than domestic credit.

Conversely, there are clear and powerful reasons for offering less generous credit overseas than for domestic sales. Firstly, as Dewdney[14] has pointed out, payments receivable for exports may be delayed longer due to sheer geographical distance, the degree of effective communication between trading nations, simple errors of documentation and even misunderstanding about contract terminology. Moreover, payments from particular countries may involve substantial lags owing to prevailing currency exchange regulations and/or the readiness, perhaps, of some customers to time their payments to exploit for themselves favourable exchange rate fluctuations. Ryder[24] has also shown that international letters of credit are not foolproof guarantees of payment. Finally, exporters tend to encounter increased difficulties and/or costs in establishing the credit ratings of new foreign customers and when confirming those of established ones although, as noted by Urbancic[25], it is possible to engage the services of an international credit rating agency. Clearly, such problems may put pressure on manufacturers to specify shorter credit periods for export customers or to discriminate against them in terms of, say, interest charges or price discounts. In this context, Hakeman[26] found that US exporters of automotive components granted considerably harsher credit terms to customers in West Germany than to US domestic buyers.

To some extent, the problems associated with export credit can be relieved through the use of international credit factoring agencies. However, the risk-shifting facilities which these offer can be costly, so that the manufacturers' problem of extracting compensatory additional revenues from his customers remains. Moreover, although institutions like the Export Credit Guarantee Department (ECGD) in the UK and the Foreign Credit Insurance Association (FCIA) in the US are often willing to bear some credit risks, few export insurance agencies of any kind provide cover against all risks. One particular source of risk against which there is usually no cover offered is adverse currency exchange rate fluctuations which can be very damaging.* However, there is available the strategy of invoicing export trade in a third currency or even a "basket" of currencies, a facility which the European ECU may soon develop and provide.

There are arguments, then, to support both more generous and more stringent credit offerings on export trade compared to domestic sales. We propose also that credit strategies might be varied according to broad product grouping.

One line of argument is based on the fact that producers of industrial goods, owing to the preponderance of fixed elements in their cost structures, typically operate at higher break-even points than "typical" consumer goods firms. This pressure to optimise capacity utilisation gives the former the incentive, perhaps, to offer more generous credit terms. Moreover, markets for industrial goods are likely to contain fewer customers, actual and potential, than markets for consumer products. This may well result in a greater incidence of oligopsony power in industrial markets which buyers can be expected to exploit in order to gain more generous credit terms, particularly when cost inflation is running at a high rate (as it was at the times of these surveys).

Conversely, producers of consumer goods often sell in batches of smaller value and to larger numbers of customers than the manufacturers of industrial products, who tend to sell in high value deals owing to their goods being indivisible in terms of product characteristics, product specification and/or shipment volumes. Hence, for a given amount of finance, the credit risks of consumer goods producers are spread over a more widely diversified body of customers than those of industrial goods manufacturers. Therefore, the former may be more able and more willing to offer attractive credit packages.

The results of the study, presented in the following section, show there to be some substantial variation in the findings concerning the credit strategies of consumer and industrial manufacturers as well as in those of domestic and export marketers. Some of the arguments presented in this section are re-examined in the fourth section in the light of the research findings.

Findings
Incidence of Credit Provision
The executives were asked, "Does your company provide credit terms for your customers?" and they were requested to choose an answer from alternatives presented

---

*Shipley[27], in fact, found that respectively 73 per cent and 29 per cent of the present UK and US export samples regard "changes in the foreign exchange value of the domestic currency" as a significant constraint on marketing performance.

to them. The responses shown in Table II are classified according to seller's domicile, location of market and broad product category.

Table II. Incidence of Provision of Credit

Type of goods	Domestic markets				Export markets			
	UK firms		US firms		UK firms		US firms	
	Con-sumer % of 40	Indus-trial % of 68	Con-sumer % of 38	Indus-trial % of 67	Con-sumer % of 31	Indus-trial % of 54	Con-sumer % of 13	Indus-trial % of 32
Never	3	9	3	6	3	7	0	16
Less than half of the occasions requested	20	18	0	12	29	19	0	19
More than half of the occasions requested	35	31	45	39	42	37	31	19
Every time requested	43	43	53	43	26	30	46	28
Insist on a letter of credit	0	0	0	0	0	7	23	19

In view of customers' requirements for credit as outlined above, the incidence of credit provision seems surprisingly limited. Fewer than 50 per cent within all but one of the groupings of firms supply credit each time it is requested. Only small proportions of the eight groupings, however, never provide credit.

In domestic markets, the US firms offer credit a little more often than the UK firms, especially in the case of consumer goods. In export markets, much larger proportions of the US manufacturers than UK firms demand letters of credit. Even so, the US consumer goods producers provide credit more extensively than the other three exporter groups. Conversely, the US exporters of industrial products exhibit the lowest incidence of credit provision among all the groupings in the study.

Rates of Interest
An important dimension of credit strategy is firms' relative interest charges since these directly affect relative effective prices. Accordingly, a company's competitiveness varies inversely with interest charges, other things being equal.

The respondents were asked, "If your company does provide credit, what rate of interest are customers usually charged?" They were asked to specify their responses in terms of the rates at which their own firms were then currently able to borrow. The responses are presented in Table III.

Majorities of all the consumer goods marketers offer interest-free credit. Indeed, in both export and domestic markets, markedly more of the UK and the US consumer products firms charge zero interest than their industrial-marketer counterparts. The UK firms apply more favourable rates than the US companies in domestic markets, while exporters' rates are more similar. However, comparatively few firms of either country charge rates above their own borrowing rates. This clearly suggests that part or all of the costs of extending credit are simply built into price structures.

Table III. Rate of Interest Charged on Credit

Type of goods	Domestic markets				Export markets			
	UK firms		US firms		UK firms		US firms	
	Con-sumer % of 40	Indus-trial % of 68	Con-sumer % of 38	Indus-trial % of 67	Con-sumer % of 31	Indus-trial % of 54	Con-sumer % of 13	Indus-trial % of 32
Zero	88	60	66	49	74	39	69	47
Between zero and the seller's borrowing rate	0	2	0	5	0	7	0	3
Same as the seller's borrowing rate	3	13	13	21	6	9	0	6
Higher than the seller's borrowing rate	8	9	18	16	13	13	8	6
Do not give credit	3	9	3	6	3	7	0	16
Discriminate between customers	0	7	0	3	0	7	0	3
ECGD rates/letter of credit	0	0	0	0	3	17	23	19

Table III also suggests that the UK domestic marketers, and especially those which make industrial goods, offer more generous interest rates than the two groups of UK exporters. The US figures, however, indicate much less variation of rates between market categories.

Table IV. International Comparisons of Attractiveness of Interest Rates

Type of goods	UK firms		US firms	
	Consumer % of 31	Industrial % of 54	Consumer % of 13	Industrial % of 32
Lower in domestic markets	10	15	0	0
Lower in export markets	0	2	0	0
Same in both	84	57	77	63
Only give domestic credit	0	2	0	13
Only give export credit	0	2	0	0
Give credit in neither market	3	6	0	3
Require letter of credit	0	7	23	19
Discriminate between customers	3	9	0	3

Further analyses of the data revealed that the variations involving firms which sell in both domestic and export markets are much less pronounced. These data are presented in Table IV which shows that large majorities of both groups of consumer goods firms offer the same rates to both home and foreign customers and that the same holds for smaller majorities of both sets of industrial goods manufacturers. A small minority of all the UK firms favours domestic customers while the number which favours export customers is negligible. None of the US companies offers more attractive rates to either foreign or domestic customers although 13 per cent of the industrial marketers provide credit in the domestic market only. Clearly, among firms which sell in both home and foreign markets, there is little evidence to support much international discrimination regarding interest strategy.

Duration of Credit Period
The duration of the credit period is another feature of credit attractiveness. This is important as it affects customers' cash flow and, depending on prevailing interest and inflation rates, it influences profitability.

The respondents were asked, "If your company does provide credit, what is the maximum period of time for which you extend credit?" The question deliberately sought to elicit information concerning the *maximum* time of credit provision since this offers some insight into how competitive firms are willing to make their credit terms in order to win contracts. It is expected that the normal or mean credit periods will be shorter than the maximum.

Table V. Maximum Duration of Credit Period

Type of goods	Domestic markets				Export markets			
	UK firms		US firms		UK firms		US firms	
	Con-sumer % of 40	Indus-trial % of 68	Con-sumer % of 38	Indus-trial % of 67	Con-sumer % of 31	Indus-trial % of 54	Con-sumer % of 13	Indus-trial % of 32
30 days or less	43	24	21	9	6	6	8	3
31-60 days	23	13	18	15	16	2	38	13
60-90 days	28	29	37	27	42	22	15	19
91-182 days	5	13	11	21	29	28	8	19
183-365 days	0	3	5	8	3	4	0	3
1-2 years	0	4	5	5	0	0	8	3
More than 2 years	0	4	0	10	0	22	0	6
Do not give credit	3	9	3	6	3	7	0	16
Insist on a letter of credit	0	0	0	0	0	7	23	19
Discriminate between customers	0	0	0	0	0	2	0	0

The responses are presented in Table V, which indicates that in all four market categories the credit period granted by the industrial marketers is, on average, longer than that allowed by the consumer goods producers. This difference is most pronounced among the UK domestic marketers. Most notable of all, moreover, is that 22 per cent of the UK exporters of industrial goods provide credit for longer than two years. Generally, though, the UK exporters offer longer credit terms than their home-market compatriots. The corresponding US variation is less marked. Nevertheless, the industrial marketers, on average, offer a credit period that is clearly longer than that of the consumer goods producers in the domestic market and similarly in export markets, but to a smaller extent.

Further analysis of the data generated the information shown in Table VI which reveals that only a handful of the UK respondents which operate in both domestic and export markets provide lengthier credit at home whereas more than 50 per cent of them do the reverse. Conversely, the corresponding US proportions are about 14 per cent and about 26 per cent. Large numbers of both the US export groups demand letters of credit whereas among UK firms this practice is limited to only a few industrial marketers.

Table VI. International Comparisons of Credit Duration

| Type of goods | UK firms | | US firms | |
	Consumer % of 31	Industrial % of 54	Consumer % of 13	Industrial % of 32
Longer in domestic market	3	0	15	13
Longer in export markets	52	54	31	22
Same in both	42	31	31	31
Only give domestic credit	0	2	0	13
Only give export credit	0	2	0	0
Give credit in neither market	3	6	0	3
Require letter of credit	0	6	23	19

Credit and price Discounts
Partial determinants of competitiveness are a firm's credit offerings and its price discount policy. However, these may be viewed as different means for influencing effective selling prices. Consequently, it might be argued that attractive credit conditions and generous discounts are direct substitutes for each other. On these grounds, it was considered that the validity of this research would be jeopardised by neglect of the credit-discount relationships. Accordingly, the respondents were asked, "If your company does provide credit, do the customers concerned receive price discounts as favourable as those received by customers not requiring credit?" The responses are shown in Table VII. In all except one category, around 50 per cent of the firms do not discriminate discounts against credit recipients. The exception is the set of US domestic sellers of industrial products where the relevant frequency is 72 per cent. In every group, however, substantial proportions of the respondents lower the discounts given to credit recipients. Overall, there is little difference in the distributions of the two groups of UK domestic marketers. The same seems to be the case with their export equivalents when consideration is given to the joint frequencies of "do discriminate" and "sometimes discriminate" (the latter response, of course, may cover

a wide variety of policies). Among the US samples, however, there is less consensus. In the domestic market the incidence of attractive credit and discounts is higher among the industrial marketers whereas in export markets it is higher among the consumer goods producers.

Table VII. Incidence of Price Discounts among Recipients of Credit

Type of goods	Domestic markets				Export markets			
	UK firms		US firms		UK firms		US firms	
	Con- sumer % of 40	Indus- trial % of 68	Con- sumer % of 38	Indus- trial % of 67	Con- sumer % of 31	Indus- trial % of 54	Con- sumer % of 13	Indus- trial % of 32
Do discriminate	35	31	42	22	26	24	15	19
Do not discriminate	48	46	50	72	42	52	54	47
Sometimes discriminate	15	15	5	0	29	17	8	0
Do not give credit	3	9	3	6	3	7	0	16
Insist on a letter of credit	0	0	0	0	0	0	23	19

Summary of Findings
(a) Credit incidence is:
  (1) substantial but less prevalent than expected among all classes of respondents;
  (2) a little more extensive among consumer than industrial firms;
  (3) more extensive in domestic than export markets;
  (4) more extensive among US than UK firms in domestic markets with the reverse in export markets. Substantially more US than UK exporters demand letters of credit.

(b) Interest rates are:
  (1) generous among large numbers of firms in all classes;
  (2) on average lower among consumer than industrial firms in all classes;
  (3) lower among UK than US firms in domestic markets with the reverse in export markets;
  (4) generally not differentiated between domestic and export markets by firms which operate in both.

(c) Duration of credit period tends to be:
  (1) longer among industrial than consumer firms in all classes;
  (2) longer among UK exporters than domestic firms but slightly the reverse for US firms;
  (3) longer among US than UK domestic marketers with the reverse for exporters.

(d) Price discounts are differentiated:
  (1) against considerable numbers of the credit recipients in all classes of respondents;
  (2) least commonly by US domestic industrial firms;
  (3) more commonly by UK firms generally than all the US groups bar the domestic consumer firms.

General Conclusions and Recommendations
The discussion and the research findings seem to offer two broad conclusions. Firstly, consumer goods firms tend to be more generous than industrial goods sellers both on a bi-national comparison and when operating in export as opposed to domestic markets, except in the matter of maximum credit duration. This would appear to reflect the considerations of diversification among customers and other points discussed in the second section. Another inference is that the length of credit period offered is seen as a major facet of competitiveness in industrial goods markets because of the size of the customer's investment often involved. In turn, credit duration seems to be regarded as a more important weapon than interest rate competition in the industrial goods sectors. Moreover, the sellers of industrial goods are more flexible between markets (perhaps because sensitivity to international differences in levels of interest rates increases with duration of credit provision).

Secondly, UK firms are rather more generous than US firms in export markets. Various explanations of this can be suggested. Perhaps, despite popular conceptions in the UK (see Baker[28]), exporting philosophy is in the UK regarded as more important than in the US. In addition, a fairly obvious observation is the differential official provision of insurance and other facilities to aid exporting from the UK. However, perhaps the significance of the operations of the British Overseas Trade Board and the ECGD should not be overstated. It is a source of some wonderment to both the ECGD and outside commentators like Clemison[29] that more use of these facilities is not made. Despite the risks they must carry, only about one-third of UK exporters insure through ECGD, even though its charges are modest. What does, however, seem clear is that many US firms are ignorant of or unwilling to use the parallel services offered by the FCIA and other institutions in the private sector. It would seem that these bodies themselves face their own domestic marketing problems.

There are also a number of credit policy recommendations which follow from this analysis. It seems clear that if US firms did examine more closely some alternative ways of financing exports, they could probably avoid some of their apparent discrimination against overseas customers. No doubt US firms could also benefit from more governmental involvement and assistance. It seems odd to the authors that there is no official US counterpart to the UK's ECGD (probably as odd to the US observer as the lack of a Small Business Administration in the UK). For UK firms which do already display more attention to customer requirements in export markets, more extensive use should be made of ECGD facilities and those of international factoring agencies, especially in the light of the present evidence that firms (particularly those selling industrial goods) are flexible as between domestic and export markets. A more fundamental observation about UK experience also arises. UK firms are more generous in their export markets than in their domestic markets and probably because they do use ECGD facilities to whatever degree. It might seem cogent to pose the question: "Would the recent sharp increase in import penetration into the UK have been accomplished quite so easily if there was an official equivalent to the ECGD for home markets (GATT probably precludes this) *or* if firms made more use of credit agencies in domestic markets?"

Finally, at a broader level, we remain unconvinced that despite some limited evidence of flexibility in credit policy, credit managers typically formulate detailed credit policy analyses (one exception can be found in Juskow[15]). Accordingly, we propose a simple model of credit analysis for the assistance of credit managers wishing to add analytical rigour to their decision making. The methodology of sensitivity analysis of capital investment projects is well known in the financial management literature — analysts can specify the impact on a project's NPV or IRR of specified percentage or absolute changes in key variables to identify those aspects which most crucially affect project profitability. We propose that this approach can also be used in the field of credit management.

Credit managers face conflicting demands. We may assume, though, that their principal aim is usually to maximise the expected profitability of contracts. However, profitability depends on a range of factors, largely connected with the generosity of credit terms which a firm offers. On one hand, there are pressures to liberalise credit terms by, for example, giving more or longer or cheaper credit in order to encourage trade. We may call this the "trade volume effect" (TVE). On the other hand, there are pressures to tighten credit by offering less or shorter or dearer credit. These are factors mainly concerned with the profitability of existing contracts and, having secured these, the discounted profitability is greater the tighter the credit policy. We refer to this as the "contract profitability effect" (CPE).

The overall expected profitability of an active credit policy depends on two opposing influences. Whereas a relaxed credit policy will, for reasons of competitive advantage, enhance sales, a tight credit policy will reduce payment risks and working capital charges. In the latter connection, the firm should consider the full opportunity costs involved. This, of course, may differ from the interest rate (if any) applied to credit accounts. We refer to firms' own opportunity cost of capital as k. However, the full charge for providing credit depends not only on the interest rate applied but may include differentials in price discounts and/or a credit component built into any cost-oriented pricing procedure as used by most firms[20]. We denote the overall charge, interest, etc, applied by the lender-seller for providing credit as C_L.

Hence, the expected profit contribution $\overline{\pi}$ of credit policy is given by:

$$\overline{\pi} = f(V, P, C_L, k)$$

where V = volume of sales

P = credit period offered, and thus the expected payment period.

A priori, one would expect that generally

$$\frac{\delta \overline{\pi}}{\delta V} > 0$$

Learning Resources
Centre

while the other relationships depend on whether one examines the TVE or the CPE. Generally, we postulate:

Variation	TVE	CPE
$\dfrac{\delta \bar{\pi}}{\delta P}$	> 0	< 0
$\dfrac{\delta \bar{\pi}}{\delta C_L}$	< 0	> 0
$\dfrac{\delta \bar{\pi}}{\delta k}$	< 0	< 0

where the variations respectively refer to "extend credit period", "raise overall credit charges" and "higher opportunity costs of capital". Clearly, some of these effects can counterbalance each other and their overall significance and magnitude is an empirical issue.

One might also expect to find that the relative importance of these effects varies between markets and by product category. However, the rational credit manager might attempt to investigate these effects in different markets to increase his awareness of the impact of the credit policy package on past profitability and, allowing for any known changes in market parameters, apply these past relationships to the future. Ideally, a picture should emerge as shown by Figure 1 where the impact of changes in, say, credit duration on profitability for hypothetical cases is shown.

With a continuation of present policies, the firm might expect these markets to offer the same profit contribution over the next planning period. However, analysis of the past behaviour of the markets may reveal how responsive profitability has been to credit policy changes. For example, profitability in Market 1 would seem to respond better than in Market 2 to a "speed up" policy change of specified size while in Market 3, "speed up" policies are counter-productive and so a "slow down" policy would be suggested.

The data requirements for an examination of credit policy in this way could often, of course, be prohibitive but analysis of this sort, where possible, can reveal where, for example, it may be most desirable to use the services of a body like ECGD or a credit factor in order to finance extended credit.

In many areas of business activity there is a reluctance to use such analytical techniques where data requirements are daunting. However, as Maffei[30] has observed, lack of information is not necessarily a problem — if it can be shown that results are insensitive to changes in a particular sphere of operation, it matters little if that sphere is also one about which little is known. For other cases, the analytical model proposed should at the very least enable credit managers to conceptualise about the implications of any policy variations they may envisage.

Figure 1. The Sensitivity of Expected Profit to Changes in Credit Duration

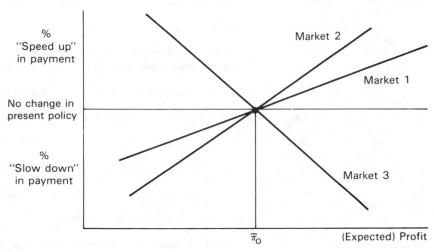

Summary

This article notes that many marketing practitioners and pedagogues seem to attach less importance to the role of sellers' credit strategy in marketing than professional buyers attach to it in purchasing. The authors compare findings about dimensions of the credit package supplied to customers for consumer and industrial goods in both domestic and export markets by US and UK manufacturing companies. Although there does appear to be much that is rational in the credit strategies of the firms surveyed, there also seems to be much that is not. A simple model based on sensitivity analysis is presented as a potential means for the improvement of credit strategy.

References
1. Michell, P., "Infrastructures and International Marketing Effectiveness", *Columbia Journal of World Business,* Spring 1979, pp. 91-101.
2. Pass, C., "Pricing Policies and Market Strategy: An Empirical Note", *European Journal of Marketing,* Vol. 5 No. 1, 1971, pp. 94-98.
3. Udell, J. C., "How Important is Pricing in Competitive Strategy?", *Journal of Marketing,* Vol. 28 No. 1, January 1964, pp. 44-48.
4. Banting, P. M. and Ross, R. E., "The Marketing Mix: A Canadian Perspective", *Journal of the Academy of Marketing Science,* Vol. 1, Spring 1973, pp. 1-11.
5. Greenley, G. E., "An Overview of Marketing Planning in UK Manufacturing Industry", *European Journal of Marketing,* Vol. 16 No. 7, 1982, pp. 3-15.
6. Greenley, G. E., "Where Marketing Planning Fails", *Long Range Planning,* Vol. 16 No. 1, 1983, pp. 106-115.
7. Saimee, S., "Elements of Marketing Strategy: A Comparative Study of US and Non-US Based Companies", *International Marketing,* Vol. 1 No. 2, 1982, pp. 119-126.
8. Kiser, G. E., Rao, C. P. and Rao, S. R. G., "Vendor Attribute Evaluations of Buying Center Members Other Than Purchasing Executives", *Industrial Marketing Management,* Vol. 4, 1975, pp. 45-54.

9. Lehmann, D. R. and O'Shaughnessy, J., "Difference in Attribute Importance for Different Industrial Products", *Journal of Marketing,* Vol. 38, April 1974, pp. 36-42.

10. Shipley, D. D., "Resellers' Supplier Selection Criteria for Different Consumer Products", *European Journal of Marketing,* Vol. 19 No. 7, 1985, pp. 26-36.

11. Dempsey, W. A., "Vendor Selection and the Buying Process", *Industrial Marketing Management,* Vol. 7, 1978, pp. 257-267.

12. Sheth, J. N., "A Model of Industrial Buying Behaviour", *Journal of Marketing,* Vol. 37, October 1973, pp. 50-56.

13. Willets, W. E., *Fundamentals of Purchasing,* New York, Appleton-Century-Crofts, 1969, pp. 82-83.

14. Dewdney, K. A., "Cashflow and Export", *Industrial Management and Data Systems,* September/October 1983, pp. 22-24.

15. Juskow, D. J., "Is your Credit Policy Effective?", *Management Accountant* (US), Vol. 64 No. 8, February 1983, pp. 34-36.

16. Ben-Horim, M. and Levy, H., "Management of Accounts Receivable Under Inflation", *Financial Management,* Vol. 12 No. 1, Spring 1983, pp. 42-48.

17. Ben-Horim, M. and Levy, H., "Inflation and the Trade Credit Period", *Management Science,* Vol. 28 No. 6, June 1982, pp. 646-651.

18. Hill, N. and Riener, K., "Determining the Cash Discount in the Firm's Credit Policy", *Financial Management,* Vol. 8 No. 1, Spring 1979, pp. 68-73.

19. Halloran, J. A. and Lanser, H. P., "The Credit Policy Decision in an Inflationary Evnironment", *Financial Management,* Vol. 10 No. 5, Winter 1981, pp. 31-38.

20. Shipley, D. D., "Pricing Flexibility in British Manufacturing Industry", *Managerial and Decision Economics,* Vol. 4 No. 4, December 1983, pp. 224-233.

21. Shipley, D. D., "Marketing Objectives in UK and US Manufacturing Companies", *European Journal of Marketing,* Vol. 19 No. 3, 1985, pp. 48-56.

22. Kotler, P., *Marketing Management: Analysis, Planning and Control,* fourth edition, Englewood Cliffs, Prentice-Hall Inc., 1980.

23. Terpstra, V., *International Marketing,* third edition, New York, CBS College Publishing, 1983.

24. Ryder, F. R., "Challenges to the Use of the Documentary Credit in International Trade Transactions", *Columbia Journal of World Business,* Vol. 16 No. 4, Winter 1981, pp. 36-41.

25. Urbancic, F. R., "How to Use an International Accounting Adviser in Export Credit Management", *Credit and Financial Management,* Vol. 84 No. 1, January 1982, pp. 36-42.

26. Hakeman, B., Seminar of the Institute for International Commerce, University of Michigan, October 1968, reported in Terpstra, V. *op. cit.,* p. 474.

27. Shipley, D. D., "Constraints on Marketing Performance", *Management Research News,* Vol. 8 No. 2, 1985, pp. 6-10.

28. Baker, M. J., "Export Myopia", *Quarterly Review of Marketing,* Vol. 4 No. 3, Spring 1979, pp. 1-10.

29. Clemison, J., "Sources of Export Finance", *The Accountant,* Vol. 189 No. 5663, 6 October 1983, pp. 416-419.

30. Maffei, R. B., "Mathematical Models, Values of Parameters and the Sensitivity Analysis of Management-Decision Rules", *Journal of Marketing,* Vol. 21 No. 4, April 1957, pp. 419-427.

12. Exploring Copywriters' Ability to Perceive Target Group Attitudes Towards Advertising Copy

by Karin Holstius

In reviews of advertising research it has been pointed out that the institutions of advertising and their creative personnel have received far too little research attention. In effect, copywriters, art directors and visualisers play an important part in the marketer's communication with the consumers because they are in charge of the design and wording of advertisements. The persuasiveness of an advertisement depends greatly on the creative personnel's ability to perceive correctly consumer reactions to different advertisement features.

In a recently completed study[7] the total population of 28 Swedish copywriters in Finland were included for the purpose of assessing their perception of different target groups' attitudes towards specific linguistic features in the body copy of advertisements.

Research Questions

Since the end of the 1960s a special style of advertising copy has been observed and syntactically analysed by linguists, e.g., in Swedish, Danish and English[1, 6, 10]. In some advertisements syntactically short-clipped sentences with abbreviated or disjunctive grammatical structures are abundant not only in headlines and slogans but also in the body copy of the advertisement.

This kind of advertisement copy has several features which distinguish it from advertising copy with grammatically regular sentences:

(1) the sentences are very short;
(2) full stops and typography disrupt syntactic units;
(3) the lexical density is high;
(4) qualifiers such as adjectives and adverbs are often preferred instead of verbs;
(5) in terms of transformational grammar the distance between surface structure and deep structure tends to be greater than for regular sentences.

As this kind of advertising copy appears to be favoured by some copywriters — perhaps depending on target group and/or product — it was decided to undertake a study of the attitudes of some Swedish target groups in Finland and to include the Swedish copywriters in the study for the purpose of assessing their ability to perceive target group attitudes.

The copywriters' ability to perceive target groups' attitudes towards different kinds of advertising copy must be related to research about person perception in general. In perception theory three categories of persons, social objects, can be distinguished:

(1) the generalised other;
(2) the face-to-face group;
(3) the particular other.

The referent, to which the judge is asked to respond, can be the object's feelings toward (a) another person, (b) himself, (c) the judge and (d) an issue[15, p. 417]. In the present study the object is the generalised other, the defined target group, and the referent is an issue, advertising copy. The outlined scheme of different social objects and referents implies that the judgements require a variety of specific skills rather than a general ability to judge others.

As it is part of the copywriter's daily work to perceive consumer reactions to the advertising copy he produces, and as previous research has shown that stereotypical predictions — without contact with the persons judged — can be very accurate[15, p. 412], it was assumed that the copywriters would be fairly skilled at rating target group attitudes. Previous findings that similarity between judge and judged aid in the accuracy of judgements [15, p. 415], and the observation that the sex of the judge and judged should always be taken into account[15, p. 428] suggested the testing of the hypothesis that copywriters' perception of target group attitudes to advertising copy is more accurate when judge and judged are of the same sex.

Method
In the instrument of measurement were included four pairs of advertising texts with each pair consisting of one version with grammatically short-clipped sentences and one version with grammatically regular sentences.

The advertising texts used in the study had originally appeared in Swedish newspapers and magazines mainly in the grammatically irregular version. To obtain paraphrase versions of the texts they were rewritten into a grammatically regular form with complete sentences. The products were given fictitious names and some minor facts in the texts were also changed in order to avoid possible prejudiced attitudes because of identification of brands or advertising campaigns.

To isolate the syntactic features of the texts and to prevent influence from other factors on the attitudes to be measured, the typography was kept neutral, no illustration was included and the texts were chosen so that they contained no slogans, rhymes or other special stylistic features.

The texts used in the study were tested for equality as regards cognitive meaning of contents in the paraphrase texts. On a scale from 0 to 10, where 10 stands for complete equality of meaning, the paraphrase texts got ratings of equality between 9.83 and 9.41 when the eight texts were presented in random order in all possible combinations, i.e., altogether $\frac{8(8-1)}{2} = 28$ presentations of text pairs. The constancy of the content variable was also controlled for with an analysis applying generative transformational grammar. The analysis shows that the paraphrase texts with different syntactic features can be derived from the same underlying structures by applying different transformations, which in the opinion of many linguists indicates cognitive synonymy[3, p. 162; 16, p. 156-160, 171; 9, p. 71-119; 11, p. 95].

The target groups for each pair of texts — with their respective products: yoghurt, hair conditioner, car seat-covers and electric razor — were defined by forty Scandinavian copywriters. The following target groups defined by two or three variables emerged: younger women with higher education, younger women, men with lower education, younger men. These are also the kind of target group definitions with which copywriters are confronted in their daily work when advertising campaigns are planned for consumer goods of the kind included in the study.

For the assessment of the copywriters' perception of the attitudes of the target groups twenty seven-point semantic differential scales were chosen. The majority of the scales, sixteen of them, were chosen from a selection of twenty-nine bipolar adjectival scales which had been previously used by Carroll in a factor analysis of prose style[2, p. 596]. The scales chosen for the present study are listed together with their reliability coefficients in the Carroll study:

(1)	serious — humorous	.92	(9) complex — simple	.82
(2)	abstract — concrete	.90	(10) clear — hazy	.78
(3)	emotional — rational	.90	(11) interesting — boring	.78
(4)	opinionated — impartial	.89	(12) pleasant — unpleasant	.75
(5)	intimate — remote	.87	(13) varied — monotonous	.75
(6)	earnest — flippant	.87	(14) good — bad	.74
(7)	personal — impersonal	.86	(15) precise — vague	.71
(8)	masculine — feminine	.85	(16) ordered — chaotic	.69

Four further scales assumed to be applicable to advertising copy were included in the instrument of measurement:

reliable — unreliable

believable — unbelievable

appealing — non-appealing

irritating — non-irritating

Two of these scales are unipolar but they were accepted for inclusion as e.g., Fishbein and Ajzen[5, p. 55] conclude that the results usually do not differ much from results obtained with bipolar scales. On the other hand, Mindak[12, p. 620] even argues for the use of unipolar scales in some instances, especially in an advertising context, as respondents might be reluctant to use negative sides of scales, which in turn frequently results in indiscriminate clustering about the middle of the scales.

The semantic differential scales are ordinarily used to assess the respondent's own judgement of the concepts to be rated. In the present study, however, the copywriters were required to shift to the viewpoint of the target groups. (For a similar use of the scales see, e.g., Stagner and Osgood[14, p. 389-401].)

Each pair of texts was followed by the definition of the target group and the twenty seven-point scales. The respondents were requested to mark both text versions on each scale, and their attention was drawn to the fact that they could give both text versions the same rating. The usual requirements as regards random order of adjectives and text versions were met.

The instrument of measurement was tested with forty Scandinavian copywriters, gathered for a conference, and it proved to be suitable for the purpose of assessing copywriters' perception of target group attitudes to syntactically different kinds of advertising copy.

Findings I: Copywriters

The results of the perception test were first interpreted as means of ratings with *t*-tests on differences between perceived attitudes of target groups to the two different kinds of advertising copy. As the same copywriters rated both text versions, the formula for dependent pairs was used to calculate the *t*-values*. The data were also searched for differences between the twenty male and eight female copywriters' perception. Altogether the findings were meagre with significant differences between the copywriters' ratings of the text versions in rather few cases, as well as between male and female ratings. It appeared that the reason for this was that the copywriters disagreed, which resulted in contrary rating patterns and distorted an interpretation based on means of ratings. It was therefore decided to conduct a factor analysis to search the data for qualitative distinctions.

To enable identification of possible different patterns in the copywriters' perception of the target groups' attitudes a factor analysis was conducted of the 28 observations on 80 scales, 20 scales each for four pairs of texts. The differences between the ratings of the paraphrase texts were calculated and used in the coding. This means that the absolute positions of the ratings on the scale were not considered, which is in accordance with the purpose of the study.

In this factor analysis the factors are loaded by persons and the indices of association are computed across variables, and thus the analysis explains a variation between individuals. The rotation principle used is varimax and the method is a principal component method.

An examination of the factor loadings shows that mainly three rating patterns can be identified. It is, however, possible to isolate five factors which have reasonably stable loadings. If three factors are considered the eigenvalues for the loadings on factors 1-3 are: 4.715, 3.519 and 2.204 respectively, which constitutes 37.3 per cent of the total variance. The eigenvalues for the loadings on five factors constitute 47.3 per cent of the total variance.

The identification of the system behind the ratings of the copywriters cannot be an analysis of their special traits or characteristics; the researcher has information only about their sex, approximate age, occupational status — full-time employee or

---

$$ * \quad \frac{\bar{x} - \bar{y}}{\sqrt{\dfrac{o^2_{x-y}}{n}}} $$

freelance — and the place where they are working. These facts do not appear to have influenced the loadings the copywriters got on different factors. That the two main factors — 1 and 2 — are not typically male or female has been controlled with a point biserial correlation analysis, where one of the variables is dichotomised in the categories men and women and the other variable consists of the loadings on one factor. For factor 1 $r = .310$ and for factor 2 $r = -.220$. Instead, the factor analysis serves the purpose of identifying different rating patterns.

Factor 1 can be identified as a rating pattern which shows that the copywriters perceive target groups to have more favourable attitudes* to three of the texts with short-clipped sentences, whereas the target group is expected to prefer the version with regular sentences only in the case of text 2 (see Figure 1). The profile shows means of ratings of persons No. 3, 5, 6, 18, 19 and 22, who have the highest loadings on factor 1. Because of perceived preference for advertising copy with impressionistic short sentences and an abundance of punctuation marks factor 1 is called "pointillism". When three factors are considered factor 1 contributes 45.2 per cent to the common variance.

Factor 2 can be identified as a rating pattern of copywriters who expect positive target group attitudes towards grammatically regular copy for all four texts. Because traditionally regular sentences are preferred the factor is called "traditionalism". Figure 2 is based on the means of ratings of persons No. 1, 4, 12 and 24, who all have reasonably high and stable loadings on the factor. The profile is more consistent than for factor 1. The perceived differences between regular and short-clipped copy are clearly noticeable for all four texts, whereas the profile for factor 1 shows smaller differences in expected attitudes especially for text 4. The contribution of factor 2 to the common variance is 33.7 per cent when three factors are considered.

Despite the somewhat lower loadings on factor 3 it can be easily identified as a rating pattern according to which the copywriters expect all target groups to be fairly indifferent to the syntactic features of the paraphrase texts. The factor is called "indifference" and it is exemplified with the profile in Figure 3 showing the means of ratings of persons No. 2, 9 and 16 on all 20 scales for text 1. When three factors are considered factor 3 contributes 21 per cent to the common variance.

When further factors are considered the loadings become less stable and are reasonably high in so few cases that they will not be commented upon in this context. It can also be observed that several copywriters have low loadings on all factors. A scrutiny of the questionnaires shows that some of the copywriters are inconsistent in their ratings — e.g., on scales like reliable/unreliable, believable/unbelievable and pleasant/unpleasant, appealing/non-appealing — and others produce a rating pattern which they have in common with nobody.

It was obvious that some of the scales caused the copywriters special difficulties and their ratings also indicate that it might not be possible to register syntactic differences in the texts with scales like abstract/concrete or serious/humorous. When

*When the instrument of measurement was tested with 40 Scandinavian copywriters the ratings were also used for a correlation analysis in order to find out which scales measure a positive-negative attitude. When the correlations with the scale good/bad were considered as well as a dimension "over-all positive or negative evaluation" isolated by Carroll[2, p. 599] the scales appearing in Figures 1 and 2 emerged as the most suitable ones for denoting positive/negative attitudes.

Figure 1. Profile for Factor 1, "Pointillism"

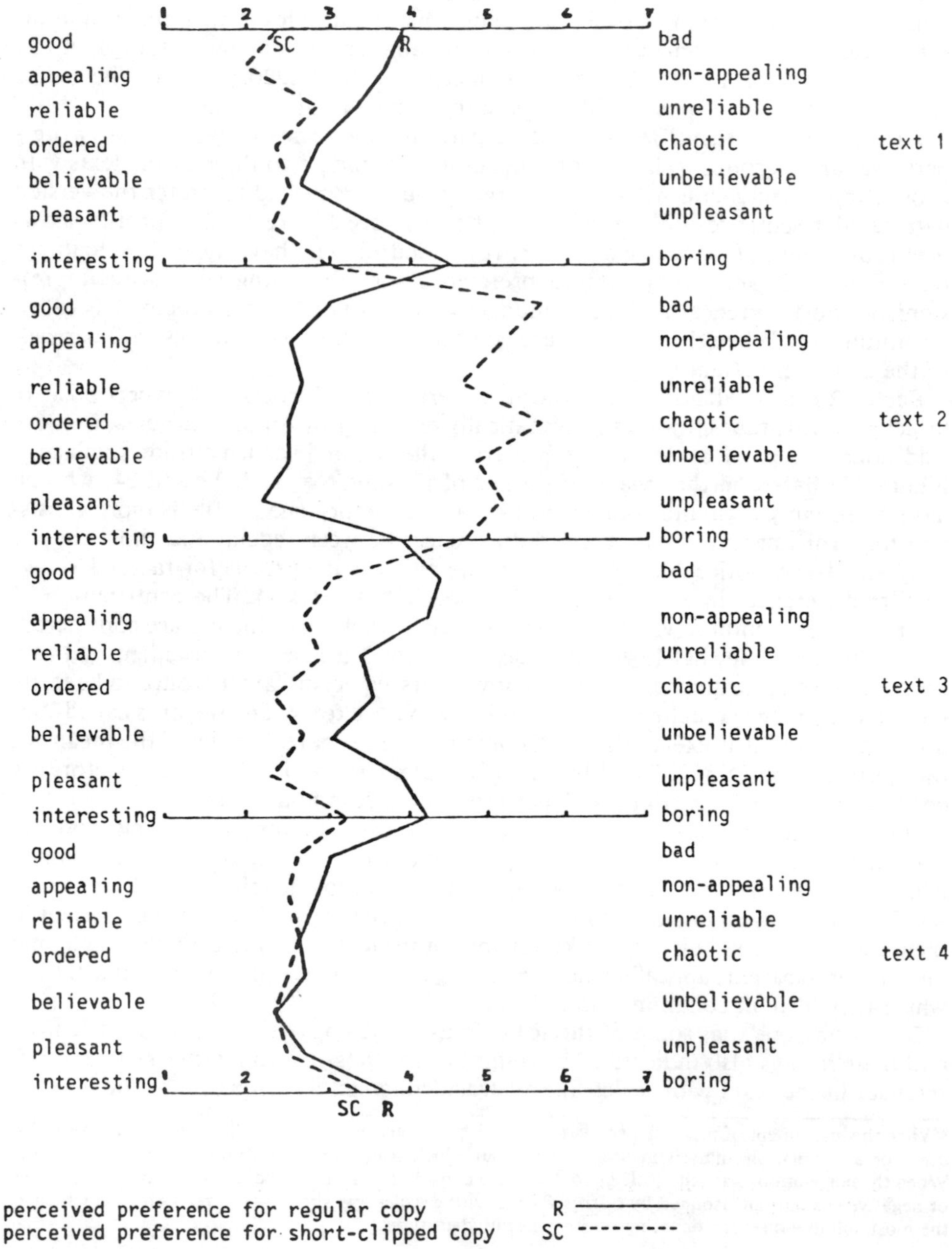

good	bad	
appealing	non-appealing	
reliable	unreliable	
ordered	chaotic	text 1
believable	unbelievable	
pleasant	unpleasant	
interesting	boring	
good	bad	
appealing	non-appealing	
reliable	unreliable	
ordered	chaotic	text 2
believable	unbelievable	
pleasant	unpleasant	
interesting	boring	
good	bad	
appealing	non-appealing	
reliable	unreliable	
ordered	chaotic	text 3
believable	unbelievable	
pleasant	unpleasant	
interesting	boring	
good	bad	
appealing	non-appealing	
reliable	unreliable	
ordered	chaotic	text 4
believable	unbelievable	
pleasant	unpleasant	
interesting	boring	

perceived preference for regular copy   R ———
perceived preference for short-clipped copy SC - - - - -

Figure 2. Profile for Factor 2, "Traditionalism"

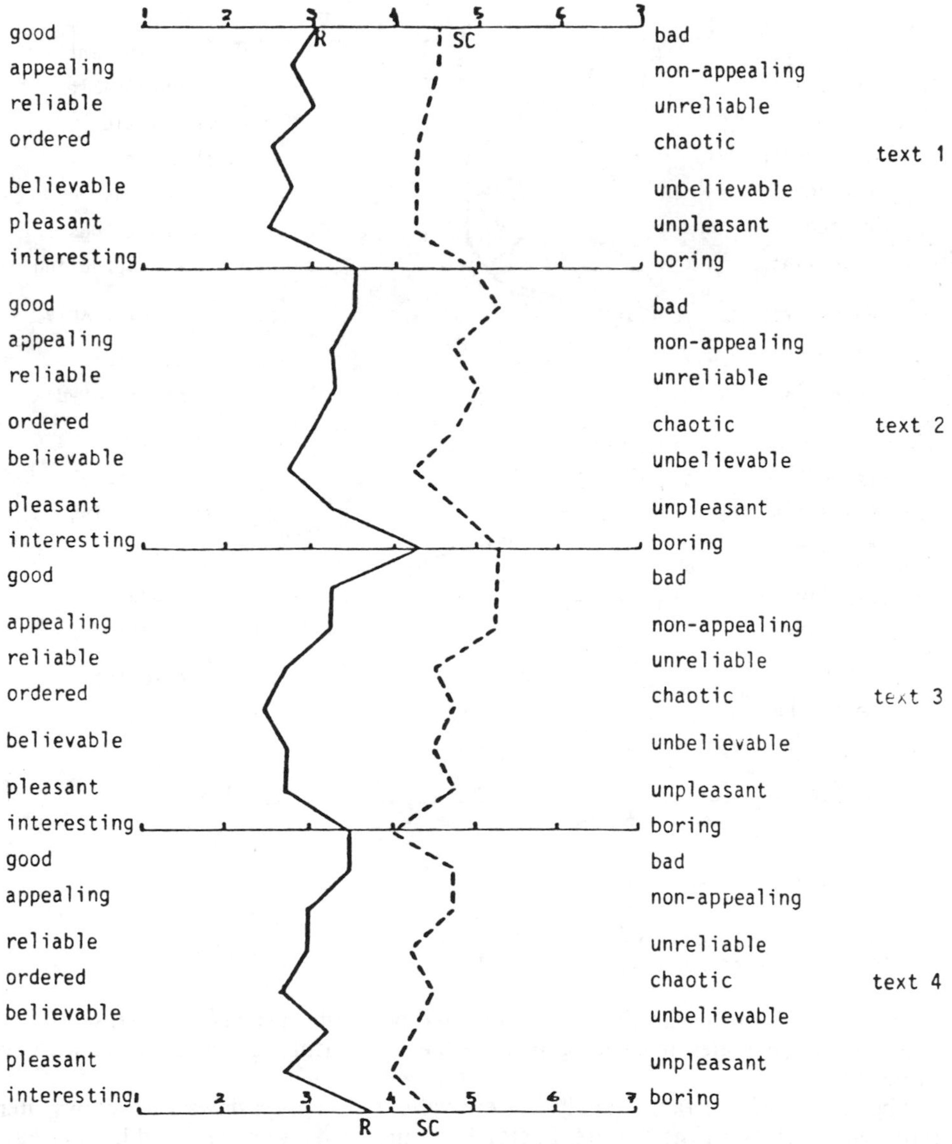

good	bad
appealing	non-appealing
reliable	unreliable
ordered	chaotic
believable	unbelievable
pleasant	unpleasant
interesting	boring

text 1

good	bad
appealing	non-appealing
reliable	unreliable
ordered	chaotic
believable	unbelievable
pleasant	unpleasant
interesting	boring

text 2

good	bad
appealing	non-appealing
reliable	unreliable
ordered	chaotic
believable	unbelievable
pleasant	unpleasant
interesting	boring

text 3

good	bad
appealing	non-appealing
reliable	unreliable
ordered	chaotic
believable	unbelievable
pleasant	unpleasant
interesting	boring

text 4

perceived preference for regular copy   R ──────
perceived preference for short-clipped copy   SC ----------

Figure 3. Profile for Factor 3, "Indifference" — Text 1

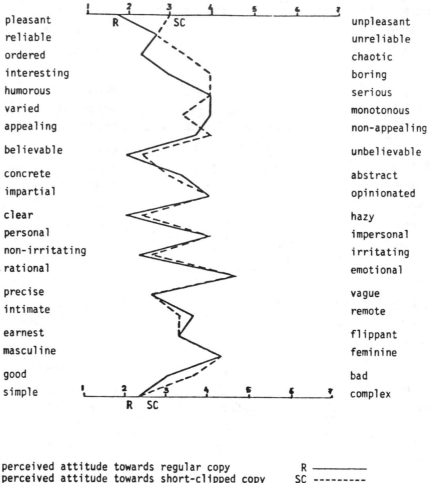

pleasant	unpleasant
reliable	unreliable
ordered	chaotic
interesting	boring
humorous	serious
varied	monotonous
appealing	non-appealing
believable	unbelievable
concrete	abstract
impartial	opinionated
clear	hazy
personal	impersonal
non-irritating	irritating
rational	emotional
precise	vague
intimate	remote
earnest	flippant
masculine	feminine
good	bad
simple	complex

perceived attitude towards regular copy   R ————
perceived attitude towards short-clipped copy   SC --------

the results of the test with the copywriters had been interpreted it seemed sensible to concentrate on scales measuring positive/negative attitudes in the tests with the target groups.

The results of the factor analysis were validated in interviews with copywriters representing three of the factors. Factor 1 "pointillism" was validated in interviews with persons No. 18 and 19. The interviewees were given the four text pairs and were requested to give their general opinion on the paraphrase versions and to specify which one of them they regarded as more suitable for each defined target group, i.e., which copy version they expected to arouse more positive attitudes. Both interviewees stated without any hesitation that they assumed the target groups to prefer the regular copy for text 2 and the short-clipped copy for texts 1 and 3. As regards text 4 they both showed some uncertainty before declaring that they expected the target group to have a more positive attitude towards the short-clipped copy. This is quite consistent with the profile in Figure 1 which shows the smallest differences between the ratings of the copy versions in the case of text 4.

Factor 2, "traditionalism", was validated in interviews with persons No. 4 and 12. After having read through all the texts the interviewees instantly selected the versions with regular sentences for all four target groups. One of them also specially pointed out that in his opinion regular copy will always be more suitable and lead to more positive attitudes because the short-clipped way of expression is unnatural.

As the interviewed copywriters expressed the same preferences during the interview as the factor analysis had ascribed to them, it can be concluded that the interviews support the presented interpretation of the results of the factor analysis. The interviews were conducted seven to nine months after the respondents had completed the questionnaires, and the answers given in the interviews might therefore also be regarded as a kind of reliability test of the scales measuring positive/negative attitudes in the study.

Findings II: Target Groups
As the positive/negative dimension was easily identified in the perception test with the copywriters, whereas scales measuring some other dimensions as, e.g., abstractness, did not seem to be suitable for differentiating between the text versions, it was decided to choose some of the scales measuring positive/negative attitudes for the tests with the target groups. Six copywriters were interviewed for the purpose of finding a suitable set of scales which in the opinion of these specialists at the same time include adjectives which they find particularly descriptive of good and successful advertising copy. It was also decided to include only bipolar scales, and not to make the test too comprehensive in order to avoid possible effects of fatigue and indifference. These considerations resulted in a choice of six scales which all have fairly high correlations with the scale good/bad, although two of them are not included in the profiles presented in Figures 1 and 2: pleasant/unpleasant, reliable/unreliable, clear/hazy, earnest/flippant, interesting/boring, good/bad. Furthermore, the scale masculine/feminine was included in the test because the only assumption it has been possible to trace about target group attitudes towards the syntactic features of advertising copy is the mention made by Leech[10, p. 196] that short-clipped copy might be thought especially suitable to a male audience.

Ideally, the sample of subjects for the target group test would be a representative cross section of the general population. As is so often the case, however, the choice was dictated by the need to save expenses and to find an easily available population. The 370 students at the Swedish Commercial College in Helsinki were willing to participate in the test. As they have very different educational backgrounds and the College therefore is divided into three main sections, no difficulties were encountered when assigning the subjects to the target groups defined by sex and education. As three of the target groups were defined to be younger by age and the fourth one had no age definition, it was decided to complement this one with a group of middle-aged men who corresponded to the educational definition of the group. In the test situation steps were taken to minimise the possibilities of hypothesis-guessing and bias because of experimenter expectancies.

The results of the tests with the target groups are shown in Tables I and II. The ratings on the scales measuring positive/negative attitudes are pretty similar for all four target groups and show a clear preference for advertising copy with regular sentences.

Table I. Means of Target Group Ratings of Regular (R) and Short-Clipped (SC) Advertising Copy

| | Female target groups | | | | Male target groups | | | |
| | text 1 | | text 2 | | text 3 | | text 4 | |
	R	SC	R	SC	R	SC	R	SC
1 pleasant/unpleasant 7	2.2	4.8	2.4	5.6	2.9	4.6	2.8	4.7
1 reliable/unreliable 7	2.3	4.0	3.2	5.0	3.3	3.9	3.0	4.2
1 clear/hazy 7	2.0	3.1	2.2	4.9	3.0	3.5	2.7	4.0
1 earnest/flippant 7	2.6	4.7	2.6	5.4	3.4	4.6	3.0	4.8
1 interesting/boring 7	3.2	5.0	3.4	5.6	3.4	5.3	3.2	4.9
1 good/bad 7	2.6	5.0	3.1	5.5	3.5	4.5	3.1	5.0

Table II. Differences Between Target Group Ratings of Regular (R) and Short-Clipped (SC) Advertising Copy Expressed in *t*-values

| | Female target groups | | Male target groups | |
| | text 1 | text 2 | text 3 | text 4 |
	R ≠ SC	R ≠ SC	R ≠ SC	R ≠ SC
pleasant/unpleasant	6.81	16.29	4.77	6.50
reliable/unreliable	5.62	10.49	1.82	4.40
clear/hazy	3.36	10.50	1.57	3.68
earnest/flippant	7.13	13.62	3.36	5.69
interesting/boring	5.02	8.88	4.60	5.96
good/bad	6.83	9.23	2.38	5.67
	$df = 63$	$df = 130$	$df = 53$	$df = 75$

The *t*-tests show that the differences between attitudes towards regular and short-clipped advertising copy are significant on the 0.05 level except for text 3 on the scale clear/hazy. With the exception of three instances the differences are also significant on the 0.001 level. The *t*-values also indicate that female target groups experience greater differences than male target groups between the two kinds of advertising copy.

On the scale masculine/feminine the direction of the ratings was the same for all four target groups: the text version with short-clipped, irregular sentences was experienced as more masculine and the differences were significant on the 0.001 level except for text 4 with the target group young men, where the difference in mean ratings did not reach an acceptable level of significance. Also in this case the female target groups differentiated more clearly between the two text versions with the differences between mean ratings being 2.4 for text 1 and 1.4 for text 2 and the t-values 8.63 and 6.24 respectively. The differences for the male target groups were 1.2 with *t*-value 3.66 for text 3 and 0.3 with *t*-value 0.93 for text 4.

A comparison of the male and female target group ratings on the positive/negative dimension as well as on the scale masculine/feminine indicates that female audiences might be even less receptive to short-clipped advertising copy.

Tentatively the questionnaire also included a seven-point scale good/bad for the rating of attitudes towards the product itself when presented with regular or short-clipped copy. The direction of the ratings was the same as for the attitudes towards the copy only: the differences with preference for the product presented with regular copy were significant on the 0.001 level for the female target groups 1 and 2 and for the male target group 4, and in case No. 3 the difference was significant on the 0.01 level.

Conclusions and Discussion
The "traditionalist" as well as the "pointillist" copywriters expected the target group younger women to have more favourable attitudes towards regular advertising copy in text 2. When the subsequent test showed that the target group rated regular copy more positively on all six scales — well above the 0.001 level of significance — it is obvious that both these groups of copywriters were able to perceive correctly the positive/negative attitude of the target group.

As regards the other three target groups, who also preferred regular copy, only the "traditionalist" copywriters turned out to have correct expectations about their attitudes, whereas the "pointillist" copywriter group wrongly anticipated more positive attitudes towards short-clipped advertising copy. The rating profiles of three of the target groups are shown together with the "traditionalist" and "pointillist" rating profiles in Figures 4-6.

The profiles show that both groups of copywriters have a correct perception of the direction of the target group attitudes on the scale masculine/feminine, although the "pointillist" copywriters seem to be somewhat less accurate on this scale as well, when they do not differentiate between the versions of text 1. The female target group for this text, however, experiences a greater difference in masculinity/femininity between the two kinds of copy than any other of the tested groups.

As the results of the tests with the target groups pointed to very clear-cut differences in attitudes towards the two text versions, it was also obvious that the "indifferent" copywriters were wrong as they did not perceive attitudes to be influenced by the syntactic features of the text. A couple of individual rating patterns — with, e.g., expected positive attitudes towards short-clipped copy in text 2 — also proved to be incorrect estimations of the effect of the grammatical structure of advertising copy.

Figure 4. Comparison of Target Group Attitudes and Copywriter Perception, text 1

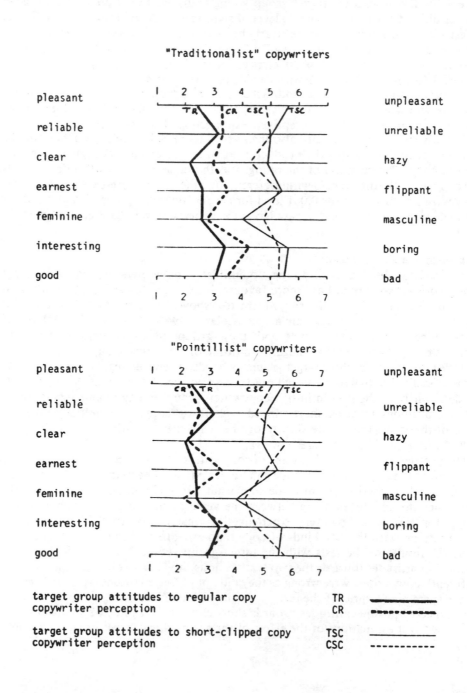

Figure 5. Comparison of Target Group Attitudes and Copywriter Perception, text 2

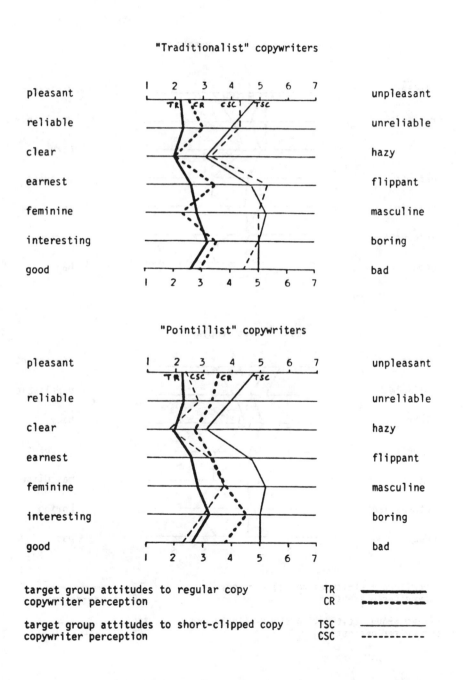

"Traditionalist" copywriters

"Pointillist" copywriters

target group attitudes to regular copy	TR	▬▬▬▬
copywriter perception	CR	▬▬▬▬
target group attitudes to short-clipped copy	TSC	───────
copywriter perception	CSC	- - - - - -

Figure 6. Comparison of Target Group Attitudes and Copywriter Perception, text 3

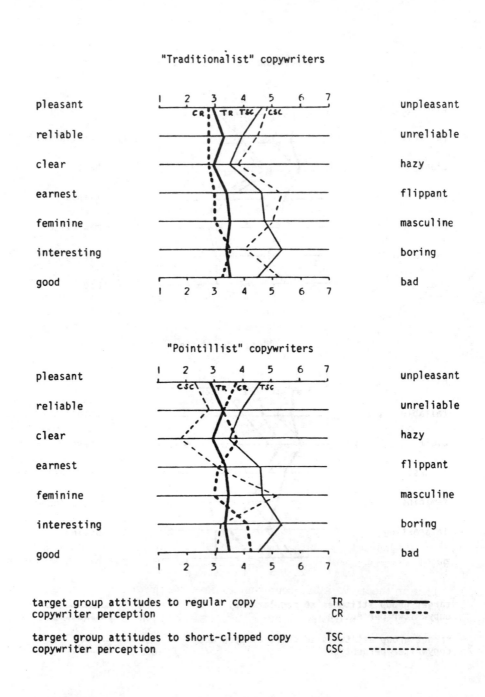

As two of the four target groups were female and the four most typical representatives of the "traditionalist" copywriters were all male, no support was obtained for the hypothesis that perception is more accurate when judge and judged are of the same sex.

The fact that the same groups of persons — copywriters as well as target groups — rated both versions of the texts might be seen as a threat to internal validity. It was, however, decided that this test design would affect the outcome less than an experimental design with different groups rating the paraphrase versions. The method used kept the context variable constant and it secured the measurement of attitudes to the syntactic structure of the text instead of, e.g., attitudes to brand names or the vocabulary of the texts. It might also be mentioned that Hughes[8, pp. 41-43] is of the opinion that paired comparisons on the semantic differential not only shorten the questionnaires but also might reduce the halo effects and solve the problem of anchoring.

The quesion of external validity is relevant for the results of the tests with the target groups, whereas the copywriters represent the total population. As the target groups were not randomly chosen from the population it is difficult to claim that the sample is representative of a greater population than the one analysed. Derbaix[4] has found that students are no good substitute for consumers when measuring cognitive and affective reactions to advertisement contents, whereas Fishbein and Ajzen[5, p. 118] refer to empirical evidence that most psychological processes are generalisable across different subject populations. The present study was conducted with four groups of students, four different texts and products were used, and in all instances more positive attitudes were expressed towards regular advertising copy. The possibilities for generalisation might be further enhanced by the fact that also a group of middle-aged respondents with a different background and in a different environment made similar ratings.

A noteworthy result of the test with copywriters was the correct perception of negative/positive attitudes towards text 2, an advertisement for a hair conditioner. Not only the "traditionalists" and the "pointillists" but also a majority of the other copywriters expected more positive attitudes towards the regular copy. A reason for this might be the fact that this advertisement was decidedly less informative than the three others. A content analysis of the advertisement shows that it contains no testable arguments for the ad-thesis, the exhortation to buy or use the product, whereas the other three advertisements contain several testable arguments with information about the product itself. Text 2 might be regarded as typically persuasive advertising which tries to create attitudes towards the product by means of non-rational influences. As the target group ratings also show the greatest differences between regular and short-clipped copy for text 2, it is possible that there is an interaction effect between persuasiveness and short-clipped syntax which results in especially negative attitudes.

In perception theory various circumstances have been found to improve perception, e.g., experience and similarity between judge and stimulus person. In several studies good judges have been found to be less social and less extroverted, and detachment has therefore often been mentioned as associated with the ability to judge others accurately. Adjectives that have been found to characterise good judges are: cautious, clear-thinking, realistic, reserved, serious, sincere and thorough. The purpose of the present study was not to attempt a penetration of the personality of copywriters and therefore no information is available that might distinguish the "traditionalist" copywriters from the others. The fact that the percentage of "traditionalists" in the whole population was so small raises the question of whether the recruitment or the training of copywriters might stress other abilities than those assumed to be correlates of ability to judge others. An interview with a psychologist conducting a central recruitment programme for advertising agencies in Finland in fact revealed that the following qualities were stressed in the suitability tests for copywriters: a natural talent for the language, flexibility, working speed, creativity, common sense, ability to work under stress and not always insist on top quality, business sense and ability to communicate and sell ideas. Some of these requirements might be incompatible with e.g., cautiousness, reserve and thoroughness.

It has not been possible, within the framework of this study, to assess the determinants of the copywriters' ability to perceive target group attitudes towards special linguistic features of advertising copy. Similarity between judge and stimulus person did not appear to improve copywriter perception, as a group of male copywriters were more accurate in their ratings of male as well as female target groups' attitudes. The possibility of experience being crucial for the copywriter population's perception was also ruled out as the experience of the "traditionalist" copywriters ranged from four to twenty years, and so did the experience of the "pointillist" copywriters.

It is possible that the ability to perceive attitudes towards special linguistic features of the body copy of the advertisement requires a more specific skill rather than a general ability to judge others. It is also possible that copywriters — and creative personnel in general — encounter difficulties in judging consumer reactions to their own or their colleagues' creative work due to their own preferences in creative styles. Derbaix[4] has also found that advertising experts — copywriters, art directors and research directors — differ from consumers in their cognitive and affective reactions towards advertising content. A comment about the syntactically short-clipped writing style was recently made in the *International Herald Tribune*[13] and the alleged over-use of sentence fragments was mainly attributed to copywriter preferences.

As the advertising world experiences fashions not only in content but also in style, the implication for marketers as well as creative professionals is that more attention ought to be paid to the linguistic features of advertising copy. The results of the present study indicate that fashions in writing styles can cause negative attitudes which cannot be predicted by copywriters.

References
1. Abrahamsson, S. E., "Fragmentarisk meningsbildning i svenskt reklamspråk, Abo: Licentiatavhandling vid Åbo Akademi, 1968.
2. Carroll, J. B., "Vectors of Prose Style", in J. G. Snider and C. E. Osgood (Eds.), *Semantic Differential Technique,* Chicago, Aldine Publishing Company, 1969.
3. Chomsky, N., *Aspects of the Theory of Syntax,* Cambridge, Massachusetts, MIT Press, 1965.

4. Derbaix, C. M., "Are Consumers Unique in Terms of Cognitive and Affective Reactions towards the Advertising Content?", *European Journal of Marketing,* Vol. 15 No. 7, pp. 12-22, 1981.
5. Fishbein, M. and Ajzen, I., *Belief, Attitude, Intention and Behaviour: an Introduction to Theory and Research,* Reading, Massachusetts, Addison-Wesley, 1975.
6. Hansen, E., *Reklamesprog,* Kobenhaven, Hans Reitzels Forlag A/S, 1970.
7. Holstius, K., *Attitudes towards Advertising Copy and its Syntatic Structure: an Empirical Study,* Ph.D. (Econ.) diss., Swedish School of Economics and Business Administration, Helsinki, 1981.
8. Hughes, G. D., "Upgrading the Semantic Differential", *Journal of the Market Research Society,* Vol. 17, January 1975, pp. 41-44.
9. Katz, J. J. and Postal, P. M., *An Integrated Theory of Linguistic Descriptions,* Cambridge, Massachusetts, MIT Press, 1964.
10. Leech, G. N., *English in Advertising: A Linguistic Study of Advertising in Great Britain,* London, Longman, 1972.
11. Lyons, J., *Chomsky,* Glasgow, William Collins Sons and Co Ltd, 1977.
12. Mindak, W. A., "Fitting the Semantic Differential to the Marketing Problem", in James G. Snider and Charles E. Osgood (Eds.), *op. cit.*
13. Safire, W., Language column in the *International Herald Tribune,* 5 April 1982, p. 18.
14. Stagner, R. and Osgood, C. E., "An Experimental Analysis of a Nationalistic Frame of Reference", *Journal of Social Psychology,* Vol. 14, 1941, pp. 389-401.
15. Tagiuri, R., "Person Perception", in G. Lindzey and E. Aronson (Eds.), *The Handbook of Social Psychology,* Vol. 3, 1969.
16. af Trampe, P. and Viberg, A., *Allmän språkteori och grammatik,* Lund, Liber Läromedel, 1972.
17. Interviews with copywriters.

13. Merchandising

by Francis Buttle

Overview

The majority of marketing and retailing literature gives only scant attention to merchandising as a means of lifting sales performance. This is a grave injustice when its power and cost-effectiveness is compared to its promotional kindred—advertising, personal selling, sales promotion and public relations. This article has been designed to fill that gap in the literature and promote its more widespread understanding and use.

We start by putting forward a definition of merchandising and explaining how and why it works so effectively. Then we discuss its extraordinary power and cost-effectiveness as a means of ensuring a vital, final pre-purchase exposure of consumers to persuasive or informative material. We then discuss five merchandising techniques—manipulation of store traffic flow, shelf positioning (location of product categories and brands), allocation of limited shelf space between competing claims, use of point-of-sale material and the mounting of special displays. We show how these techniques can be used profitably by both the retailer and the manufacturer.

Merchandising—The Silent Salesman?

A sales volume increase of 400 per cent is just one of many successes attributable to effective merchandising. Details of this and other merchandising triumphs appear in a later section of this article. However, this example serves to emphasise the major point that it can be highly effective. Additionally, merchandising can be cheap and in some cases can actually cost nothing.

It is worthwhile trying to define the term "merchandising" because a much clearer picture of its scope will emerge. It is one of a selection of promotional tools available to both retailer and manufacturer. To communications professionals this selection is known as the "promotional mix"; it contains advertising, sales promotion, personal selling, public relations and merchandising.

Where merchandising differs from other tools of the promotional trade is that it is exercised exclusively at the retail store or other point of sale such as a car yard or showroom. The definition of merchandising which I prefer—"merchandising is any form of on-store or in-store promotion other than personal selling which is designed to trigger purchasing behaviour"—clearly distinguishes our subject matter from all other forms of promotion. Merchandising has been nicknamed the silent salesman, and, whilst this may appear true, it is equally true of packaging, print advertising and the vast majority of public relations. Thus, the nickname is not wholly and exclusively appropriate.

Merchandising has come into its own with the advent of self-service and has become a "scientific art". It is scientific in the sense that universal rules govern merchandising activity and that shopper behaviour may be modified in predictable ways, but artistic in the manner in which these rules are implemented.

Some commentators believe that self-service only developed because retailers recognised the power of merchandising and were prepared to operate with reduced staffing levels. In effect, they claim that merchandising caused self-service rather than the reverse.

Both manufacturers and retailers are interested in motivating purchase behaviour. However, whilst manufacturers want to stimulate sales of their own brands and depress sales of their competitors, retailers are usually more interested in increasing store traffic, total sales turnover per square metre of floor space (a few retailers calculate sales on a "volume per cubic metre" basis in the belief that air space should be regarded as a productive asset), and volume sales per customer.

These two aims may conflict. For example, Brand Z is a low-profit line for the retailer who is therefore not keen to devote much shelf-space to it. The manufacturer, on the other hand, is likely to press for just that; some manufacturers, realising the importance of good retail presentation, employ merchandising representatives who not only sell the product, but, by applying the techniques described later, help to move the product off the shelves.

The merchandising representative is primarily an educator. His first task must be to convince the retailer of the value of merchandising by pointing out the lost sales and profit resulting from sub-optimal stock turns caused by poor merchandising. The better the stock turn figures, the greater the turnover per square metre of floor space and the better the retailer's bottom line at the end of the financial year.

The merchandiser's wages are paid by the manufacturer, and, although working in retailer education, his objective must be to so stimulate stock turn that manufacturing and marketing economies are achieved by his employer, thus producing more profitable trading.

Some multiple stores agree facing (product on display) and stock levels with manufacturers before each season, and permit merchandisers or sales representatives to maintain those levels. Few retailers will allow merchandisers total freedom in their stores. Above all, merchandisers must not allow their educational role to become instructive; the risk of losing customer goodwill is too high.

An American merchandising magazine had this to say about the role of the salesman:

"The day of the sales representative as order-taker is gone for ever. In order to become as sophisticated as other packaged goods industries, where the scientific principles of marketing and merchandising have become the steadfast rule, new disciplines must be applied. Today, as well as knowing his product line, the sales rep. must be a knowledgeable, if not expert, merchandiser."[1]

In some industries the sales representative and merchandiser are two different people. The main advantage of having specialised merchandisers is that expertise can be nurtured. Further, in cases where sales representatives do a lot of prospecting or new business selling, they can be freed from shelf-stocking or mounting displays. However, some retailers are not happy with more than one company representative calling on them. Many feel that their day is already interrupted too often.

Under the general heading of merchandising come a variety of behaviour-triggering devices. The list in Table I shows the most common. A full list would be as limitless as your imagination.

Table I. Merchandising Techniques

Store fronts	Shelf talkers
Name signs	Display cards
Dump bins	Crowners
Open/shut signs	Swing tickets
Window stickers	Packaging outers
Door stickers	Trundler panels
Working models	Mobiles
Stack cards	Bottle collars
Leaflets	Brochures
Price tickets	Carrier bags
Paper bags	Posters
Store layout	Shelf space allocation
Shelf positioning	Lighting
Music	Balloons
Demonstrations	Free standing display units

All these techniques have applications in the non-durable sector of the supermarket, hypermarket and other self-service trade.

Durables are not beyond the scope of merchandising. Televisions can be excitingly displayed and hi-fis demonstrated; washing machines can be sold with the offer of free installation and cars can be sold with the assistance of a trial run. Even houses can be merchandised with a show-home.

Industrial goods are less frequently merchandised, simply because there is more face-to-face selling. However, exhibitions and warehouse displays, mobile showrooms and cut-away models do have a role to play in merchandising products like gear boxes and electric motors.

Most manufacturers of well-known branded consumer goods not only use merchandising. They rely on advertising to pre-sell the product. Occasionally, however, there are outstanding successes achieved by merchandising alone. McVities, the British biscuit manufacturer, once introduced a range of cakes to the UK market using merchandising only and achieved sales second to Lyons, which was market leader with 25 per cent. McVities' share was a highly profitable 15 per cent.

How Merchandising Works
There is no accepted body of knowledge about how merchandising influences in-store behaviour. However, all successful merchandising has two simple factors in common: visibility and appeal:

- the more visible a product is, the more likely it is to be seen and therefore bought;
- the more appealing a product is made to appear, the more likely it is to be purchased.

A manufacturer's salesman may work hard to establish retail shelf domination, but few retailers are likely to offer just that one brand. Food retailers, unless deliberately pursuing a limited range policy, generally do stock more than one brand in most product categories because they believe that consumers prefer to buy from a selection. In these circumstances, the manufacturer's merchandising aim must be to increase the probability that the shopper will buy his brand. He does this by ensuring that it is more visible and appealing than competitive products. Hence, a customer who has no brand preference or who chooses from several alternatives will be more likely to buy that manufacturer's brand.

Why Merchandising Works
The basic reasons why merchandising works have been intimated in the preceding section. Some consumers do not have firm product or brand intentions in mind when they enter a retail outlet, whilst others change their minds after entering the store. Put another way, many purchases are made on impulse. Such shoppers are frequently highly susceptible to in-store influence.

There is some empirical evidence to support this generalisation. Consumer behaviour experts, Engel, Blackwell and Kollat, provide figures which suggest that impulse or unplanned purchasing is commonplace:

"50% or more purchases are made on this basis in supermarkets, and the unplanned purchase represents over 33% of all transactions in variety stores and drugstores"[2].

As though recognising this phenomenon, many food retailers happily offer and promote essential everyday purchases like bread, not because of its profit margin which is relatively low, but because it provides the basis for additional store traffic and subsequent impulse buys.

Engel, Blackwell and Kollat also refer to research evidence which shows how 25 per cent to 30 per cent of in-store brand substitution decisions derive from exposure to merchandising influence. Expert opinion claims that:

"The key to any successful merchandising programme lies in its ability to generate impulse sales, or sales which the consumer did not plan to make until stimulated by some point-of-sales material or display. It is stated that between 35% and 70% of all purchases are impulse sales. According to POPAI (Point-of-Purchase Advertising Inc.) approximately 67% of wine and spirit purchases in supermarkets...were unplanned/impulse purchases."[3]

There seems little reason to doubt that similar figures would apply wherever sophisticated retail distribution systems have developed. Even the relatively conservative book trade can benefit from merchandising. In one study, 5000 book purchasers, questioned immediately after making a purchase, reported their reasons for entering the bookshop. The results appear in Table II.

Table II. Reasons for Entering a Bookshop[4]

	Reasons	%
(a)	To buy a specific title	48
(b)	To browse	23
(c)	To buy a book on a specific topic	18
(d)	To buy a present	3
(e)	To buy a magazine	3
(f)	Other reasons	1
(g)	Don't know	4
		100

A total of 31 per cent of book buyers (b),(e),(f),(g) made unplanned purchases. This is very significant for the book retailer because it shows how buyers are susceptible to in-store influence. Another 21 per cent of customers (c),(d) were also influenced within the store to buy the title with which they left. Therefore, a total of 52 per cent of shoppers were receptive to the influence of merchandising.

To summarise:

(1) Some customers will buy from a category from which they had no prior intention of making a purchase.

(2) Other customers will have decided, prior to store entry, to buy from a given product category. They do not make up their minds about brand until they are in the store. This may be because they have inadequate information about the alternatives or because they consider several brands to be perfect substitutes.

(3) Some shoppers, having decided before entering the store to buy a particular brand will purchase a competitive product or will allocate their limited resources to a brand selected from an entirely different product category.

The Advantages of Merchandising
The two most important advantages of merchandising are as follows:

(1) It is one of the most cost-effective tools of the promotional mix. It can generate surprisingly large sales increases at relatively low cost.

(2) It influences shoppers in the final stages of purchase decision-making—at the point of sale.

Cost-Effectiveness

Merchandising is a very inexpensive tool, particularly if a company is skilled and experienced in its use. In a company with limited promotional funds, merchandising can be vital because many of the techniques, such as better shelf positioning and product facing control, may involve no additional expenditure. These tasks can be performed by a sales representative whose salary is already being paid. He may have to reduce his call rate to perform these new tasks, but this is of little consequence if his overall productivity increases.

Some merchandising does involve a cash expenditure, for instance, shelf talkers (product information cards attached to the shelf), display backing cards and working models. However, there is no reason why this expenditure should not be rigorously controlled. Some of the most effective shelf talkers are not the pre-printed variety, but blanks upon which messages are hand-printed.

Cost is only one part of the cost-effectiveness equation. Only if merchandising is effective in producing incremental sales can the claim of cost-effectiveness be upheld.

Evidence concerning the sales impact of the various merchandising techniques is drawn mostly from the United States. An experiment upon matched sets of supermarkets conducted over a five-month period highlighted the following effects of merchandising:

(1) Special displays of new health and beauty-aid items achieved between 100 per cent and 400 per cent more sales than did normal on-shelf locations.

(2) Related-item displays sold as much as 418 per cent more than when the component items were displayed separately. A related-item display is one where logically related products such as cheese and crackers or ice cream and wafers are displayed together rather than separately.

(3) "As advertised" signs, "cents off" signs and product identification signs increased sales by 124 per cent, 23 per cent and 18 per cent respectively.

An experiment to test the effectiveness of end-of-aisle displays in 12 drugstores showed increased sales of between 142 per cent and 217 per cent. End-of-aisle displays are situated at the end of a row of gondolas where the shopper is normally moving from one aisle to the next.

Another study audited 734 displays of 360 grocery products in five supermarkets. Unit sales of items on special display were significantly higher than those in normal shelf positions.

An experiment was conducted in a wide variety of store types (supermarkets, grocers, drug stores, stationers, photographic outlets) on a wide variety of product lines including juice, cigarettes, liquor, personal care items, pens and cameras. Special displays without motion netted a gain of 37 per cent over normal shelf positions; those with motion netted an average of 83 per cent.

Canned corn which was moved from the bottom shelf to just below eye-level increased its unit sales by 200 per cent.

A macaroni-and-cheese dinner was moved from eye-level to the next-to-bottom shelf and suffered a 60 per cent sales drop.

A product accustomed to two shelf facings was given four for an experimental period and experienced a 40 per cent increase in weekly unit sales.

Another product which had four facings and was not moving in sufficient numbers to warrant the space was reduced to two facings. Whilst sales of that product remained unchanged, an adjacent product which absorbed the two facings increased 39 per cent.

The pioneering study into the effectiveness of merchandising was conducted in the USA in 1959. Five Kansas supermarkets, owned by J.S. Dillon & Sons were scrutinised to discover how floor layout and self-service operations could be changed to increase profitability. Amongst the recommendations made were these:

(1) similar products should be located together;

(2) gondolas should use adjustable shelving so that the shopper is not presented with a visually monotonous rank of merchandise;

(3) space should be allocated to product categories and brands according to their sales turnover;

(4) the best positions should be offered to the most profitable lines;

(5) gondola ends should be used for displays;

(6) coloured price tickets should be used to help shoppers find product categories.

Influence at the Point of Sale
Most marketers will do everything possible financially to establish an awareness of, and preference for, their brands before the shopper enters the store. They try to pre-sell the consumers so that they will specify their brands at the point of sale. Hence, many firms resort to the advertising and public relations components of the promotional mix to achieve this preference, which is known as consumer franchise. Enlightened manufacturers are not willing to risk losing the sale in the store but instead supplement their expensive pre-sell with relatively inexpensive merchandising.

This is particularly the case when competition amongst the brands is fierce. The "Battle of the Brands" is just as intense in the store as it is in the media as the following quotation about the American canned soup market makes abundantly clear:

> "In the beginning there was just Campbell's Chicken with Rice soup. Today, besides Chicken with Rice soup, Campbell Soup Co. makes Chicken Gumbo, Chicken Noodle, Chicken Noodle Os, Curly Noodle with Chicken, Cream of Chicken, Creamy Chicken'n'Mushroom, Chicken Vegetable, Chicken Alphabet, Chicken Stars, Chicken'n'Dumplings and Chicken Broth. Rather than undercutting one another on price the manufacturers are locked in a big bucks battle to see which can spew out most new products, advertise and promote the most heavily, and tie up the most shelf space."[5]

But the benefits of merchandising need not be experienced only by the big firms. It is equally important, if not more so, for smaller manufacturers and retailers who cannot afford to employ heavy media advertising in their promotional strategy. If they do not merchandise well, then they are placing their commercial destiny almost entirely in the hands of brand loyal shoppers. It is in the store that the Davids can fight it out on almost equal terms with the Goliaths. The word "almost" has been judiciously used because some heavyweights have been known to apply considerable pressure to prevent effective merchandising by minor competitors. This is particularly so where the merchandising equipment is owned by the manufacturer instead of the retailer, as in the case of freezers and cool cabinets.

The retailing scene is in constant metamorphosis; manufacturers are well advised to adapt their merchandising techniques to these changes. For example, there is the recent advent of the discount store which will only display merchandise in the outers in which it is delivered. In order to keep their costs to a minimum, they will only cut cases or break open pallets. An appropriate merchandising response would be to develop easily cut and stacked outers featuring specially designed graphics incorporating a selling message or product information.

Merchandising Techniques

In this section, we give more detail about the five most powerful forms of merchandising:

- manipulation of store traffic flow
- shelf positioning
- space allocation
- point-of-sale material
- special displays.

Manipulation of Store Traffic Flow

Store traffic is the term used to describe the movement of shoppers in the store between the times of entry and departure.

In the USA and, to a lesser extent, Europe, Australasia, Africa and Asia, stores are specifically designed to guide shoppers though as many areas of the store as possible. There are three main reasons behind this:

(1) customers who shop in an entire store buy far more than those who shop in only selected areas;

(2) the longer a shopper spends in the store, the greater the purchase volume;

(3) traffic tends to concentrate on the store perimeter if not manipulated by the store.

The following example of store redesign shows the benefits of traffic management quite dramatically. Before redesign a liquor store was planned as in Figure 1.

Beer and spirits were stocked in the quick service area. Beer was stacked on rollers and was requested by the customer at the quick service checkout. Spirits were stacked above and alongside the rollers. Liqueurs, table wines, sherries and non-liquor lines such as nuts and snacks were stocked on gondolas in the self-service area of the store.

An analysis of sales dockets and observation of traffic flow revealed that a large percentage of customers was buying beer and spirits only. Traffic would enter through the doors in the quick service area, buy the beer and spirits and pay at the quick service checkout.

Figure 1. Liquor Store Layout—Before

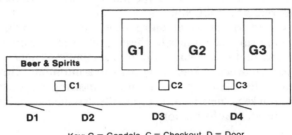

Key: G = Gondola, C = Checkout, D = Door

A large number of customers were not being exposed to some 90 per cent of the floor area and the lines carried, thereby severely reducing the opportunity for impulse sales. The required change was simple. The beer fixtures were immobile but the spirits were moved to the back of the store in order to draw traffic past the other product categories. The floor layout was changed to that shown in Figure 2 and traffic flow was also improved by removing one checkout and closing up one door.

Figure 2. Liquor Store Layout—After

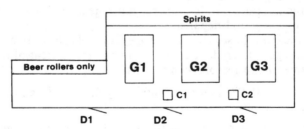

Key: G = Gondola, C = Checkout, D = Door

The effect of these changes was an upturn of 6 per cent in sales per customer.

The solution of a store layout problem begins with balancing the demands on finite space of both selling and non-selling areas. Non-selling areas incorporate office, despatch, storage, checkout, bagging and aisle space although some experts consider the last three to be integral parts of the selling area.

In starting with a new building, the problems are easier to solve; real skill is needed by operators in existing premises where modifications to the shop floor are impossible. Lighting, power points, pillars, uneven floors, varying ceiling heights, doors and stairs are all constraints.

Maximisation of selling space means that retailers must rigorously control stock levels in the store room. Similarly, window backs and counters may need removal. In some stores counters and the space behind them occupy as much as 40 per cent of available selling space.

Retailers who build their own stores are well advised to plan the optimal internal layout and then erect the walls around it. Ideally, such a store could have separate entry and exit doors so that shop front congestion, which can discourage some shoppers from entry, is reduced. The two-door principle also permits better traffic circulation.

The two main considerations in layout of the selling area are aisle design and merchandise location.

Aisle Design

Aisles must be designed for maximum exposure of the shoppers to the merchandise. Traffic movement studies can be used to show how shoppers move around the store. A "shopper-tracking study" has shoppers unobtrusively followed around the store with an observer noting the route followed and where movement stops for the purchasing process to begin. The purchase may begin with the scanning of a shelf, or by picking up a product or questioning an assistant. Studies like these show which areas of the store receive little exposure.

The conventional layout of a supermarket is the grid pattern. The shopper generally enters at one corner and moves up and down the aisles which run in parallel. The longer the store the more likely there are to be cross aisles. However, these diminish traffic circulation and, therefore, product exposure. Continuous aisles promote traffic flow, exposure and sales.

Figures 3 and 4 show the "before-and-after" floor plans of a small neighbourhood supermarket. Before the change in layout the central island gondolas were not well patronised; the categories which were located on the inside shelving moved very slowly. Additionally, the entry/exit was often congested and the merchandise located behind the hinged door sold poorly.

Figure 3. Supermarket Layout—Before

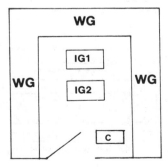

WG = Wall Gondola, IG = Island Gondola, C = Checkout

Figure 4. Supermarket Layout—After

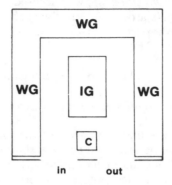

Key: WG = Wall Gondola, IG = Island Gondola, C = Checkout

With the loss of half a day's sales as the shop closed for alterations, a new gondola was installed in the central area. This opened up the shop making the merchandise much more visible from the street. The shop front was altered to induce a clockwise traffic flow. Two retractable doors were installed and the checkout located between them. This gave the shop proprietor complete control over the movement of shoppers once they had entered. The result of these inexpensive alterations was a net gain in turnover in the first year of 11 per cent. A portion of this was due to increased patronage; the balance was earned by greater sales per shopper.

A variation of the grid design is the angular layout shown in Figure 5. Minor aisles are angled off the main artery.

Figure 5. Angular Store Layout

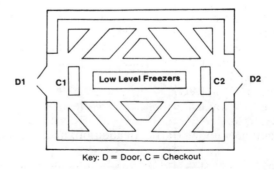

Key: D = Door, C = Checkout

Where the physical limitations of the store prohibit good traffic flow, the angular layout enables a shopper passing down the main artery to see more of the merchandise.

However, in some neighbourhoods where theft (euphemistically included in shrinkage figures) is a problem, this variant gives the potential thief ample opportunity to exercise his skill.

Aisle widths need not be fixed. Indeed, there are sound reasons for variance. The seasonality of the merchandise and the height of the gondolas flanking the aisle are two main considerations. Winter lines such as gloves and Christmas trimmings are often located alongside wider aisles during the season. Wider aisles are especially important in waiting areas, particularly checkout and bagging areas or when the customer wishes to compare alternatives, as is the case in butchery departments.

Shoppers do not like to be dominated by stacks of merchandise in tall gondolas. It makes them feel small and uncomfortable. Wider aisles overcome this problem. High gondolas also increase security problems; since they obscure vision theft is likely to increase. In any event, lower gondolas let the shopper see more of the store and encourage impulse sales. The minimum width in supermarkets is two trundler widths plus an allowance for overtaking, about 1.75 metres.

Pillars represent psychological barriers which can stop shoppers passing down an aisle. It is better to incorporate them into displays. Where gondolas cannot be used to direct traffic, barriers may be of value.

Department stores traditionally have not attempted to route shoppers scientifically. The "department scatter" approach, which is still dominant, may well encourage browsing, and, providing the merchandise is located according to the principles explained later, there is no reason why a high level of sales per customer should not be achieved.

A recent British department store development employed a loop walkway on which shoppers were routed past the entire stock of merchandise and were assailed by displays on either side. The walkway linked the escalators and staircases so shoppers had no way of avoiding exposure.

Merchandise Location

The prime issue in locating merchandise is the amount of pull a line exerts. "Power" or "demand" lines attract customers to the store. They are often perishables such as dairy products, or sugar, bacon, biscuits, cheese, flour and cereals which many shoppers buy every trip. "Loss leaders", which are sold at below cost and specials such as temporary price deals are also demand lines.

Strong traffic stimulators such as these should be located so that shoppers must walk past other lines. The general tendency in supermarkets which are not laid out according to these principles is for customers to shop in the perimeter. Known as "wall-shopping", it is encouraged by locating demand lines along the wall, Unfortunately, this is not helped by equipment maintenance requirements. Cool cabinets, whose contents are often demand lines, are usually located along the walls so that repairs can be carried out without interrupting traffic. In addition, many cool cabinets are loaded from the rear.

Wall shopping was the subject of this remark by a major American liquor retailer.

"Wine is an enormous impulse item for us. If you hide wine it won't sell. In four separate tests in four different states, we found that every time we moved wine from an interior aisle location to a perimeter aisle location, sales improved materially. The overall result was a documented sales increase of 93 per cent within a 120-day period." [6]

Some items such as silverware and china, which require deliberation before purchase, are better located away from the main arteries. Otherwise, congestion occurs.

As more and more households acquire freezers, space devoted to frozen foods in supermarkets will increase. Vertical freezers have the same restocking problems as cool cabinets and are, therefore, generally located along the walls. Chest freezers, if located in central aisle areas can open up a store making adjacent gondolas more visible and creating a more spacious feeling. They can also be placed along the windows so that passers-by can see into the store and get a feel for the type of merchandise carried.

Some areas are habitually poor sales producers. Corners are notoriously bad, as are blind gondola ends (those which the shopper does not pass as turning into a parallel aisle). However, these areas, appropriately known as coffin corners and dead ends, can be used effectively. Demand lines or special displays can be placed there, with attractive streamers, mobiles or public announcements used to draw shoppers.

Multi-storey stores face special problems. Traffic tends to decrease with altitude. Merchandise with limited appeal, non-impulse lines and demand lines should be located on the upper floors.

Impulse lines should be where the population is densest, or the lower levels. The department store development to which we referred on p. 115 was a three-storey block. Fashion items, which are huge impulse lines, were located on the ground floor. On the first floor were home and housewares; in the basement were men's and children's clothing.

Shelf Positioning
There are two aspects of shelf positioning which have a bearing on sales. These are:

- positioning of product categories;
- subsequent positioning of brands.

Positioning of Product Categories
Shelves should be stocked according to some method in which all the brands in a category are grouped together in order to help shoppers make comparisons. There are two basic ways in which this can be achieved—either by horizontal or vertical positioning. In horizontal positioning, individual sizes and brands within the category are positioned along the length of the shelf. In vertical positioning, they are stacked on all levels of the gondola.

Of the two, vertical positioning is certainly the better from the shopper's viewpoint because he can find the brand he wants without having to walk the length of a gondola. The retailer also benefits from vertical positioning. Firstly, he is still able to position demand categories in such a way as to draw customers' attention to other lines and induce impulse sales. Secondly, he can position the most profitable sizes and brands at eye level in order to sell more.

Customers tend to look at eye level first and, if they do not see what they want, they will then scan the shelves above and below. Eye level positions are hotly contested by merchandisers. Retailers often like to put larger or more profitable sizes and brands at eye level.

What is eye-level for one customer need not be eye level for all. Sweets and toys aimed at the child do not sell well when stacked five feet above ground level. Supermarket operators will cleverly place chocolate novelties on the lower shelves of gondolas so that children pick them up. It is axiomatic that touch and sight sell children's lines. For this reason, many checkouts, where bored and fractious children wait with their harrassed parents, have a low-level display selling novelties.

The depth of upper and lower shelves often means that merchandise at the back is not visible to the passing shopper. Wire racking overcomes this to a degree as does the use of gondolas which slope away from the shopper. Figures 6 and 7 show designs for both island and wall gondolas which let the shopper see the merchandise on non-eye-level shelves.

Figure 6. Island Gondola

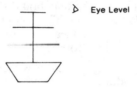

Figure 7. Wall Gondola

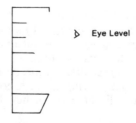

An alternative is to angle up lower shelves and to angle down upper shelves.

Some retailers prefer to rotate both product categories and brands to encourage shoppers to search the shop for the items they have on their shopping lists. One supermarket operator had this to say:

"I believe in constant rotation of brands on the shelf. If a customer buys the same brand every week from the same shelf, he doesn't see anything else in the store. I constantly rotate brands on the shelf so that the customer has to look for his brand. This increases the impulse factor. I even rotate entire categories. I want the customer to walk around".[7]

This retailer is the exception rather than the rule. Most believe that there are other ways of persuading shoppers to shop through the entire store without presenting them with this sort of frustration. Indeed, most actually flag or signpost the main categories so that they can be conveniently located.

Positioning of Brands
The fact that some brands are more popular than others can be used to advantage by both retailer and manufacturer.

(1) The retailer who places a sought-after brand on a non-eye-level shelf causes exposure to other brands. The customer wanting this brand starts at eye level and continues to scan the shelves until he finds it. Many retailers, however, prefer to make hot brands even hotter by stocking them where visible and attractive. A high-margin, popular line is undoubtedly better at eye level.

(2) The retailer can place a popular brand next to an overstocked, and therefore cost-incurring, slower mover. This guarantees a higher level of consumer exposure to the product. Brand leaders should always be placed by the shopkeeper next to high-margin lines to encourage impulse sales.

(3) The manufacturer of a slow mover will frequently try to persuade the retailer to position his product next to a popular brand so as to gain exposure.

Space Allocation
Many manufacturers and retailers believe that shelf space should be allocated between brands in proportion to their sales. For instance, a leading preserves manufacturer with a major share of the glass-packed preserves market exhorted retailers thus:

"At least 50% of your shelf space should be allocated to glass pack jams and marmalades."

Not only do some marketers claim that shelf space should equal market share but that forward stocks should also equal market share. This position is primarily held by market leaders, of course, who want maximum exposure for their brand and as little exposure for pretenders as possible.

Brands with lower market share argue, convincingly, that space should be allocated according to future sales potential, not according to past sales achievements. Future sales potential is generally greater for new brands which are attacking the position of the leader.

However, retailers do reap considerable benefits from allocating space according to market share. If they do not, the consequences are:

(1) inefficient use of staff who spend too much time re-stocking shelves with fast-moving items instead of erecting displays, selling or being more productive elsewhere;

(2) a lower unit volume sales return per metre of shelf space because slower moving lines are occupying too much space.

However, there are valid reasons why this principle should not be adhered to.

(1) A strict sales criterion may prevent a product or brand from having even one
facing.

(2) Some shoppers insist on being offered a selection.

(3) The fastest selling lines may not produce the best profit for the retailer. Slower
movers with higher margins may be better.

(4) For various reasons a retailer may want to push a particular line. One way of
doing this is to increase its facings. Although the point of diminishing returns
is undoubtedly reached at some time, the sales of a product generally increase
with facings.

The manufacturer's merchandising staff fight for increased facings for this very reason.
They must convince retailers that there is more profit in allocating space to their own
brand at the expense of competitive brands. Many merchandisers capitalise on a
weakness of some retailers who are not adept at shelf management. Slow-moving lines
tend to drive out fast-moving lines. This occurs because shop staff tend to fill up shelf
space with nearby products. If this tendency is not carefully policed, then slower moving
lines gradually creep into more and more spaces on the shelf, causing lost sales.

Merchandisers who want increased facings only need to identify which lines fall
into this category and suggest to the retailer that they reorganise the shelf. The result
is increased facings for their own brands and reduced facings for competitors.

Point of Sale
There is huge variety of point-of-sale (POS, also known as point-of-purchase or POP)
materials of which the most popular are shelf talkers (materials attached to the shelf
bearing the brand), window banners, price tickets and posters.

There are three main purposes of this material. First, many marketers use it to restate
their advertising message in the store. This extends the impact of the advertising to
the store and may recall a sound or visual element of the advertisement to the mind
of the shopper. Second, POS is used to attract the shopper's attention to a particular
item. Bearing in mind that a shopper may spend only ten minutes in a store and that
there may be over 6,000 lines on the shelves, POS needs to stand out from the sensory
noise level in the store. A recent innovation has retailers offering manufacturers the
opportunity to make announcements over their public address systems. Third, and
perhaps the most important role for POS, is to provide a motive for making a purchase.

American researchers have investigated the power of signs at the point of sale. There
is strong indication that signs advertising a price special cause sales to increase by
close to 30 per cent. The increase in sales due to a sign stressing a benefit is somewhat
less, at 17 per cent. At regular price, price signs increased sales by 66 per cent, while
benefit signs moved them up by 27 per cent. The research took place in department
stores[8].

Signs can only do their job if they are visible. They must stand out from the mass of visual stimuli. Size, location, colour, movement and illusion help to attract the eye.

Some of the more common abuses of POS are:

(1) leaving the material too long, so that it becomes a fixture and loses visibility;

(2) leaving the material in position when it is torn, soiled, sun-bleached, damp or mildewed which is hardly good publicity for the product or store;

(3) leaving the material in position when the occasion for which it was used has passed;

(4) using too much POS so that impact is lost.

Special Displays

A special display is an arrangement of a quantity of merchandise separate and apart from its normal location on the shelf. The aim of special displays is to attract the attention of shoppers and to stimulate impulse purchases. According to the American Point-of-Purchase Advertising Inc's survey of 7000 shoppers in mass merchandise stores, 30 per cent made unplanned purchases. Half of these were caused by exposure to displays—this is clear evidence of the power of display.

The two most popular types of packaged food display are case stack displays and bin displays.

● *Case stack displays.* The product is left in the outer and the sides of the outer cut away. A message card is generally placed over the display.

● *Bin displays.* The bin may be cardboard, plastic or metal. It is assembled by a salesman or shop assistant who loads the bin with product and erects a message card.

Each type has advantages. The case stack is more versatile and capable of translation to the needs of differing outlets. A small display of one cut outer might suit a small outlet. A palletised load may be cut in a discount store. The bin display requires more space as a rule.

Retailers themselves may not be able to install the types of self-selection fixtures so readily provided by many manufacturers—the L'eggs stocking merchandiser is an example—simply because of cost. Manufacturers order in economic quantities.

Merchandisers (the same name is used to describe both fixture and person) allow manufacturers who have attained maximum penetration of retail outlets to obtain additional off-shelf sales. The L'eggs example is an exception; the merchandiser was offered to the trade at the product launch. To persuade retailers to use these fixtures, marketers will often feature them in media advertising.

Despite the fact that they complain of lack of floor space, retailers generally find merchandisers to be good impulse sales generators because of the heightened visibility they afford the product.

Four main principles govern the use of special displays.

(1) Displays should be located where most people pass, slow down or stop. Location is very important. Normally, displays sell well at gondola ends.

(2) The display must attract the shoppers' attention. The same factors which draw attention to point-of-sale material also work for displays. However, three aspects are worthy of special mention—size, message card and lighting. Big displays are more successful than small especially if message cards are used to spell out a selling message.

Lighting is important even in normal circumstances. On wall gondolas, integral overhead lighting can be used fully to illuminate the merchandise. In aisle positions gondolas are more often illuminated by strip lighting located over the aisles. Were the strips placed directly over the merchandise, shadows would be cast over the lower shelves.

Some stores, especially those carrying up-market lines, such as delicatessens and high-fashion clothing stores, use a general low lighting level and subsidiary lights for interest areas.

(3) The product must be easy to pick up and look as if it is selling well. If the display is full, neat and tidy it is unlikely to move merchandise. This is because many customers believe the product is not selling well or feel reluctant to disturb the order. Therefore, astute retailers leave a few gaps to give the impression that the line is popular. These empty spaces are called "starter gaps".

Equally, it is a good idea to tumble the contents of bin displays. Experience shows that the easier a product is to pick up the better it will sell. The day of the pyramid of perfectly placed product is past.

(4) Displays should be frequently changed; otherwise they lose their dramatic appeal and become fixtures.

Non-food displays lend themselves to a little more variety.

A vignette, a scene showing the product in use, often with related products, is frequently used to good effect by furniture retailers. A display of kitchen units in a conventional kitchen layout, together with appliances, cupboards filled with dummy packs, wall-mounted spice racks and dishes on the sink drainer gives added interest to the display and gives shoppers an idea of how the units might look in their own home.

Self-selection racks, used by clothing retailers, emphasise the choice available to the shopper and draw attention to the variety of ways in which separates can be combined.

Related-item displays are frequently used by department stores. Instead of displaying men's toiletries only in the cosmetics department, they are also on display in the menswear department together with shoes, socks, nightwear and so on. It is sometimes known as the 'shoppe' approach and it is valuable in moving otherwise slow-selling lines.

Even a supermarket shelf is amenable to related-item displays if use is made of shelf extenders and J-hooks. Small tubs of dye for use in washing machines have been displayed on narrow racks attached to the front of shelves carrying detergents. J-hooks have been used to associate tin openers with canned fruit, tea strainers with tea leaves and pets' toys with pet food.

Non-food items also lend themselves more to item and assortment displays. An item display, where a single specimen of a product is put on isolated display can dramatically emphasise its uniqueness. Assortment displays, which are often used by luggage and footwear retailers emphasise breadth and depth of variety. These are important considerations for shoppers who like to choose from an assortment as is normally the case with shoes.

A variation of the in-store display is the window display. These are the "eyes of the store" looking out on the shopper. The main objective is to attract pedestrian or car-carried traffic into the store, or "to make the passer buy". This is commonly achieved by displaying new products where novelty arouses interest or by posting bills announcing loss leaders or specials.

Window dressers always attempt to attract the pedestrian's attention and arouse his curiosity. To do this they need the skills of both lighting technician and stage designer. They need not regard the shape of the window as a major constraint since masking tape, paint, drapes or blinds can be used to obscure parts of the glass. The major item, such as a product on temporary special, should serve as the focal point and act as a guide for positioning peripherals. The designer should bear in mind the type of shopper the store is targeting, use of colour and movement, harmony of shape, the symmetry of the display, lighting intensity and location, the depth of the display area and topicality. For instance, a display could be seasonal or tie in with local events.

Attempts to measure the power of a dressed window can be made. Some retailers count the number of pedestrians who stop to look; others go further and count the numbers entering the shop having previously looked in the window.

It is worth noting that not all shops have window displays. As mentioned earlier, some food retailers prefer to let the passer-by see right into the store. Other retailers have fully retractable doors. This is most common in fresh fruit and fish retailing, although some clothing stores have also adopted the idea.

The Merchandising Plan

An organised approach to merchandising calls for a plan. Whilst the contents of each plan will vary according to the needs of the planner and his organisation, there is much to be said for adopting the format I suggest below. At least it forces the retailer to examine his merchandising problems and adopt a systematic approach to their solution. The plan is a 10-part document.

(1) Fact gathering:
    (a) sales performance by product category;
    (b) stock turn rates;
    (c) traffic flow pattern;
    (d) profit contributions by product category.
(2) Identification of merchandising problems.
(3) Objectives for the coming trading period.
(4) Merchandising techniques to be used.
(5) Timing of implementation.
(6) Departments, staff and material suppliers involved.
(7) Training requirements.
(8) Likely competitor reaction.
(9) Budget.
(10) Means of evaluation.

Review

(1)   Merchandising is any form of on-store or in-store promotion, other than personal selling, designed to trigger purchasing behaviour.

(2)   Merchandising works because it makes merchandise more attractive and visible.

(3)   Estimates show that about half the items bought in supermarkets are impulse buys.

(4)   Merchandising has two main advantages—it is cost-effective and it influences the shopper at the point of sale.

(5)   The five main merchandising techniques are manipulation of store traffic flow, shelf positioning, space allocation, point-of-sale material and special displays.

(6)   Store traffic flow should be managed so that shoppers are exposed to the largest proportion of the selling area as possible.

(7)   The two prime considerations in planning store layout are aisle design and merchandise location.

(8)   Demand lines should be used to draw traffic past impulse merchandise.

(9)   There are two forms of shelf positioning—horizontal and vertical. The latter is more effective.

(10)   The two dimensions of shelf positioning are product category and brand locations.

(11)   Many retailers believe that shelf space should be allocated in proportion to market share. This is not necessarily the most profitable.

(12)   Special supermarket displays are most frequently of two types—case stack displays and bin displays.

(13)   Other forms of display are self-selection racks, item displays, assortment displays, vignettes and window displays.

(14)   Displays work well when traffic is slow, where the product is legibly priced, easy to pick up and where attention is drawn to the display.

References

1. *Impact Two*, Vol. 1, March 1979, p. 1.
2. Engel, J.F., Blackwell, R.D. and Kollat, D.T., *Consumer Behaviour*, Holt, Rinehart, Winston, 3rd edition, 1978, p. 483.
3. *Impact Two, op. cit.*, pp. 1-2.
4. "In-store Survey of Book Purchasers", Massey University Market Research Centre, 1978.
5. "The American Nightmare: 80 Varieties on Every Shelf", *Dominion*, 16 May 1979.
6. *Impact Two, op. cit.*, p. 7.
7. *Ibid.*
8. "Sales Go Up With Signs", *Retail News*, October 1979.

14. Industrial Sales Forces – Organisation Strategy

by C. D. Moss

The information presented in this article was collected in the course of a continuing research project on the role of the industrial salesman as a gatherer and reporter of market-place intelligence. An article[1] published last year derived from the research programme revealed that the industrial salesman played an important part in acquiring various types of intelligence, i.e., concerning customers; the product; competition; buyer behaviour, etc.,—such information being a useful input into the corporate planning process of an organisation. Further investigation since has shown that the way in which sales forces are organised affects the quantity and quality of the intelligence feedback generated to the company. Consideration is given in this article to looking at the following:

(1)   the developments and trends taking place in how companies organise their industrial sales forces;

(2)   the reasons why companies have re-structured their sales forces—what marketing objectives have been sought when making organisational changes: and

(3)   the marketing information generated from salesmen working within different organisational patterns.

It has to be recognised that in many companies the organisation of the sales force remains static, changing only when forced to do so by movement of company personnel, or pressure from the market. In deciding the way in which manpower resources should be organised, the Marketing Manager's initial consideration must be the type of contact and degree of service necessary to satisfy the market's needs. Changes in the structure of markets; demand for specialist advice; the requirement to negotiate major contracts at high level; and the need for a particular ancillary service all force more rigorous examination of how the sales force should be disposed.

Geographical Structures
By far the most common method of industrial sales force organisation in the past has been allocating salesmen by geographical area. Hardy[2] and Fisher[3] defend such allocations on the grounds that savings in travelling expenses can be made, and that salesmen can acquire better local and customer knowledge. However, this type of organisational allocation assumes that the product range being marketed is reasonably homogeneous and within the salesman's technical capability to handle. This research, however, has demonstrated that in the industries that have to be responsive to ever-quickening technological change and in industries beginning to

190

concentrate on the development of "systems" packages for the market-place, it is imperative for the salesman to acquire a high level of technical expertise in demonstrating product benefits and applications. This expertise cannot be developed without providing a more specialised role for the salesmen. From my investigations it was noticeable that salesmen working in confined geographical territories generated a less valuable input of customer intelligence than salesmen who were organised in specialist ways—markets have magnitudes or size bounds; they have contours (large buyers and small buyers), and salesmen working within a geographical structure did not seem to recognise the existence of such bounds and contours. Many companies have, therefore, taken the opportunity of exploring the possibilities of organising their sales forces in accordance with the differing importance of particular accounts or on the basis of different sizes of customers, in order to focus the salesman's mind on the need to recognise the requirements and problems of clearly defined groups of customer.

It is being gradually recognised that a specialised knowledge of different kinds of customers, their organisations, attitudes, and product applications is essential for developing future marketing plans—particularly for the purpose of identifying trends and growth rates in individual market segments. Salesmen working in defined geographical territories, covering all types of customer, were weak in interpreting buyer behaviour patterns, and in reporting about changes in the operational circumstances of customers, whereas salesmen working within specialised boundaries could acquire an understanding of buyer behaviour and customer processes because they were exploring problems in greater depth within a defined range of customers. Within such a range the salesman could identify a commonalty of activities which would help to give him a framework within which he could gather appropriate intelligence. For the reasons outlined above allocation of sales force duties on a geographic basis is on the wane in the companies surveyed, and considerable restructuring of sales organisations is taking place.

"Key" Account Structures

In instances where sizes of contract have been varying widely, some companies have organised their sales forces by size of account. The significance of large customers in relation to total market size has given rise to the practice of creating a sales force to handle "key" accounts. Behind this lies the belief that the larger customer needs better service in terms of expertise. His problems tend to be more complex; the availability of alternative processes, usually not practical for the smaller company, leads to difficult decisions in which expert advice may be needed. Increasingly, note Lidstone and Melkman[4], companies are structuring not only their field organisations, but also their internal sales administration on the basis of allocating specific responsibility. The research demonstrates that several electronics companies operating in rapidly-changing technical environments, for example, have teamed their internal desk sales staff with their outside staff around "key" customers. Salesmen working within such a structure have been noticeably able at monitoring the technological developments and changes taking place at the "key" customer location. Such salesmen also were most capable when forecasting likely future volume levels at the "key" location. Within this organisational pattern the salesman develops a relationship with a large number of individual decision-makers at the customer location and can investigate their particular problems in depth. The salesman knows who makes what decision and who influences the various factors impinging on the decision. He is in a position to supply marketing staff with intelligence which enables them to adapt and improve products, and to permit efficient planning of the advertising and promotion effort.

Functional Patterns of Organisation

Specialisation of the role of the salesman has also led to duties being allocated by function in some companies investigated (particularly in the chemicals, plastics, and scientific instruments industries). The point behind such an allocation seems to be that a total selling job necessitates a different type of salesman at different stages. Also Smackey[5] has justified this type of specialisation with reference to differences in required communicative skills. For instance, specialisation may be attained by separating out pioneer work from the regular maintenance work of the salesman and putting this in the hands of a specialised team of representatives. Pioneer work in this context means something more than routine prospecting—it is concerned with finding new applications for established products and developing the market for new products. This means that initially a product has to be brought to the attention of a few major customers and considerable time spent working with each of these few companies to overcome commercial, technical and installation problems. Also there may be problems in negotiating price arrangements which are not necessarily within the responsibility and capability of the regular salesman in many sales teams. For such reasons approximately a quarter of the companies covered in the research programme were actively re-structuring their sales forces by placing pioneer development work in the hands of a small number of specialists (usually highly educated, having a wide range of selling experience in allied environments, and occupying an élite status within their organisations). The pioneer salesman can often discover valuable evidence of product acceptability either regionally or nationally and so provide a series of unbiased tests for alternative sales presentations, so that a future product when finally used by a company's own sales force has maximum chance of success. Such salesmen gave a knowledgeable input on likely product applications and were capable of reporting useful intelligence about competitor activities. I was also impressed with their ability to estimate the potential size of the market for the new product they were canvassing.

Other pioneer salesmen were selling a product which had yet to be designed or made (merely an idea or concept)—the salesman is selling a technical capability. For this reason he must be skilled in the firm's own technology to the point where he can almost draw up the specifications. Numerous examples were seen of this type of pioneer operation. One company involved in the manufacture of industrial gases adopted a pioneer sales force organisation to sell the idea of using particular gases for the freezing of food. The sales force was described as a technological mission sales force—once customers had accepted the practicalities of freezing food by means of industrial gas, this sales force handed the order-taking over to a regular sales force that could concentrate on the maintenance of business. Many companies marketing sophisticated machinery had "Future Products" sales forces operating within a time span of five to ten years—at a certain point in development the operational plan would be taken over by the "Present Products" sales teams.

In several cases companies have adopted such a structure because of the Marketing Manager's belief that one of the leading causes of new product failure is the inadequacy of the sales force to introduce the product. There are numerous underlying reasons for the inadequacy—field coaching, sales force calibre, training on the new product, etc., but even conceding the adequacy of these, usually too little attention is devoted to a vital psychological block each salesman faces, i.e., the future difficulties in his relationships if the product does not live up to its promises. His dependability in the eyes of each customer as a source of reliable intelligence is a principal feature of the relationship, and it took him a long time to develop it. Realising that each customer can have a differing point of view, the salesman is inclined to doubt the wisdom of giving an unknown product his unqualified support in his presentations. Where a company continuously introduces new products, if it is large enough to afford a special new product sales force on a full-time basis, this will alleviate the problem and also gain other advantages such as singleness of purpose of the salesman, clearly defined responsibility, execution of the presentation as prescribed, and more reliable feedback from the market-place.

Very reliable data from pioneer salesmen on market size, product applications, rates of product acceptability, competitor activities, etc., resulted from adopting a division of sales force activities between pioneer selling and maintenance selling. The maintenance salesman, whose product was already designed and made could concentrate on feeding back knowledge on customers' problems and modes of operation. For 10 per cent of the companies re-structuring their sales forces in accordance with such principles, it was precisely the need for relevant, useful intelligence from the market-place that prompted the changes. It has to be recorded that in pursuing this primary intention companies have been the recipients of much more beneficial marketing intelligence than was received prior to the structural changes.

New Accounts Sales Forces

This same intention—to increase feedback—was also noticeable in companies adopting other organisation patterns. Companies had sales forces whose prime function was to increase penetration within existing customers, while leaving other salesmen to seek further penetration in new accounts. Behind this structure lies the view that gaining ground at the new account location requires more ingenuity, patience, persistence, flexibility and enthusiasm than is needed to obtain a little more business out of regular customers. In some instances, salesmen tend to approach new customers in the same way as they do their established customers. Others avoid "prospecting" because they know they are not reasonable at it and see it at the expense of "servicing" time where there is a reasonable hope of more orders. Palmer[6] has noted that this type of "new accounts" sales force is feasible for a large company with many end-users and usually a continuous turnover of the better and more prestigious customers. Those customers, of course, have to be replaced quicker than they drop out if the long-term welfare of the company is to be assured, and to ensure it the solicitation of the best prospects might better be planned and deliberate, and not left in competition with servicing. Thus, a group of specialist salesmen can answer the need by exploring new account possibilities. Using a new acount sales force, companies found that much more feedback was contributed about prospects' activities and operations than had been the case when their sales forces were organised in generalised ways. The new account salesmen seemed to focus more attention on the exploration of a prospect's needs than did salesmen operating within a fixed, geographic territory looking after a diverse range of established and new customers. The constant and heavy pressure on the salesman to acquire new business caused him to take a more critical look at the reasoning behind the purchase of a product by a new customer. Much more intelligence about buyer behaviour was reported by new account salesmen. Such salesmen also proved more able than colleagues in other structures at estimating the proposals made by competitors and at analysing the crucial areas of proposals upon which the success of negotiations with prospects depended—see Robertson[7] who has drawn attention to the particular value of sales force feedback on competitive activities within this pattern of organisation. Companies re-structuring their sales organisations in order to create a new account sales force were not only recognising the principle that a different type of personality was needed to explore potential prospects, but also recognising the fact that feedback—about the buying behaviour and activities of the prospects together with an evaluation of competitor proposals submitted—could be greatly improved.

Product Specialisation Sales Teams
Other companies endeavouring to increase the specialisation of their sales forces have found a need to concentrate on making salesmen specialists in particular products. Traditionally, an industrial salesman has had to be acquainted with all his company's products, but it is being recognised that where products differ in type of technology this may require a width of knowledge which is not obtainable at a cost proportionate to the potential business. Companies were seen specialising salesmen by product in circumstances where the products marketed were diverse, requiring different types of technical knowledge, and also where the key members of the decision-making unit in the prospect companies were different from one category of product to another. This type of organisation was commonplace throughout all the various categories of company investigated—originating from the position that in many firms different factories manufactured different products—and there had been the tendency to create distinct sales forces for each product category, without serious review of the alternatives. Often the roots of such an organisational pattern were historic—firms with independent sales teams have merged, but the past selling arrangements have continued in existence. The structure meant that one buying company would have maybe two or more salesmen for the same firm calling—thus causing customers to become irritated, with consequent waste of time and effort to both parties. Rohan[8] has discussed the problems of acquiring feedback from salesmen operating in such circumstances. However, the research has demonstrated that salesmen operating within this specialised role brought back to their companies a beneficial feedback concerning product problems; product price policies; strategies to be adopted in marketing the product; and developments in the product range. However, in companies re-structuring their salesmen into specialised product forces I did not detect that the prime intention of such changes was to increase the

quality and quantity of feedback from the market-place (in direct contrast to the intentions observed in some companies making the structural changes mentioned earlier). The primary reason for having product sales forces was the undoubtedly correct belief that the salesman became an expert on his product, and, more importantly, had less need of technical support from other corporate functions. Companies in establishing these specialised forces, therefore, tended to be looking for substantial reductions in the cost of back-up services provided to salesmen rather than for specific improvements in feedback of information.

Market-Centred Sales Forces

Marketing managers are gradually becoming aware that absence of specialisation amongst their salesmen will detract from selling effectiveness, because the salesman will lack the detailed knowledge to support his selling claim. Another approach used by companies to deal with this problem has been to base the organisation of the sales force around the industries which they serve. Hanan[9] has pointed to the effectiveness of this approach in giving the salesman a knowledge in depth of the industry he serves. Within this market specialisation approach each salesman is assigned an industry or group of industries, rather than a product or a region, and so acts as a market manager. A market is a group of customer needs—thus a scientific instruments firm was observed to focus around such areas as leisure industries, laboratory facilities and research establishments, while an engine manufacturing firm focused around such areas as lorry manufacturers, generator manufacturers and shipbuilding companies. The salesman has an opportunity to become exceptionally well informed on factors of derived demand, impending technological developments and product applications. These are the areas where such salesmen generated appropriate feedback for future planning purposes.

Development of market-centred sales forces was observed in three particular situations. Firstly, in those companies where new product famine had hampered the product development function—in such an instance, companies were adopting this market specialisation approach for their sales forces in order to obtain feedback on the extent to which the current product range could be supplemented by new and modified products. Secondly, such sales forces were being created in companies desiring either to diversify into high margin services or to concentrate on the marketing of systems—feedback was required on the potential size of market segments that might take the services and systems. Thirdly, instances of this approach were also observed in companies where a change in marketing strategy was contemplated to highlight the financial benefits of customer profit improvement—detailed sales force feedback was needed upon the customers' methods of operation and weaknesses in usage of the purchased product. These companies referred to above were re-structuring their sales forces as a result of particular needs—it was, however, recognised that actions arising from these needs could not be evaluated without improved market-place feedback.

Conclusion

The research has noted how companies are continually reviewing the need to specialise further their sales teams against a background of change affecting the technological parameters of existing product ranges. The investigations reveal that companies are questioning whether their current sales force organisations are suitable given the rapidly-changing nature of the market-place. Most recent developments in industrial sales force organisation have flowed from the necessity for organising in the face of a quickening rate of innovation. Where innovation is most rapid the problem of maintaining a concerted marketing plan strains sales management to the limits. It is noticeable that when a change in the organisation of the sales force is made more time is being allocated for salesmen to acquire intelligence helpful to the marketing planning effort. Under the traditional geographical and product allocation of duties salesmen have limited opportunities to report intelligence. With the creation of the new account sales forces, pioneer sales forces, etc., there is greater scope for the salesmen to generate intelligence. Within the new sales force structures the customer-contact strategy requires that the salesman asks more questions about his prospects' needs at the time of his calls, and about determining factors which influence these needs. He needs to ask the questions for "self-use" purposes—the answers to the "self-use" questions are, however, valuable as an input to his own company's future plans.

Moss[1], Robertson[10], Wotruba and Mangone[11] have testified that marketing managers are becoming aware of the need to develop reporting systems to bring intelligence from the market-place via their increasingly specialised salesmen. Methods of doing business have radically altered in the past decade, and the ways of organising sales forces have to be seen in this context. Many sales force structures have evolved over time and changes are often made on an *ad hoc* basis in response to particular situations. However, as more and more companies begin to realise what particular types of information they need in order to develop effective future plans, one is seeing that sales forces are being re-structured with the specific objective of increasing the flow of intelligence from the market-place.

References
1. Moss, C. D., "Industrial Salesmen as a Source of Marketing Intelligence", *European Journal of Marketing*, Vol. 13 No. 3, 1979.
2. Hardy, L. W., "The Sales Force—Structures and Organisation", *European Journal of Marketing*, Vol. 12 No. 6, 1978.
3. Fisher, L., *Industrial Marketing*, Business Books Ltd., 1976.
4. Lidstone, J. and Melkman, A., "Make Marketing Plans for Major Customers", *Marketing*, October 1977.
5. Smackey, B. M., "A Profit Emphasis for Improving Sales Force Productivity", *Industrial Marketing Management*, Vol. 6 No. 2, 1977.
6. Palmer, O. W., *Management Structures in Modern Marketing Systems*, unpublished study, 1971.
7. Robertson, D. H., "Sales Force Feedback on Competitive Activities", *Journal of Marketing*, No. 38, 1974.
8. Rohan, T. M., "Getting and Using Good Feedback from Salesmen", *Industry Week*, 19 January, 1976.
9. Hanan, M., "Reorganise your company around its Markets", *Harvard Business Review*, November/December, 1974.
10. Robertson, D. H., "Management Can Make Better Use of Feedback from Sales Force in Marketing Plans", *Industrial Marketing*, March, 1975.
11. Wotruba, T. R. and Mangone. R., "More Effective Sales Force Reporting", *Industrial Marketing Management*, No. 8, 1979.

15. Sales Strategies for the On-Licence Trade

by Peter S. Oxford

Distribution and product mix in the on-licence sector is not necessarily the consequence of consumer demand but the result of the activities of the owners and controllers of the distribution channels who need sales strategies to make their products and services attractive to the distribution channels.

Introduction and Background

In recent years there have been significant changes in the structure of alcoholic drinks distribution. These are a consequence of changing lifestyles, economic conditions and a more flexible approach towards granting retail licences. The overall effect has been a shift from drinking in pubs to drinking at home.

The change in drinking habits is evidenced by a dramatic increase in wine consumption — 65 per cent through the off-licence sector. The increase in wine consumption has coincided with a decline in beer sales and in the consumers' use of the public house.

Another influencing factor is the European Economic Commission's intervention in the form of Regulation 84/83, which released 45,000 tenant publicans from the "tie" system. The tie was an almost feudal agreement whereby the brewer landlord stipulated what products the tenant sold and where he purchased them. The on-licence sector is composed of 124,000 pubs, clubs, hotels and restaurants attracting $13.8 billion of consumer spending. Pubs accounted for 75 per cent of turnover in the on-licence sector in 1983. The brewers own 61 per cent of all pubs.

Brewers with a heavy dependence on beer sales and a major involvement in pub ownership will be faced with grave economic problems if current trends continue. The brewers have been slow to react but are embarking on an investment programme to win back custom for the pub[1].

Brewers who act as wine and spirit brand owners through their subsidiaries are competitors of IDV (UK) Ltd. Unlike the brewers, IDV (UK) does not own retail outlets in the on-licence sector. Watneys and Berni are associated companies of Grand Metropolitan but the trading relationship is as the free market. The bulk of IDV (UK) sales to the pubs has been the result of reciprocal trading arrangements.

It is a view that, as a consequence of reciprocal trading, the tie system and the growth opportunities in the off-licence sector, marketers have not had to pay very much attention to distribution channels to the on-licence sector. Marketing skills, therefore, have been devoted to brand building through the off-licence sector. In the years 1972-1983 the greatest area of growth (63 per cent), was in grocery supermarkets. The power of the supermarket chains in the marketplace manifests itself in the growth of private labels and in pricing. In some instances, volumes are sufficient for retailers such as Sainsbury, Marks and Spencer and the Co-op to deal directly with their sources. This accounts for Sainsbury and Victoria Wine being the largest importers of wines into the UK.

Supermarkets, as well as cash-and-carry groups, are able to flex their buying muscle especially during such peak seasons as Christmas time. At the peak demand time the retailers sell selected brands at a loss, an activity which seldom benefits the brand owner.

The brewers, for their part, are determined to lure consumers back to the pub. The releasing of the tie is of little help, though, because the tenant publican is exposed to a free trade environment for the first time. This combination of market activities suggests that the time has come for brand owners and marketers to consider the potential and the functions of the on-licence trade.

Can Sales Strategies Solve a Marketing Problem?
Fundamentally, there are two approaches to marketing: product marketing and trade marketing. Product marketing is primarily concerned with product-consumer relationships, while trade marketing addresses the problem of distribution.

Both premises encompass the marketing mix of product, place, promotion and price. The difference is the weighting given to the individual parts. Product marketing concentrates on consumer needs and awareness while trade marketing is concerned with the marketplace as well as consumer needs[2]. What the manufacturer must do, therefore, is to cultivate the development of his marketing policy through the trade by equal attention both to the needs of the consumer and the needs of the distributive trade.

An extension of trade marketing is channel management in which case the bias is towards the distribution route. Channel management is more operational than conventional marketing or brand management and could be designated the task of sales management[3].

The channel manager is aware of the dynamics of the distribution channel and, by careful monitoring, can anticipate market changes. This sounds a defensive or reactive posture and may be more applicable to sales management. The marketer's proactive approach is to question the performance criteria of the distribution channel[4]. He may do this by posing such questions as:

— What products are sold in the distribution outlet?
— What products could be sold in the distribution outlet?
— What must the company do to sell through this distribution outlet?

Sales strategies are the result of market appreciations with a trade marketing and channel management approach. The appreciation will analyse the functions of the various distribution channels, identify channels that can best serve the product and recommend how they can best be motivated to co-operate and work for the product.

The sales strategies are positive directions to the whole organisation as to how, where and at what cost particular products get to particular consumers. Products demand different requirements of the distributer or retailer. A strategic approach identifies channels that are cost-effective in getting products to target consumers.

IDV (UK) will have sales strategies for each brand and for each sales company as IDV (UK) do not own distribution outlets in the on-licence trade. The sales companies must plan how they can make their service as well as their product acceptable to the customer.

An immediate problem for IDV (UK) is not the product-consumer relationship but the distribution channel-consumer relationship. The consumer has a high awareness of IDV brands as evidenced by purchase levels through the off-licence sector. Generally, sales have increased through the "off sector" at the expense of the "on sector".

The significant growth of wine through grocery supermarkets in comparison to the on-licence sector is, in part, the consequence of protective policies by the brewers. The supermarkets, never slow to seize an opportunity, have sold wine at competitive prices direct to the consumer. The concern is for beer and maintaining a unit price for drink. The main fear of the brewer is a consumer shift to a product of lower value than beer. If the wine producers and shippers want to make the product available through the pub, the onus is on them to make it an attractive proposition to the brewer.

IDV (UK)'s record suggests that its strategies have been successful but changes in control and attitudes of the distribution channels warrant a change of emphasis. The opportunities are for wine in the on-licence sector; the threat is that brewers may become more involved in wine. Wine is consumed at home and with meals but is only now beginning to make inroads into the pub.

Historically, the brewers have resisted the move to wine to protect their beer interests; this attitude is changing. The brewer will want the profit from wine which is a single margin commodity.

The On-Licence Trade

There are five main categories of operating licence for the distribution and sale of alcoholic drink.

(1) *Full on-licence:* authorised to sell alcohol for consumption on or off the premises. Pubs and many hotels fall into this category.

(2) *Restricted on-licence:* (a) a "restaurant licence" for the sale of alcohol for consumption on the premises by customers paying for a meal; (b) a "residential licence" is where alcohol can only be sold to residents and their guests.

(3) *Registered clubs:* a licence to run a non-profit club normally organised by an elected body.

(4) *Off-licence:* a licence to sell alcohol.

This article is concerned with the on-licence sector which consists of full on-licensed, restricted, licensed and registered clubs.

Table I. Structure of Licensed Trade in England and Wales (000's)

	1962	1977	1980	1983
Full on-licence	68.0	65.5	67.1	96.1
Restricted	2.8	16.7	20.6	23.7
Licensed club	1.1	2.9	2.1	3.3
Registered club	21.5	25.8	26.9	27.2
Off-licence	24.6	33.8	37.2	40.9
Total	118.0	144.7	153.9	164.2

Source: Home Office.

The increase in the number of on-licensed premises is not reflected in consumer expenditure statistics.

Table II. Customer Expenditure on Alcohol, 1980 Prices (£ million)

	All alcoholic drinks		Alcoholic drinks other than beer	
	Off-licence	On-licence	Off-licence	On-licence
1980	2,616	7,455	1,925	2,561
1981	2,697	7,132	1,948	2,529
1982	2,707	6,870	1,934	2,452
1983e	2,955	7,000	2,000	2,512

Source: Central Statistics Office/Euromonitor.

e = estimated.

In 1983, the share of the on-trade in volume terms was 85 per cent compared to 75 per cent of value. This is largely explained by the fact that there is much less difference in the price of beer between off-licences and on-licences. In on-licences, beer consititutes a greater value than wines and spirits.

The on-licence trade accounts for 89 per cent of beer sales, 60 per cent of cider sales, 46 per cent of spirit sales, 21 per cent of fortified wine and 35 per cent of wine according to returns for 1983. Estimating the value of individual drinks markets is difficult because of the wide range of mark-up practised in the on-trade. The value figures in Table III are calculated on the basis of the volume figures using an average price per litre[5].

Table III. Liquor Sales by Licence Type 1983 Exposed as Percentage of Total

	Volume			Retail value		
	Total (MC)	% of total On	Off	Sales £M	% of total On	Off
Cider	300.0	60	40	418	76	24
Beer	6,224.0	89	11	6,846	89	11
Spirits	227.2	46	54	3,558	66	34
Fortified wine	153.0	21	79	760	39	61
Table wine	351.0	35	65	1,666	53	47
Sparkling wine	21.8	37	63	208	65	35
Total	7,277.0	82	18	13,456	75	25

Source: *Retail Business.*

It is difficult to isolate hotels from licensing data because a number of hotels have full licences and are locked in with pubs in government statistics. Consequently, the alcoholic drinks trade through the hotel segment is not well documented. Many brewers own hotels and these are often included in the returns for their estates.

Over 90 per cent of the on-licence premises are pubs producing over 95 per cent of the liquor turnover. The high figure is due to the comparatively low volume of beer going through hotels where the bias is towards wine.

Distribution Channels: Pub Ownership/Club Loans

The pubs and clubs combine to make the most important segment of the on-licence trade in terms of volume of trade, value and in number of outlets.

The number of on-licence premises has shown a steady increase since 1946 but the pub sector has declined from 80,000 to 77,000 in 1984. The increase is the result of growth in clubs and restricted licences for restaurants and small hotels.

Table IV. On-Licensed Premises, England and Wales

	1962	1977	1980	1983
Full on-licence	68.0	65.5	67.1	69.1
Clubs	22.6	28.7	29.0	30.5
Restricted	2.8	16.7	20.6	23.7

Source: Home Office.

In formulating a strategy, it is important to appreciate the influence of the brewers who collectively own 61 per cent of the full on-licence premises.

Table V. Ownership of Full On-Licences

	1976	1978	1980	1982
Brewery-owned as % of total UK on-licences	69.0	66.6	64.1	61.4
No. of brewery-owned (000s)	51.2	50.1	48.9	47.8
Non-brewery-owned (000s)	23.1	25.1	27.5	30.0

Source: Brewers' Society/Key Note Publication.

The decrease in brewery ownership has been, in part, the result of policies to dispose of uneconomic units. Population movement has closed premises in rural areas and in redeveloped urban areas planning has effectively reduced the number of pubs. High-rise developments resulted in an increase in population density within a pub's catchment area.

Historically, the brewers have always owned the majority of pubs, but the 1960s saw a polarisation of the brewing industry. Takeovers and mergers resulted in regional brewers closing down because production became centralised. The situation by 1984 was that 34,000 outlets were owned by six major brewing organisations known collectively as the "big six".

Table VI. Pub Ownership by Major Brewer

Brewer	Tenancies	Managed	Total
Bass	5,071	2,327	7,398
Allied-Lyons	5,200	1,800	7,000
Whitbread	4,806	1,754	6,560
Grand Metropolitan (Watneys)	4,806	1,754	6,560
Courage Imp.	3,596	1,927	5,523
Scottish and Newcastle	627	757	1,384
Total	23,900	10,015	33,915

Source: Statistics MR/Wood Mackenzie.

In addition to the "big six", 38 regional brewers own 11,978 pubs and small brewers another 1,500 giving a total of 47,393 in brewery ownership.

Managed outlets are owned by the brewer and run by salaried employees of the brewer. The brewer has complete control over stocking policies and retail prices.

Tenanted outlets are owned by the brewer and the property is leased to the tenant. A condition of the tenancy is that the tenant purchases his alcoholic and non-alcoholic drink from the brewer at a wholesale price set by the brewer. EEC Regulation 84/83, introduced in January 1984, decreed that tenants would no longer be obliged to purchase non-beer products from the brewer. Currently the bulk of tenants remain "tied" because existing agreements are being allowed to remain in force until January 1989.

The full effect of the EEC regulation will be covered in a later section. What has to be appreciated is the position of the brewers as owners of distribution channels. Not only have they controlled the price into the tenanted estates but also the retail price to the consumer. Through their manager estates the brewers have set the consumer price.

Distribution for spirit products has been further enhanced through reciprocal arrangements between the brand owners. IDV has taken advantage of such arrangements through W. & A. Gilbey and Peter Dominic, the wholesale and retail sales companies within IDV. The brewers give favoured status for such brands as Smirnoff, Gilbey's Gin and Hennessy in their outlets in return for IDV's selling the brewers' brands through W. & A. Gilbey and Peter Dominic.

The practice of reciprocal trading will become less and less prevalent as the tie for wines and spirits weakens with the implementation of EEC Regulation 84/83.

In addition to their own estates, the brewers have major investments in free trade outlets. In the main, these are clubs and pubs which are, in effect, tied to the brewer. In exchange for an agreement to purchase agreed volumes of the brewer's beer over a designated period, the licensee is offered a low interest loan. There is evidence that some brewers include wine and spirits in the agreement. According to one estimate, the brewers have £400 million out on loan[5].

Ironically, it is the clubs that have experienced growth over the years and it is clubs that take up the greatest share of the brewery loans. The brewers have been competing with each other to absorb surplus beer capacity and, in addition to loans, have discounted above the rate for the tenanted estates.

The success of the club can be attributed to setting its prices lower than those of the publican. Clubs are non-profit-making and, as a result, can not only be competitive in pricing but can re-invest profit into improving accommodation and facilities.

Table VII. Licensed Clubs — England and Wales

	1962	1971	1980	1983
Full on-licence	68.0	64.1	67.1	69.1
Licensed clubs	1.2	2.6	2.1	3.4
Registered clubs	21.4	24.0	26.9	27.2
Clubs as % of full licences	33	41	43	44

Source: Home Office.

With their all-male membership, clubs have historically been beer-orientated. Increasingly, however, women are being allowed to attend functions and, in some instances, family membership is permitted. This, plus the move away from beer, will increase the off-take of wines and spirits. Currently, loan agreements incorporating wines and spirits are in the minority, but escalation is a possibility.

If the brewers lose wine and spirit volume from tenants free from the tie, the brewers will be tempted to turn to the clubs for their growing wine and spirit trade. Such a strategy would further restrict the opportunites for the independent wholesaler such as W. & A. Gilbey and, in turn, affect IDV brand sales in a lucrative segment.

Distribution Channels: Hotels and Restaurants

While the hotel business is an important part of the huge catering industry, alcoholic drink is a small proportion of the total turnover. The growth in this segment has come from an increase in the number of small hotels and restaurants. Neither group offers an opportunity for the national wine and spirit supplier.

The target market must be premises with over 50 bedrooms. Generally, the facilities will boast more than one bar and restaurant. According to the Data Research Group, 1,259 hotels fall into this category while 8,632 have between ten and 50 rooms.

A listing by the English Tourist Board by region can be found as Appendix 1. The majority of the hotels are in London and the south-east, while a high percentage of those in the south-west are seasonal.

The secondary target group are those forming consortia. Hotels forming consortia are usually independently owned and look to the consortia for marketing support and nation-wide exposure.

Hotels and restaurants are notorious for looking to the supplier for same-day service. Few restaurants or hotels have large cellar areas and need the assurance of a local supplier if only to cover emergiencies. One hotel manager admitted that, on reviewing his purchasing records, the majority of purchases had been made at the emergency source. It had not been planned that way and the centrally negotiated prices were competitive.

IDV Distribution supports W. & A. Gilbey and Morgan Furze in this segment. The distribution service centres on four stock-holding depots strategically placed up the backbone of the UK. Such a network serves the IDV (UK) agency customers needing central delivery in bulk. Selling the notion that such a system is not so big and distant and that it can meet the individual needs of the local pub or restaurant is an additional task for the W. & A. Gilbey sales force.

Government Intervention: Release of the Tie and the Effect on Distribution

EEC Regulation 84/83 has had an enormous impact on the market. The European Commission has struck at the heart of a system dating back centuries and has significantly changed the relationship between landlord and tenant.

The Commission accepted the principle of a tie agreement and has allowed it to remain for draught beers. The concern was the lack of an element of fair trading with non-beer products. The physical distribution and keeping characteristics of draught beer are reasons enough for a tie, but draught beer is unique to the brewery and can only be purchased from that source.

Bottled and canned products such as spirits can be bought from many sources and the tenant should be free to buy these from wherever he chooses. The regulation lays down rules difficult to police. All products subject to a tie must be listed individually. Secondly, the tenant can purchase outside the tie should the brewer not be able to supply within a "reasonable time" or if the tenant can prove he can purchase on more "beneficial terms" elsewhere.

The brewers' problem is the time likely to be spent in arbitration and what constitutes a better deal. The brewers see a loss of profit and control and spent a torrid

1984 considering their sales strategies and negotiating new agreement. They have until January 1989 to complete the negotiation of new tenancy agreements.

Watneys was the first to react and stole a march on other brewers by freeing all its tenants from the tie. The strategy was to sell the tie by increasing rents to compensate for the loss of profit. The immediate effect was to erode the customer base of W. & A. Gilbey which was nominated as a supplier in the tie agreements. Some of the tenants will become customers of Peter Dominic, the retail arm of IDV, and in many ways will be better served. The brand business through the Watney-tenanted estates is at risk. Having rejected W. & A. Gilbey and Peter Dominic, the tenant will use the cash-and-carry and not all IDV brands have sufficient distribution to ensure the business is not lost.

The small brewers will consider turning their estates over to management or to complete freedom from the tie. This will result in the closing of their respective wine and spirit departments. Those brewers with managed estates will consider entering agreements with national wholesalers such as W. & A. Gilbey whereby the latter services the brewer with its wine and spirit needs. In all, this will mean a distribution channel to 11,000 outlets.

The immediate reaction in distribution will be an increase in the cash-and-carry sector, where keen prices on a limited range of leading spirit brands will be the magnet. This will particularly suit the small pub, but the larger outlets and multiples will need the range of services a national wholesaler can give.

After the cash-and-carry, the tenant is most likely to consider the local wholesaler. Freed from one major organisation, he is likely to believe all large organisations are the same and, understandably, he may want to move away from any organisation that reminds him of his landlord.

The Licensing Laws and Flexi Hours

The present law, as it affects England and Wales, is contained in the Licensing Act, 1964; Scotland introduced new legislation in 1976. The main concern is opening hours, which vary from one licensing authority to another and can vary by type of licence.

The government is under pressure from the Flexi Hours Action Group (FLAG) to review the licensing laws in accordance with the recommendations of the Errol Report, 1972. FLAG is an action group made up of brewers, Tourist Board, publicans and hoteliers. In opposition to FLAG is Action on Alcohol Abuse (AAA), consisting of religious, temperance and health groups.

The current move is towards less restrictive licensing regulations which would allow publicans to choose the hours of opening within a fourteen-hour day. The debate centres on whether such a change will result in an increase in alcohol abuse. When Scottish legislation in 1976 extended pub opening hours, initial reports claimed that convictions from drunkenness declined in Scotland and the general attitude of the Scottish public favoured the new licensing hours[7].

Consumer Trends, Lifestyles and Leisure

Since the 1950s young people have been a major target market for the drinks trade. Vodka, lager and the new soft spirit products owe their growth to an early acceptance by this group. Alcohol retains a high priority in spending particularly in the 18-24 age group. Older groups show a higher concern for health, drinking and driving laws and are constrained by mortgages and family responsibilities.

Wood Mackenzie (May 1984), in their analysis of trends, argue that, in spite of unemployment, spending on alcohol remains at a high level of discretionary spending. The younger age groups visit the pub more frequently than older age groups. Trendy pubs and wine bars are aimed to meet the fashion-conscious needs of the younger drinker.

Increased leisure time and a better standard of living led to an increase in dining out during the 1960s and 1970s. The promise of the 1970s, however, has not been realised in the 1980s. Stainland Hall (*Survey and Forecasts to 1988*) and Mintel (*British Lifestyle,* April 1984) confirm a decline in dining out. Public opinion tends to differ. The confusion is caused by the growth in fast food and take-away establishments in particular; there is a tendency to confuse meals not prepared at home and dining out. Appendix 2 is the result of research by BMRB and shows the demographic location of people who regularly eat out. It may not be a surprise to note that the section of the population AB and the south-east top the league.

There is an opinion in the trade that the consumer will tire of entertaining at home, become bored with the video and computer and will look to the pub for entertainment and social contact. The brewers certainly hope so.

The decline in manual intensified industries has led to a lessening in the demand for thirst-quenching beer. In addition, the increasing use of pubs by women has influenced the range of products stocked; vermouth and wine have prospered as a result of this trend.

The opportunities in the pub sector are in wine, now that the brewers are encouraging the publican to diversify into catering. Watneys has launched its own wine range to its pubs; low alcohol drinks are on-licence products and the new cooler type drink is aimed at the thirst-quenching market.

The on-licence sector is often the place where new tastes are acquired, especially for more expensive spirit-based products; the consumer is not likely to spend seven pounds on a bottle of spirit he has not tasted. There is growing evidence of the drinker being less conservative and being prepared to experiment with drink and the pub gives the consumer that opportunity.

The On-Licence Trade and IDV (UK)
The on-licence trade is in a state of turbulence and has gone through a period of decline. In truth, only the pub business has suffered and that mainly through the decline in beer. The brewers have not always used their power wisely and have been jolted into action by the European Commission and its ruling on the tie system.

There are opportunities for IDV (UK) and signs that the pub trade will survive. The consumers like the products, as evidenced by the off-licence trade. The problem is in making the products attractive to the distribution channels. An analysis of strengths, weaknesses, opportunities and threats will point the way to the sales strategies.

Strengths

(1) *Marketing orientation:* mission to market IDV-owned and agency brands — marketing led.

(2) *Brand portfolio:* arguably the best brand portfolio of a UK-based liquor organisation: Smirnoff, Croft, Piat, Malibu, Baileys, Hennessy, J & B, Gilbey's Gin — all have on-licence exposure to varying degrees.

(3) *Reputation for developing new brands:* Volari and St. Leger new brands have on-licence potential.

(4) *Four sales companies:* IDV (UK) Sales, W. & A. Gilbey, Morgan Furze, Peter Dominic, all operate in the on-licence sector.

(5) *National distribution service:* service offering trunking and local delivery supported by telesales and local order offices.

(6) *Not brewery-owned:* free to operate across the whole market without obligation through direct ownership to a national brewer.

Weaknesses

(1) *Images:* big company image not always accepted by the small independent business units that make up the on-licence sector.

(2) *Distribution:* linked to big company image. IDV must question the ability to meet the needs of wholesale customers who often need emergency strikes and small orders frequently.

(3) *Cash-and-carry trade:* brands such as Gilbey's and Hennessy do not have good cash-and-carry or off-licence distribution.

(4) *No control of distribution channel:* do not own on-licence outlets; much executive time spent on Grand Metropolitan Group synergy.

(5) *Wine in on-licence sector:* Piat d'Or the exception; IDV (UK) sales performances in wines through brewers negligible.

Opportunities

(1) *Market size:* huge market attracting £8.5 billion of consumer spending. Brewers making big investments at £1.2 billion.

(2) *New products;* need for drinks to compete with beer.

(3) *Consumer profile:* all social groups and ages use one segment of on-licence trade or other. Young people using pubs give IDV an opportunity to develop new products as this sector is prepared to experiment and acquire new tastes.

(4) *"Ons" versus "offs":* need for products which are unique to on-licence premises, especially wine and low alcohol beverages.

(5) *Wine:* consumer trend is moving towards wine. Growth is likely to accelerate as brewers recognise demand for wine.

(6) *Tenants free of tie:* freedom of tenants to purchase brands of choice through distributor of choice.

(7) *Flexi hours:* new legislation will encourage use of pub.

(8) *Small brewers wine and spirit divisions:* some small brewers will find it uneconomical to continue to operate wine and spirit divisions as their tenants are freed from tie; they will look elsewhere for support.

Threats

(1) *Brewery control:* big brewers are not going to give up control and will compete in free market to maintain volume and to compensate profit lost with tenant going free.

(2) *Brewery wine:* brewers becoming increasingly interested in growth potential of wine; e.g., Watneys own wine range.

(3) *Wine margins:* wine is single margin, a commodity with profit at the retail end.

(4) *Health and drinking and driving:* the pub trade may not recover because the consumer restricts his drinking to home to avoid drinking and driving.

Problems in Distribution and Wholesaling

As brand marketers, IDV (UK) need to have influence in the on-licence trade and, in such a competitive environment, must be committed. The conclusion is that IDV (UK) is in a good position to exploit its opportunities.

Each brand and sales company will devlop its own sales strategy and IDV (UK) strategy is important in setting the ground rules and allocating channel management responsibilities. The key objective is to develop brands. IDV (UK), therefore, must decide whether it needs to be involved in wholesaling. The strategy could be one of buying distribution and relying entirely on others for distribution. The main objection to such a measure is a loss of control over brand positioning in the market. A secondary objection is that many of the distributors are themselves brand owners and will always favour their own.

IDV (UK) Sales with its Brewery Support Team is the main vehicle for getting the brands to the brewers and the cash-and-carry trade. Peter Dominic, with 480 retail units, is respected as one of the leading specialist off-licence chains and an important component in the IDV mix. The companies under scrutiny are W. & A. Gilbey and Morgan Furze.

It can be argued that IDV does not need a level of involvement in the wholesale trade to warrant W. & A. Gilbey. Although contributing a profit, Gilbey's sales have seen a decline as its customer base is eroded by Watneys freeing its tenants from the tie.

If W. & A. Gilbey did not sell the other factored products IDV (UK) would lose some buying power which will affect Peter Dominic's ability to compete on price. To concentrate on brewery-owned pubs and cash-and-carry customers is to ignore the free trade operations.

Peter Dominic's greatest investment would be in convincing the trade that a high street retailer can wholesale. It is not a question of stock holding, credit or promotional support but whether the wholesale customer will be confident that the service will always be available. If forced to choose Peter Dominic would protect its retail custom. As a result, its wholesale customer profile would be the lower end of the market, consisting of the small pub and restaurant neither of which is likely to have a level of trade that justifies a national wholesaler.

Key areas which these strategies do not address are wine, national account business, the Grand Metropolitan Group business, hotels and restaurants It is difficult to see how strategies concentrating on IDV (UK) sales or Peter Dominic can accommodate the 14,000 W. & A. Gilbey and Morgan Furze customers who want the services of a wine and spirit wholesaler.

The on-licence sector is turbulent and a difficult market in which to operate. W. & A. Gilbey may well be the IDV company most at risk, but that is not to say that there are no long-term prospects[9].

The time an organisation needs sales strategies is when the environment becomes turbulent. The aim of solid organisational strategies is to plan a way through this turbulence and to be in a position to influence the market, or at least to capitalise on the opportunities it offers.

Sales Strategies for W. & A. Gilbey and Morgan Furze

W. & A. Gilbey is probably better placed than the competition to compete in the new free market. It is not likely to suffer any further erosion of its customer base by tenants being free of the tie. The opportunity is for growth competing for the tenants of brewers other than Watneys. The key objective of the strategies is to increase the quality of the customer profile and position W. & A. Gilbey away from the cash-and-carry trade.

The target market has two distinct segments: pubs and clubs, hotels and restaurants. W. & A. Gilbey are nation-wide and specialists in the former segment and will concentrate in this area. With regard to the hotel and restaurant trade, the UK can be divided into the south-east region and the remainder of the UK. Excluding the south-east, the hotel segment will be covered by a small, specialised sales team basically in support of the national account team. The target market will be national account business and major independent hotels.

Morgan Furze are London-based and specialists in servicing the hotel and restaurant trade. Morgan Furze should expand into the south-east of England with its current number of personnel.

Both companies will favour wines. This is particularly important as consumer tastes mature and move into generic and better quality wines where margins are higher.

The need for W. & A. Gilbey to have control of wine purchasing and the limitations in distribution to meet wholesale requirements in certain parts of the country were latterly discussed. Dependent on those two key service functions is the policy on press and trade relations.

Historically, neither company has invested in the trade press or exhibitions of functions, particularly in the hotel and catering trade. It is recommended that a two-year investment programme be undertaken to establish on-licence trade confidence in W. & A. Gilbey and Morgan Furze.

Summary of Recommendations

(1) There should be concentration on the free trade pub, club, hotel and restaurant segments and to maintain current off-trade business.

(2) IDV should increase its wine offering and also develop a range of services as wine shipper and supplier.

(3) A two-year programme should be implemented, actively promoting W. & A. Gilbey and Morgan Furze as wine and spirit merchants to target market segments. The programme will involve trade press, attendance at selected trade exhibitions, functions and education grants.

(4) W. &. A. Gilbey will look to improve the distribution service, where necessary, by joint distribution with regional brewers, acquiring local wholesalers or extending the emergency services of IDV Distribution.

(5) The key objective is to maintain the size of the customer base but to improve the quality by offering an efficient and reliable service.

References

1. "Brewing Industry will Invest £1.58 bil", *Financial Times,* 2 March, 1984, p. 8.
2. Lawrence, A., "The Management of Trade Marketing UK", pp. 1-33.
3. Piercy, N., "Departments Face up to the End of the Line", *Marketing Week,* 14 December 1984, pp. 39,40,46.
4. Michman, R. D., "Marketing Channel: A Strategic Planning Approach", *Managerial Planning,* November/December 1983, pp. 38-42.
5. "The Distribution of Alcoholic Drinks", *Retail Business,* Special report No 1. February 1985, pp. 22-23.
6. "EEC Talkback", *Licensee,* August 1984, p. 6.
7. White, I., "Comment: Time for Change", *Brewing Review,* Summer 1985, pp. 1-8.
8. Merier, R., "The Five-point Fight Back Strategy", *Marketing,* October 1984, p.7.
9. Davidson, "Management by SMURF", CMB Directors & Board, Spring 1984, p. 22.

**Appendix 1. Hotels in England and Wales by
ETB (English Tourist Board) Regions**

	ETB All hotels	Hotels over 10 bedrooms	Hotels over 50 bedrooms
Wales	1,207	764	62
South West	3,277	2,519	250
South	2,521	980	101
South East	1,795	425	68
Yorkshire/Humberside	1,563	646	86
North West	1,511	730	119
East Anglia	1,447	737	64
Heart of England	1,415	391	78
Cumbria	907	294	27
East Midlands	866	235	34
Northumbria	666	232	36
Thames & Chiltern	549	185	19
London	336	726	315
Totals	18,062	8,632	1,259

Source: English Tourist Board/Jordans/Data Research Group.

Appendix 2. Eating Out (% of Sample)

	%
Sex	
Men	16
Housewives	19
Working women	9
Age	
15—19	8
20—24	17
25—34	19
35—44	16
45—54	22
55—64	14
65+	17
Social groupings	
AB	32
C1	24
C2	13
D	9
E	9
Geographic locations	
London/South	23
Anglia/Midlands	12
Wales/South-West England	16
Yorkshire/North-East	11
Lancashire	14
Scotland	17

Source: BMRB/Mintel.

16. A Framework for the Use of Power

by Jack J. Kasulis and Robert E. Spekman

Marketing channel decisions are among the most difficult facing a firm. Primary among the factors contributing to the importance of these are the facts that:

- the outcome of channel decisions affects the long-term relationships with other channel members;
- the degree of co-ordination among the members of a marketing channel is likely to influence the competitive position of that system.

This article focuses on ways in which channel co-operation and co-ordination can be improved, and unnecessary dysfunctional conflict reduced.

Traditionally, marketing channels of distribution have been composed of loosely aligned members who behave rather autonomously [1]. In short, channel behaviour has traditionally been a consequence of the "rule of self interest". Each firm concentrates on its own activities without a great deal of regard for those of the other channel participants. Thus, other channel members are viewed as independent entities — as suppliers or markets for one's products — but not as partners in the distribution process. This orientation may be viewed as the "independent firm perspective".

Increasingly, many channel members have recognised the importance of others to their own success. Unwilling to have their performance determined by the behaviour of others in the channel, many have tried to co-ordinate channel activities. Co-ordination has been attempted through aggressive leadership (administered systems), legal means (contractual systems), and integration (corporate systems) [2]. A vast majority of sales today are obtained through such vertical marketing systems which include firms like: Kraftco, Corning, and Hallmark (administered); McDonalds, Holiday Inn, and Shell Oil (contractual); and Sears, Sherwin Williams, and Hart, Schaffner and Marx (corporate) [3].

From a managerial perspective, these vertical marketing systems are established in order to effect a degree of order and control over the cost and quality of the functions performed by various channel participants. The administered, contractual, and corporate approaches represent what may be viewed as the "systematic perspective". These approaches accept the notion that their system is in competition with other channel systems, not just other manufacturers, wholesalers, and retailers. Thus, a firm like Schwinn is not only in competition with other bicycle manufacturers, but also with Sears, Wards, and other retailers of bicycles. In essence, the success of Schwinn is a function of how competitive its *total* distribution system is in comparison to the Sears and Wards systems as well as the Raleigh and other manufacturer-led systems.

Stern has suggested examining the power relationships among firms as an approach to study channel behaviour [4]. Power is viewed here as one channel member getting another to do something he would not otherwise do [5]. Power is commonly used by firms who follow the "independent firm perspective" as well as the "systems perspective". Though power is common to both, there is a difference in thrust between the two. If acting from the "systems perspective", the power attempt is primarily designed to enhance the competitive posture of the channel system, and consequently may even strengthen channel bonds. In this instance, the exercise of power may be viewed positively. On the other hand, when acting from the "independent firm perspective", the exercise of power is designed to accomplish an objective of one channel member and does not necessarily result in the betterment of the channel system as a whole. The danger of this approach lies in one channel member pursuing self interests to such an extent that fellow channel members may be so adversely affected that the channel itself suffers. In this instance, the use of power has a negative connotation.

The purpose of this article is to provide a better understanding of power relationships in marketing channels so that the likelihood of positive outcomes is increased. This insight is important for both the systems and independent perspectives. Few firms are totally dedicated to the systems perspective. However, even if one is, improper execution of power in a channel of distribution can lead to unnecessary conflict, decreased co-operation, inefficiencies, and even to the termination of channel relationships. Even for those who are pursuing the independent channel perspective, a better understanding of power outcomes may help to avoid unnecessary adverse consequences.

It is imperative that the marketing manager fully appreciates the subtle, yet significant, aspects of this problem. To this end, a series of propositions are presented to serve as a framework for anticipating responses which may result from the exercise of power. It is the authors' premise that a deeper understanding of the power construct will enable the marketing manager better to administer the channel. That is, the ability of a firm to anticipate and/or predict the behaviour of other channel participants in response to its power attempts should serve to lessen the amount of uncertainty accompanying channel decisions.

Power in the Marketing Channel

Power is the vehicle by which the range of variability in channel behaviour is limited, and a measure of predictability and dependability is established. There have been two approaches to studying power in the channel of distribution. One set of researchers have dichotomised power into coercive and non-coercive sources [6]. While the parsimony of this approach is acknowledged, merely factoring power into two major components does not readily permit a full analysis of the many facets of the power construct. Moreover, it inhibits a more complete understanding of the varied responses which can accompany a power attempt. This rather simplistic approach leads to the predictable conclusion that coercive means create greater conflict in the channel and therefore should be avoided wherever possible. This orientation implicitly assumes that all non-coercive sources are the same, and ignores the more useful analysis of *what* non-coercive sources should be used.

Other researchers have investigated power dependent relationships by utilising a typology developed by French and Raven [7]. These social scientists have posited six bases of power — reward , coercive, legitimate, expert, referent, and informational. Table I presents definitions and examples of each of these power bases as adapted to a channel of distribution. The French and Raven typology is richer than the coercive/non-coercive approach in that it includes five non-coercive bases of power. Such an approach allows for a more detailed analysis of alternative non-coercive strategies available to a firm trying to exert control over the operations of the channel.

By definition, each of the bases of power is capable of inducing overt behaviour. Consequently, the power alternatives may appear on the surface to elicit equivalent responses. Thus, marketing managers frequently view the success of a power strategy in terms of a prompt, overt response to an influence attempt. The actual selection of one of the afore-mentioned power bases emerges partly from a perception that immediate action would follow, and partly from the personal preference or the distinctive competence of the influencing agent. However, this behaviour may only be considered a success in the sense of accomplishing a short-term objective, such as obtaining dealer participation in a particular promotional campaign. There often may be a lack of concern regarding other, less discernible, consequences which are equally as important to the influence agent. For instance, will there be enthusiastic support during the promotional campaign? Will this exercise of power adversely impact on the nature of the channel relationship itself?

"Power myopia" is quite common. For example, when service station games were prominent, many dealers became participants, but begrudgingly "played the game" to the detriment of its overall success in stimulating sales as well as in some cases even affecting the channel relationship itself. Thus it is important to be sensitive to all consequences associated with the use of power. It is particularly important that the influence agent be cognisant of, and alert to, the less overt outcomes of a power-based channel management strategy. In this way, he can more effectively execute powerbased marketing strategies.

Responses to Power
Of help in understanding the consequences of using power is a categorisation developed by Kelman [8]. Table II summarises Kelman's three general consequences of an influence attempt: compliance, identification, and internalisation. It is a basic tenet of this article that this schema enhances one's understanding of the consequences of the exercise of power. This increased understanding will assist a channel member better to anticipate the reaction of others, thereby reducing the probability of unintended adverse effects.

Table I. Definitions and Examples of Bases of Power

Bases of power	Definition	Examples
Reward	A's ability to mediate rewards to B	Providing financial incentives or support services such as: —Goodyear's ability to give allowances for returned tyres —McDonald's promotional support
Coercive	A's ability to punish B	Withholding important support or threatening termination of the relationship such as: —a franchisor terminating a contract with a franchisee —a retailer diminishing shelf space for products from a particular distributor
Legitimate	The perceived right of A to dictate to B Legal Legitimate-contractual agreement of A to dictate to B	Contractual requirements mandating behaviour such as: —Mobil requiring particular franchisees to stay open 24 hours —Sears requiring a manufacturer to conform to product specifications
	Traditional Legitimate-institutionalised behavior that becomes accepted role	Philosophical acceptance of channel roles such as: — Coors' right to establish temperature controls for its distributors to maintain beer quality —an oil company's prerogative of allowing only its oil display on the service isle
Expert	Superior knowledge or insight attributed to A by B	Acquiescence in suggestions because of unique expertise and trust such as: —a supermarket following merchandising suggestions made by the Procter and Gamble representative —a pharmacist following a drug wholesaler's stocking suggestions
Referent	B's desire to share the attractiveness of A	Seeking to share the image or reputation of another such as: —department store carrying Dior, Cardin, and Estée Lauder cosmetics to portray a fashion or prestige image —an automotive dealer carrying Pontiacs and a lesser known foreign car
Informational	A's ability to explicate information or contingencies not adequately considered by B	The ability to persuade others as to the merits of one's position such as: —a full line wholesaler offering a complete inventory management programme as a way or reducing a client's investment in inventory at the store level —a sales agent demonstrating the savings incurred by purchasing the same volume but in larger orders at a time

Table II. Consequences of an Influence Attempt

Consequences of the Use of Power	Conceptualisation	Operationalising
Compliance	B conforms to A's influence solely because B expects to achieve a favourable reaction from A	Short-lived, erratic response which is only enacted when B's behaviour is monitored by A
Identification	B conforms to A's influence because B wishes to establish or maintain a desired association with A	A prolonged, fairly predictable response limited to B's source of identification with A
Internalisation	B comforms to A's influence because A's demands are consistent with B's values	Long-lasting co-operation based upon similar perspectives

Kelman's schema concentrates on the cognitive determinants of a response rather than focusing on the response itself. By understanding these *causal factors,* a more complete understanding of all the ramifications occurs [9].

Cognitive involvement may be viewed as lying along a continuum ranging from compliance to internalisation. If a channel member attributes his response to the incentive alone, this action typifies compliant behaviour. If a channel member behaves primarily to maintain an association with another, this represents identification-related behaviour. If a channel member views the cause of his action as stemming from an agreement on values and goals among the channel participants, this exemplifies internalised behaviour. A central point of this article is that the source to which behaviour is attributed is likely to vary across the bases of power. Thus, the consequences of an influence attempt will tend to be associated with a particular power base.

Table III lists three propositions and seven sub-propositions which tie the bases of power to Kelman's outcomes. It should be emphasised that the connection is in probabilistic terms. For example, coercive behaviour is *more likely* to result in compliance than in identification or internalisation. Furthermore, the causal determinants result from a variety of factors including other power attempts, industry practice, the availability of alternative channels, etc. Any one instance of coercion does not necessarily lead to compliance when the relationship has traditionally been one based on internalised values. Rather, successive uses of coercion will ultimately move one from internalisation to compliance. In fact, previous behaviour may even colour the perceptions of the type of influence used.

Compliance

Much channel behaviour is closely tied to the existence of an inducement, the threat of the withdrawal of an incentive, or another form of sanction. However, the exercise of power along these lines can be quite costly both in terms of the size of the incentive necessary to gain compliance and the constant surveillance required to monitor the level of co-operation. Further, the withdrawal of either the incentive, or the surveillance, is likely to result in reversion to the previous behaviour. In the service station example, the dealers who are unwilling participants in the oil company games were always the ones who were "inadvertently" out of game coupons until the oil company representative arrived.

The problem with compliant-related behaviour is further exemplified by the diminishing utility of an inducement. Over time an inducement loses its potency. For example, a dairy may sell cottage cheese in re-usable storage containers for those grocers who prominently display their brand. The increased sales from the premium are satisfying to both the retailer and dairy. However, the increased sales may become the standard for the grocer's next period sales while the novelty of the premium for the consumer may be wearing off over time. Thus, the dairy has to incur the additional costs of developing another incentive to ensure its prominent display by the grocer in the long run. This is further complicated when expected increased sales do not occur, thereby making subsequent influence attempts (increased rewards) less credible.

Proposition 1 in Table III indicates that coercive, reward, and legal legitimate power are most likely to foster compliant-related behaviour. The perception of external control is most apparent here. In response to coercion or rewards, a channel member is likely to perceive that behaviour is prescribed for him by the incentives of obtaining rewards or avoiding punishment. Similarly, in the case of legal legitimate power, the less powerful channel member is apt to perceive that aspects of his behaviour are mandated by a legal document. Thus, the channel member is likely to attribute his behaviour to external factors and not to a belief that he should, regardless of the incentive or sanction, perform as desired. As a result, there is a greater probability that the induced compliant-related behaviour will revert to its previous pattern as soon as the inducements are removed, the surveillance is slackened, or the legal constraints are lifted.

Each of three power bases is likely to result in a different level of co-operation among the channel participants. Of the three, coercion is the least productive. Coercion is most notable for (1) its inability to mollify any underlying source of conflict in the channel [10]; (2) its tendency to enlarge a conflict [11]; and (3) its ability to hasten an abandonment of a channel relationship [12]. In each of these instances, coercive power is expected to result in counterproductive behaviour, including only short-term compliance.

Though the use of reward power is more appealing to the recipient, this power strategy is limiting since channel members will probably attribute their behaviour to the incentive and not to the innate desirability of the behaviour. Sales promotion

Table III. Proposition Linking the Bases of Power with Kelman's Consequences of an Influence Attempt

Proposition 1: The use of *coercive, reward,* or *legal legitimate* power
by a dominant channel member will probably foster *compliance*
by other channel members.
(1a) Of the compliance-related bases of power,
    coercive power will tend to result in
    the lowest level of long-run co-operation.
(1b) Of the compliance-related bases of power,
    reward power will tend to result in
    a more moderate level of long-run co-operation.
(1c) Of the compliance-related bases of power,
    legal legitimate power will tend to
    result in the highest level of long-run co-operation.

Proposition 2: The use of *referent* or *expert* power by a dominant
channel member will probably foster *identification*
by other channel members.
(2a) Of the identification-related bases of power,
    referent power will tend to result in a lower
    level of long-run co-operation among the channel
    members.
(2b) Of the identification-related bases of power
    expert power will tend to result in a higher,
    level of long-run co-operation among the
    channel members.

Proposition 3: The use of *traditional legitimate* or *informational* power by a
dominant channel member will probably
foster *internalisation* by the other channel members.
(3a) Of the internalisation-related bases of power,
    traditional legitimate power will tend to result
    in the lower level of long-run co-operation.
(3b) Of the internalisation-related bases of power,
    informational power will tend to result in the
    higher of long-run co-operation.

tools aimed at the retail trade are an excellent example of the outcome of using reward powers. Once the deal period is over, the end cap displays are usually removed and the co-operative advertising is frequently halted. The retailer simply does not share the same long-term objectives with the manufacturer as well as other manufacturers offering lucrative sales promotion programmes. While reward power is more apt to lead to increased co-operation since the channel recipient finds the relationship pleasing, it can be seen that the result is only short-run complicity with little channel commitment.

Of these three power bases, legal legitimate power has the greatest probability of long-run co-operation. Though this channel relationship may not be based on shared values, it is dependent on the legal rights and obligations of the channel participants. The co-operation, however, may be confined only to the text of the contract. Conflict quickly arises when one member violates the contract or oversteps its basic tenets. The recent wave of franchisee dissatisfaction in the US stemming from the franchiser's attempt to enforced system constraints which lie outside of what the franchisee perceives to be the legal bounds of their relationship is illustrative [13].

Identification

In comparison with compliance, identification-related behaviour is more predictable and dependable. There is a degree of shared values which stems from the desire of one channel member to associated with another or by one channel member's use of another as a frame of reference. However, the range of goal compatibility may be rather narrowly defined and somewhat limited in scope. That is, the further removed an activity is from the source of the identification, the less likely the channel member will perform as prescribed. For example, a retailer may desire to identify with a manufacturer because the manufacturer is recognised as the innovative and technical leader in its industry. But the retailer is less apt to acquiesce in the manufacturer's power attempts aimed at influencing the retailer's merchandising and/or promotional programme if the retailer perceives these decisions to lie outside the bounds of the manufacturer's area of competence. On the whole, however, identification-based relationships are less volatile than those relationships based upon compliance and will result in a greater degree of co-ordination and efficiency in the operation of the channel.

Proposition 2 of Table III indicates that referent and expert power are endemic to identification-related behaviour. Expert and referent power bases are much more subtle in their impact than are the power bases associated with compliance-related behaviour. Perhaps an explanation is that referent power, and to some extent expert power, are used in conjunction with other bases of power and are consequently difficult to isolate [14]. A more important factor, however, refers to the role played by the powerful channel member with respect to the exercise of expert and referent power within the channel. Specifically, reward, coercive and, to a degree, legal legitimate power necessitate direct, overt action in order to gain compliance. Referent and expert power, on the other hand, primarily stem from the less powerful channel member's desire for association and not from explicit administration of rewards or punishments. The striving to benefit from another's expertise, image, or reputation suggests a certain amount of shared values and goals among the channel members. This commonality is expected to result in a greater commitment to the marketing channel than is found in those dependency relationships based upon compliance-related bases of power.

Propositions 2a and 2b indicate that expert power is expected to result in more long term co-operation than referent power. Referent power connotes a somewhat more nebulous power base since a firm's image or reputation is less easily quantified than a firm's technical competence or marketing expertise. Expert power conveys a notion of a possession of knowledge or technical know-how upon which a dependency relationship is built. While it is possible that the attraction to the expert could wane because his trustworthiness becomes suspect due to self-serving gains, or the needed expertise becomes available elsewhere, there are ample instances where the power-holder occupies a unique position in the channel or possesses unusual skills. For instance, a small manufacturer of surgical equipment may turn to the American Hospital Supply

Corporation for their noted marketing expertise in, and extensive sales coverage of, the health care field. It is difficult, in this case, to distinguish clearly between American Hospital's expert and referent bases of power since their reputation is based, to a great extent, upon their marketing competence. As referent power is more dependent upon the other bases of power, expert power is seen to be more stable and, consequently, is likely to manifest more co-operation in the long run than referent power.

Internalisation

In most instances, the internalisation of the channel's norms and values by the participants serves to improve the efficiency of the channel, and places this marketing system in a better competitive posture *vis-à-vis* other marketing systems. Because the prescribed behaviour is consistent with the channel member's value system, it tends to be performed regardless of continued surveillance, without the reimposition of other power attempts, and with little concern for a channel member encroaching upon the exclusive domain of another channel participant. Consequently, there is likely to be a much greater level of predictability and dependability in the behaviour of the channel members. Moreover, conflict among channel participants is likely to be relatively low and, therefore, the costs associated with maintaining the effectiveness of this channel of distribution are expected to be minimised. Thus, internalisation embodies many of the advantages of having a corporate vertical marketing system. Like a truly integrated channel of distribution, members who have internalised the common norms and values can view their performance as a team effort and can effectively improve the system's competitive posture through its increased co-operation and co-ordination.

Proposition 3 in Table III indicates that traditional legitimate and informational power lead to internalisation. Traditional legitimate and informational power tend to result in the highest level of dependability and predictability of behaviour among the channel members. Not only does the induced behaviour become perceptually independent of the influencing agent, but responsibilities become routinised into tacitly agreed upon roles and norms. In both instances, the influence attempt is sufficiently subtle for the prescribed behaviour to be attributed to internal rather than external causes so as to be readily assimilated as part of the channel member's own value system.

Informational power is said to be likely to result in more long-run co-operation than traditional legitimate power. The notion of long-run co-operation emanating from traditional legitimate power stems from an inculcation of established behaviour that has developed over a period of time. The extent to which there is long-run co-operation is a function of the stability of the relationship and is limited to those situations in which the relatively powerless channel member accepts the basis for legitimacy. It should be clear that the acceptance of traditional roles is not necessarily enduring and that conflict over a single issue may escalate to a point where the entire relationship is jeopardised [15]. Avoidance of economic obsolescence, dissatisfaction with existing operations [16], and a desire for more self-detemination through the acquisition of countervailing power [17] are factors influencing the dynamics of the channel relationships

Informational power is felt to provide the marketing channel with the highest level of channel co-operation. The provision of useful information, in accordance with intended behaviour, is a sufficiently subtle influence attempt that causation is perceived to be internal. Further, the dissemination of information can be manipulated so as to make this power base more flexible than traditional legitimate power and, therefore, better able to deal with potential conflict among channel participants. For example, the firm of O.M. Scott offers its retailers training programmes, technical and merchandising support, and point-of-purchase material which are intended to make the retailer rather knowledgeable regarding lawn care products and problems. This programme of "systems selling" enables Scott to instill in its retailers a total marketing channel perspective. The retailer comes to view himself *and* Scott in competition with other retailers who sell other brands of lawn care products. In this fashion, the prescribed channel behaviour is attributed to the power recipient's own value system.

Summary and Implications

Power has been acknowledged as a means by which the conduct of the channel members can be co-ordinated so as to achieve a higher level of channel efficiency. The use of power within the marketing channel is not, however, without its problems for there are certain adverse consequences which can result from the improper use of power. The purpose of this article has been to present a framework which serves as a guide to the marketer in outlining the response which may ensue from the exercise of power. It is a major premise of this article that if a firm has the ability to anticipate and/ or predict the behavioural responses of the other channel members, it is able more efficiently to administer the marketing channel.

To the marketing manager, the schema presented in this article suggests that the exercise of certain bases of power (i.e., reward, coercive, legal legitimate, referent, expert, traditional legitimate and informational) results in varied degrees of channel co-operation. Compliance-based behaviour resulting from the use of coercion, reward and legal legitimate power often leads to a network of firms which is primarily self oriented and thus has little if any commitment to the goals of the marketing channel as an integrated whole. Compliance is often gained at great cost to the influencing agent both in terms of the administration of sanctions (both positive and negative) and in terms of the surveillance required to monitor the behaviour of the channel members. As the channel participants attribute their prescribed behaviour to the inducement, there is little inculcation of system-wide values or goals. In fact, once the surveillance is lifted, it is expected that the channel behaviour will revert to its previous state.

The exercise of expert or referent power bases, resulting in identification-related behaviour, is conducive to the establishment of a higher level of channel co-operation.

Such power dependent relationships are maintained at lower costs to the influence agent since it is not necessary for him to monitor the conduct of the other channel members. An interpretation of these two bases of power is, however, subject to some confusion for they are often utilised in conjunction with other power bases. Nonetheless, it is more advantageous for a firm to develop its own unique image, noted expertise or competence with which channel members choose to associate than to rely on its ability to control inducements for the channel participants as a means of obtaining long-run channel co-operation.

Traditional legitimate and informational power, resulting in internalisation-based behaviour, lead to still higher levels of longer periods of channel co-operation. Power resides in the ability of the influencing agent to manipulate the value systems of the channel participants so that the prescribed behaviour appears to be highly congruent with their internal goals and values. In this fashion, the prescribed conduct is attributed to internal motives and is dissociated from the influencing agent. In those cases, for instance, in which the influencing agent can provide information (i.e., informational power) to the other channel members that shows that co-ordinated channel conduct results in greater profitability to the participants, there is a greater probability of prolonged channel co-operation.

Channel relations provide frequent opportunities for one member to influence another's behaviour. The ultimate objective of any channel management strategy is to develop a degree of co-operation in channel participant behaviour. The efficiencies gained from a co-ordinated channel effort are expected to improve the channel's competitive stance *vis-à-vis* other distribution networks. This means that the channel administrator should not myopically view half-hearted and forced complicity among channel members as a successful power outcome; but should, instead, strive to cultivate those power bases which tend to elicit an internalisation of and an identification with the system's goals and values. While in some instances firms must rely on coercion, rewards, or contractual agreements, firms should develop, and more extensively use, those bases of power which produce the greatest amount of long-run co-operation

References

1. McCammon, B. C., Jr., "Perspectives for Distribution Programming", in *Vertical Marketing Systems,* Bucklin, L. P. (Ed.), Glenview, Ill., Scott, Foresman and Co., 1970, pp. 32-52.

2. *Ibid.*

3. McCammon, B. C., and Hammer, W. L., "A Frame of Reference for Improving Productivity in Distribution", *Atlanta Economic Review,* Vol. 24, September-October 1974, quoted in Stern, L. W., and El-Ansary, A., *Marketing Channels,* Englewood Cliffs, Prentice-Hall, 1976, Chapter 10.

4. Stern, L. W. (Ed.), *Distribution Channels: Behavioural Dimensions,* Boston, Houghton Mifflin Company, 1969.

5. Dahl, R., "The Concept of Power", *Behavioural Science,* Vol. 2, July 1957, pp. 201-18.

6. Hunt, S., and Niven, J., "Power in a Channel of Distribution: Sources and Consequences", *Journal of Marketing Research,* Vol. 11, May 1974, pp. 186-93; Lusch, R., "Sources of Power: Their Impact on Intrachannel Conflict", *Journal of Marketing Research,* Vol. 13, November 1976, pp. 382-90; and Walters, G., *Marketing Channels,* New York, Ronald Press, 1974, pp. 434-55.

7. El-Ansary, A., and Stern, L. W., "Power Measurement in the Distribution Channel", *Journal of Marketing Research,* Vol. 9, February 1972, pp. 47-52.

8. Kelman, H. C., "Processes of Opinion Change", *Public Opinion Quarterly,* Vol. 25, 1961, pp. 57-78.

9. Raven, B., and Kruglanski, A., "Conflict and Power", in Swingle, P. (Ed.), *The Structure of Conflict,* New York, Academic Press, 1970, pp. 82-3; and Bem, D. J., "Self-Perception Theory", in Berkowitz, L. (Ed.), *Advances in Experimental Social Psychology,* Vol. 7, New York, Academic Press, 1972, pp. 1-62.

10 *Ibid.*

11. Stern, L. W., and Gorman, R. H., "Conflict in Distribution Channels: An Exploration", in Stern, L. W., *Distribution Channels: Behaviour Dimensions, op. cit.*

12. Baldwin, D., "The Power of Positive Sanction", *World Politics,* Vol. 24, October, 1971, pp. 19-38.

13. "Cramping the Style of Franchisers", *Business Week,* June 15, 1975, p. 82.

14. Beier, F. J., and Stern, L. W., "Power in the Channel of Distribution", in Stern, L. W. *Distribution Channels: Behavioural Dimensions, op. cit.*

15. Palamountain, J. C., Jr., *The Politics of Distribution,* Cambridge, Mass., Harvard University Press, 1955.

16. Little, R. W., "The Marketing Channel: Who Should Lead this Extra-corporate Organisation", *Journal of Marketing,* Vol. 34, January 1970, pp. 31-8.

17. Galbraith, J. K., *American Capitalism,* Boston, Houghton Mifflin Co., 1952, pp. 27-75.

Part 4 Marketing Management

17. An Understanding of Marketing Strategy

by Gordon E. Greenley

This article is concerned with an understanding of marketing strategy and with the differentiation and clarification of concepts used in conjunction with marketing strategy. The impetus for this research arose out of a major programme of research, which has been carried out by the writer, the results of which are separate to this article and which have already been published elsewhere[1,2,3]. The research highlighted that, although all the respondent companies claim to have a marketing strategy, the marketing executives responding all exhibited great difficulty in explaining this strategy, and definitions varied widely, with little commonality of response. Hence the impetus to develop an overall understanding of marketing strategy, within the framework of a journal article.

In order to develop this understanding an exhaustive search of the literature has been completed. The outcome of this reference to the literature also exhibits wide variations in the understanding of marketing strategy by the writers concerned, with the utilisation of many concepts and phrases, resulting in many varied explanations as to its nature. Therefore, confusion on the part of marketing executives is, perhaps, to be expected. Hence, further impetus to develop an understanding within the framework of an article. However, the body of knowledge within the literature has been taken as being the source for developing this understanding, as it represents the development work of marketers within this area.

The understanding of marketing strategy developed in this article is through a process involving three different levels of treatment. The first two levels arise out of the overall strategic planning of the company and provide the framework out of which marketing strategy should be developed. However, as these two levels provide the framework for developing the actual marketing strategy, they are not considered to be part of it. The third level of the process is the actual marketing strategy, which is considered to be composed of five component parts. The article concludes that, in defining its marketing strategy, a company needs firstly to establish the two levels from the strategic planning framework, then from this define each of the marketing strategy component parts. It is also concluded that failure to follow this process leads to ineffective definition, implementation and effectiveness of marketing strategies.

The article is presented in four sections. The first discusses explanations of marketing strategy from the literature. The second section examines strategic planning as a basis for developing levels one and two of the process, whereas the third section explains the resultant understanding of marketing strategy. The last section summarises the article and suggests consequential implications.

Explanations from the Literature

Most writers on the subject of marketing strategy start with a broad encompassing statement of what they consider it to be. For example, Chang and Campo-Flores[4] refer to marketing strategy as being crucial and central issues to the use of the marketing function. Similarly, Baker[5] sees it as being a broad means of achieving given aims, Luck and Ferrell[6] as being fundamental means or schemes and Kotler[7] as being the grand design to achieve objectives. Similar broad statements were also given by the companies participating in the previously reported research. Several companies claimed that their marketing strategy was a long-term activity, others that it provided for the overall achievement of objectives and others that it provided a broad plan of action. Other comments were given as even wider statements, such as to sell as large a quantity as possible or to maximise profits.

Having made such a statement, most writers then move on to explain the detailed issues, means or schemes which they prescribe as constituting a marketing strategy. Here there are four major bases that are used in the literature to explain the detail of marketing strategy. These are the marketing mix, the product life cycle, market share and competition, and positioning. In addition, some writers also advocate special marketing strategies for both international and industrial markets. The remainder of this section is concerned with an explanation of these approaches.

The Marketing Mix Base

A common approach in the literature is simply to link these issues to the elements of the marketing mix. Indeed, Foxall[8] defines marketing strategy as being an indication of how each element of the marketing mix will be used to achieve the marketing objectives. This definition gives a complete reliance on the mix and therefore the utilisation of the elements is the strategy. This is, however, a very simplified and restricted approach to marketing strategy, as will be illustrated later in the article. Chang and Campo-Flores[4] also develop this theme, suggesting a range of marketing component strategies which constitute the total marketing strategy. These they give as product strategy, distribution strategy, sales promotion strategy and pricing strategy. This approach is also followed by Jain[9], who gives the same breakdown, again following a simple approach of relating marketing strategy to the mix elements. A modification of this approach is prescribed by Udell[10], who splits the issues into price and non-price strategies. Yet another modification is that by Foster[11], who puts an emphasis on the companies' product mix and, in particular, reducing product prolification.

The PLC Base

Other writers extend this theme of the marketing mix to the concept of the product life cycle. For example, Kotler[12], Baker[5] and Doyle[13] outline that the marketing strategy for a particular product needs to be modified as the product moves through the various stages of its PLC. This is based upon a change of the mix at the different stages, so that a change is made in the relative degree of reliance of each element, giving a different mix, and hence a different marketing strategy, at each stage. This treatment is extended by other writers, such as Scheuing[14], who defines a specific strategy for each stage of the PLC, labelling them life cycle marketing strategies. However, there are two major problems associated with this approach. The first is that it is difficult for the company to be able, at a particular point in time, to identify the stage at which a product is within its life cycle. The other problem is that the specific strategies for each stage do not always allow for application to all products, given the wide variation experienced by companies in market and product conditions.

The Market Share Base
Another approach used in the literature to explain the issues involved in marketing strategy is to link the latter to market share and competition. A major example here comes from the work of Bloom and Kotler[15]. Their approach is firstly to explain how a company can identify its optimal market share, given a particular set of conditions. Having identified this level the company needs a marketing strategy to achieve the optimum. The second stage is to select a strategy from a range of strategies that are designed to build, maintain or even reduce market share. However, within each of these share-linked marketing strategies they also advocate a range of further strategies, again based upon the elements of the marketing mix. A similar approach is also advocated by Buzzell, Gale and Sultan[16], although they label the alternatives as being building, holding and harvesting strategies. Alternatively, strategies for companies with low market shares are given by Woo and Cooper[17]. Similarly, Doyle[18] also links marketing strategy to market share. Here the approach is simply to equate one strategy as the pursuit of market share and another strategy as its non-pursuit. However, overall this approach of linking marketing strategy to market share appears to be merely the utilisation of the elements of the marketing mix, linked with an objective or aim (and therefore not a strategy) which is concerned with a pre-determined level of achievement (being market share).

In addition to the market share link, competitive marketing strategies have also been described by Kotler[12], with a revision in a later publication[19]. In the earlier work he prescribed a range of nine competitive marketing strategies, prescribing that the company chooses, at a particular point in time, that which relates directly to the activities of its competitors. In the later work he advocates an approach in which the company has a range of competitive marketing strategies from which to choose, depending upon which of four strategy ranges the company's market share dictates that it falls into. Here there is a liberal use of the word "strategy"; there are strategies within strategies and application of the approach is perhaps not immediately apparent.

The Positioning Base
Another approach from the literature in the explanation of marketing strategy is to utilise the concept of positioning. The major overall problem here is the variation given in the literature as to the meaning of positioning. For example, Wind and Claycamp[20] explain a product's position as its overall situation in the market relative to its sales, market share and profitability. Cravens[21] sees positioning as being the selection of a marketing strategy from a range of alternatives, although the latter can be considered to be component parts of corporate strategy, as developed by Ansoff[22].

Yet another variation of the interpretation of product positioning is reflected in the articles of Alpert and Gatty[23] and Holmes[24]. Here a product's position is related to its customers, in that it explains the user profile and how they perceive the image of the product.

The concept of positioning can also be explained in terms of both market and product positions, as illustrated, for example, by Kotler[7]. Here the company investigates the segmentation of a particular market and then decides which segment or segments to participate in. This selection is referred to as market positioning. For each segment the company requires a product, or products, and the number of products developed, plus their overall nature, is referred to as product positioning. This is developed for a range of products in an article by Warwick and Sands[25] and the application of market segmentation in marketing strategy for UK Building Societies is illustrated by Doyle and Newbould[26].

International Markets
Although several references are made in the literature to international marketing strategies, these tend to relate to the elements of the marketing mix. The basic tenet here is that these need to be varied for different countries, based upon variations in market conditions in these countries. For example, Keegan[27] gives a range of five alternative marketing strategies for a particular overseas market, based upon the elements of the product and communications. This range allows for variation in the product and the communications mix, but is never the less based on the marketing mix. Similarly, Halfill[28], in reporting the results of a survey, uses the phrase multinational marketing strategy, but again is basing this on the marketing mix, with the emphasis on advertising. In a survey to investigate the nature of international marketing strategies in American companies, Samli[29] also illustrates this emphasis on the marketing mix, but identifies an orientation of the mix towards competitors within each market.

Industrial Markets
In the case of industrial marketing strategies which are described in the literature, a similar situation exists. Copulsky[30] describes industrial marketing strategies as also being based upon the marketing mix, but with an emphasis on the product and price. A similar emphasis was also reported by Cunningham and Hammouda[31], from their investigations into a UK engineering company. Two other articles on industrial marketing strategy also emphasise the orientation to the marketing mix, but broaden their base to utilise the concept of positioning. In the article by Forbis and Mehta[32] the use of market segmentation is advocated and hence market positioning is included in their industrial marketing strategy. Similarly Corey[33] utilises market segmentation, but advocates both market and product positioning within industrial marketing strategies.

This completes the discussion of the explanations of marketing strategy from the literature. The next section is concerned with a review of strategic planning, as a basis for developing levels one and two of the marketing strategy process.

A Review of Strategic Planning

As levels one and two of the marketing strategy process developed in this article are from the company's strategic planning, a review of both the nature of, and stages involved in, strategic planning is necessary. This will provide a basis for developing levels one and two, being the framework for developing the actual marketing strategy as level three.

Corporate planning is a concept which represents the summation of the total planning to be carried out in a company and writers such as Taylor and Sparks[34] and Hussey[35] split corporate planning into strategic planning and operational planning. Strategic planning is seen by Hussey to be the process which defines the overall objectives of the company and the means by which these objectives are to be obtained. The emphasis given by Ackoff[36] is that strategic planning is differentiated from other planning in that its consequences have an enduring effect on the firm and are broad issues which relate to the long term. Due to the influence of the effects of strategic planning, Higgins[37] identifies the responsibility of strategic planning as lying with top management, as opposed to the functional managers. The various stages involved in strategic planning will be discussed later in this section.

Figure 1. The Relationship of Marketing Strategy to Corporate Planning

Operational planning, however, is seen by Denning[38] to be a projection into the future of plans which cover existing company operations. Here the plans are the responsibility of functional managers, as the concern is seen to be the operation of these functions into the future. The marketing function is seen to predominate in this area of planning, as for example given by Higgins[37], and therefore marketing planning is taken as being part of operational planning. Although strategic planning is seen by Ackoff[36] to be concerned with the long term, operational planning, due to its very nature, necessarily relates to the short term, in that it is based on the firm's present operational base of resources. However, looking into the long-term future necessitates not only the setting of objectives and strategies, but must also include, as suggested by the Society for Long-Range Planning[39], "translating strategy into detailed operational programmes", which is very much the responsibility of operational planning. Therefore, operational plans are also needed in the long-term situation, which leads Scott[40] to identify both strategic long-range plans and operational long-range plans. Short-term operational planning is also labelled tactical planning by many writers, such as Hussey[35], although Higgins[37] sees operational planning and tactical planning as being synonymous. However, tactical planning is seen by Winkler[41] as being specific action and by Chang and Campo-Flores[4] as being specific action designed to execute strategies. In the context of this article, marketing strategy is seen as being part of the long-term operational planning of the marketing function. The relationship of marketing strategy to these forms of planning is illustrated in Figure 1.

Review of the Stages of Strategic Planning
Although writers within the literature give various stages within the strategic planning process, writers such as Taylor and Sparks[34], Hussey[35] and Kollat, Blackwell and Robeson[42], tend to follow the stages given in Figure 2.

The approach starts with a specification of the overall direction which the firm wishes to pursue, given in the form of a corporate mission plus corporate objectives. The latter relate to certain levels of achievement or performance, refer to the total company and are applicable to the long run. After determining the strengths and weaknesses of both its internal and external environments, plus any gaps between its objectives and current base likely performance, the company moves on to consider its corporate strategy. This is seen by Hovell[43] as being the means of directing resources to achieve the objectives. The strategic planning process given advocates the identification and evaluation of alternative strategies, before the company chooses that to be pursued. Within these stages of strategic planning, level one of the marketing strategy process is seen as being the corporate mission and level two is seen as being the corporate strategy. Therefore, in order to develop these levels as being the overall framework for determining marketing strategy, further consideration will be given to both corporate mission and strategy.

Kollat, Blackwell and Robeson[42] explain the concept of corporate mission as being concerned with a long-term vision of what the business is, or is striving to become. Chang and Campo-Flores[4] describe it as being the scope and direction of business endeavours. The scope of business is taken to be defined in terms of customers,

Figure 2. The Stages of Strategic Planning

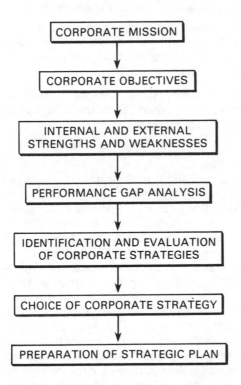

products and business areas. Therefore, the purpose of establishing a mission is to develop an encompassing understanding of the company's purpose and overall direction. In developing the mission, Drucker[44] suggests that a series of questions about the company need to be posed, such as; what is our business? what will be our business? what should our business be? The establishment of such a mission, in which these areas are defined, is seen by Kotler[45] as providing personnel with a shared sense of opportunity, direction, significance and achievement.

A major contribution to the understanding of corporate strategy is the well known work of Ansoff[22]. The view taken by Ansoff is that corporate strategy is made up of four component parts, from which it is possible to develop a range of alternative strategies. These four components are summarised as follows:

(1) *Product—market scope:* this specifies the particular industries to which the firm is to restrict its business, defining the broad areas of product and market participation.

(2) *Growth vector:* this relates to the alternatives available to the firm to achieve growth of sales and output, giving the alternatives of market penetration, market development, product development and diversification.

(3) *Competitive advantages:* concerned with how the firm will be able to develop advantages over its competitors within these industries and vectors.

(4) *Synergy:* in simple terms, this is concerned with evaluating how the firm's strengths and weaknesses will affect its market participation. In the words of Ansoff, "it is concerned with the desired characteristics of fit between the firm and its products—markets."

This section has reviewed strategic planning as a basis for developing levels one and two of the marketing strategy process and these levels have been identified as being corporate mission and corporate strategy.

The Resultant Understanding
As already mentioned, levels one and two of the understanding provide the framework for developing the marketing strategy which is given as level three.

As the corporate mission provides an encompassing understanding of the company's purpose and overall direction, it is considered as being level one of the process in developing a marketing strategy. Hence the mission provides the broad scope of the business in terms of customers, products and business areas, which is the starting point for making decisions on marketing strategy, in that the central issues of the total marketing operation must follow the company's central theme. Within this scope the framework is prescribed in the form of the classes of customers the firm wishes to serve, giving the scope for market positioning and examining suitability of variations in the marketing mix. Similarly the scope of products provides a framework for product positioning as well as giving ramifications within the marketing mix. The scope of business areas also gives a framework to market positioning, in that the supply of products to different areas (such as industrial, consumer, or international business areas) will each have different ramifications on the decisions to be made on marketing strategy. The theme of purpose also needs to be reflected in the marketing strategy. This may vary from company to company as it could be based upon the development of a particular technology, a particular raw material, a particular section of society, or indeed on any other similar theme. However, whatever the specification of the purpose, the components of the marketing strategy must support it. Finally, the direction of the company also has ramifications for marketing strategy. Directions aimed at growth, stability or contraction would each result in different decisions being made in the components of marketing strategy, as would a diversification direction as opposed to a non-diversification direction.

Level two of the understanding is the established corporate strategy, which is considered to be the second part of the marketing strategy framework. The product-market scope component of corporate strategy is itself an extension of the corporate mission as it gives more detail in specifying the scope of the business. Although this component is narrower in its definition of scope than the corporate mission it still allows for decision making within marketing strategy, in the selection of markets, market segments, product lines and individual products. However, the point is that the product-market scope component defines the framework for these decisions, giving the range to be pursued. The growth-vector component also provides a decision-making framework for marketing strategy. Here the selected alternatives for pursuing growth will each affect the marketing mix to be determined within the marketing strategy. Each growth alternative will also affect decisions on product positioning and the very nature of the market within each growth alternative will require a different approach to market positioning. The component of competitive advantage will dictate the approach to be taken in each element of the marketing mix and indeed will affect their interrelationship. Overall approaches to competitors may also necessitate making decisions on both market and product positioning. Finally, the corporate strategy component of synergy will affect marketing strategy in that identified company strengths and weaknesses, in relation to the approaches the company is to take towards these, may provide either restrictions to the development of marketing strategy, or, indeed, may provide an improvement to its effectiveness.

Level three of the understanding is the actual marketing strategy. The approach taken in this article is to specify marketing strategy as being composed of five component parts, three of which have been discussed in section one, and two of which have not yet been discussed. The first three components relate to market positioning, product positioning and the marketing mix, and are discussed further as follows.

Market Positioning
This part of the strategy is concerned with deciding which approach to adopt relative to the segmentation of the market and the selection of the segments in which the company is to participate. Depending upon the range of product-market scopes, or strategic business units (SBUs) adopted, each scope may require a different approach to segmentation within the market. In selecting the segments for participation the company has the choice of pursuing all segments, only one segment, or several. This choice could well be affected by the rate of growth required, the nature of competitors within the segments and the corporate approach to them, plus the synergy developed by the relative strengths and weaknesses. This component is seen as being logically the first decision to be made in establishing a marketing strategy.

Product Positioning
Having selected the market segments for each product-market scope, the number of products which the firm is to offer to each segment must be determined and their overall nature must be specified. Again this decision area can be affected by the corporate strategy components of growth, competition and synergy. However, the major considerations are obviously the market requirements within each segment. The understanding of these requirements obviously provides a basis for deciding whether each segment of participation requires one or several products, as well as determining the overall nature of each product. However, specific details of product specifications are not considered to be part of the marketing strategy, but are considered to be decisions relative to the tactical planning of marketing. This point will be pursued further in the summary.

Marketing Mix
Having determined the range of segments in which they will participate, plus the nature and number of products to be offered, the next decision in formulating the marketing

strategy is to determine the utilisation of the individual elements of the mix, plus the relative degree of reliance to be placed upon each. Again the distinction needs to be made between the role of the marketing mix within marketing strategy and its role within marketing tactics. In the former, decisions are required to determine which of the elements given by McCarthy[46] are to be used in order to market the selected products, as well as deciding the relative degree of importance or reliance to be placed on each in order to satisfy the market requirements. However, the role of the marketing mix within marketing tactics is in the specification of details, such as product features, brand name and image, price structure, copy platform and selling techniques. Again the finalisation of this component is affected by market requirements, so that the marketing strategy may need to vary with product market scope. In addition, the corporate approach to competitors may also affect decisions, as could the corporate approach to growth, plus effective synergy.

The two additional components not yet discussed are market entry and timing. These are discussed as follows.

Market Entry

This component is concerned with how the company intends to enter, re-enter, position itself, or re-position itself within each of the selected market segments. Here Kotler[7] gives the alternatives of acquisition, collaboration and internal development. In the former the approach of acquiring an existing product(s) or company is well documented, as, for example, given by Fogg[47]. The selection of this strategy would be affected by the overall direction of the company as specified within the corporate mission. Also the corporate strategy components of growth, competitive advantage and synergy would also relate to such a decision. Collaboration with another company that can provide expertise in marketing, or indeed any other business area, can be similarly affected by corporate strategy. The purpose element of the corporate mission would provide the guideline for such a strategy, but the overall level of synergy within the company would give a major indication of the need to adopt a collaboration strategy. Finally, internal development means that the company does not need to involve other companies, so that the marketing operations are developed by the company through its own resources. Adoption of such a strategy would again be affected by the purpose element of the corporate mission, the level of synergy and also the stipulated rates of growth.

Timing

Here the component relates to the point in time at which the other components of the marketing strategy are to be implemented, plus the points in time when particular tactics within the marketing mix are to be implemented. One approach here is to link the strategy to competitors' activity, as, for example, outlined by Jain[9]. Here the strategy can be to be first to implement, or to be early but following the first company, or to take a laggard position, being one of the last companies to implement. Here the competitive advantage component of corporate strategy is likely to have a bearing, as is the purpose element of the corporate mission. Another approach of selecting times is to follow relevant indicators from the external environment. These can range from economic indicators, to industry trends, to seasonal trends, to trade exhibitions. Here there is probably less effect from the corporate mission and strategy, although the immediacy of required growth would need to be considered. The timing component of marketing strategy also relates to selecting the optimum time to exploit a particular market or market segment. Abell[48] has identified the importance of recognising the time period associated with a particular opportunity within a market, which he labels the "strategic window". Here he offers an approach in the decision-making process, to determine when the particular implementation of strategy or tactics should take place. Here there can be consideration of the corporate strategy, in relation to the immediacy of required growth, the impact on such a strategic window of the corporate approach to competitors and the level of synergy within the company.

The rationale for finalising marketing strategy as being composed of these five components is that they represent the central issues of the marketing operation. These vary from the specific activities to be carried out within each of the elements of the marketing mix, which, as previously discussed, represent the marketing tactics. The PLC base is rejected due to its inherent weaknesses, which make it unsuitable as a basis for strategy, although it is recognised that at the tactical level adjustments to the mix are valid relative to the PLC. The market share base is rejected as it is considered to be an objective at which to aim strategy performance, as opposed to being a marketing strategy basis itself. Also, particular attention to competitors as a marketing strategy base is rejected. This is because full consideration of competitors is, by necessity, given in the formulation of the five selected component parts. In addition, more direct consideration is taken of competitors in both the planning and implementation of marketing tactics. Finally, the international and industrial market bases are also rejected, as the principle established is that the five components of marketing strategy can be applied as a general rule. Therefore all can be applied in any market situation, regardless of the nature of the market profile and regardless of the particular market requirements. However, what is obviously important in formalising the five components for any market situation is a full understanding of the total environment of the marketing operation. This includes both internal aspects, plus the external environment of not only the market conditions, but also the full macro-environment. This, therefore, gives the variation in the application of the five components within any specific market, as opposed to a stereotyped market *per se*.

In section two a split was identified between long-range operational planning and short-range operational planning. The five components of marketing strategy are considered to be enduring in nature and therefore are considered to be the marketing element of long-range operational planning. Market positioning can be considered to be enduring in that, once a company has selected market segments for participation, the consequential commitment to capital investment and other resources means that it is likely to be for a relatively long period of time. This also applies to product positioning, where both customer expectations and production commitment need to be catered for over a relatively long period of time. Also, once the reliance is established within each element of the marketing mix, then commitment to investment and the organisational structure mean a relatively long-term involvement. In the case of both market entry and timing, again there is an enduring effect. Once these decisions have been made, then again commitment is established for a relatively long period of time. Alternatively, marketing tactics are considered to be transient in nature and are therefore considered to be the marketing element of short-range operational planning. Hence the tactics relate to the annual marketing plan, within the framework of marketing strategy, and can be adjusted throughout the annual plan relative to market conditions. The outcome of such a classification is that the marketing tactics are the prime means of achieving the annual marketing objectives, even though they are developed within the framework of marketing strategy. However, the marketing strategy is seen as being a means of achieving the corporate objectives, with only a contribution to the marketing objectives by providing the framework for the marketing tactics. However, this does not mean to say that marketing strategy should be located within strategic planning, as tends to be suggested by writers such as Abel and Hammond[49]. Indeed, marketing strategy is seen as being very much the concern of the marketing function, in that, as already established, it constitutes the marketing element of long-range operational planning.

Summary and Implications

The aim of this article was to develop an understanding of marketing strategy. The approach was to survey the literature on marketing strategy and then to review the strategic planning process. The latter provided a basis for developing levels one and two of the understanding, which were specified as being the corporate mission and the corporate objectives. These two levels provided the framework for the development of the third level of the understanding, which is the actual marketing strategy to be developed. This was specified as being composed of five component parts, being market positioning, product positioning, the marketing mix, market entry and timing. It was also argued that marketing strategy is the marketing element of long-range operational planning and relates directly to the attainment of the corporate objectives. Alternatively, marketing tactics are seen as being the marketing element of short-range operational planning, giving a direct contribution to the attainment of the marketing objectives.

Therefore the outcome of the understanding is that, in defining its marketing strategy, a company needs firstly to establish the two levels from the strategic planning framework, then from this define each of the marketing strategy component parts. Failure to follow this process must lead to ineffective definition, implementation and effectiveness of marketing strategies, as supported by the nature of the presented process.

Finally, two observations from the literature which relate to the utilisation of marketing strategy need to be emphasised. The first has been reported by writers such as Hayes and Abernathy[50], Anderson[51] and Piercy[52]. These writers report that the marketing emphasis in companies in recent times has been orientated towards short-term gains in revenue and profits. Therefore the emphasis is being placed on the marketing tactics of short-range operational planning. Although the latter is obviously important, full consideration of marketing strategy is of equal importance, not only to contribute to future performance and success, but also to provide a framework for the operation of the annual marketing plan. The final observation comes from the work of Carroll[53]. This observation is that the word strategy has been abused by many writers, having become "a grandiose synonym for the word important". Hence the word strategy has been unjustifiably included in the title of many articles and books in an attempt to improve their importance and academic respectability. To a certain extent this trend appears to be in the opposite direction to the first observation. However, the danger is that, as reflected by Carroll, a true understanding and application of strategy within marketing (or indeed within any other business function), can become confused by the very body of knowledge which is attempting to clarify it.

References

1. Greenley, G.E., "An Overview of Marketing Planning in U.K. Manufacturing Companies", *European Journal of Marketing*, Vol. 16 No. 7, 1982, pp. 3-16.
2. Greenley, G.E., "Where Marketing Planning Fails", *Long Range Planning*, Vol. 16 No. 1, February 1983, pp. 106-15.
3. Greenley, G.E., "Effectiveness in Marketing Planning", *Strategic Management Journal*, Vol. 4 No. 1, March 1983; "An overview of Marketing Planning in U.K. Service Companies", *Marketing Intelligence and Planning*, Vol. 1 No. 3, 1983, pp. 55-68.
4. Chang, Y.N. and Campo-Flores, F., *Business Policy and Strategy*, Santa Monica, Goodyear Publishing, 1980.
5. Baker, M.J., "Limited Options for Marketing Strategists", *Marketing*, June 1978, pp. 23-27.
6. Luck, D.J. and Ferrell, O.C., *Marketing Strategy and Plans*, Englewood Cliffs, Prentice-Hall, 1979.
7. Kotler, P., *Marketing Management: Analysis, Planning and Control*, 3rd edition, Englewood Cliffs, Prentice-Hall, 1976.
8. Foxall, G.R., *Strategic Marketing Management*, London, Croom Helm, 1981.
9. Jain, S.C., *Marketing Planning and Strategy*, Cincinnati, South-Western Publishing, 1981.
10. Udell, J.G., "The Perceived Importance of the Elements of Strategy", *Journal of Marketing*, Vol. 32, January 1968, pp. 34-40.
11. Foster, D.W., "Product—Market Strategy", *Long Range Planning*, Vol. 3, March 1970, pp. 70-77.
12. Kotler, P., "Competitive Strategies for New Product Marketing over the Life Cycle", *Management Science*, Vol. 12 No. 4, December 1965, pp. 104-119.
13. Doyle, P., "The Realities of the Product Life Cycle", *Quarterly Review of Marketing*, Summer 1976, pp. 1-6.
14. Scheuing, E.E., "The Product Life Cycle as an Aid in Strategy Decisions", *Management International Review*, Vol. 4 No. 5, 1969, pp. 111-125.
15. Bloom, P.N. and Kotler, P., "Strategies for High Market-Share Companies", *Harvard Business Review*, Vol. 53 No. 6, November-December 1975, pp. 63-72.
16. Buzzell, R.D., Gale, B.T. and Sultan, R.G.M., "Market Share—a Key to Profitability", *Harvard Business Review*, Vol. 53 No. 1, January-February 1975, pp. 97-106.
17. Woo, C.Y.Y. and Cooper, A.C., "Strategies of Effective Low Share Businesses", *Strategic Management Journal*, Vol. 2 No. 3, July/September 1981, pp. 301-318.
18. Doyle, P., "Market Share and Marketing Strategy", *Quarterly Review of Marketing*, Autumn 1975, pp. 1-3.
19. Kotler, P., *Marketing Management: Analysis, Planning and Control*, 4th edition, Englewood Cliffs, Prentice-Hall, 1980.
20. Wind, Y. and Claycamp, H.J., "Planning Product Line Strategy: A Matrix Approach", *Journal of Marketing*, Vol. 40, January 1976, pp. 2-9.
21. Cravens, D.W., "Marketing Strategy Positioning", *Business Horizons*, December 1975, pp. 53-61.
22. Ansoff, H.I., *Corporate Strategy*, New York, McGraw-Hill, 1968.
23. Alpert, L. and Gatty, R., "Product Positioning by Behavioural Life-Styles", *Journal of Marketing*, Vol. 33, April 1969, pp. 65-69.
24. Holmes, J.H., "Profitable Product Positioning", *MSU Business Topics*, Spring 1973, pp. 27-32.
25. Warwick, K.M. and Sands, S., "Product Positioning: Problems and Promises", *University of Michigan Business Review*, November 1975, pp. 17-20.

References

26. Doyle, P. and Newbould, G.D., "Marketing Strategies for Building Societies", *Management Decision*, Vol. 13 No. 1, 1975, pp. 41-50.

27. Keegan, W.J., "Multinational Product Planning: Strategic Alternatives", *Journal of Marketing*, Vol. 33, January 1969, pp. 58-62.

28. Halfill, D.S., "Multinational Marketing Strategy: Implications of Attitudes Towards Country of Origin", *Management International Review*, Vol. 20 No. 4, 1980, pp. 26-29.

29. Samli, A.C., "International Marketing Strategy Decisions and the Growth Rate of Major American Firms", *European Journal of Marketing*, Vol. 8 No. 2, 1974, pp. 108-118.

30. Copulsky, W., "Strategies in Industrial Marketing", *Industrial Marketing Management*, Vol. 5, 1976, pp. 23-27.

31. Cunningham, M.T. and Hammouda, M.A.A., "Product Strategy for Industrial Goods", *Journal of Management Studies,* Vol. 6 No. 2, May 1969, pp. 223-242.

32. Forbis, J.L. and Mehta, T., "Value-Based Strategies for Industrial Products", *Business Horizons,* Vol. 24 No. 3, May/June 1981, pp. 32-42.

33. Corey, E.R., "Key Options in Market Selection and Product Planning", *Harvard Business Review,* Vol. 53 No. 5, September/October 1975, pp. 119-128.

34. Taylor, B. and Sparks, J.R., *Corporate Strategy and Planning*, London, Heinemann, 1979.

35. Hussey, D.E., *Corporate Planning*, Oxford, Pergamon, 1979.

36. Ackoff, R.L., *A Concept of Corporate Planning*, New York, Wiley, 1970.

37. Higgins, J.C., *Strategic and Operational Planning Systems,* London, Prentice-Hall, 1980.

38. Denning, B.W., *Introduction to Corporate Planning: Selected Concepts*, London, McGraw-Hill, 1971.

39. Society for Long-Range Planning, "Editorial Definition", *Long-Range Planning*, Vol. 14 No. 1, 1981.

40. Scott, B.W., *Long-Range Planning in American Industry,* American Management Association, 1965.

41. Winkler, J., *Winkler on Marketing Planning*, London, Associated Business Programmes/Cassell, 1972.

42. Kollat, D.T., Blackwell, R.D. and Robeson, J.F., *Strategic Marketing,* New York, Holt, Rinehart and Winston, 1972.

43. Hovell, P.J., "The Marketing Concept and Corporate Strategy", *Management Decision,* Vol. 17 No. 2, 1979, pp. 157-167.

44. Drucker, P., *Management: Tasks, Responsibilities, Practices,* New York, Harper and Row, 1973.

45. Kotler, P., "Strategic Planning and the Marketing Process", *Business,* Vol. 30 No. 3, May-June 1980, pp. 2-9.

46. McCarthy, E.J., *Basic Marketing,* seventh edition, USA, Richard Irwin, 1981.

47. Fogg, C.D., "New Business Planning: the Acquisition Process", *Industrial Marketing Management,* Vol. 5, 1976, pp. 95-113.

48. Abell, D.F., "Strategic Windows", *Journal of marketing*, Vol. 42 No. 3, July 1978, pp. 21-26.

49. Abell, D.F. and Hammond, J.S., *Strategic Market Planning,* Englewood Cliffs, Prentice-Hall, 1979.

50. Hayes, R.H. and Abernathy, W.J., "Managing Our Way to Economic Decline", *Harvard Business Review,* Vol. 58, July-August 1980, pp. 67-77.

51. Anderson, P.F., "Marketing Strategic Planning and the Theory of the Firm", *Journal of Marketing*, Vol. 46, Spring 1982, pp. 15-26.

52. Piercy, N., "Cost and Profit Myopia", *Quarterly Review of Marketing*, Vol. 7 No. 4, July 1982, pp. 1-12.

53. Carroll, P.J., "The Link between Performance and Strategy", *The Journal of Business Strategy,* Vol. 2 No. 4, Spring 1982, pp. 3-20.

18. Marketing Objectives in UK and US Manufacturing Companies

by David D. Shipley

Much has been written about marketing objectives. However, during recent years empirical findings on this topic have been sparse. This leaves a gap in the literature that is important because now, more than ever, marketing practitioners need guidance on this pivotal matter. Objectives provide management with direction through the specification of particular requirements, activities and achievements. These, of course, enhance the quality of strategic management and effective marketing planning and control. In turn, these raise the probabilities of survival and success for companies operating in the harsh and turbulent contemporary business environment.

The desirable attributes of sound objectives are well known. They should be clearly defined[1] and hierarchical[2] with the corporate mission at the apex[3]. Objectives should be measurable so as to be made quantitative[4] and they should be time-specific[5]. Finally, they should be realistic and, where possible, consistent[6] and ideally they should be set in a flexible framework.

The purpose of this article* is to report information relating to some of these properties as provided by marketing executives. Specifically, the article focuses on the nature of marketing objectives and on facets of their time-relatedness, flexibility and consistency with each other. The nature of objectives is compared as between domestic and export markets and, throughout, comparisons are formed between UK and US companies.

The Surveys and the Samples

The data were collected in two interview surveys carried out by the writer among the marketing heads of manufacturing firms. Usable responses were obtained in 108 UK and 105 US companies in, respectively, 1979 and 1980. All of these organisations operate in their own domestic markets and 85 of the UK firms export significantly as do 45 of the US companies. A ten-firm pilot study was undertaken in the UK to cleanse the questionnaire of ambiguities and other problems and it was subsequently assessed by four US expatriates before being taken to their country. Small amendments were made on both occasions. Generally, technical terminology was omitted

*This article draws from an ongoing comparative study of marketing strategy which has received generous financial support from Shell UK Ltd, Hallmark International Inc., Western Litho Plate Company, The Foundation for Management Education and North Staffordshire Polytechnic.

from the questions and the face-to-face nature of the surveys enabled clarification to be provided when necessary. The interviews were arranged by telephone and their median time was 2-3 hours. The US firms were located in a trapezoidal area with Atlanta, Houston, Omaha and Chicago at its corners whereas the UK companies were dispersed fairly representatively across the country.

Table I shows the configurations of the two samples. These are generally quite well matched and although there are a few inevitable disparities they are unlikely seriously to distort the relative significance of the responses.

Table I. Characteristics of the Samples

	UK Firms (N = 108) %	US Firms (N = 105) %
Broad product type		
consumer non-durable	19 } 38	22 } 36
consumer durable	19	14
manufactured materials	12	12
components	26 } 63	30 } 64
machinery	25	22
Number of employees		
fewer than 201	20	27
201 to 1000	53	42
more than 1000	27	31
Manufacturing experience		
less than 11 years	5	3
11 to 20 years	10	8
21 to 50 years	32	39
more than 50 years	54	51
Product concentration		
single product-type	27	17
multiple product range	73	83
Ownership		
independent	44	56
subsidiary	56	44

Nature of Marketing Objectives

Common business objectives relate to survival, profitability, costs, revenue, volume, market share, risk-reduction, innovation, social responsibility, public image, etc. Objectives referring specifically to quantitative performance in the marketplace, however, usually include appropriately one of, or a combination of, profits, revenue, volume and market share.

Table II. Rank Orders of Marketing Objectives

| | Domestic Markets | | | | | | | | | | Export Markets | | | | | | | | | |
| | UK Firms | | | | | US Firms | | | | | UK Firms | | | | | US Firms | | | | |
	R1 %	R2 %	R3 %	R4 %	TR %	R1 %	R2 %	R3 %	R4 %	TR %	R1 %	R2 %	R3 %	R4 %	TR %	R1 %	R2 %	R3 %	R4 %	TR %
Specified level of profit or rate of return on capital employed	54	15	3	0	72	56	16	5	3	80	49	15	7	1	72	40	13	13	0	66
Real terms growth of profit or rate of return on capital employed	36	22	6	2	66	22	25	11	6	64	32	20	8	4	64	27	18	11	7	63
Specified amount of sales revenue	4	13	7	7	31	6	11	11	3	31	4	13	4	7	28	11	9	4	2	26
Growth of sales revenue in real terms	4	6	18	8	36	5	10	15	8	38	8	7	20	7	42	7	16	16	7	46
Specified market share of sales	3	6	13	7	29	5	9	16	8	38	1	6	9	6	22	7	13	7	9	36
Growth of market share of sales	2	8	15	7	32	8	10	12	11	41	5	7	16	7	35	9	9	13	11	42
Specified volume of sales	2	9	14	7	32	2	7	6	6	21	2	8	12	9	31	4	9	4	4	21
Growth of volume of sales	7	4	10	12	23	11	6	6	4	27	9	6	11	11	37	11	9	9	2	31
Others (please specify)	3	2	1	5	11	0	3	1	1	5	2	2	1	5	10	0	4	4	4	12

R1, R2, R3 and R4 respectively indicate ranked first, second, third and fourth in importance. TR indicates the total of ranked percentages.

The UK and US executives were asked to consider the potential marketing objectives shown in Table II and, where relevant, rank up to four of them in order of importance to their companies. Some respondents in both samples cited fewer than four and others ranked some of the objectives equally. Consequently, the columns in the response presented in Table II do not sum to 100 per cent.

Overall, there is much similarity in the findings from the two samples. This suggests that the reasons for setting the various objectives are non-random.

Predictably, profit objectives are the most frequently cited and generally the highest-ranking objectives. It is proposed that this indicates the importance of profits, the difficulties of achieving them in the prevailing hostile environment and the penalties for failure. This seems to be supported by the higher incidence and rank in all four market types of the achievement of a specified profit level as compared to real profit growth which, in turn, is consistently more than twice as prevalent as, and higher-ranking than, any of the individual non-profit objectives.

Further analysis showed that in domestic markets, only three per cent of the UK and eight per cent of the US enterprises ranked neither of the two profit objectives and, respectively, 40 per cent and 50 per cent ranked them both. When both were ranked and allowance made for their incidence of equal rank, 22 per cent of the UK firms rated the profit target above profit growth whereas only 12 per cent did the reverse. The equivalent statistics among the US companies were, respectively, 29 per cent and 11 per cent. More significantly, when one or both profit objectives were ranked, 54 per cent of the UK respondents rated specified level above growth and 38 per cent did the opposite. The corresponding US figures were, respectively, 58 per cent and 24 per cent.

These data indicate several points. First, few firms in either sample omit profit from their objective functions. Second, large numbers of respondents in both countries regard each of the profit dimensions as being relatively and absolutely important. Third, small majorities of both samples rate profit target achievement above profit growth and substantial minorities of both samples express the reverse preference. As stated, these points probably reflect the difficulties of, and pressures for, the achievement of profits in the contemporary austere environment.

Despite the predominance of profit considerations, all of the other objectives listed were ranked by substantial proportions of the firms in all the four market categories. The author has described elsewhere a number of reasons why firms pursue revenue, volume and market share objectives[7]. At the risk of inflaming writers with different opinions, however, the author subscribes to the common view that these "alternative" objectives are pursued in the belief that their achievement is conducive to profit-making. Attainment of these "alternatives" will almost certainly bring pay-offs like salary, perquisites, status, power, etc, but in the absence of revenue, volume and share there can be no profits at all.

Generally, the "alternative" objectives occupy the lower rankings in Table II and none of them is ranked first by more than 11 per cent of the firms in any of the four market classes. This, of course, is attributable to the importance of the two profit objectives.

It is interesting to compare the relative importance of the profit and "alternative" objectives in domestic and export markets. The traditional view is that in domestic markets, firms will be concerned mainly with the pursuit of profits, whereas in foreign markets they will be primarily motivated by volume objectives[8, 9, 10].

In a recent article, Piercy[11] has reported findings which contradict this view. Those findings are compared to the present data in Table III. Piercy's results were confined to his respondents' major (first priority) objectives and they were reported in aggregate form as "profit" and "volume". To facilitate a comparison, the current findings were also aggregated. The frequencies where either of the profit objectives were ranked first were summed and, as proxies for "volume", all the "alternatives" ranked first, excluding "other", were aggregated.

Table III. Top Priority Objectives in Domestic and Export Markets

Top priority objective	Domestic market			Export markets		
	Piercy's UK firms %	Present UK firms %	Present US firms %	Piercy's UK firms %	Present UK firms %	Present US firms %
Profit	79	90	78	67	81	67
Volume	19	22	37	30	29	49

The author's findings are somewhat distorted because some of the UK and US respondents ranked multiple objectives equally. Notwithstanding this, Table III shows that in all three samples, profit objectives are of top priority to large majorities of the firms in both domestic and export markets. Consequently, to varying extents, all three samples run counter to the traditionally conceived view of firms being predominantly volume-orientated in export markets. That view is challenged most strongly by the present UK companies and least strongly by their US equivalents. In all three samples, the proportion of firms which attach top priority to volume objectives overseas exceeds the proportion which rank volume first in home markets. Nevertheless, in none of the export markets is the profit objective of principal importance to fewer than 67 per cent of the firms.

All of Piercy's respondents were exporters and he reported that the vast majority set identical objectives in UK and foreign markets. Fewer than 100 per cent of the present firms are significant exporters. Of those which are, 74 per cent of the UK and 78 per cent of the US companies set identically ranked combinations of objectives in both domestic and overseas markets. Hence, in none of the three relevant samples is there strong support for the contention that firms differentiate objectives such that profits are sought domestically and volume is pursued overseas. Rather, with regard to the nature and rank of objectives, most firms appear to adopt an inflexible approach to home and export markets.

Consistency among Objectives

A task of major importance for management is to try to avoid the existence of conflict among their objectives. Indeed, the successful implementation of this task would greatly enhance the probability of attainment of any given objective. This follows from the view first expressed by Simon who observed that business objectives often do conflict and that, consequently, they become constraints on one another[12]. Moreover, these constraints collectively define feasible areas of activity rather than outcomes to be aimed for.

The factors which cause objectives to conflict are their nature and their multiplicity. Potential conflicts abound. For example, long-term growth versus short-term profits, growth versus stability, profit margin versus competitiveness, profits versus social responsibility. Similarly, there is clear scope for conflict among the objectives listed in Table III. For instance, although the acquisition of revenue, volume and market share is necessary for profit-making, an objective to increase profits is not necessarily consistent with objectives to increase any of the other three variables. Achievement of the latter might require larger marketing expenditure or lower prices, either of which could forestall the attainment of a profit objective. Although this may appear a very obvious point, it is not a trivial one, bearing in mind experiences which indicate that many business persons sometimes forget either the cost or the revenue sides of the profit equation.

As for multiplicity of marketing objectives, nearly all the firms in the entire study cite more than one. Indeed, 99 per cent of the US companies and 93 per cent of the UK enterprises specify multiple objectives and the mean number cited was 3.4 in each sample. These data mirror the author's earlier findings whereby 93 per cent of a postal sample of 728 UK companies specified multiple pricing objectives, with 2.9 being the mean[7].

Time Dimensions of Objectives
Failure to attach time horizons to objectives seriously detracts from their usefulness. For instance, an objective stated as "increase volume by 25 per cent" is far less instructive than "increase volume by 25 per cent before the end of the period of the new three-year plan".

A major disadvantage of overlooking the time dimension is that there is less pressure and so probably less effort applied to pursue an objective which lacks a deadline. Moreover, even if only one of a firm's objectives is not time-related, the whole set of objectives may remain unattained if their achievements are interdependent, as many of them are very likely to be.

On a related tack, the more distant the time specified for achievement, the less urgent is the immediate pressure to exert effort for the attainment of the objective. Hence, it is important that firms develop annual objectives and that they construct monitoring procedures for these, as well as for shorter- and longer-range objectives, so that progress can be reviewed at frequent and regular intervals. In these circumstances, any divergence of achievement from objective can be observed, diagnosed and controlled before "things get seriously out of hand".

The UK and US interviewees were not asked about monitoring mechanisms. They were, though, asked whether they set annual objectives. They were also asked whether they set longer-range objectives and, if so, over how many years.

It was found that 95 per cent of the US and 92 per cent of the UK firms set annual objectives. There is nothing startling about these high frequencies other than that both are below 100 per cent. It was established that the few companies which do not set annual objectives do not replace them with shorter-term ones. It is surmised, therefore, that short-term planning and control in these firms is at best *ad hoc* and clumsy while, at worst, non-existent.

The time distributions of the respondents' longer- and long-range objectives are shown in Table IV. What is most notable is that as many as 44 per cent of the UK firms and 32 per cent of their US counterparts do not set objectives of more than one year's duration. This presumably indicates that they do not engage in long-range planning. It might well be that the austerity of the modern environment causes these companies to allocate all of their resources to short-term survival. The plight of such firms is deserving of some sympathy. However, it would be ironic if it has been engendered by their earlier failure to plan further ahead and set long-range objectives. Be that as it may, their long-term prospects would, no doubt, be much enhanced by the introduction of some long-range orientation.

Table IV. Duration of Long- and Longer-Term Marketing Objectives

	UK Firms* 108 %	US Firms 105 %
2 years	3	2
3 years	14	14
4 years	7	4
5 years	32	46
6 to 10 years	2	3
Do not set objectives for periods longer than 1 year	44	32

*Two UK firms set both three- and five-year objectives.

The other commentable feature of Table IV is that, of the firms in both samples which do specify objectives beyond one year, most specify a five-year period and most of the rest define a three-year horizon. This accords with the texts on strategic management and marketing planning.

Flexibility of Objectives
It was noted above that many of the present firms and those of Piercy[11] set the same objectives in export markets as those they set for domestic markets. This might be tenable practice. However, environmental conditions as well as customer wants and preferences vary across countries. Consequently, it may well be more appropriate to adjust the nature of objectives as well as desired levels of achievement across a firm's different national markets. Indeed, this type of reasoning is at the centre of the literature on strategic marketing planning[1, 13].

A flexible approach to objectives is also necessitated because, among other considerations, objectives are formed on the basis of predictions about likely external environmental conditions and internal resources, both of which are susceptible to temporal change. Accordingly, if these improve substantially after objectives have been set, the level of desired achievement could be gainfully raised. On the other hand, if conditions deteriorate badly, it may be appropriate to make objectives less stringent in order to accommodate the essential quality of realism in objectives.

Alternatively, from time to time it becomes necessary to replace particular objectives, as when products move from stage to stage in the life cycle. Thus, in the growth stage the first priority may be to build market share, whereas in the decline stage the predominant objective may be to innovate. Hence, when objectives become less apt than alternatives or become otherwise inappropriate they should be replaced.

In slightly different vein, corporate objectives can be achieved through the attainment of any of several alternative objectives that may be set for or by marketing management. For example, a corporate objective to increase profits can be satisfied by the achievement of a higher revenue objective and/or a tighter costs objective. Switching priorities from one to the other as opportunities and threats arise may facilitate the attainment of a corporate objective that might otherwise remain unsatisfied. Thus, willingness to adjust the orders of hierarchical importance of marketing objectives adds a different dimension to flexibility.

The respondents in the current study were asked about this important facet of planning and control. Only 47 per cent of the UK enterprises do adjust the order of importance of their marketing objectives over time and even among the US companies only 66 per cent do. These UK data are supported by the author's earlier study on pricing objectives, where it was found that 43 per cent of the firms changed their pricing priorities through time[7]. Various explanations might account for this type of rigid approach to objectives but it seems that there is much room for improvement among the firms in both countries and particularly among the UK manufacturers.

Summary and Conclusions

This article compares several aspects of marketing objectives among UK and US manufacturing companies. It finds much binational similarity. Majorities of the firms in both countries specify profit variables as their principal objective in both domestic and export markets. This contradicts the traditional view that firms are predominantly concerned with volume in foreign markets and profits in domestic markets. Notwithstanding this, substantial proportions of the UK and US firms do specify revenue, volume and market share objectives in both their domestic and export markets. Large proportions of the two samples specify identical sets of objectives for both foreign and domestic markets.

Very large majorities of the UK and US companies pursue multiple objectives and this, along with the types of objectives sought, is conducive to conflict and some probable loss of effectiveness. Nearly all the firms specify annual objectives. However, substantial numbers of firms in both samples do not set longer-range objectives and it is contended that this impairs effective marketing planning and control and, through that, performance. Substantial proportions of the UK and US companies do not adjust the hierarchical importance of objectives over time. Arguments are posited which suggest that this form of rigidity of policy can have serious detrimental effects.

In short, although many of the firms demonstrate commendable aspects of their approach to objectives, many of them also reveal considerable scope for improvement. Little difference obtains in the apparent acumen of the US and the UK firms. The higher incidence of long-range objectives among the latter firms, though, along with their somewhat more prevalent flexibility, shows them in a more favourable light than the UK companies.

References

1. Kotler, P., "Strategic Planning and the Marketing Process", *Business,* May-June 1980, pp. 2-9. Reprinted in Cox, K. K. and McGinnis, V. J. (Eds.), *Strategic Market Decisions: A Reader,* Englewood Cliffs, Prentice Hall, 1982.
2. Granger, C. H., "The Hierarchy of Objectives", *Harvard Business Review,* May-June 1964, pp. 63-74.
3. Argenti, A. J. A., "Objectives", in Kempner, T. (Ed.), *A Handbook of Management,* London, Penguin, 1976.
4. Eilon, S., *Aspects of Management,* Oxford, Pergamon, 1979.
5. Kotler, P., *Marketing Management: Analysis, Planning and Control,* fourth edition, Englewood Cliffs, Prentice-Hall, 1980.
6. Wilson, R. M. S., *Management Controls and Marketing Planning,* London, William Heinemann, 1979.
7. Shipley, D. D., "Pricing Objectives in British Manufacturing Industry", *Journal of Industrial Economics,* Vol. XXIX No. 4, June 1981, pp. 429-43.
8. Cooper, R. A., Hartley, K. and Harvey, C. R. H., *Export Performance and the Pressure of Demand,* Allen and Unwin, 1970.
9. PEP, *Attitudes in British Management,* London, Penguin, 1966.
10. Tookey, D. A., "Factors Associated with Success in Exporting", *Journal of Mangement Studies,* Vol. 1, March 1964, pp. 48-66.
11. Piercy, N., "Export Marketing Management in Medium-Sized British Firms", *European Journal of Marketing,* Vol. 17 No. 1, 1983, pp. 48-67.
12. Simon, H. A., "On the Concept of Organisational Goal", *Administrative Science Quarterly,* Vol. 9 No. 1, June 1964, pp. 1-22.
13. Abell, D. F., "Metamorphosis in Marketing Planning", in Cox, K. K. and McGinnis, V. J. (Eds.), *Strategic Market Decisions: A Reader,* Englewood Cliffs, Prentice-Hall, 1982.

19. A Multinational Approach to New Product Development

by James Espey

Introduction

No company, no matter what its historical dominance or its present assets, can survive the scrap heap if it isn't, on the one hand, aware of change and, on the other, active in reacting constructively to take advantage of the opportunities that change presents. In essence, this is what new product development is all about. It is not just a question of finding new products but rather of building new businesses. On the other side of the coin, the only certainty about new products is that most of them fail — yet they are the lifeline to business survival.

This latter statement in itself spawns one of the greatest problems facing management, namely inertia or fear, or probably both. It is axiomatic that, if most new products fail, the way to avoid personal failure is never to support new product launches. One might facetiously say: become a good committee man, avoid sticking your neck out and you will rise through the ranks of the organisation. Sad, but often true. The fact remains, however, that only those companies that have the courage to launch new brands and make things really happen will survive in today's competitive world.

Various A. C. Nielson reports indicate that companies that introduce new products show a much faster profit and sales gain rate than those that do not. As far back as 1961 A. C. Nielson found in the UK that during the previous 12 months 46 per cent of all detergent sales, 34 per cent of all margarine sales, 26 per cent of all ready-to-eat cereals and 20 per cent of all toilet soap sales were made by brands and types introduced since 1950. In other words, little has changed in over 30 years.

Taking the correct positive view of new product development, not only are new products the lifeblood of a company but they encourage and foster excitement, pleasure and ultimately fiscal reward.

Wind[28] in a recent work remarks that idiosyncratic personal, interpersonal, organisational and environmental conditions preclude the prescription of a single best organisational design.

Perhaps the key in all of this is to create the right environmental climate where new product development is actively fostered with a degree of failure to be expected. The crime is not the failure of the new brand, but the failure to try.

This study seeks to outline one solution to the problem by analysing the successful efforts of International Distillers and Vintners, a multinational corporate group specialising in alcoholic beverages.

Corporate Structure

For IDV the answer was to develop a simple but logical central group structure which permitted free, flexible and innovative marketing management, especially in the area of product development. Silver[16] explains this emphasis on new products: "By 1986 nearly one third of a company's total profits will be supplied by products that are not in the marketplace today (1982)".

The necessity to restructure is best explained in terms of mechanistic and organic structures as proposed by Taylor[25].

The more common mechanistic structure lies in the formal hierarchical positions of the firm leading to individual conformity and a reduction in the diffusion of creative behaviour. An organic structure is one of high complexity, low centralisation, low formalisation and low stratification.

For marketing to function effectively, communication between Production, Accounts and Sales is a necessity. A company operating a mechanistic structure is likely to learn from Production what a company can and cannot do; from Sales what the company can and cannot sell; and from Accounts what the company can and cannot afford. Mason[18] predictably determined that such a structure inhibits innovation. Miller[20] researched further to conclude that firms with an organic structure are more innovative.

To reap the benefits of internal corporate flexibility and co-ordination, IDV established a Group Marketing Division at the pivotal centre of corporate operations, charged with the responsibility for stimulating and controlling new product development at the centre and in the localities. Set aside from the usual inherent mechanistic problems this group benefits as an organic sub-system.

The success of this formula has been realised through the development of a number of brands — Piat d'Or, Malibu and Dunhill Whisky, etc. However, the best known of these new brands and the clearest example of the success of this approach to creative marketing is Baileys Irish Cream, a cream and whisky-based liqueur which created its own brand category as it rose rapidly to world-wide success.

To put in perspective the dramatic impact of the Group Marketing Department on IDV new product development and especially Baileys Irish Cream, a brief history of IDV is necessary.

Corporate Background

IDV was formed in 1962 from the merger of two major wine and spirit companies, W. & A. Gilbey and United Wine Traders. It brought together the production knowledge of the former with the marketing skill of the latter. The two companies combined an impressive but unstructured portfolio of long-established and prestigious brands in various stages of international maturity. Economic, social and political fluctuations, at home and overseas, meant many of the brands had become particularly vulnerable; of particular concern were J & B Rare Whisky in America and Gilbey's Gin in the UK. At the time of merger both companies needed a period of stability in which to undertake rationalisation.

In the 1960s IDV continued to expand its portfolio of brands. In conjunction with the success of Croft Original and Black Velvet, IDV became agents for Smirnoff, a brand that was to experience substantial and rapid growth, aided by increased distribution gained through an agreement with Watneys to sell through their outlets.

During these years IDV's technical proficiency grew to the point that in many parts of the world its technical know-how was unequalled. However, little was happening from a marketing perspective. Money that could have been spent on brand development was spent elsewhere. The result was a portfolio of established brands that was in danger of relying too heavily upon existing strengths and consumer tastes. Needed was an injection of funds to stimulate growth in these brands, and a commitment to new product development.

IDV was drifting. Direction from top management was often lacking. J. White[27] makes the point that employee behaviour is influenced by the organisation's expectations of how employees act. Therefore, if there is no change in the "organisation's expectations", employees continue as before. Each IDV company continued to operate much as it always had done, with little co-ordinated policy or attempt to build international brands or rationalise existing activities. There was no visible central marketing structure or strategic marketing direction. Brand marketing was stated to be important, but there was no central definition of what a brand might be. From a marketing perspective IDV looked like an uneasy confederation of fiefdoms, each one at odds with the others, rather than a rationally organised business enterprise.

Another major problem was the lack of innovative direction from the centre. With Research and Development situated outside Marketing, it was looked on as a department of intellectual "boffins". This structure constituted a drag on the process of innovation: not only were these "boffins" looked on with scepticism by top executives, but the distance of R & D from the marketplace resulted in products being produced not geared to the market or consumer needs.

In 1972 IDV was acquired by Grand Metropolitan, a UK-based international corporation with holdings in various consumer products and services. The take-over did little at first to improve the lack of direction within IDV.

Group Marketing Policy

In 1976 the first sign of a new philosophy emerged through the appointment of a new IDV Managing Director with a strong marketing background. It took him little time to reach the conclusion that IDV was nothing more than a collection of different operating companies bound together essentially by history, some brands, and with little real central co-ordination or direction. In effect, IDV was a very loose confederation with perhaps the only significant link being the central company operating as the banker.

On the positive side, the company had a number of successful brands and many good executives, both in the UK and overseas, who each in their respective operations were diligently endeavouring to maximise profit. On the negative side, however, it was readily apparent that the company had no clear cut sense of direction. What was the very reason for being in business? The answer to this question was definitely not clear, and there was little cohesion — if any — in the Group itself. This manifested itself through a mediocre profit track record.

It was also evident from consultation with a great number of executives that IDV was truly ready for change. Not only were most people looking for clear cut leadership but, frankly, the uncertainty of the 1970s was not conducive to management effectiveness and generally people were looking for the company to have a clear sense of direction.

Essentially the task was to give closer direction to an international group in order to maximise the synergy available whilst retaining entrepreneurial flair in each subsidiary company.

The strength of IDV rested upon its small brand portfolio and, in particular, J&B Rare. It seemed obvious, therefore, that a greater preoccupation with brand building and a reduced dependence on J&B Rare made commercial sense. With this in mind, early in 1977 a new director was appointed to the Main Board with prime responsibility for directing the group's marketing thrust.

The new Group Marketing Director's primary function was to set priorities for international brands and on new international brand development. In so doing it was made clear that his job was to operate as a catalyst and not as a line manager pulling together the strands of the company's brand activity. Whilst he enjoyed the leverage of being a Main Board Director, too heavy-handed an approach would obviously have been counter-productive. In fulfilling his role he took charge of a number of departments which were already operative but very much in isolation, in particular the New Product Department and Research & Development. Both of these elements operated independently and enjoyed limited top management support. As such, without someone to support them at Board level it was obvious that many ideas would and did fall to the ground.

Shortly after the establishment of the Group Marketing Division the company put together its first formal corporate strategy which essentially defined IDV's prime objective as *to maximise long-term profit through the marketing of a wide range of profitable international brands*. In achieving this objective a limited number of brands was selected which would be actively supported to maximise their world potential. In addition, the strategy formalised the need for an active new product development programme; on the one hand to develop a wide range of new potential brands and, on the other, to speed up the decision-making process to determine whether or not they were viable.

This change signalled a major shift in corporate philosophy from a production orientation, in which the major goal was to maximise the utilisation of existing production facilities, to a marketing orientation, a philosophy unanimously supported at Board level. This strategy put a premium on the development of existing brands and new products and on marketing synergy within the IDV world-wide group.

Having stated a commitment to brand building and new product development the next problem was to devise a corporate structure which would centralise marketing direction but preserve tactical executional autonomy within subsidiary companies.

Each subsidiary operates in a different cultural, social, economic and political environment and is a specialist in recognising and reacting to short-term problems specific to its market, often without the need to involve Group head office. However, there are problems and opportunities not specific to a particular market that, if solved jointly by subsidiary divisions and corporate head office, would save duplication of resources. It therefore became central management's task to harness and co-ordinate overall effort to benefit local interests and the larger interests of the Group: "with co-ordination comes control".

The centre was to become a solid base providing corporate direction whilst at the same time encouraging the free flow of ideas to and from the subsidiaries. If IDV personnel at the centre could develop a structure to balance this combination of interests, the result would be a more open and improved communication and information flow; IDV at the centre would be a catalyst for new ideas. It has been shown[22] that organisations dependent on a larger parent are more willing to innovate than others, especially if the internal climate is conducive to change — an important goal for IDV. However, there is no single best organisational design to stimulate innovation. Ultimate success is bound up in the management of change in human relationships that results from structural transformation.

The newly appointed Group Marketing Division had a challenging task, for whilst in principle it was warmly welcomed there was always the danger that companies accustomed to operating independently would now see central support as "Head Office interference". For the first time ever there was a Main Board Director backed by a small team who now had formal power to become involved in each company's marketing and product development strategy.

Specifically Group Marketing was set up to institute central marketing direction and to propagate a greater concentration on brand building and new product development. Its major duties include:

(a) providing product development input to any member company in the Group, drawing upon IDV's technical expertise and extensive experience in all major markets;

(b) funding product development work from R & D to the preliminary phases of market research, thereby co-ordinating under one authority the many steps involved in this long process;

(c) providing new product input based on directives from central IDV management.

These directives blended the federalised arrangement of member companies within a multinational corporate group and the needs of central management for tighter control over Group operations.

New Product Development Policy

Prior to 1977, R & D had been a separate department headed by an executive who lacked the necessary authority to translate ideas into practice. It was also regarded as a team of backroom technicians who should be kept away from the marketplace.

With the formation of Group Marketing, R & D was incorporated into the new structure to work directly alongside New Product Development. Hopkins[13] emphasises the benefits:

— the marketing department is close to the marketplace and therefore sensitive to marketing opportunities, so products are likely to meet customer needs;

— planning and control of new product activities are centralised in competent hands;

— development of new products is likely to be carried out with urgency and drive;

— management commitment to new product development is emphasised, making product innovators feel an integral part of the organisation.

In IDV the new product development function is a small team responsible for conceiving new products, formulating them, studying the marketing possibilities and taking them through the pilot production and testing phases, thus emulating the venture team structure.

Cannon[4] states that the use of a venture group within a large organisation is an attempt to recreate the environment of a small company that allows entrepreneurial freedom with the additional benefit of resource availability. Also implicit is the fact that the team is outside the regular organisational structure, enabling more freedom and flexibility than other departments.

> A venture team is created with the freedom to carry through a project in a climate of entrepreneurship.

The benefits are therefore held to be:

> . . .a self-sufficient and highly motivated and committed permanent group, a high degree of visibility and close contact with top management[11].

The IDV New Product Development team adopted this structure for these very reasons. The rationale behind it is clearly stated by Peters and Waterman in their book, *In Search of Excellence* — small firms produce about 24 times as many innovations per R & D dollars as large firms.

The New Product Development team's functions also include setting up and administering research projects on behalf of member companies within the Group, visits to member countries for consultation and exchange of ideas, and help in package design and product optimisation.

The principle that the more people involved in a project the more successful the result does not work. The creative people responsible for a new brand concept are likely to be the most enthusiastic, and therefore should keep responsibility for the project as long as possible. Setting up committees to pronounce on individual elements in a brand mix merely aggravates problems.

David[9] expands:

— committee performance is seldom at the level of its best member;
— below optional performance results even when the tasks can be allocated to sub-groups;
— members do not work together to maximise the total effectiveness of the group. The result is often an excessive outlay in time, market research and money.

At the head of this New Product Development team is a senior executive known in company jargon as "The Resident Madman"; as described by Sands and Warwick[24]:

> 'a corporate revolutionary', an unorthodox individual with acute powers of observation and concentration.

He is an in-house entrepreneur supposed to look beyond corporate obstacles. Yet he starts with far more resources than most entrepreneurs. Not only has he been employed in a similar capacity for a number of years, thus bringing his own unique style and experience to the job, but he is also given direct access to key personnel in IDV companies and all specialised units (e.g., R & D).

The task of the madman and his team is to survey the world wine and spirits industry in search of opportunities. Verhage[26] explains:

> Being open to ideas from many different sources may stimulate the creative process and favourably influence both the quantity and quality of ideas.

However, control is maintained by a hurdle system which requires review of the team's efforts by top marketing management at each stage in the brand development process, thus co-ordinating innovative ideas with commercial guidelines,

> Successful innovation is founded, not in a committee process, but on the motivation and energies of entrepreneurs. The marketing input must inform the judgement of the entrepreneurs, not replace it[19].

Besides the resident madman, the team includes a highly qualified R & D man and a small outside consultancy company. The consultant brings experience in fields other than the liquor industry. He must be sufficiently experienced and professional to be aware of the company's resources and limitations, but detached enough not to be too constrained by existing principles and practices. The Group can also call upon the services of the entire Group Marketing and Group R & D departments.

The resident madman reports directly to a Main Board Director, thus ensuring that, in contrast to the structure prior to 1977, the top executive responsible for new product development has "clout" at the highest level. He also acts as a source of motivation to the Group and lends a commercial dimension to new ideas. Millman[21] calls this person "the sponsor".

> A senior executive who takes on the role of protector; he is given the job of seeing new ideas are not condemned to death before receiving a fair hearing.

The importance of a positive attitude towards development amongst IDV's management and especially at Board level is crucial. Even if IDV has an excellent organisation for new product development or excellent new product opportunities, the launching of new products would fail without the necessary management support.

The development of new markets and products involves inherent risk. The willingness to accept this risk is dependent on the climate established by senior management. This climate affects the corporate character of IDV. With top management supporting a climate of creativity, innovation and risk taking has been established in the new product development group.

A number of studies have been done which positively correlate new product development success with top management support. Goulding[12] sums them up:

> Management attitudes prevailing within an organisation are of vital importance to successful new product development. Not only must senior management negotiate the finance for the project, but also they should provide the creative atmosphere, judgmental abilities and a willingness to take risks.

In IDV's case the importance of the Board member in terms of financial control at each stage of the development process cannot be overstressed. Davidson[8] found that corporate egocentricity, lack of objectivity and arrogance could bring about failure. With the top executive having to justify commercially his decisions at Board level the likelihood of these factors becoming predominant is reduced.

The key to this corporate structure of a small new product group headed by a resident madman who reports directly to a Main Board Director is that whilst the latter controls, represents and protects the Group, the former is left to act as an entrepreneurial innovator free to seek new opportunities and ideas unhindered.

The history of Baileys Irish Cream illustrates the workings of IDV's marketing philosophy. Baileys resulted from the combination of corporate and marketplace opportunity. Whilst the brand was launched in 1974 it really took off from 1977 onwards which coincided with the R&A Bailey Company enjoying the active support of the consolidated Group Marketing Division and, through them, the senior directorate of IDV.

The Example of Baileys
In the 1970s external research of the wine and spirit environment showed a number of changes likely to affect the direction of future development. These were:

— the traditional market segments (gin, whisky, vodka, etc) were maturing rapidly — further growth seemed unlikely;
— a move towards lighter alcohol products;
— an increase in women buying alcohol;
— the existence of a diverse and relatively under-developed liqueur segment;
— a liqueur segment not dominated by one strong brand.

Initial analysis of market trends and opportunities, therefore, strongly suggested there was a gap in the market for a pleasant-tasting light liqueur. IDV followed up this line of research due to two factors. Firstly, in the liqueur market alcohol content is a less significant factor in determining preference. Since IDV could conceivably reduce alcoholic strength to a minimum acceptable level (for a liqueur) without significantly affecting consumer response, a new liqueur product could be offered at a highly attractive price whilst at the same time increasing the profit margin. Consumers purchase liqueurs for their taste, not for their alcoholic content. A liqueur also promised to be the easiest and least expensive kind of product to introduce:

— market research could be carried out with little difficulty and at low cost;
— consumer reaction to new drink types is relatively quick;
— heavy expenditure on media advertising is not always necessary due to the uniqueness of the product.

Secondly, most liqueurs (Benedictine, Drambuie) have a low "use up" rate (the speed at which a product is consumed); they are high proof, difficult to drink and therefore take a long time to finish. IDV's notion was to produce an instantly palatable liqueur that invited rapid consumption.

Coincidentally a compatible corporate opportunity presented itself. In Ireland, Grand Metropolitan not only owned a small and successful Gilbey's subsidiary, but also Express Dairies. At the time the dairy company was in the process of looking at new markets for its products and Gilbey's of Ireland were looking to develop a brand for export.

A consultant liaising with Gilbey's of Ireland and Group Marketing had previously done some work on Irish dairy products (Kerrygold butter) and suggested the possibility of combining some of Express Dairies' surplus cream with whisky produced by Gilbey's of Ireland. Although it was not yet clear how to combine the two, the new environment within product development at the centre ensured that the idea was accepted in true entrepreneurial spirit; the "madman" and his team set to work!

Concurrently Gilbey's of Ireland assured Group Head Office that both they and Express Dairies had plentiful supplies of raw materials — raw whisky and cream. The result was cross-fertilisation of resources between Group (finance and technical expertise), subsidiary (whisky and local knowledge) and the external consultant (dairy experience) which led to the introduction of the most successful brand IDV has ever developed.

As well as being responsible for the raw products and local knowledge, the Irish connection also provided the "brand champion", a person who "facilitates change by accepting personal risk and making personal commitment"[2].

The brand champion is an informal organisational role that is considered an important factor in achieving success:

> Such a person appears to have a personal stake in the future of the development. [He provides] an enthusiastic and zealous approach[that is] required to nurture the project[6].

David Dand, the Chairman of Gilbey's of Ireland, fulfilled this role to the ultimate. He pushed Baileys along with drive and enthusiasm from initial concept to pilot production. When distributors were initially lukewarm about the product it was David Dand's persistence that overcame their reluctance.

With David Dand and IDV's consultant working closely with Group R & D and with the embryonic Group Marketing Division, the liqueur went through several stages of development. There were problems in producing a cream and whisky mixture that would remain stable without requiring refrigeration. These were quickly overcome by the technical staff. There were other problems deciding on a flavour. Eventually chocolate was chosen. Then there was the question of a name for the new brand. Gilbey's of Ireland selected "Baileys Irish Cream" to exploit fully the product's Irish heritage and image.

Helped by the enthusiasm of the brand champion and the Irish subsidiary, Group Marketing was now ready to move into the next phase. Here again IDV's commitment to international co-operation and co-ordination came to the fore through the use of the subsidiaries in the UK and USA — focus group studies were carried out in London and New York on product and packaging.

The results were mostly inconclusive, although there was reasonable evidence that consumers liked the taste of the new product. These first tests of Baileys did not make the decision to go ahead with further testing in the UK market any easier.

In 1974 the decision was made to install a pilot plant in Dublin with a total annual capacity of 25,000 cases. Dand sought out importers to distribute the product in key markets: Britain, Germany, Scandinavia, Canada, Australia and South Africa. By 1975 exports had reached 18,000 cases. Five years later sales would exceed one million cases a year. Thus, within a few years, the success of this innovation made Gilbey's the largest exporter of spirits and liqueurs in Ireland.

As early as 1977 IDV management was asking Gilbey's of Ireland how it would handle a million cases a year as it was necessary to ensure that production could keep pace with demand. With the best forecasts for Baileys somewhere between 50,000 to 100,000 cases by the end of the fifth year, the phenomenal growth of the brand caused problems for Group management. It was decided not to open up any new markets until sufficient production capacity had been installed.

Planning for the future of Baileys quite clearly required a decision to acquire plant and equipment. However, there was no certainty that Baileys was to be a long-term success. Despite the earlier research that pinpointed consumer demand for such a product there was no guarantee that Baileys was not a fashion brand that would only satisfy a short-term change in consumer tastes.

Before making a commitment to new and expensive production facilities, Group Marketing needed to be certain that Baileys was no short-term fad. A long-term marketing plan was put together by Group Marketing and Gilbey's of Ireland that laid the basis for future direction by emphasising strict regulations and controls for the brand:

— on the production side the aim was to ensure Baileys became a product highly reliable and consistent in quality;

— on the marketing side the plan outlined a consistent premium brand image designed to enforce the unique selling proposition of Baileys.

It was acknowledged that long-term growth and stability could be achieved only by a strict system of international brand management. The central goal through life-style advertising was to project the consistent image of Baileys as a quality product and a complement to the good life; an extract from *Advertising Age* sets the scene: "Baileys is a very secure, very comfortable non-threatening psychological place to be"[1].

Life-style advertising was seen as the most effective way to promote the new brand. However, despite commitment to a predetermined image, initial advertising was cumbersome; for example, a pub setting used for a TV commercial was inappropriate for a brand largely drunk at home. Any fear that the belief held by Kotler[17] — only 4-8 per cent of the world's products can be globally branded — might be correct was soon refuted as Baileys continued its international growth; consumers liked the taste and the image:

Liqueur brands are consumer driven. When someone buys a spirit they are buying more than taste. They are buying fashion, value and status[1].

As Baileys continued to evolve, two factors helped the brand grow internationally. Firstly, in the UK market the product benefited substantially from tastings in retail outlets; research has shown that consumers who tasted were quite likely to purchase. Secondly, as Baileys moved into overseas markets the product had become so well known through word of mouth and duty free sales that significant demand often preceded national launch.

In early 1979 the decision was made to go ahead with a new production facility in Dublin with a projected annual capacity in excess of three million cases per annum. With this in place, Baileys entered the United States market in that year. Its reputation had preceded it, and US sales therefore quickly shot up from 10,000 cases in 1979, to 150,000 cases in 1980, and 900,000 cases in 1982.

US sales this year will be comfortably in excess of one million cases and world-wide sales more than 2.5 million, making it the biggest selling international liqueur brand.

As it had done in Europe, Baileys immediately created its own brand category. Consumers who were put off by the high alcohol content of traditional liqueurs regarded Baileys as a more palatable alternative. Others who would not ordinarily buy a liqueur or speciality spirit came to think of Baileys as an affordable bit of the good life, a suggestion strongly reinforced by Baileys advertising.

Inevitably, imitators sprang up everywhere. The trend was so noticeable that *Time Magazine* devoted a whole story to the sudden vogue for cream-based liqueurs, paying special attention to Baileys. Since 1979 many of its imitators have quit the market. In many cases consumers disliked their artificial taste.

Regardless of their quality, Baileys' imitators suffered because they were clearly perceived as "me too" products, a perception which helped cement Baileys' image as *the* quality product.

Implications

IDV's success is a result of the organisation's ability to restructure in the light of environmental pressure, whilst at the same time encouraging management to accept change as an opportunity, not a threat.

Along with timing and some luck there are five other predominant internal factors that explain why IDV's restructure and renewed commitment to brands and brand building ensured the success of Baileys Irish Cream.

(1) *Structural Freedom*

> The structure of any organisation inevitably determines the communication and consequently the information flow[24].

The integration of New Product Development and Research and Development, with the creation of Group Marketing in a pivotal position meant the former became a flexible department open to all sources of new ideas. This simple structure, coupled with the support and commercial control of top management, enabled decisions to be made more quickly, and acted upon more effectively than would otherwise have been the case.

(2) *The Brand Champion*

> He possesses a combination of company and market knowledge, technical competence, drive, aggression and political astuteness[6].

In such an environment it is not enough to have a good idea. Baileys would have either died in the concept development stage or would have lingered in the pre-production stages of development if it had not been for David Dand of Gilbey's of Ireland assuming the role of brand champion. His commitment, vitality and enthusiasm were crucial.

(3) *Entrepreneurial Spirit*

> The development of new markets and/or new products involves inherent risk. The willingness to accept this risk is to some extent dependent on the corporate character[12].

The existence of a small New Product Development section allowed the team to reap the benefits of the venture group structure; namely, the creation of entrepreneurial freedom in an atmosphere conducive to innovation and risk taking.

(4) *The "Resident Madman"*

> He has the mentality of an entrepreneur who enjoys taking risks to achieve success[5].

Predominant in the entrepreneurial function was the "madman". His role was to maintain a creative compromise between the intimate world of the New Product Development team, with its need to preserve a free, informal and relaxed exchange of ideas, and the requirements of mainstream management.

He protected the team from unnecessary management interference and passed on their best ideas to his superior — the Main Board Director.

(5) *Corporate Culture*

> Important from the company's viewpoint is the ability to recognise the potential of inventive and useful ideas, and provide the organisational climate for their development...climate influences behaviour[22].

It was the Board Director's duty, along with his colleagues, to provide a secure yet dynamic culture which would achieve the balance between benefits of a secure environment and benefits of an entrepreneurial environment hungry for change and success. The result in this case was a reduction in obstacles stifling product development and an enthusiastic response from those involved.

The outline of management structure described above suggests, wrongly, that new product development takes place only at the centre of IDV's multinational corporate enterprises. As the example of Baileys shows, the central position of Group Marketing and the New Product Development team allows it to function as a catalyst for product development efforts throughout the Group's many companies.

It is easy for Baileys to overshadow all other brands but it was also during this period that Malibu, invented in South Africa as Coco Rico, was transplanted to the UK under its new name and has since become a significant international brand in its own right. Then, again, there is Piat d'Or, now the top-selling bottled French wine in the UK and rapidly becoming a global success story. In the field of product revitalisation the repackaging and relaunch of Gilbey's Gin was also strongly motivated by Group Marketing support.

There are, of course, numerous other examples but the fact remains that during the period from 1978 until 1984 IDV has exhibited unprecedented growth, largely as a result of a clear cut sense of direction and a strong emphasis on brand development.

The existence of a closely united international network affords various organisational benefits. The company is able to monitor market trends on a global as well as local basis. It also has the means to control the manufacture and marketing of developed brands in their countries of origin, and, in addition, to accelerate their diffusion across an international network, thereby achieving world brand status rapidly and effectively. Again, Baileys is a classic example.

The IDV Group Marketing structure has reduced the negative effects of the NIH factor (Not Invented Here) emanating from the member companies. The frequency of inter-group contact concerning new product development has increased with warnings of new product introduction well in advance of launch dates. These moves enable Group New Product Development to withdraw gradually from a project and concentrate on its primary task of preparing future brands. A parental eye can still be kept on new ideas for an indefinite period, but the day-to-day running of the brand is left to the subsidiary.

Sometimes an idea originates from Group headquarters; sometimes it emerges from a subsidiary company. Wherever it comes from, the crucial point is that IDV's strategy enables it to generate the most promising new ideas for a given marketing environment and to implement them as efficiently as possible.

For marketing professionals, one clear lesson emerges from the spectacular history of Baileys Irish Cream. It is this: invent your own product category and if it is successful you will remain way ahead of all future competition. However, without the right internal environment and organisational structure it should never be forgotten how easy it is for the finest seeds to fall on barren ground.

Last but not least, it must also be appreciated that in all the aforementioned the Group Marketing Director enjoys the support of the Chief Executive of IDV and his entire Board.

References

1. "Liquor Marketing", *Advertising Age,* 26 July 1984.
2. Booz, Allen and Hamilton, *New Products Management for the 1980s,* 1982.
3. Brand, D., *Corporate Culture: IDV in Perspective,* unpublished, 1985.
4. Cannon, T., "New Product Development", *European Journal of Marketing,* Vol. 12 No. 3, 1978.
5. Carson, J. and Rickards, T., *Industrial New Product Development: A Manual for the 1980s,* Gower Press, 1979.
6. Chakrabarti, A., "The Role of Product Champion in Product Innovation", *Californian Management Review,* Vol. 17 No. 2, 1974.
7. Cooper, R., "Introducing Successful New Industrial Products", *European Journal of Marketing,* Vol. 10 No. 6, 1976.
8. Davidson, J., "Why Most Consumer Brands Fail", *Harvard Business Review,* March/April, 1976.
9. Davis, J., *Group Performance,* Addison-Wesley, 1969.
10. Espey, J., *The Development of a Worldwide Strategy for IDV,* unpublished dissertation, November 1981.
11. *Financial Times,* 25 October 1984.
12. Goulding, I., "New Product Development: A Literature Review", *European Journal of Marketing,* Vol. 17 No. 3, 1983.
13. Hopkins, D., *Options in New Product Organisation,* New York, The Conference Board, 1984.
14. Kennedy, A., "The Adoption and Diffusion of New Industrial Products: A Literature Review", *European Journal of Marketing,* Vol. 17 No. 3, 1983.
15. Krausher, P., *New Products and Diversification,* Business Books, 1977.
16. Kuczmarski, T. and Silver, S., "Strategy: The Key to Successful New Product Development", *Management Review,* July 1982.
17. Quoted in Lorenz, P., *Financial Times,* 19 July 1984.
18. Mason, R., "Product Diversification and the Small Firm", *Journal of Business Policy,* Vol. 3 No. 3, 1973.
19. McIntyre, S. and Statman, M., "Managing the Risk of New Product Development", *Business Horizons,* May/June, 1982.

20. Miller, R., *Innovation, Organisation and Environment,* Sherbrooke University.
21. Millman, A., "Understanding Barriers to Product Innovation at the R & D/Marketing Interface", *European Journal of Marketing,* Vol. 16 No. 5, 1982.
22. Payne, R. and Mansfield, R., "Relationships of Perceptions of Organisational Climate to Organisational Structure, Context and Hierarchical Position", *Administrative Science Quarterly,* Vol. 18, 1978.
23. Peters, T. and Waterman, R., *In Search of Excellence,* Harper & Row, 1982.
24. Sands, S. and Warwick, K., "Successful Business Innovation: A Survey of Current Professional Views", *Californian Management Review,* Vol. 20 No. 2, 1977.
25. Taylor, J., "A Striking Characteristic of Innovators", *Journal of Market Research,* February 1977.
26. Verhage, B. *et al.,* "New Product Development in Dutch Companies: The Idea Generation Stage", *European Journal of Marketing,* Vol. 15 No. 5, 1981.
27. White, J., "Corporate Culture and Corporate Success", *Management Decision,* Vol. 22 No. 4, 1984.
28. Wind, Y., *Product Policy, Concepts, Methods and Strategy,* Addison-Wesley, 1982.

20. Marketing Asset Accounting: Scope and Rationale

by Nigel Piercy

ORIGINS AND OBJECTIVES

The source of the project represented by the articles in this volume was an initiative by Gordon Wills in 1983, when he wrote:

> My own most recent concern has been with what I call 'Marketing Asset Accounting', i.e., attempting to identify what marketing assets (like brand names, distribution penetration, quality perceptions, and the like) are worth really. We know accounting convention writes them off in year one normally[1].

Since the present writer had for some time been interested in the organisational interface between marketing and accounting, and in particular its implications for marketing decision making, our joint objective was to collect major reviews of knowledge relating to the question of the valuation of marketing assets (however those assets might be conceived) as a contribution both to the armoury of the practical marketing analyst and decision maker, and as a way of isolating and identifying avenues for useful research efforts.

Inevitably such ambitious goals are only partly achieved, but what is presented here amounts to a rigorous attack on various aspects of a problem which has major practical significance, of value both to practitioner and researcher.

The structure of what is attempted in this volume pursues the following logic.

This present introduction to the area seeks to define the scope of marketing asset accounting and to compare this with the current literature of the marketing/accounting interface, and concludes by developing the structure and rationale linking the articles presented in this volume.

MARKETING ASSETS OR MARKETING COSTS?

On one hand, our aim here is supportable by the recognition by others that marketing expenditures and activities are both "asset-based" and "asset-creating". On the other hand, it would seem that the bulk of the literature is concerned primarily with the measurement and control of marketing costs — a phenomenon earlier described by this writer as "cost and profit myopia in marketing"[2] to which we return shortly. Consider the following studies to substantiate this point.

264

Marketing Costs

Over the years a large number of studies have concentrated on the problems of measuring, evaluating and controlling marketing costs. While this is not an exhaustive review, the received model of the marketing/accounting interface may be obtained by considering the following studies.

Sevin's[3] classic examination of marketing productivity analysis in 1965 has provided the foundation for much current thinking in this area. He was concerned with the issue of productivity and, by implication, the measurement and allocation to segments of marketing costs, proposing frameworks for functionally classifying marketing costs, allocating them to various bases, and thus to products, markets, customers, and so on.

By contrast, Hise and Strawser[4] in 1970 reported on the application of capital budgeting techniques to marketing operations, seeking the measurement of return on investment of sales, channels, marketing research and advertising, essentially as a control and evaluation mechanism for marketing expenditures.

Stephens[5] has proposed the concept of a "profit-oriented marketing information system" emphasising the profit contribution of individual sales areas resulting from the variables over which the salesman had some control, based on the concept of treating each sales area as an individual business. In 1974 Mossman et al.[6] continued the theme of measuring the "profitability" of marketing, through analysing marketing costs to attach them to the relevant marketing segments, the profitability of which could then be measured.

A widely-quoted paper published in 1973[7] by Kirpalani and Shapiro focused on the "financial dimensions" of marketing management, again drawing on the conceptual tools developed in accounting and finance to highlight the possible benefits in contribution accounting and segmental analysis, marketing-oriented financial reporting, and break-even analysis, to propose the application of "rate of return" analysis to marketing operations. The ethos remained one of cost allocation and control.

Similarly, from the management accounting field, Buzby and Heitger[8] in 1976 advocated the allocation of costs to report on profit contribution by market segment, and Warner[9] in 1979 wrote about customer costing as an extension to product costing for management control. In the same vein, Rayburn[10] wrote in 1977 about the use of accounting tools for analysing and controlling marketing performance, again through the medium of reporting the costs of marketing segments to arrive at the assessment of return on investment, although also suggesting the use of other financial tools.

On the marketing side, Dunne and Wolk[11] also pursued the notion of marketing cost analysis to allow managers to assess the profitability of products, territories, and customer types, through their "modular contribution-margin income statement".

By 1980, Nduna[12] in the UK, was in a position to review the field of "marketing accounting", although still primarily as a vehicle for cost analysis and reporting. In 1983, Sheth and Frazier[13] proposed a "margin-return model for strategic marketing planning" as a way of costing and evaluating the product portfolio, and Macintyre[14] proposed a "new look" at marketing costs, reaffirming the ethos of segmental and distribution cost analysis.

Although the studies above represent only a sample of works on the marketing/accounting interface, that sample is large enough to suggest that the major focus has been on the analysis and division of marketing costs to evaluate the performance of marketing segments and ultimately to control the allocation of marketing efforts and expenditure to those segments.

While such aims are worthy enough, they ignore, and even worse obscure, what is created by marketing efforts — assets in the marketplace whose benefits are difficult to measure and which are unlikely to coincide conveniently with accounting periods.

In 1982 the present writer published a paper entitled "Cost and Profit Myopia in Marketing"[15], which had gained the 1981 UK Marketing Author of the Year Award, and which was a determined attack on the philosophy inherent in such developments in marketing theory and practice as those cited above. In fact, this paper has attracted some controversy (e.g., Griffin[16]) and, given the nature of this present exercise, there seems some value in revisiting the argument.

Cost and Profit Myopia in Marketing

On a recent consultancy visit to a multinational chemicals manufacturer (where, incidentally, until the present time the term "marketing" had itself been forbidden by Board dictat) the problems faced in developing and co-ordinating European sales and marketing were in large part undermined by such attitudes as: the products are commodities which cannot be differentiated and are sold on price; sales should ideally be run to the same controls as operate in the factory; and any changes must be evaluated in terms of the annual "bottom-line". The struggle for marketing development continues in that organisation, but the case makes a significant point — cost and profit myopia in marketing is alive and well!

The argument supporting the idea of cost and profit myopia (CPM) pursued the following logic.

CPM was defined as "a morbid, short-sighted obsession with short-term measurable costs and short-term profits", or as an attitude where:

> If cost and profit analysis in marketing leads to the use of an invalid base for decisions; if financial periods dominate our thinking; if we over-emphasise short-term financial profit and become risk-aversive and defensive in our policies; if we are tempted to drop operations (like export markets) which seem 'unprofitable' in the terms of short-term, full-cost accountancy fiction; then surely we will destroy the central core of what marketing is about. If this is true to any significant extent, then are we not in danger of becoming 'marketing bureaucrats' at the expense of entrepreneurial vigour and dynamism?[15]

Instances of such attitudes were cited from the UK engineering industry — inappropriate product deletions for small savings in direct costs leading to weak product-mixes and through overhead allocations lower "profitability" and higher prices for the remaining products; and the Boston Group study of the now-extinct UK motorcycle industry to identify a "British marketing philosophy".

The CPM argument stressed the importance of *volume* management in marketing, suggesting that:

> Marketing affects company profitability not by virtue of cost accounting and the penny-pinching of accountants attempting to control marketing, but that *marketing determines the potential for profit by managing demand and achieving sales volume targets*[15].

We cited the now-classic PIMS and Boston work and Japanese business successes in support of this point, to conclude that:

> For present purposes, these findings offer support to the claim that the most advantageous role for marketing in modern markets is to fight for volume — through action-oriented marketing research, fierce and thorough product differentiation, and effective communications — rather than to be concerned with the measurement and assessment of operations on the basis of short-term costs and profits. In terms of the BCG theories, the role of marketing in profit making is to achieve volume and market position for the company, and thus strengthen long-term profitability. In short, the specialist marketing function is seen as the management of demand, rather than cost-control in the management of supply|15|.

Finally, we argued for the separation of corporate strategy and integration from marketing, to facilitate the development of marketing as the demand/volume/revenue managing function of an organisation, and concluded on the point that:

> The case has been argued strongly, and some may see this as an attack on marketing — in fact, it is intended to be an assertion of the need to strengthen our marketing through a change in philosophy and a concentration of our efforts on volume and demand management. In some ways, perhaps the message of the paper is that we started with the marketplace and that we should re-orient ourselves towards its exploitation. Real organisational power stems from managing the 'critical uncertainties' faced by the company. The argument in this paper is that our interest should be in the 'critical uncertainties' of a marketplace recovering from recession, rather than in cost accounting. It seems that only thus may we allow the practice of entrepreneurial marketing — with vitality, creativity and innovation — rather than the bureaucratic marketing of cost-cutting, cut-back and decline. Perhaps the most important question for the individual executive to ask is: 'Are we guilty of "cost and profit myopia" in our marketing — could the case-study of "British Marketing Philosophy" have been written about us?'|15|.

In fact on reviewing the CPM argument some five years later, the basic thesis still seems attractive — an obsession with costs, particularly arbitrarily allocated costs, is at the root of a major deficiency in marketing.

However, it now appears timely to attempt to extend the case to incorporate an answer to the following argument. If we accept that marketing is, at least in part, focused on the management of demand-related variables, that process involves the expenditure of large amounts of resources. Indeed, this writer has recently estimated that of the order of five per cent of UK GNP is expended on direct marketing activities[17]. If this is so, and if marketing executives are to be able to give voice to such necessary claims for corporate resources — how can they show what is being achieved with those resources? In other words, without reneging on CPM, what values do our marketing outlays create? Indeed, if CPM is to be avoided in the practical setting, one vital and unavoidable need is to conceive of marketing *investments* rather than costs.

Marketing Assets
One of the major purposes of the present book, is, in fact, to turn attention away from the concept of marketing as a cost centre, or even a profit centre, and towards the creation of marketing assets.

In justice, the management accounting field at least offers some recognition of this difference. Smiddy[18] in 1983 raised the question of whether accounting could justifiably continue to ignore the brand as an asset, since it creates long-term profits, although such contributions to the accounting literature are rare.

Certainly, some recent contributions in the marketing field have made some moves towards recognising the notion of marketing assets. In 1983, Hugh Davidson[19] wrote about "asset-based marketing" to which we return in the next section. Earlier, King[20] contrasted "real marketing" with "accountant's marketing", the latter leading to the sacrifice of long-term brand strength to gain short-term financial savings. Similarly, Gabor's work[21] demonstrated the difference between the higher values attached by consumers to branded products compared to the price placed on them by accounting-based cost allocations.

In this sense, it may be suggested that while the marketing/accounting interface has been dominated by issues of cost allocation and control, it is implicit in the literature of marketing that efforts directed at the marketplace create intangible assets which produce income. The problem we face is how to account for such intangible assets.

THE MARKETING ASSET ACCOUNTING PROBLEM

If we take as a working definition of an asset that it is a value-producing resource, then, on the one hand, we may relatively easily identify tangible resources such as land, property, plant and so on, but also, on the other hand, almost as easily, intangible resources of various types like research and development, personnel, and most importantly what we may term, for the moment, market franchise. While techniques for evaluating tangible assets are considered to be limited in validity for strategic purposes[22], they are far more so in relation to intangible assets.

Prime among these intangible assets is what we have termed above market franchise — or marketing assets. Let us consider the nature of these assets, their importance, and the need for their evaluation in decisions with strategic implications.

The Nature of Marketing Assets

Although the specific concept of marketing assets has received little explicit recognition, as we have seen above, it is true that certain examples exist. For instance, King[23] suggested that in identifying the assets and strengths of a company, we should consider:

(a) *marketing expertise* — customers, trade goodwill, contracts, distribution, transport, sales force people and skills, experience in marketing branded goods, advertising, packaging, merchandising, consumer research, knowledge of special techniques (e.g., mail order), and management skills; and

(b) *relations with consumers* — direct experience or research knowledge of the structure of consumption, people's behaviour and motivations, and, most important, company and brand reputations — in terms of extent, coverage and meaning.

We may expand shortly on the importance of such assets, but certain characteristics emerge from the listing above. Marketing assets are: intangible; apparently measurable only in intermediate terms such as brand awareness or sales force productivity; normally created only through the investment of resources; largely outwith the normal scope of financial evaluation, other than crudely as "goodwill" to be written off as quickly as possible; and yet central to any concept of the distinctive competence of a business unit.

To recognise the significance of the Boston Consulting Group and PIMS (Profit Impact of Marketing Strategies)[24] work, we should probably add to King's list, a third factor:

(c) *market share* — relative to major competitors, as it relates to experience effects and hence to prices and profitability.

Similarly, we might add the concept of franchise with buyers, or loyalty:

(d) *brand loyalty* — an enduring relationship between the buyer and a brand personality or identity.

Indeed, one might add, too, the resource represented by distribution expertise:

(e) *logistical expertise* — skill, experience and scale in order processing, handling, delivery, storage, etc.

For instance, at Amersham International, marketing radioactive compounds throughout the world, one of the most significant marketing assets is the logistics system taking orders directly into the computer system, which both produces the necessarily complex documentation and links orders to the packaging and stock control systems, and integrates deliveries with airline schedules.

Further, if one follows Levitt's[25] prescription of "marketing success through differentiation — of anything", then one should include:

(f) *marketing organisation* — structural arrangements to interface with the environment and to promote social exchange.

Indeed, one might continue adding further to such a list and amending it for some time and adapting it to particular product-markets according to which are the critical success factors, but enough has been said to establish our present point: that many of the intangible outputs of marketing efforts may be conceived as enduring, valuable assets.

Importance of Marketing Assets

The importance of marketing assets *per se* is easily demonstrable in the sense that they provide the basis for continuing to do business and the foundation for developing a company. For instance, King[23] demonstrated how, for a manufacturer of upholstered furniture, marketing and consumer assets could be used to suggest directions for business development, as in Table I.

Similarly, Davidson[19] has described Kellogg's strategy of strengthening its long-term consumer franchise by exploiting the *Corn Flakes* brand image and identity (a product with a high market share though in long-term decline) in the launch of *Crunchy Nut Cornflakes* at a premium price. By contrast, another company described by

Table I. Marketing Assets in a Furniture Company

Marketing assets		Business directions to explore
Marketing Expertise		
Customers	Department stores	Other furniture, durables Fabrics Floor and wall coverings
	Furniture stores	Other furniture Household goods (lamps, etc)
Salesmen		Most durable products
Techniques	Order/delivery	Most durable products
	Mail order/catalogue	Wide range of household products
	Advertising	Any household goods with strong design content
Warehousing/ Transport		Removals Carrier service Container
Relations with consumers		
Understanding needs and wants	Physical comfort	Bedding Other furniture Appliances
	Social needs	Leisure products, storage Office equipment
	Decoration/prestige	Decorations House planning "Home" furnishing
Company reputation/image		Household products linked by design concept

Source: Adapted from King[23].

Davidson, rather than exploiting its marketing assets, responded to threats to its sales volume of established me-too brands, first by price-cutting in an attempt to maintain sales to the trade, second by cutting investment in plant, R & D, media spending and product quality, and finally by launching a range of private-label brands in direct competition with its own brands. Davidson concludes:

> To a stock market analyst, this company may appear reasonably successful, since it has a progressive profit record. In reality this has been achieved at a terrible cost. While Kellogg's asset-based solution strengthened its long-term consumer franchise, company X's reactive efforts severely weakened its branded position. Kellogg was practising asset-based marketing. Company X was groping along, using capacity-based or fiscal year marketing, which involves cutting the muscle as well as the fat[19].

Indeed, many cases exist exemplifying the successful use of branding and marketing strengths to develop business — Cadbury's exploitation of an identity with food quality to move from confectionery and chocolate-based food and drink into less heavily branded food markets such as instant potato, instant milk, packaged cakes, and the like, the exploitation by Marks and Spencer and Sainsbury's of buying strengths and market reputation to develop incrementally over time into new product-markets increasingly removed from their original bases[23].

The Importance of Measuring Marketing Assets

In short, the single most telling point which must be made about the importance of the concept of marketing assets, and hence by implication the techniques of marketing asset accounting, is that in the absence of explicit recognition and measurement marketing assets may be squandered.

On the one hand, marketing assets are squandered when the opportunities they represent are ignored — as shown in the case histories cited above. On the other hand, this occurs equally and possibly more subversively where decisions are made which ignore the impact of outcomes on the marketing assets which have been created possibly at great expense: a price-cut destroys an image of quality and reliability; a decision on minimum order quantity and drop size reduces the intensity of distribution; abandoning an export market writes off distribution and end-user loyalty achieved through advertising and social exchange; and so on.

For such reasons it is claimed that marketing asset accounting is central to developing "asset-based marketing" of the type formulated by Davidson[19], and to making explicit a major outcome of marketing efforts.

In addition, one has to recognise the corporate setting for marketing and strategic decision making. One source of organisational power has been described as "paradigm development", or the strength achieved by groups through developing a common conceptual framework, a common language, and so on. In the same way, the conflict between departments such as marketing and finance may be conceived as "paradigmatic competition" — a competition among organisational participants to determine whose view of the world will prevail. At its simplest level there is a danger that the marketing viewpoint in developing corporate strategies will be heard less because of the lack of a paradigm or language in which to enter the advocacy of market-oriented policies. While it might be said that this has always been the case, this factor is of increasing concern for two reasons which are of growing significance. First, the environment faced is hostile — and organisational decline and cut-back is inevitably more political than is a situation of growth — and, second, the departmentation of marketing and the corporate status or standing of the marketing department would seem to be declining. Thus, we are looking for a language, or a frame of reference, to safeguard marketing assets in the politics of decline and a weakening of corporate marketing.

If the nature and significance of our topic are accepted, let us consider the contributions which are made in this volume.

The Attack on the Marketing Asset Accounting Problem

To begin, Ken Simmonds approaches the question of how accounting may cope with the concept of a firm's *competitive position* in the marketplace — i.e., its power relative to its competitors — as an asset which is capable of being built-up or run-down. The critical point upon which he builds is that conventional accounting assessment of performance ignores the degree to which that performance is achieved at the expense of (or contributes towards) changes in competitive position. In this sense he suggests that conventional accounting provides a poor indication of the true position. Simmond's attack on this shortfall is through his concept of "strategic management accounting" to track the changing positions of competitors through a group of basic indicators, which are relatively easily operationalised. He concludes that such an approach enables the strategic analyst to estimate how alternative strategies will interact with those of competitors to change a firm's competitive position and profitability.

Second, Timothy Barrett turns to the operational issue of actually valuing the *intangible* assets created through marketing efforts, that is "all non-separable assets which yield a future advantage in the output markets of competitive organisations" — the elements subsumed within Simmonds' holistic approach to "competitive position". Barrett, too, is concerned with developing competitive strategy and criticises the traditional accounting approach for ignoring marketing assets, and thus for misrepresenting performance. He examines the traditional accounting argument and its implicit assumptions, and contrasts this with "modernalist" accounting theory. He then proposes and illustrates through a case history an approach to valuing marketing assets, based on economic value accounting, which allows the organisation to focus on intangible marketing assets, while retaining compatibility with the net present value approach to investment appraisal and which does not include the values of intangible marketing assets until there is market evidence of their economic existence.

Third, Richard Wilson approaches the general question of *accounting for marketing assets* by focusing on the shortfall between what is offered by accounting to the marketing practitioner or manager and what the latter requires and needs in information for planning, decision making and control. His basic thesis is that at the operational level a significant step forward would be simply for accountants to think in terms of investing in marketing assets rather than taking marketing outlays as current expenses. Wilson's approach is to consider the nature of assets in the general literature and way in which accountants classify assets; to review the process of asset valuation, based on traditional exchange value concepts such as historical cost, replacement cost, net realisable value and net present value of future cash flows, to draw attention to how that process leads to the neglect of marketing assets; to address the issue of investment in marketing assets and the ways in which marketing assets may be classified, and the problems of their intangibility, with particular reference to goodwill and advertising. His conclusion is that a strong case is made for taking marketing outlays as investment in assets, in the terms he has developed, as a first stage in the development of a suitable framework of operational measurements.

Fourth, Gayle Rayburn attacks the specific problem of the *time-lag of benefits* flowing from marketing investments — advertising and other marketing outlays are typically treated as current-period expenses even though their productivity may be delayed until later time periods or spread over many — in spite of developments with other intangible assets as in the case of human asset accounting. Rayburn examines the impact of traditional accounting principles on the treatment of marketing expenses, in terms of the marginal principle and conservatism, arbitrary allocation devices, and the intangibility of certain asset types, and explains the accountant's problems in reporting such outlays as advertising as a defined asset. She turns then to the availability of marketing models usable by accountants to overcome these problems and highlights the advantages gained through recognising marketing assets in this way. She concludes that it is no longer justifiable for accountants to ignore the issue of marketing assets.

Next, Harry Robinson provides a marketing view of the related issue of conceiving *marketing expenditure as capital investment*, and examines the obstacles and opportunities involved in treating marketing outlays in this way, structured around the elements of the marketing programme and the existence of models to analyse and techniques to measure their marketplace effects, and draws attention finally to the organisational implications of such changes.

Finally, Charles Moss explores further that organisational theme emerging out of Robinson's comments and the earlier points made by Simmonds and Barrett by identifying the *role of the marketing accountant* in industry. He focuses on the marketing/finance interface in organisations as one potentially fraught with conflict which it is important to resolve. He reports on his research into the emergence of the marketing accountant role in industry and the benefits which may be associated with that organisational function. The author notes the areas of policy in which the marketing accountant may have influence, although drawing attention to the practical limitations surrounding this role.

The volume closes with a review of what we believe has been achieved and what we hope will be the way forward.

References
1. Wills, G., correspondence with the writer, August 1983.
2. Piercy, N., "Cost and Profit Myopia in Marketing", *Quarterly Review of Marketing*, Summer 1982, pp. 1-12.
3. Sevin, C.H., *Marketing Productivity Analysis*, New York, McGraw-Hill, 1965.
4. Hise, R.T. and Strawser, R.H., "Application of Capital Budgeting Techniques to Marketing Operations", *MSU Business Topics*, Summer 1970, pp. 69-76.
5. Stephens, H.V., "A Profit-Oriented Marketing Information System", *Management Accounting*, September 1972, pp. 37-42.
6. Mossman, F.H., Fischer, P.M. and Crissy, W.J.E., "New Approaches to Analyzing Marketing Profitability", *Journal of Marketing*, Vol. 38, April 1974, pp. 43-48.
7. Kirpalani, V.H. and Shapiro, S.S., "Financial Dimensions of Marketing Management", *Journal of Marketing*, Vol. 37, July 1973, pp. 40-47.
8. Busby, S.L. and Heitger, L.E., "Profit Contribution of Market Segments", *Management Accounting*, November 1976, pp. 42-46.
9. Warner, W.A., "Costing for Customers", *Management Accounting*, November 1979, pp. 19-22.
10. Rayburn, L.G., "Accounting Tools in the Analysis and Control of Marketing Performance", *Industrial Marketing Management*, Vol. 6, 1977, pp. 175-182.
11. Dunne, P.M. and Wolk, H.I., "Marketing Cost Analysis: A Modularized Contribution Approach", *Journal of Marketing*, Vol. 41, July 1977, pp. 83-94.
12. Nduna, A.J., "A Pragmatic Approach to Marketing Accounting for Decision Making", *Quarterly Review of Marketing*, Vol. 6 No. 1, 1980, pp. 8-14.
13. Sheth, J.N. and Frazier, G.L., "A Margin-Return Model for Strategic Marketing Planning", *Journal of Marketing*, Vol. 47, Spring 1983, pp. 100-109.

14. Macintyre, D.K., "Marketing Costs: A New Look", *Management Accounting*, March 1983, pp. 21-28.

15. Piercy, N., *op. cit.*

16. Griffin, T., "Marketing Management — The Top and Bottom, Short and Long of It All", in *Back to Basics: The 4Ps Revisited*, Proceedings, Marketing Education Group Conference, Cranfield, 1983.

17. Piercy, N., *Marketing Budgeting — A Political and Organisational Model*, Beckenham, Croom Helm, 1985.

18. Smiddy, P., "Brands — An Asset to be Ignored?", *Accountancy*, July 1983, pp. 95-97.

19. Davidson, H., "Putting Assets First", *Marketing*, 17 November 1983, pp. 35-40.

20. King, S., "Has Marketing Failed, Or Was It Never Really Tried?", in Thomas, M., *Marketing: Bridging the Gap Between Theory and Practice*, Proceedings, Marketing Education Group Conference, Lancaster, 1982.

21. Gabor, A., *Pricing: Principles and Practices*, London, Heinemann, 1977.

22. Wensley, R., Barwise, P. and Marsh, P., *Strategic Investment Decisions: The Meeting of Marketing and Finance in the Search for Exploitable Market Imperfections*, Research in Marketing Series, No. 83/4, London Business School, 1983.

23. King, S., *Developing New Brands*, London, Pitman, 1973.

24. Abell, D.F. and Hammond, J.S., *Strategic Market Planning*, Englewood Cliffs, New Jersey, Prentice-Hall, 1979.

25. Levitt, T., "Marketing Success Through Differentiation — of Anything", *Harvard Business Review*, Vol. 58 No. 1, 1980, pp. 83-91.

Part 5 Selected Marketing Applications

21. A Service Quality Model and its Marketing Implications

by Christian Grönroos

The Missing Service Quality Concept

In order to be able to develop service marketing models and service management models one has to have a clear picture of what customers in the marketplace really are looking for and what they are evaluating in the customer relation of service firms. Nevertheless, publications on service marketing—research reports, scientific articles and books—do not include any explicit model of how the quality of a service is perceived and evaluated by consumers[1]. What we need is a model of service quality, i.e., a model which describes how the quality of services is perceived by customers. When we know this, and the components of service quality, we will be able to develop service-oriented concepts and models more successfully.

The term "service quality" is frequently used by both academicians and practitioners. However, it is never defined in a way which could guide management decisions. Too often the term "quality" is used as if it were a variable itself, and not a function of a range of resources and activities. To state that service firms, for instance, will have to develop the quality of their services to be able to compete successfully in the future is meaningless, unless one can: (1) define *how service quality is perceived* by the consumers; and (2) determine *in what way service quality is influenced*.

Today we have no service quality concept. Therefore, the purpose of the present report is to develop a service quality model. This model is tested on a sample of service business executives.

Expected Service and Perceived Service

To answer the first question of how service quality is perceived, we may find some guidance in the literature on consumer behaviour. However, theories and models of consumer behaviour and buying behaviour do not explicitly consider services. Still, literature from those areas is of some help to us.

Consumer researchers have not explicitly considered the effects of consumers' perceptions of a product after consumption to any considerable extent[2]. However, several researchers have studied the effect on expectations about product performance on post-consumption evaluations of the product[3]. Among other things, it has been found that higher levels of performance lead to higher evaluations, if expectations are held constant[4] and that conflict arousal, in relation to the consumption of a product, depends on product performance relative to the expectations of the consumer[5].

According to one writer[6] the outcome of a product will be more important to post-consumption evaluations, the higher the degree of the consumer's personal involvement in the consumption process. Higher involvement leads, for instance, to a greater degree of noticing.

Typically, services are products which require high consumer involvement in the consumption process. In the buyer-seller interactions, during the simultaneous parts of production and consumption, the consumer usually will find a lot of resources and activities to notice, and evaluate. As an example we could think of an airline company or a provider of conference services. Hence, the consumer's experience of a service can be expected to influence his post-consumption evaluation of the service quality which he has experienced, i.e., the perceived quality of the service[7].

Consequently, it is reasonable to state that the perceived quality of a given service will be the outcome of an evaluation process, where the consumer compares his expectations with the service he perceives he has received, i.e., he puts the *perceived service* against the *expected service*. The result of this process will be *the perceived quality of the service*.

Hence, the quality of the service is dependent on two variables: expected service and perceived service. Therefore, in a service quality model we need to know the resources and activities, under the control and outside the immediate control of the firm that have an impact on these variables, i.e., an answer to the second question stated in the first section of this article. We shall turn to this question in the following sections.

Promises and Performance

Traditional marketing activities—advertising, field selling, pricing, etc.—can be used in order to give *promises* to target customers[8]. Such promises influence the expectations of the customers, and have an impact on the expected service. Moreover, traditions ("we have always done so") and ideology (religion, political involvement, etc.) may also have an effect on a given customer's expectations. The same goes for word-of-mouth communication.

Furthermore, previous experience with a service also influences the expectations of a customer. The perceived service, on the other hand, is the result of the consumer's perception of the service itself. We shall now turn to the issue of how the service is perceived.

Swan and Comb have suggested that the perceived performance of a product can be divided into two sub-processes; namely, instrumental performance and expressive performance[9]. In empirical tests of these concepts and their impact on consumer satisfaction, made by these two researchers and by others[10], mostly consumer goods have been considered. The tests and the results of them are, however, of considerable theoretical relevance to services, too.

The instrumental performance of a product is the technical dimension of the product. In the context of services, it would be the technical result of a service production process: e.g., a passenger has been transported from one place to another, a medical problem has been attended to in a hospital, financial transactions of a firm have been performed. It is, so to speak, what the customer is left with, when the production process is finished. *Expressive performance* is related to "psychological" level of performance. In a service context, the expressive performance would be related to the buyer-seller interactions, i.e., to the contacts the consumer has with various resources and activities of the service firm, during the service production process when the technical outcome, the instrumental performance, is created. As an example, we may think of an airline passenger's contacts with the employees of the company, physical and technical resources, such as in-checking desks, the plane itself, seats, meals and the passenger's contacts with other passengers. The passenger's interactions with such human and non-human resources during the pre-flight, in-flight, and post-flight production processes will certainly have an effect on his evaluations of the service, and on the service he perceives he has received.

Swan and Combs argue that satisfactory instrumental performance of a product is a prerequisite for consumer satisfaction, but that this is not enough. If the expressive performance of a product is not considered satisfactory, the consumer will still feel unsatisfied, irrespective of the degree of satisfaction caused by the instrumental performance[11].

For example, a bank may manage the affairs of a customer perfectly in a technical sense—the instrumental performance is satisfactory—but if the customer is dissatisfied with the performance of the manager or the teller, or if he does not accept the idea of an automatic teller machine he is supposed to use, he will probably feel unhappy with the service he gets from the bank. Similar examples can easily be found from other areas of the service sector, such as hotels and restaurants, transportation, health care, repair and maintenance, shipping and consultancy.

In a service quality model, the different kinds of product performance ought to be translated into quality terms. In the next section we will develop the quality model.

Technical Quality and Functional Quality
The service is basically immaterial and can be characterised as an activity where production and consumption to a considerable extent take place simultaneously. In the buyer-seller interactions the service is rendered to the consumer. Clearly, what happens in these interactions will have an impact on the perceived service.

The hotel guest will get a room and a bed to sleep in, the consumer of a restaurant's services will get a meal, the train passenger will be transported from one place to another, the client of a business consultant may get a new organisation scheme, a manufacturer may get its goods transported from its inventories to a customer by a transportation firm, a bank customer may be granted a loan, etc. As we have noticed earlier, this mere technical outcome of the production process corresponds to the instrumental performance of the service. And clearly, this technical outcome of the process, i.e., *what* the consumer receives as a result of his interactions with a service firm, is important to him and to his evaluation of the quality of the service. This can be called the *technical quality* dimension. Frequently, it can be measured by the consumer in a rather objective manner, as any technical dimension of a product.

However, as the service is produced in interaction with the consumers, this technical quality dimension will not count for the total quality that the consumer perceives he gets. Obviously, he will also be influenced by the way in which the technical quality is transferred to him functionally.

The accessibility of a teller machine, a restaurant or a business consultant, the appearance and behaviour of waiters, bank tellers, travel agency representatives, bus drivers, cabin attendants, business consultants, plumbers, how these service firm employees perform, what they say and how they say it do also have an impact on the customer's view of the service. Furthermore, the more a consumer accepts self-service activities or other production-related routines, which he is expected to perform, the better he will, probably, consider the service. Moreover, the other customers simultaneously consuming the same or similar services may influence the way in which a given customer will perceive a service. Other customers may cause queues, disturb the customer, or they may, on the other hand, have a favourable impact on the atmosphere of the buyer-seller interactions.

In summary, the consumer is not only interested in what he receives as an outcome of the production process, but in the process itself. *How* he gets the technical outcome—or technical quality—functionally, is also important to him and to his view of the service he has received. This quality dimension can be called *functional quality*. Functional quality corresponds to the expressive performance of a service. Hence, we have two quality dimensions, which are quite different in nature: technical quality which answers the question of *what* the customer gets, and functional quality which, on the other hand, answers the question of *how* he gets it. Obviously, the functional quality dimension cannot be evaluated as objectively as the technical dimension. As a matter of fact, the functional dimension is perceived in a very subjective way.

The perceived service is the result of a consumer's view of a bundle of service dimensions, some of which are technical and some of which are functional in nature. When this perceived service is compared with the expected service, we get the perceived service quality. This is schematically illustrated in Figure 1. However, the figure includes a third quality dimension, the corporate image, which in some cases can be viewed as a third variable in the quality model. We shall turn to image as a quality dimension in the next section.

Image as a Quality Dimension

Usually, a service firm cannot hide behind brand names or distributors. In most cases the consumers will be able to see the firm and its resources during buyer-seller interaction. Therefore, *corporate image*, or sometimes local image of an office or another organisational unit, is of utmost importance to most service firms[12]. The expectations of the consumers are influenced by their view of the company, i.e., by the image.

The corporate image is the result of how the consumers perceive the firm. The most important part of a firm, which its customers see and perceive, is its services. Therefore, the corporate image can be expected to be built up mainly by the technical quality and the functional quality of its services. Of course, there are other factors, which also may influence the image, but they are normally less important. One may choose between two types of such factors: external factors, such as tradition, ideology and word-of-mouth, and on the other hand, traditional marketing activities, such as advertising, pricing and public relations.

Figure 1. The Service Quality Model

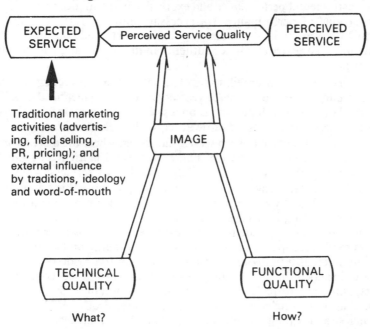

When a service firm wants to inform new target markets about its image, traditional marketing activities like image advertising can be the most effective means of doing so. Moreover, if customers in an existing market, for some reason or another, have an image of the firm which does not correspond with reality, traditional marketing activities can again be expected to be an effective way of communicating the real image to the market. In our opinion, however, advertising campaigns, or other traditional marketing activities, should not be launched, if the picture of the firm that is given the customers does not reflect an existing technical quality and functional quality. All traditional marketing efforts have an impact on the expectations of the customer, and an advertising campaign which gives the impression that the technical and/or the functional quality of the service are better than they really are, will result in an increased expected service level. If the perceived service remains on the same level as before, the gap between the expected service and the perceived service will grow, which may lead to conflict arousal. The firm will get disappointed customers. Finally, disappointed customers may cause the image to deteriorate.

However, the image may be a quality dimension. If a consumer believes that he goes to a good restaurant and the meal, for instance, is not perfect, or the behaviour of the waiter is irritating, he may still find the perceived service satisfactory. His positive image of the restaurant makes him find excuses for his negative experiences. Obviously, if he is disappointed many times, his image of the restaurant will deteriorate. In a corresponding manner, a negative image may easily increase perceived problems with service quality. Moreover, the bad image will probably become even more unfavourable.

Some Empirical Evidence Concerning the Service Quality Model

Tests in the instrumental performance and expressive performance of products indicate that the first kind of performance is a necessary, but not sufficient, condition for satisfaction[13]. Swan and Combs also argue that a satisfied consumer will be more likely to mention expressive attributes, rather than instrumental attributes, as a reason for his satisfaction.

As far as services are concerned, these observations would suggest that functional quality is more important to the perceived service than the technical quality, at least as long as the latter quality dimension is on a satisfactory level. Informal case studies, which we have done as pilot studies, lead us to the same conclusion.

This is especially important to such service industries, where the mere technical quality is very similar among firms in the marketplace, and is difficult to differentiate. As we know, this is the case for a very large number of services.

The hypothesis stated above was tested on a sample consisting of Swedish service firm executives in 1981. A random sample was drawn from a population consisting of persons participating in a series of service marketing seminars, and a questionnaire was mailed to the respondents on the average six months after the seminar. The respondents represent top management as well as marketing and other business functions, mainly internal training and personnel. Moreover, a wide range of service industries are included in the sample: e.g., banks, insurance companies, hotels, restaurants, shipping, airline companies, cleaning and maintenance, car rental companies, travel agencies, engineering consultants, architects, business consultants, advertising agencies, and a range of institutions from the public sector.

The items concerning service quality and corporate image are one part of the total questionnaire only. Approximately 60 per cent of the questionnaires were returned. This equals 219 respondents. As most service industries are very personnel intensive, and are likely to stay so in the relevant future, the performance of the employees involved in the buyer-seller interactions—the contact personnel—was used in order to operationalise the functional quality dimension. The terms contact personnel, technical quality and functional quality were familiar to the respondents.

The items used, as well as the results, are illustrated in Table I. The answers were given on Likert-type scales with five points ranging from "agree strongly" (5) to "disagree strongly" (1). The scales were analysed separately, and the results are given separately. In the table the results for all respondents are given. The picture did not change when the data were broken down according to the background variables used, such as industry, size, position of the respondent, and type of customers.

As we may see from Table I, a very large proportion of the respondents agree strongly or partly with the five first items. The buyer-seller interaction, where the functional quality emerges, is considered a more important part of marketing than traditionl marketing activities. This stresses the view that the quality-generating process, and especially the buyer-seller interaction, is of utmost importance to service marketing. We have, in other contexts, defined the management of the buyer-seller interaction as the *interactive marketing function*[14] of service firms as a complement to the traditional marketing function.

Items 2 through 4 indicate that traditional marketing activities are considered

Table I. Items and Results Concerning Service Quality and Corporate Image

Item	(1) Proportion agreeing strongly/ partly(%)	(2) n	(3) No answer
In most cases the everyday contact with customers (the buyer-seller interaction) is a more important part of marketing than traditional marketing activities, such as advertising, mass communication, etc.	94.1	218	1
The corporate image is more the result of the customer's contacts with the company (the buyer-seller interaction) than the result of traditional marketing activities	88.8	216	3
Traditional marketing activities are of marginal importance only to the view of the corporate image of the customers *the firm has today*	74.0	218	1
Word-of-mouth communication has a more substantial impact on *potential customers* than traditional marketing activities	83.5	216	3
The contact personnel's way of handling the contacts with the customers, if it is customer-oriented and service-minded, will compensate for *temporary problems* with the technical quality of the service	91.3	219	0
The contact personnel's way of handling the contacts with the customers, if it is customer-oriented and service-minded, will compensate for an overall *lower technical quality level*	37.9	217	2

Comments: The proportions in column 1 are significantly larger than 50 per cent on any significance level, except for the last item. The frequency distribution is U-shaped for this item. Consequently, no statistical tests have been applied on the total data material.

marginally important to corporate image, whereas the buyer-seller interaction and word-of-mouth is considered more effective. The fifth item indicates that functional quality is considered very important; in fact so important that a high level of functional quality (contact personnel performance) may compensate for temporary problems with the technical quality. One may also notice that more than one-third of the respondents agree strongly or partly with the sixth item, which says that good contact personel performance may even compensate for an overall lower technical quality level.

Conclusions and Marketing Implications

We may conclude that the functional quality, in fact, seems to be a very important dimension of the perceived service. In some cases it is more important than the technical quality dimension. Successful service management may, therefore, mean that attention is paid to improving the functional quality of a firm's services. Managing the buyer-seller interaction, and thus creating good functional quality, may be a powerful marketing function (interactive marketing), more important than traditional marketing activities.

The importance of traditional marketing activities to corporate image should not be over-estimated. The image is mainly the result of the perceived service. Moreover, the importance of word-of-mouth ought to be remembered.

Managing the perceived service quality means that the firm has to match the expected service and the perceived service to each other so that consumer satisfaction is achieved. In order to keep the gap between the expected service and perceived service as small as possible, two things seem to be critical to the service firm:

(1) The promises about how the service will perform given by traditional marketing activities, and communicated by word-of-mouth, must not be unrealistic when compared to the service the customers eventually will perceive.

(2) Managers have to understand how the technical quality and the functional quality of a service is influenced, and how these quality dimensions are perceived by the customers.

The first consideration has implications for advertising and other traditional marketing efforts. By such activities a view of the service which is not based on reality should not be given to the customers. Moreover, for the firm's present customers such activities are probably far less effective than the impact of the customers perceptions of the service. As potential customers are concerned, traditional marketing is more powerful.

The second consideration brings us back to the service quality model, illustrated in Figure 1. Management has to understand the importance of the functional quality, and how the two quality dimensions can be developed. The technical quality dimension is obviously a result of the know-how which the firm has. This means good technical solutions, technical abilities of the employees, etc. By appropriate use of machines and computer-based systems the technical quality may be improved.

However, as we have seen this is not enough. To ensure that the consumers are satisfied an acceptable functional quality is demanded. The contact personnel are often of vital importance to functional quality. Moreover, customer-oriented physical resources and technical resources, as well as the accessibility of the firm's services, the consumer orientation of self-service systems, and the firm's ability to maintain a continuous contact with its customers are examples of ways of influencing the functional quality dimension.

In conclusion, one should notice that the quality dimensions are interrelated. An acceptable technical quality can be thought of as a prerequisite for a successful functional quality. On the other hand, it seems as if temporary problems with the technical quality may be excused, if the functional quality is good enough. Finally, the importance of the image should be recognised.

Of course, much more research is needed, especially research on the consumers' view of service quality.

References

1. See, for example, publications by Wilson, Rathmell, Levitt, Eiglier and Langeard, Berry, Bateson, Gummesson, George, Thomas, Lovelock, Grönroos and others.

2. Bettman, J.R., *An Information Processing Theory of Consumer Choice*, Reading, Mass., Addison-Wesley, 1979, p. 275.

3. See, for example, Lewin, K. *et al.*, "Level of Aspiration", in Hunt, J.M. (ed), *Personality and Behaviour Disorders*, Vol. 1, New York, Ronalds, 1944; Cardozo, R.N., "An Experimental Study of Consumer Effort, Expectation and Satisfaction", *Journal of Marketing Research*, August, 1965; Cohen, J. and Goldberg, M.E., "The Effects of Brand Familiarity and Performance upon Post-Decision Product Evaluation", Paper presented at the American Marketing Association's Workshop on Experimental Research in Consumer Behaviour, Ohio State University, 1969; Olshavsky, R.W., and Miller, J.A.,

"Consumer Expectations, Product Performance and Perceived Product Quality", *Journal of Marketing Research,* February, 1972; Anderson, R.E., "Consumer Dissatisfaction: The Effect of Disconfirmed Expectancy on Perceived Product Performance", *Journal of Marketing Research,* February, 1973; and Oliver, R.L., "Effect of Expectation and Disconfirmation on Post-exposure Product Evaluations: An Alternative Interpretation", *Journal of Aplied Psychology,* August, 1977.

4. See Oliver, R.L., *op. cit.,* 1977.

5. Hansen, F., *Consumer Choice Behaviour: A Cognitive Theory,* New York, The Free Press, 1972, p. 179.

6. Bettman, J.R., *op. cit.,* p. 272.

7. In the area of industrial services, Johnston and Bonoma have found that firms which successfully have rendered or currently render a service, often are the only one solicited when a repeat purchase is to be made. See Johnston, W.J. and Bonoma, T.V., "Purchase Process for Capital Equipment and Services", *Industrial Marketing Management,* No. 4, 1981, p. 261.

8. Calonius, H., "Behövs begreppet löfte?", *Marknadsvetande,* No. 1, 1980 and Calonius, H., "On the Promise Concept", unpublished working paper, Swedish School of Economics, 1983.

9. Swan, J.E. and Combs, L.J., "Product Performance and Consumer Satisfaction: A New Concept", *Journal of Marketing,* April, 1976, p. 26.

10. See Maddox, R.N., "Two-factor Theory and Consumer Satisfaction: Replication and Extension", *Journal of Consumer Research,* June, 1981.

11. Swan, J.E. and Combs, L.J., *op. cit.,* p. 26.

12. Bessom, R.M., "Unique Aspects of Marketing of Services", *Arizona Business Bulletin,* November, 1973, p. 78, and Bessom, R.M. and Jackson, D.W. Jr., "Service Retailing: A Strategic Marketing Approach", *Journal of Retailing,* Summer, 1975, p. 78.

13. Swan, J. E. and Combs, L.J., *op. cit.,* pp. 27 and 32.

14. See Grönroos, C., "A Service-oriented Approach to Marketing of Services", *European Journal of Marketing,* Vol. 12 No. 8, 1978, and Grönroos, C., "Strategic Management and Marketing in the Service Sector", Helsingfors, Finland, Swedish School of Economics, 1982, p. 136ff.

22. A Re-examination of Marketing for British Non-Profit Organisations

by C. M. Octon

"Marketing is an evolving discipline that must develop new answers as new problems arise."[1] Despite a period of 15 years between this statement and Kotler and Levy's first suggestion that further developments in marketing thought and practice were necessary in the context of non-profit organisations, evolution has been slow[2]. The trend over these years has been one of repetition of conventional wisdom in the American environment in contexts which bear a strong resemblance to commercial exchange relationships. This is not a true broadening of the marketing concept as claimed by Kotler but a transfer of techniques between one situation and another where the characteristics and problems appear very similar.

The British non-profit sector, however, appears to exhibit rather different characteristics and problems both from those discussed in the American literature and those identified in the British commercial sector. Developments in traditional thinking are, therefore, necessary if the marketing concept, marketing and marketing management are to be applicable to this sector of operations.

British non-profit organisations can be classified into two main groups: public sector and voluntary sector organisations. Whilst definitions are not commonly agreed for organisations of either type, the following outlines read in conjunction with the diagram present a tentative attempt at a comprehensive, although not definitive, description of the sector.

The public sector, perhaps the more familiar of the two terms, can be defined as comprising "that part of the nation's economic activities which comes within the scope of central government including nationalised industries and other public corporations"[3].

The complexity inherent in the voluntary sector[4], however, precludes such a neat outline as the above. At a general level, these organisations can only be described by exclusion from any other sector in the following manner. Voluntary organisations are non-commercial, in that their primary objective is not profitability; the services they provide are for the benefit of clients, members, or the public at large and not for shareholders; they are not established by statute nor are they under statutory control as are the public corporations; but neither are they simply informal groups as they exhibit a formal structure of responsibility and authority. This leaves a range of organisations which abound under a number of different titles: charity, industrial and provident society, association, trust, friendly society. These terms, however, merely represent the status of the voluntary organisation for tax rating and legal purposes and are not of relevance to this discussion.

Figure 1. The British Non-Profit Sector

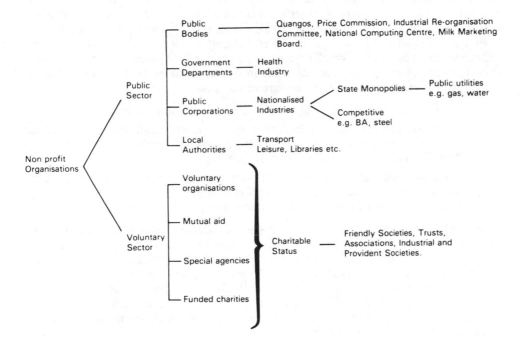

Nevertheless, if both public and voluntary sector organisations are examined carefully, they can be seen to possess certain characteristics which differentiate them from commercial organisations and which are of importance when discussing marketing theory and practice. Examples of such characteristics in the public sector might be the problematic formulation and evaluation of strategies concerning social objectives, the need to serve many publics, often on a non-discriminatory basis, and lack of continuity of policies due to a changing political environment. In the voluntary sector such characteristics are identified as servicing of dual publics for resource attraction and allocation, the nebulous nature of benefits to donors and pricing complexities when the price decision is taken by donors rather than the organisation.

If, therefore, the characteristics of non-profit organisations are different from those of commercial organisations it may not be possible to transfer conventional marketing theory and practice between the two sectors. A re-examination of conventional definitions of the marketing concept, marketing and marketing management is necessary and tentative adaptations are suggested.

Marketing

Whilst it might be generally agreed that the marketing concept is transferable from the commercial sector to the non-profit sector in its present form, the ease with which marketing can be transferred is dependent upon the nature of the exchange process. Kotler defines marketing as "a human activity directed at satisfying needs and wants through exchange processes"[5]. In the commercial field, exchange is characterised by a transaction undertaken by two parties, each of whom perceives that which is received to be of greater value than that which is given in exchange.

In a public non-profit organisation it is difficult to identify the value of the exchange to the organisation which is providing a service in the public interest. In addition, the consumer's perceptions of value in conventional terms may also be questioned in, for example, the following circumstances:

— when consumption of a public sector offering is compulsory, e.g. education;

— where payment is made indirectly by everyone although any one consumer may not need or choose to use the offering subsequently provided, e.g., the Health Service, local authority leisure services;

— where offerings are made available on a monopoly basis only and the consumer, therefore, has no choice between offerings of competing organisations, e.g., domestic power and lighting, the postal service.

In the voluntary sector, the exchange process is confused by a separation in many cases, of those who provide financial resources and those who receive the benefits. In such instances, determining the value of the exchange process to donors is problematic and is not contingent upon the beneficiary providing the rewards. This is supported by Yavas *et al.,* who claim that "it is a fact that donors to charitable organisations receive few, if any, tangible rewards; donor rewards are primarily psychological and spiritual in nature"[6]. How such rewards are measured is, as a consequence, a difficult research issue.

The voluntary organisation and, indeed, a number of public sector organisations can, therefore, perhaps best be described as intermediaries between the two parties rather than direct participants in an exchange process. It is perhaps partly because of the catalytic role of the organisation in the exchange process that the emphasis in both sectors appears to remain firmly on the provision of the offering or the nature of the cause rather than on the value of the offering as defined by the individual, whether contributor, user, donor or client. Difficulties when discussing marketing are thus compounded and the necessity to understand the exchange process is increased in importance. However, if both types of organisations can view themselves as intermediaries in the system they may achieve a more realistic perception of the relationship.

Marketing Management

Similar difficulties are encountered when discussing the transfer of marketing management between the commercial and non-profit areas. As distinct from marketing — the description and analysis of exchange processes — marketing management, as expressed by Kotler, takes place when at least one party to a potential exchange gives thoughts to objectives and means of achieving desired responses from other parties[7].

When exploring the longer-term aspects of marketing management, i.e., setting objectives and determining strategy, in both sectors, the traditional priority accorded to profitability has been subsumed by social objectives. Social objectives, however, are not easily definable, defy quantification and present problems in evaluation.

The public sector, in addition to its social responsibilities, may have financial criteria to satisfy and the importance of the latter relative to social objectives may vary significantly with prevailing political policies. It is this changeable emphasis which has posed considerable problems for public sector strategies. As the political focus changes, as it does on a frequent basis, so strategies must be shelved and new ones developed to achieve recently formulated objectives. A flexibility in planning is required which many business organisations would find difficult to achieve. A public sector organisation may experience even greater problems due to the inbuilt rigidity of the structure and atmosphere of the system.

Notwithstanding the variable political climate, criticism can be made of public sector organisations that their objectives are never likely to be socially orientated in reality whilst they appear to persist in defining the scope of their operations in product-based terminology. Levitt has identified this deficiency in the approach of the American railways and the same trait can be identified in many organisations in the British public sector[8]. This view is supported by Christopher's article about rail freight marketing[9].

However, there is a conflict inherent in this situation. For objectives to be socially orientated a market-based definition may be required, such as transportation and energy, rather than trains and gas or electricity. To operate, however, in a socially responsible manner, these organisations must provide a basic level of service, where required, to the population. To do this is an enormous and complex operation which requires a product or service emphasis if it is to be accomplished at a satisfactory level. Whilst recognising that public sector organisations may have neglected to perceive the growing competitive elements, e.g., increasing popularity of cars and motorcycles supplanting train travel and the use of the telephone and telex instead of mail, their failure to do so does not necessarily imply a failure in marketing management terms. These organisations are perhaps less concerned with growth opportunities and more with social services implying a different orientation of marketing management activities than has been suggested elsewhere from a traditional view point.

Voluntary organisations in their role as intermediary between donors and clients have found themselves in a situation where multiple objectives exist and place conflicting demands on and within the organisation. The basis for this lies often in the structure of the membership of the organisation. Often formed by those with a personal interest in a particular cause, as the organisation expands professional and perhaps more disinterested individuals are recruited to assist with the management of the organisations. This latter group lack the personal involvement of the original membership and is likely to hold and pursue rather different objectives. Such a separation within the organisation can place strains upon it which result in the sub-optimisation of any set of objectives and present problems in strategy formulation.

The reconciliation of conflicting aims for either type of organisation may require an acceptance within it that sub-optimisation will occur. The delicate balance which must be maintained between, for example, social and financial objectives in public sector organisations and resource attraction and research progress in voluntary organisations, can only be obtained through careful planning and scheduling of activities and monitoring of progress towards objectives.

Marketing management in the shorter term is concerned with decisions about the marketing mix. Issues which are of particular relevance to this discussion are the offering, segmentation of the market, market research, promotion, pricing and distribution.

The Offering and Segmentation
In the public sector, the offering is often perceived as a necessity which is provided for the public at large on a non-discriminatory basis. This requirement of wide availability demands the commitment of substantial financial resources. Ideally these are obtained by direct payments by those who consume the offering. However, certain offerings cannot be fully supported in this way as realistic pricing policies would effectively exclude lower income segments of the population, hence they are subsidised by general taxation. Other offerings, e.g., education, health service, are considered to be so essential that no pricing policy is followed, and they are financed by the total population from taxation regardless of whether they are used or how much is consumed.

As the attraction of resources and production of offerings is spread so widely across the population, it might appear that market segmentation is not applicable in the management of public sector activities. Market segmentation is considered to be a useful concept in marketing strategy formulation to ensure that organisational resources are utilised most effectively by identifying groups of individuals in the market who share unsatisfied needs and allocating efforts and resources accordingly. Public sector organisations would be strongly criticised if attempts were made to segment the market either in the area of resource attraction or provision. To restrict resource attraction to certain segments of the general public, principally those utilising the services offered or consuming the goods, would not be socially acceptable or financially viable in many instances. In the provision made by these organisations, however, although a conscious segmentation strategy is not suggested, the market does seem to segment itself naturally into users and non-users, e.g., those undertaking sports activities in local authority sports centres, those using telephone services. It would, however, seem to be contrary to public policy to permit this situation to continue without an investigation of the remaining segments whose leisure, communications or other needs may not be adequately served at the present time by the provision available. This is not to imply that the current non-user segments should be approached in a manner which might be considered discriminatory as regards the remaining population but that different strategies might be developed which might encourage utilisation. An example of an attempt to undertake this venture is illustrated by the introduction of prepayment stamps for telephone, gas and electricity services. This strategy has facilitated the use of these services by segments whose financial circumstances previously prohibited or restricted their use but may have been instituted, not for this reason, but to facilitate more efficient collection of charges from lower income sectors of the population. It is suggested, however, that this technique could be extended in its application, to enable consumers to access the service more easily.

In the voluntary sector, the offering may again be viewed as a necessity as the existence of the organisation is often based on the provision of a service not currently undertaken by the state and in which private concerns have shown little interest. Although the final target market may be more closely defined in terms of potential clients, e.g., those suffering from a particular disease or those who are disadvantaged in some other respect, there may be some confusion and conflict concerning the service which is to be provided. Should, for example, the organisation provide services directly to clients to alleviate present suffering or would clients be better served in general by a concentration on research activities?

Segmentation of the donor market is, additionally, a difficult area as shared needs are not so readily discernible. Conventional segmentation variables such as benefits sought, demographics and sociographics are of less relevance in the donor context. Yavas *et al.* suggest that psychographics, i.e., values, personality traits, attributes, interests, needs and opinions should be used to profile potential donors[10]. They develop their proposition from earlier work by Manzer and Miller who suggest that the attention of non-profit organisations (voluntary) "should focus on the values held by the individual and the various attitudes of the individual towards the organisation and its mission as correlates of donors behaviour"[11]. How useful this approach is in operational terms has yet to be demonstrated.

Marketing Research
In the tradition of marketing, the need to obtain information about the market and the whole range of marketing activities has been well established.

In the public sector there may be resistance to the instigations of large-scale information collection for two reasons:

(1) There is often a prevailing attitude amongst providers of public goods and services that the provider can best determine what is good for the population. This is well illustrated by the following quotation:

> "The official approach (to public service provision) tends to be radically different; social planners usually have a firm view about the kind of thing it would be good for people to have. This view may have emanated from a political source or from the planner's personal value system. What the community may really need does not necessarily coincide with such presuppositions. The social planner should be willing to adopt the more objective posture of commercial firms."[12]

(2) Public suspicion may be aroused if official information collection is undertaken. Although this might be ostensibly to enable improvements to be made to public services, such endeavours may be misconstrued as the assimilation of facts about the community for purposes of manipulation.

Additionally, in this sector and in the voluntary sector, criticisms could be made of the expenditure of public funds on information collection, whether voluntarily donated or subtracted from income at source, on the grounds that this money would be better spent on provision of goods or services, the stated rationale for its collection.

These points would seem to imply a more sensitive approach to the commissioning and handling of marketing research than is normally the case in a commercial enterprise. The social aspects of public and voluntary organisations suggest that information about the market and the effectiveness of resource attraction and allocation is of primary importance. To obtain this information, it may be necessary to develop, more fully, the available techniques in the interviewing field and give much less emphasis to mass collection of data using the more impersonal questionnaire format. The first stage in the process, however, must be to convince management of the necessity for such information and then subsequently, to ensure that the consumer is reassured about the usage of such information.

Promotion

This is the most visible of marketing activities and can be readily observed as an important function of many public and voluntary organisations. Buzby has promoted the telephone service and celebrities lend their support to causes undertaking fundraising activities. As in the case of marketing research a major problem to be faced by an organisation in either sector which is undertaking a promotional campaign is the criticism which may be levelled at the use of financial resources for the more commercial types of promotion, e.g., television advertising. Oxfam has attempted to overcome this problem by developing a corporate advertising campaign aimed at illustrating the efficiency of the organisation to large business concerns[13].

In the public sector, although promotion can be considered unnecessary as a method of maintaining present market positions, because competition does not exist in all circumstances, it can be justified for its informative qualities. It can encourage mass awareness of, and interest in, those goods and services which are commonly available to the public, dispel misconceptions and promote the image of public sector organisations. Where competition does exist, for example between gas and electricity as a course of power for domestic heating and cooking, serious doubts arise as to the rationale behind promotional strategies of a persuasive nature to increase demand for the service. Both of these industries are reliant on finite resources and an increase in demand will serve only to deplete these more rapidly. Might it not be preferable to concentrate more of the promotional budget on the efficient utilisation of energy sources by promoting the benefits of insulation and double glazing as started in a small way by the electricity industry rather than allocating these resources to a competitive struggle for increased demand.

Further examples can be cited concerning the attempts of public sector organisations to use promotional techniques to counter competition and increase demand, but these examples are ones where the industry finds itself in competition with goods or services not provided by the public sector. Again, the traditional promotional emphasis on competition would seem to be inappropriate. Promotional strategies should be devised to solve a particular problem and this implies that the problem has been identified correctly. British Rail and public bus transport organisations have not, it would seem, looked closely enough at the cause of declining demand. Price promotion is the widely used technique in this area with little consideration given to the fact that this variable may be less important to the consumer in choosing his mode of travel than other factors more directly related to the service being offered. If the service itself is inadequate, no amount of promotion will attract the car owning public to public transport. The important point about promotion in the context of public provision would seem to be one of emphasis. It is perhaps more justifiable and efficient in terms of resource utilisation to use promotion for informative purposes than, in effect, to increase competition between goods and services either in the same sector or in different sectors of the economy. If the service or product is adequate to satisfy the consumer, persuasion should not be necessary.

In the voluntary sector, promotion does, however, have a dual role to play. It needs to be educational to inform the public about a particular cause or need but must also be persuasive to attract resources. There is perhaps greater scope in this sector for the use of the various promotional techniques available. Personal selling, for example, can be effective in persuading organisations to donate large sums of money to a charitable cause. Leaflets and posters can also have a marked effect on contributions from institutions and the public. Two points should be appreciated, however. Firstly, as with marketing research greater sensitivity is required when constructing a message or delivering a presentation. There is a very fine line between an effective message and one which is distasteful or offensive. Secondly, the promotional medium used may often present the donor with a channel for his contribution. Voluntary donations must be made as convenient and simple as possible. Promotional literature or personal collection can facilitate this.

In both public and voluntary sectors, however, further difficulties may be experienced when selecting media to reach under-privileged groups in the population. Webster cites this as a major problem which differentiates the methods of promotion available in this context from those used in commercial organisations[14]. New channels of promotion may be necessary which utilise media not normally considered by the business firm as communication devices. An examination, for example, of where such sectors are normally to be found on a regular basis, e.g., social security offices, doctors' and dentists' surgeries, public transport, etc., may indicate new and effective vehicles for communication.

Pricing

Traditional ideas about pricing strategy must change in non-profit sector management. The commercial focus of profitability is not the main one in the organisation. Public sector pricing policies exhibit variations which range from no price, i.e., completely subsidised services, to a price which covers cost and contributes to a general reserve fund for reinvestment in the future. Completely subsidised services are generally those where a measure of consumption is compulsory or at least extremely likely, e.g., education and health, and where the welfare of the individual might be in question if a charge was levied which the individual could not pay. Those services where charges are applied range from those where subsidies are made in addition to charges, e.g., local authority leisure facilities, realistic charges per unit of consumption, e.g., passenger transport, to charges per unit plus a standing charge, e.g., gas and electricity.

Where charges are made, organisations of this nature in the public sector face a complex problem. They are under a general obligation to provide goods and services which the population can afford to consume; they are directed not to discriminate between classes of customers according to their ability to pay; they are expected to generate sufficient revenue to cover their costs and if possible produce a surplus for reinvestment (in certain industries financial targets for returns are stipulated). To achieve those first two objectives, prices must be set at the lowest level that any consumer can afford. However, due to the increasing costs of merely maintaining not even improving the goods and services provided, the possibilities of attaining the third objective are remote.

It should be noted, however, that a certain amount of discrimination is practised in pricing policies. For example, industrial users of certain public services are charged higher prices than domestic users. This is justifiable on the basis that in such cases as gas and electricity large customers are using up finite resources more quickly than small consumers and they should therefore compensate for this financially and hence provide additional revenue to finance research into alternatives. Due to heavy increases in recent years, strategies have been used to facilitate the consumption of lower-income consumers by permitting them to spread payments over a longer time period as prices have been rising. However, the arguments against discriminatory pricing policies in these sectors do not weigh so heavily when such policies are discernable in other areas of the public sector, e.g., differential charges for children and pensioners for the use of leisure facilities. A greater flexibility in pricing throughout would seem to be suggested; however, it is not clear that this is a viable strategy if pricing objectives remain in conflict as outlined above.

In the voluntary sector, pricing has a different perspective. If donations are to be attracted, the amount contributed remains at the discretion of the individual donor and, as such, prices are not set. Pricing, in these situations, is more concerned with segmenting the market by donation potential, i.e., organisations, wealthy individuals and the general public. The remaining task is one of communicating the benefit which can be provided by certain monetary units, e.g., for a certain sum the organisation can undertake specific relief activities or research programmes. There is a great need, in addition, to justify expenditure and publicise results of activities undertaken in terms which are easily comprehended by the majority. Where voluntary organisations are providing goods or services to the public in general which are not essential, however, (e.g., a zoo), pricing policies may operate on a more commercial basis than is normally acceptable in the non-profit sector if surpluses are required for reinvestment in facilities.

Distribution

One of the major problems facing many organisations in the public sector is the issue of adequate distribution of goods or services to all members of the population who wish to use them as no system exists which is comparable to the retail structure available for products and some commercial service organisations. A higher level of financial resources is necessary to provide national services and vast networks to distribute them, e.g., gas and electricity. Herein lies one of the justifications for nationalisation. At the local level, where it is necessary to make provision for a local community which requires performance of the service in one location, distribution becomes a question of where best to locate provision for ease of access for the whole community rather than the more traditional view of the distribution function taking the offering as close to the consumer as possible. Examples can be found in the siting of post offices and leisure facilities. Provision of these services in conjunction with other service provision, to achieve economies of distribution effort and resources, has only been considered on a minor scale in the case of sub-post offices run jointly with a general store. In the main, provision is made at a separate physical location.

Distribution strategies within a voluntary organisation may be concerned either with the above question of siting of facilities, or, in the case of many charitable causes, in making the organisation accessible to the donor to facilitate collection of money. Many different strategies can be identified in this area including the street collector, the placement of collecting tins in public places, publicity citing addresses to which contributions can be sent, convenant directly from the bank to the organisation. If it is accepted, as proposed earlier, that voluntary and public sector organisations may be viewed as intermediaries in an exchange process between two parties, the emphasis placed on distribution, to date, would seem inadequate. It is suggested that more diligent attention to facilities presently available and usage of such premises to give better access to the organisation might accord the distribution function its proper role in the marketing mix.

In addition to physical facilities, however, the distribution function may require the use of voluntary personnel, either to collect financial resources, to distribute services or to supplement paid labour directly employed by the organisation. Webster suggests that organisations utilising such labour, or indeed, those working closely with volunteers in a complementary role, may encounter a range of problems concerning the organisation, supervision, compensation and control of volunteer labour which a commercial organisation would not have to consider[15]. The role of the salesman in a commercial organisation could perhaps provide guidelines in this area, but more important, would indicate departures from that situation and, as a result, where new methods are required, utilise fully and effectively the manpower available.

Conclusion

Although the broadening process described by Kotler has been disputed in this article, this should not be interpreted as condemnation of the principle. It is sound and relevant in the context of the British non-profit sector. This sector comprises a number of organisations, the ownership, structure and objectives of which do not correspond to the traditional model of business organisations. They exhibit characteristics and experience problems which are of a different nature to those found either in the same sector in America or in the commercial sector in either country. It is unlikely, therefore, that traditional marketing thought and practice will be directly applicable to this sector. Consequently, conventional marketing wisdom has been questioned and some indications have been given for the direction of evolution of marketing and marketing management in the future. American authors are perhaps fortunate in the apparent similarity between their commercial and non-business sectors. British authors, however, should view the dissimilarities between their two economic sectors as an opportunity to develop the marketing concept, marketing and marketing management in a much wider context than that of business management.

References
1. Kotler, P., *Marketing Management: Analysis, Planning and Control,* fourth edition, London, Prentice Hall, 1980, p. 708.
2. Kotler, P. and Levy, S., "Broadening the Concept of Marketing", *Journal of Marketing,* Vol. 33, January, 1969, pp. 10-15.
3. *Everyman's Dictionary of Economics,* compiled by A. Seldon and E. Pennance, London, Dent, 1965.
4. See, for example, Hatch, S., *Outside the State,* London, Croom Helm, 1980.
5. Kotler, P., *op. cit.,* p. 19.
6. Yavas, U., Rieken, G. and Parameswaran, R., "Using Psychographics to Profile Potential Donors", *Business,* Vol. 30 No. 5, 1980, pp. 41-45.
7. Kotler, P., *op. cit.,* p. 22.
8. Levitt, T., "Marketing Myopia", *Harvard Business Review,* July-August, 1980, pp. 45-56.
9. Christopher, M., "Rail Freight Marketing: Some UK Perspectives", *European Journal of Marketing,* Vol. 9 No. 3, 1975, pp. 178-187.
10. Yavas, U., Rieken, G. and Parameswaran, R., *op. cit.,* pp. 41-45.
11. Manzer, L. L. and Miller, S. J., "An Examination of Value — Attitude Structure in the Study of Donor Behaviour", *10th Annual Conference: American Institute for Decision Sciences,* in R. J. Ebert and R. J. Munroe, (Eds.), Columbia, University of Missouri, 1978, pp. 204-206.
12. Chisnall, P. M., "Marketing Surveys and Social Planning", *The Hospitals and Health Service Review,* May 1977, pp. 158-160, incorporating an idea from: Tuck, M., "How methods of commercial research can help social planners", Budapest, *Esomar Conference,* 1973.
13. Fisher, D., "Oxfam Appeals to Big Business", *Marketing,* Vol. 4 No. 9, 1981, pp. 18-20.
14. Webster, F. E., "Social Marketing", *Management Decision,* Vol. 13 No. 1, 1975, pp. 70-77.
15. Webster, F. E., *op. cit.,* p. 708.

23. The Evolution of Marketing in Small Firms

by David J. Carson

Introduction

How does any small firm get involved in marketing? Surely every firm needs customers, therefore every firm, if it is to become established and thrive, must automatically be involved in some aspect of marketing? Such marketing may be instinctive and intuitive and without pre-planning or forethought, but only by performing certain marketing functions will a firm continue to exist. For example, only by providing a "product" that satisfies some need or other for some customers, somewhere; by selling this at a "price" which some customers are willing to pay; by delivering as and when some customers find acceptable, and so on, does any firm approach survival.

Marketing activities which are performed instinctively are of undoubted importance to a firm's survival. But the question of why small firms are not more considerate of their marketing function must be asked. Why don't they give it the same rating of importance as, say, finance and accounting functions? The answer may lie in the very characteristics of small firms and how these characteristics influence the marketing undertaken by the small firm at the various stages of its development.

In this article, the characteristics of small firms are considered from a marketing perspective. In addition, the marketing undertaken by firms at different stages of development, from start-up through to the relative sophistication of a medium-sized firm, is examined.

What are the Marketing Characteristics of Small Firms?

It is well recognised that small firms have different characteristics from those of large companies, but what specifically are the characteristics of small firms? Schollhammer and Kurilof[1] put forward five sets of qualitative attributes of small businesses.

— *Scope of operations.* Small firms serve predominantly a local or regional market rather than a national or international market.

— *Scale of operations.* Small firms tend to have a very limited share of a given market; they are relatively small in a given industry.

— *Ownership.* The equity of small firms is generally owned by one person or, at most, a very few people. Small firms tend to be managed directly by their owner or owners.

— *Independence*. Small firms are independent in the sense that they are not part of a complex enterprise system such as a small division of a large enterprise. Independence also means that the firm's owner/managers have ultimate authority and effective control over the business, even though their freedom may be constrained by obligations to financial institutions.

— *Management style*. Small firms are generally managed in a personalised fashion. Managers of small firms tend to know all the employees personally, they participate in all aspects of managing the business, and there is no general sharing of the decision-making process.

Management as a Weakness

It is this last characteristic of small firms' management style that dominates much of the literature and is often cited as the single most significant factor influencing the development of a business. Indeed, there is statistical support for the argument that the calibre and experience of management are the most important factors in determining business success. One example of such statistical evidence is Dun and Bradstreet's *Business Failures Record*[2].

Similarly, Tate, Megginson, Scott and Trueblood[3] list amongst the characteristics of small business managers that of "limited formal business education". This is reiterated by Broom, Longenecker and Moore who state that small business problems and failures arise out of: "lack of managerial skill and depth; and personal lack and misuse of time"[4].

Woodruff[5] goes further and puts forward 18 management traps to avoid in small business management. These range from inadequate records through lack of development and information to internal conflicts.

Lack of Financial Resources

The other, well documented, inhibiting characteristic of small firms is the lack of financial resources due to a limited equity base. For example, Hodgetts[6] states that "owners put only a small amount of capital into the business" which becomes quickly exhausted. Consequently, according to Hodgetts, the biggest problem faced by small businesses is under-capitalisation.

The Need for "Specialists" and "Experts"

The problem of finance is fairly obvious and widely recognised. But there is another, less immediately apparent, problem which is a significant issue when considering marketing in small firms. This issue concerns not only the style of management in a small firm, but also the very size of the business operation and the ability to employ specialists.

All the standard marketing texts appear to assume the existence of a marketing manager and imply that a prerequisite of successful marketing is the existence of a specialist in the field. Clearly most small firms do not have a marketing specialist.

Broom, Longenecker and Moore[7] have observed a general weakness in marketing by small firms and have suggested that this may be a consequence of the difficulty small firms have in attracting and affording qualified personnel. In similar vein,

Gaedeke and Tootelian[8] comment that an owner of a small firm needs to be, or become, his own "expert" in many areas because, unlike a large company, he is not usually in a position to employ experts. It is because of this need to be a general specialist that Schollhammer and Kuriloff[9] have noted that an essential difference in managing small and large firms is that, in the former, the focus is on the pragmatic use of techniques as aids to problem solving, whereas in the latter it is on achieving "high co-ordination of control of specialists".

Marketing Constraints on Small Firms
Looking at the characteristics of small firms above from a marketing perspective, three broad types of constraints on marketing by small firms may be identified. They are:

— limited resources,
— lack of specialist expertise,
— limited impact on the market place.

Limited resources, such as limitations on finance, marketing knowledge, time, may all contribute to limited marketing activity relative to large companies and large competitors.

Specialist expertise may be a constraint because managers in small businesses tend to be generalists rather than specialists. Traditionally, the owner/manager is a technical or craft expert; he is unlikely to be an expert trained in any of the major business disciplines. In addition, marketing expertise is often the last of the business disciplines to be acquired by an expanding small company. That is, finance and production (if the company is a manufacturing unit) experts usually precede the acquisition of a marketing counterpart.

Limited impact on the market place may be a constraint because small businesses have fewer orders, less customers and fewer employees than large companies. Consequently, the impact of a small firm's presence in an industry, geographic area, or whatever, is likely to be limited due to its size alone. Similarly, because of limited resources and lack of marketing expertise, the impact on the media through advertising and publicity will often be negligible in relation to large company activities.

The Basis of Evolution of Marketing in Small Firms
Accepting that these marketing limitations broadly exist and apply to most small firms, consideration can be given to the actual practice of marketing in small firms, and how it evolves from when a new company is established through to when it is about to break through the threshold to being a medium-size firm.

The basis of this "evolution" lies in the widely documented concept of the business life cycle. Some writers put much store on the significance of this life cycle to small business success. Justis[10], for example, argues that the business life cycle acts as a guide to small firms for working through different stages of business life. More significantly, Schollhammer and Kuriloff[11] draw attention to the need for awareness of the changing role of top management as the organisation grows. Essentially they see the role changing from one of task-orientated activities and line responsibility to one of co-ordination, strategic planning and public relations.

This life cycle and resulting shift in management emphasis as it relates to marketing is described by Tyebsee, Bruno and McIntyre[12] who argue that growing ventures can anticipate their marketing stages. They suggest that a "company passes through a four-stage marketing development process. In the initial stage, entrepreneurs sell customised products to friends and contacts. They must then exploit a larger market place through the stages of opportunistic marketing, responsive marketing and finally diversified marketing."

Marketing Evolution in Practice
Observation of, and involvement with, small business marketing in Northern Ireland suggests a pattern of evolution of marketing in small firms that has many similarities with the evolutionary process proposed by Tyebsee *et al.,* but which is, nevertheless, significantly different. Both models, for example, identify a four-stage evolutionary process — but the stages are not directly comparable. In particular, the model described here identifies a different development process for firms moving from reactive to proactive marketing.

The four stages of marketing evolution to emerge from study of the small business economy of Northern Ireland are as follows:

Stage (1) — initial marketing activity;

Stage (2) — reactive selling;

Stage (3) — the DIY marketing approach;

Stage (4) — integrated proactive marketing.

Stage (1): Initial Marketing Activity
New firms enter markets and find customers in ways largely dictated by specific industry norms. For example, a newly established small firm in the engineering industry will often start with one major customer which is usually a large firm; a new firm in the distribution field may be based on the procurement of a franchise; and a new service firm may begin operations with a few "familiar" clients. The overriding common denominator for any new firm's customers is that, in almost every case, they are known personally to the entrepreneur and initial transactions have commenced either by the firm making contact with the customer on a *personal* basis, or by the customer making a *personal* request for supply.

At this stage of operation, the main marketing ingredients are product quality and function, price and delivery. In most cases there is virtually no promotional support and minimal selling activity. Furthermore, these marketing components are unlikely to be co-ordinated or performed in an integrative fashion. Indeed, the main concern of the new firm is usually the production of the product, since this is where the expertise of the owner mostly lies. Even factors such as delivery are considered secondary to getting the product right, because delivery only matters when and if production of the product is satisfactorily completed. It is also likely that prices are set low, often too low, hence the frequently encountered problem of poor profitability amongst new firms.

Thus it can be said that marketing, as it is generally recognised and accepted, does not exist, or at best is performed in a very primitive fashion, in most new firm start-ups. What does exist is the use of a few marketing elements in a haphazard and un-conscious way — that is, without the benefit of co-ordination. If the combination of the marketing elements are satisfying a market need, the new start-up firm will probably benefit from a small firm's most important and effective promotional tool, word-of-mouth recommendation. It is, perhaps, stretching a point to suggest that word-of-mouth recommendation be utilised as a marketing tool, since it is not, by any means, a controllable factor. On the other hand, it is fair to say that the performance of the small firm in terms of its product price and delivery, its marketing elements or tools which are controllable, will be strong influences on, and contribute towards, the word-of-mouth activity by customers.

How do new small firms increase sales and expand business? Obviously, by satisfy-ing the requirements of existing customers a new firm can often increase its business with these customers. This is usually achieved by two main means. Firstly, the word-of-mouth recommendation of existing customers as mentioned above; and secondly, by enquiries from potential users who have seen or had secondhand experience of the product. Many new firms continue to expand at an acceptable pace for quite a long time on this basis.

Stage (2): Reactive Selling

As the number of customers increases, and their industrial and geographic spread expands, it is probable that the small firm will begin to include more marketing com-ponents in its operations. Because new enquiries are increasingly coming from strangers who may not even have mutual acquaintances as introductions, it becomes necessary for the small firm to provide more formal information on its products, prices, delivery dates, etc. To do this, the small firm may produce an embryonic brochure and some standard promotional letters. At the same time it will tend to develop and refine the sales patter it uses both on the telephone and in the promotional letters.

Such marketing activity can be deemed to be almost totally *reactive* to enquiry and demand. There is seldom any question of the firm going out and looking for customers; rather, customers are secured by reacting to their initial enquiry. The owner of the small firm may never be aware of it, but it is likely that as much potential business, indeed more, is lost than won through lack of attention to detail and lack of apprecia-tion for the potential customers' request for information. Unless potential customers are furnished with the information they want when they want it, many will fade away or lose interest.

With time the small firm will tend to secure more business from enquiries. This is because the accumulated experience of dealing with enquiries teaches the small firm the best way to react to them and the need for adequate printed material to enable potential customers to be furnished with reliable initial information quickly and efficiently.

Reactive marketing is perfectly suited to many small firms as long as competition is minimal and there is a buoyant demand. As long as enquiries come streaming in, and as long as existing customers demand larger repeat orders, then the small firm will continue to thrive. But what happens when these sources begin to stagnate or decline? What must the small firm do to market itself?

Need for more Sales
The need for more sales will probably arise from a number of factors which can either occur separately, consequently or together. Some such factors are:

— Overheads begin to increase. Gaedeke and Tootelian[13] suggest that one of the weaknesses of small firms is that at a certain stage there is a tendency to have "too much fixed capital going into fixed assets".

— Gaedeke and Tootelian also state a weakness to be that of unplanned expansion. This can easily result in too many employees being taken on under one of the numerous employment grant schemes which may then expire.

— Sales activity, especially in one area of industry, may have reached a level that attracts the attention of the main competitor. This competitor may begin to move in for himself, or begin to react in defence, by using his greater marketing muscle and resources.

— The market niche that the small firm has carved out for itself, and in which it has existed until now, may be nearing saturation.

— With unplanned growth, the product range may well have expanded without any concurrent rationalisation. The small firm may thus offer a wide range of products with many lines making only a minimal contribution to profit but which still tie up valuable scarce resources.

All of the above factors will result in a squeeze on profits, and whilst some rationalisation can be carried out in areas such as the product range, the real need is for increased sales. As a general rule, the small firm must continue to expand because it is too small and usually too young to stagnate. And the soundest basis for expansion is a consistent growth of sales revenue.

Change in Attitude
It is this pressure for more sales that can bring about a fundamental change in attitude towards marketing in the owner/manager of the small firm. Until now it is likely that he has paid only lip service to marketing and will undoubtedly have felt that the firm did not really need "fancy marketing". But with the need for more sales he will probably look more seriously to marketing and, hopefully, will even recognise the value of seeking out new customers. Certainly it appears that he will look upon marketing with less misgiving and suspicion than previously.

This change in attitude seems crucial to the future expansion and development of the small firm — and the approach the small firm adopts towards marketing issues.

The Small Business "Catch 22"
How does the small firm set about improving its marketing to achieve the desired sales growth? It is at this stage that consideration may be given to employing a marketing person. But what type of marketing person?

Initial thinking may well suggest a junior executive with little or no marketing experience, since this is often the least costly alternative. This, however, is seldom a very satisfactory solution because it is often quite some time before the junior executive makes any real contribution to the marketing effort of the firm. Then, just as some definite benefits are being realised, the junior executive tends to move on to bigger and, as he perceives, better pastures. Furthermore, these junior executives need training that the small firm has neither the resources nor the expertise to provide.

Another alternative is to employ an experienced marketing executive who is able to make an immediate impact on the marketing of the firm. However, such people are both in demand and (as a consequence) expensive. This raises two issues for the small firm:

— Can the firm afford a marketing "expert"?

— Will there be enough marketing activity, initially, to justify and satisfy such a person?

It is likely that the answer to both these questions will be "no", at least, not until sales activity increases.

So, here we have the Catch 22 situation. The small firm needs to increase sales and has reached the point when to do so requires the contribution of marketing expertise to develop a more proactive approach to marketing and selling. But limited resources and marketing activity cannot usually support the employment of such an expert — until sales have increased. In other words, an increased level of sales is needed to be able to afford or justify a marketing specialist; but a marketing specialist is needed to increase sales to this level!

Stage (3): The "DIY" Marketing Approach
The Catch 22 situation usually means that the owner/manager of the firm tries to find out something about marketing and starts to dabble in new marketing activity. Bearing in mind the change in attitude towards marketing that has frequently occurred, this is a logical and natural development.

The performance of the small firm in marketing will thus depend to a large extent on the aptitude for marketing of the owner/manager. Often this is a problem because, as already noted, he frequently has a production-orientated or craftsman background which tends to mean a way of thinking, an approach to business, which is incompatible with a marketing orientation. Against this possible weakness there are the strengths of the vested interest and the commitment of the entrepreneur to his creation, his firm. This means that the experiments in marketing are undertaken with optimism controlled by caution. After all, it is his money that is being "spent"!

These first steps into marketing, as marketing is usually thought of, will be tentative in most cases owing to the unfamiliarity of the task. Some observers have noted this with implied criticism, but in fact it can be a saving grace as it mitigates against over-indulgence in the trimmings of marketing. Any such over-indulgence can easily mean the use of ineffective but expensive marketing methods which leave a legacy of scepticism about marketing that can taint all future activity.

Very often, the actual direction taken by this marketing initiative is strongly influenced by the grants and assistance available from the small business support agencies of the Government. This can, and does, lead to imbalances in the overall marketing package, but on the positive side it encourages experimentation with different marketing tools and in so doing increases awareness and understanding of the various aspects of marketing.

However, although a favourable marketing attitude may be developed alongside the working knowledge of various marketing tools, there is rarely any co-ordination or integration of the marketing effort. On the contrary, the marketing mostly comprises a series of spasmodic and disjointed initiatives. This is wasteful and weakens the impact of the marketing — but rarely is this recognised by the owner/manager of the firm, especially if he is achieving a "satisfactory" increase in sales.

Stage (4): Integrated Proactive Marketing

This final stage is reached when the firm has developed an integrative and proactive approach to marketing which is characterised by each marketing activity supporting the others with the whole effort working towards the achievement of clear short-, medium- and long-term objectives. In other words, the fourth stage represents professional marketing.

Most firms find difficulty in moving from the DIY approach of stage (3) to the professionalism of stage (4). Again, consideration may be given to employing a marketing expert to effect the transition, but immediately the small firm comes up against the Catch 22 unless sales can support such a person which typically they cannot until stage (4) is reached.

One solution is buying-in marketing expertise on a part-time basis. In this way the small firm obtains the necessary marketing assistance at a cost that matches the available limited resources; whilst the marketing expert generates an appropriate "salary" from a number of sources, and has the challenge of dealing with several different marketing situations.

Some small firms have clubbed together under the auspices of a co-operative and employed a marketing expert whom they share. The concept and practice of co-operative marketing is not new and, indeed, there are many successful examples to draw on from throughout the world[14].

Another approach is for a marketing consultant to provide a service specifically geared to the requirements of the small firm. The time at which such a consultant is brought in seems crucial to the overall success of the relationship. If it is too soon then neither the small firm nor its owner will be ready for, or receptive to, the input of the consultant expert; if too late, the part-time service will be unable to satisfy the marketing needs of the firm.

Many, even most, small firms that have survived long enough to reach stage (3) do eventually progress to stage (4). What differs is the ease with which they do so. When stage (4) is reached the firm is normally in a position to employ a marketing expert of its own, full-time. This appointment then becomes the start of a future marketing department and the move away from being a small firm to being a medium firm, with its own set of characteristics and problems.

Figure 1 summarises the four stages of marketing evolution identified.

Figure 1. Four Stages of Marketing Evolution

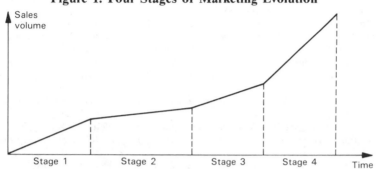

(1) This reflects the initial sales surge due largely to repeat orders and word-of-mouth activity.

(2) This reflects the reactive marketing stage which leads to the levelling of sales and the need for more sales .

(3) This reflects the haphazard marketing activity of the owner/manager and ends with his having to address the same problem as at the beginning of this stage — how to acquire marketing expertise.

(4) This is the stage at which sales will justify and support a marketing expert on a full-time basis. The problem facing many small firms is how to progress to stage (4), that is, how to overcome the "Catch 22".

Conclusion

This article has put forward a four-stage model of the evolution of marketing in the development of small firms which, it is argued, is the norm for *most* firms. As such it provides a framework, and starting point, for further analyses of small business marketing. But, in addition, and on a more immediate and practical level, the model provides indicators for consultants and educators working with small businesses of the most appropriate types of assistance they can give at each stage of marketing development.

Obviously not all small firms will conform to this model. Some will introduce, and benefit from, a marketing approach from the beginning. It is interesting to note, however, that in Northern Ireland (and there is no reason to suggest that this area is any different to the rest of the UK in this respect) the small businesses that do introduce marketing from inception, and that owe much of their development to sound marketing, nearly always have an entrepreneur with some prior marketing education or training. This suggests that it may be preferable to provide some marketing education to *potential* entrepreneurs *before* they launch a new business, rather than concentrate all marketing educational efforts on the entrepreneur already in business.

References

1. Schollhammer, H. and Kuriloff, A., *Entrepreneurship and Small Business Management,* John Wiley and Sons, 1979, p. 179.
2. Dun and Bradstreet, *Business Failures Record,* 1978.
3. Tate, C. E., Megginson, L. C., Scott, C. R. and Trueblood, L. R., *Successful Small Business Management,* Business Publications Inc., 1975, pp. 3-14.

4. Broom, H. H., Longenecker, J. and Moore, C. W., *Small Business Management,* sixth edition, South Western Publishing Co., 1983, p. 585.

5. Woodruff, A. W., "Traps to Avoid in Small Business Management", *Management Aids for Small Manufacturers,* Annual No. 6, Washington, DC, US Small Business Administration.

6. Hodgetts, R. M., *Effective Small Business Management,* Academic Press, 1982, pp. 33, 34.

7. Broom, H. N., Longenecker, J. and Moore, C. W., *Small Business Management, op. cit.,* p. 574.

8. Gaedeke, R. M. and Tootelian, D. H., *Small Business Management,* Goodyear Publishing Co., 1980, p. 15.

9. Schollhammer, H. and Kuriloff, A., *Entrepreneurship and Small Business Management, op. cit.,* pp. 179-181.

10. Justis, R. T., *Managing Your Small Business,* Prentice-Hall, 1981, p. 404.

11. Schollhammer, H. and Kuriloff, A., *Entrepreneurship and Small Business Management, op. cit.,* pp. 229-239.

12. Tyebsee, T. T., Bruno, A. V. and McIntyre, S. D., "Growing Ventures Can Anticipate Marketing Styles", *Harvard Business Review,* January-February 1983, pp. 64-66.

13. Gaedeke, R. M. and Tootelian, D. H., *Small Business Management, op. cit.,* p. 19.

14. Economists Advisory Group Ltd, *Co-operative Marketing and Joint Trading for Small Firms,* Vol. 1: *Summary and Recommendations,* 1984.

24. Export Marketing Management in Medium-Sized British Firms

by Nigel Piercy

Introduction

The aim of this paper is to examine the export market strategy decision and the base for export competition in medium-sized firms, while taking the internationalisation of the firm and its export objectives as important situational influences. The hypothesis on which this approach is founded is that decisions on export strategy and competition (whether they are explicit or implicit) underpin and shape the operational policies which are possible. For example, many of the prescriptions to exporters to employ more export specialists are based on the assumption that the firm has, or should have, an objective of export-led growth. The common recommendation to adapt products and marketing communications to individual export markets rests on the supposition that exports are best developed by market penetration and specialisation.

It may be that in many cases such assumptions, and the recommendations based on them, are wholly appropriate, but the contention in this article is that the present state of marketing knowledge, especially in exporting, is inadequate as a foundation for universal truths and general prescriptions. Rather, the approach taken here is based on the notion that greater attention should be focused on differentiating export cases and situations to determine the appropriate policies in particular circumstances. Such descriptions may contribute to an empirically based normative body of export marketing theory, although the aim here is more modest. The article draws on the results of a recent survey of export marketing policies in medium-sized manufacturing companies in the north of England, to challenge the "accepted wisdom" of the prescriptive theories of export marketing. The technical details of the survey are summarised in Appendix I. It should be borne in mind that the survey reported was essentially of an exploratory nature, and the results of the survey should be read in the light of the fact that the majority of the responding companies (75 per cent) were in the 100-500 employee category, and gained a relatively small proportion of total sales from exporting: 55 per cent of the firms obtained less than 20 per cent, and 75 per cent of the firms gained less than one-third of total business from overseas.

Internationalisation and Export Objectives

The literature of export management contains various suggestions that firms behave

307

differently towards the problems and opportunities of the export market-place, according to the stage of the development of their non-domestic business:

> "as the firm progresses from exporting to international marketing to international business, the objectives, policies and organization are adapted" [1].

The general proposition that there are various stages in, or at least types of, internationalisation is found in a number of works. A more detailed review of the literature of internationalisation has been provided elsewhere by this writer [2], but in this present context the extant literature leads to a crude but effective empirical device.

On the basis of the exploratory interviews conducted, and using the general internationalisation concepts of passivity/activity and centrality/peripheral role for exporting, a scale question was used leading to the division of exporting firms in the survey into two categories: *reactive,* responding to unsolicited orders from abroad, or to a need to make up volume shortfalls in UK sales; and *active,* where exporting has a central, growth role [2].

While this is a relatively crude form of analysis, reflecting the exploratory nature of the study, it was found that various generalisations could be made about companies in the different internationalisation groups. These generalisations are summarised in Table I. Generally it seems that exporters adopting active and reactive stances towards exporting differ in terms of size, the contribution of exports to total sales, export strategy, export price discrimination, export pricing methods and pricing currency. The suggestion which these data support is that export behaviour is related to the firm's stage of internationalisation, as suggested by the general literature, but in the specific ways noted above. This is significant in evaluating the

Table I. Active and Reactive Exporter Marketing Policies

	Active Exporters	Reactive Exporters
Company size	Larger (501-2000 employees)	Smaller (100-500 employees)
Export contribution to total sales	High (More than 11%)	Low Low (0-10%)
Export price discrimination	More discrimination	Less discrimination
Export pricing method	Market-based	Cost-based
Export pricing currency	More foreign currency invoicing	Less foreign currency invoicing

policies pursued by the individual exporting company, since the implication is that policies should be judged in the context of the firm's internationalisation. In many ways it is this differentiation which seems to be missing from the general, prescriptive models advanced in exporting.

The closely related question of corporate objectives in exporting is also worthy of attention.

The most important implications of the general literature of corporate objectives, for exporting, lie in the recognition of non-maximising behaviour and non-profit aims. Tookey [3] has suggested that exporting is mainly concerned with the disposal of surplus production capacity, and others concur in the claim that volume issues may be more important than short-term profit in export marketing [4,5,6,7,8,9]. However, Bilkey [10] points out that the findings about the export goals that firms pursue are mixed, and that in addition to the emphasis on volume noted above others have found that exporting was used as a means of gaining high profits and increasing profitability when the home market was depressed [11,12].

To some extent, variability in findings throughout the world may reflect the problems in measuring objectives reliably and with validity.

In the survey reported here, respondent choice of major objectives was constrained to the single major aim in export and in the UK, to overcome the measurement problem, although necessarily at the expense of obscuring the multiple objectives pursued. Conclusions are therefore restricted to broad categories of objectives and the contrast between UK and export objectives.

As shown in Table II, it was found that both UK and export objectives were primarily associated with profit, and apparently in both cases with satisficing. It is true that a higher proportion of firms pursued volume as the major aim in exporting than was the case for the UK, but the fact remains that two-thirds of the exporters associated international sales mainly with profit objectives.

It was found that the vast majority of firms pursued the *same* goals in UK and export marketing, and very few of the responding companies reflected the traditional view advanced, for example, by Silberston [13], where domestic business involves the pursuit of profit and exporting the pursuit of volume. Thus, under current conditions, it seems that firms emphasise profit in both UK and export markets. The implications of this will be pursued later, but lie mainly in challenging the traditional view of exporting as "marginal" business [14].

Table II. Objectives in UK and Export Markets

Major Objectives	%	In the UK	%	%	In Exports	%
To earn maximum short-run profit	—	Profit	79	2	Profit	67
To earn maximum long-run profit	26	Profit	79	18	Profit	67
To earn a satisfactory rate of profit	53			47		
To gain the highest possible market share	8			7		
To sell as much as possible	11	Volume	19	19	Volume	30
To sell surplus capacity not taken by the UK	N-A					4
Others	2 N = 223			3 N = 235		

Export Market Strategy

Perhaps the most widely propagated normative theory in export management is the prescription of concentration on key markets and it is, after all, difficult to dispute the fundamental importance of market numbers in determining the policies possible in all areas of the export marketing mix. An earlier conceptual paper in this journal [15] compared the available prescriptions and the weaknesses in their logic. The present survey attempted to assess empirically some of the underlying assumptions of the key market principles in exporting.

Market Numbers

To begin, the export market numbers pursued by firms in the survey were significantly and substantially lower than those found in the earlier studies [16,17]. This comparison is shown in Table III, and shows that considerably fewer exporting firms dealt with the large market numbers claimed by other writers to be typical of UK firms, and attracting their severe criticism. One explanation for these differences is methodological: both the earlier studies cited used non-probability samples of large, "successful", "committed" exporters, while this present survey by the writer was based on a random sample, which has greater claims to being representative of medium-sized firms. In fact, confirmation of the finding in this survey is provided by a recent Industrial Market Research Ltd survey [18], which also used a random sampling method, and produced similar results to those in this survey, as far as market numbers were concerned.

The conclusion reached is that medium-sized exporting firms in the industries studied here sell to far fewer export markets than has been claimed by those concerned with developing a case for key market concentration. This contrast is explained partly by the bias in earlier surveys towards larger firms with higher export contributions to total sales, and the finding here thus undermines the basic premise of the key market concentration thesis and dilutes its power as a panacea for UK export ills.

Table III. Export Market Numbers

Number of Export Markets	This Survey %	Barclays Bank Report* %	BETRO Report **	%
Less than 50 markets	82	34	Less than 60 markets	60
51 to 100 markets	15	26	61-100 markets	16
More than 100 markets	3	40	More than 100 markets	24
	(N = 250)	(N = 120)		(N = 122)

* ITI Research, *Barclays Bank Report on Export Development in France, Germany and the United Kingdom: Factors for International Success,* London, Barclays Bank International Ltd, 1979.

** BETRO Trust Committee, *Concentration on Key Markets,* (2nd ed), London, Royal Society of Arts, 1976.

Concentration and Limitation

Further to the last point this survey found that while the majority of the exporters deal with as many markets as they can, and thus do not limit market numbers, on the other hand almost two-thirds of those selling to more than twenty markets concentrate *efforts and attention* on a relatively small number. The major implication is that the number of export country markets is at least partly invalid as a criterion for assessing export strategy, since it ignores differentiation in efforts between markets, that falls short of actually not dealing with a particular market.

Once this premise has been established, it is then possible to combine the concepts of limitation and selectivity to distinguish between those firms pursuing an export strategy of market concentration (i.e. limiting the type or degree of managerial effort as well as simply limiting market numbers) and those pursuing an alternative, which has been earlier called *market spreading* [19].

Using this approach, in the survey, slightly more than half the exporters pursued some degree of market concentration, whether or not this is obvious in crude market numbers, leaving a smaller but substantial group of market spreaders. The conclusion advanced is that market concentration may not be as rare as some commentators have claimed, if it is once accepted that simply counting country market numbers is inadequate in providing a criterion.

Given the existence of substantial groups of exporters following the alternative strategies, there is some interest in the practical implications of the strategic alternatives for export policies and behaviour.

The differences between market concentrators and market spreaders are summarised in Table IV, and begin to show a pattern of quite distinct approaches to exporting, associated with different company characteristics and export objectives, and thus export marketing actions. The implication drawn from this is that if the policy mixes relevant to concentration and spreading differ in the ways demonstrated, then a further and serious doubt is cast on the general, prescriptive theories which are offered to management as guidelines for action.

Table IV. Export Strategy: Marketing Policy Differences

Export Marketing Policies	Market Concentrators	Market Spreaders
Export Objectives	Profit	Volume
Company internationalisation	Active	Reactive
Market information	More primary research	Less primary research
Export price discrimination	More discrimination	Less discrimination
Export pricing methods	Market-based	Cost-based
Export price rank	Low	High
Export pricing currency	More foreign currency invoicing	Less foreign currency invoicing

Reasons for Large Market Numbers

Respondents were asked in this survey to explain their reasons for exporting to large numbers of country markets (that is, more than 20), since no investigation of the managerial aims in market spreading had been included in the earlier empirical work by others. The summary in Table V shows that four major themes emerged, together with a number of more minor points.

Table V. Reasons for Large Export Market Numbers

Reasons for large export market numbers	% of firms
Concentration plus other markets	29
Product specialisation	22
Sales volume maximisation	20
Risk reduction	13
Small markets are future potential	6
Small market shares are gained at low cost	3
Lack of management control	1
Other reasons	6
	(N = 110)

Nearly one-third of the respondents argued that, in spite of exporting to large numbers of markets, they concentrated on a small number within this total; or, in other words, it was argued that concentration and large market numbers were not mutually exclusive in practical terms. This category included cases where a lower level of marketing effort was used in dealing with minor markets, but also those where demand was stimulated by a company's reputation and word-of-mouth recommendation, leading to unsolicited orders. Using the definition of terms adopted and developed in this paper, these firms may be seen mainly as those "hidden" market concentrators, who *are* concentrators in real terms, in spite of having large market numbers. It is primarily the other response groups which provide a rationale or situational logic for market spreading, as a strategic alternative to market concentration.

In this area, the first element was the argument that product specialisation led to large market numbers, particularly in the sense that specialised products tend to have a large number of small geographical markets throughout the world. To this may be added the point that for the firm with a broad product-mix, there may easily be large market numbers for the firm, but not for any particular product. The underlying logic here was that the product-market is often more fundamental than the country-market in managing exports, particularly with specialised and technical products. In more technical terms, it may be that clusters of similar country-markets make more valid and approachable targets, than do separate country-markets. For example, this is arguably the case for the European market for medical products, where there is relatively little differentiation between the demand characteristics in the separate European countries, but the European market is quite different in demand terms for the USA or Japanese markets. This view is developed in the literature of international market segmentation [20,21,22,23].

The next group of responses put forward the argument that exporters found large market numbers necessary to gain adequate or maximum volume. To some degree this may reflect the product specialisation issue discussed above, but more noticeably it results from the impact of international competition.

The restriction on real export potential facing the individual firm, on which the above argument rests, may arise in many ways. For example, if it is true that overseas competitors have grown by taking major shares of key markets, then in some cases this may leave only small shares of the same markets for others; if it is true that UK exporters tend to compete on price more than international rivals who rely on non-price competition, then it may be necessary to attack the price sensitive segments of a number of export markets to gain volume; if it is true that exporters have little or no market information, then they may not be in a position to make rational choices between markets; and if it is true that foreign buyers have poor opinions and negative attitudes towards British products through national stereotyping, then the *available* market in each country may be small.

The last of the major groups of responses was concerned with the fact that larger market numbers represented a greater degree of security, and thereby a strategy of risk spreading. This case was based on the instability of export markets, for example in the developing countries and the eastern bloc, and the consequent problems of forecasting. This view amounts to a statement of simple risk avoidance or satisficing, and should be assessed in the light of the lack of marketing information in exporting, which is considered shortly. Smaller numbers of managers explained large market numbers in other ways: the need to cultivate presently small markets for their future growth; the benefits of gaining low-cost exports through a low market share strategy; a lack of management control; and various kinds of policy constraints, such as the obligation to supply medical products to any market requiring them.

It is concluded that the major managerial consideration in explaining large market numbers is volume, either in taking all available business as a supplement to key markets, or in maximising or satisficing sales through large market numbers. Closely related to this first point, is the issue of product specialisation, with the implication of competing in a world market, possibly composed of a large number of separate national markets. Smaller numbers of firms emphasised risk reduction and risk aversion as the attraction of large export market numbers, and the issues of low-cost business and future potential.

In the present context these conclusions are put forward as an empirical foundation for a logic of market spreading, as an alternative to the widely recognised strategy of market concentration, and as a rejection of the country-market criterion as a method of assessing export strategy.

Export Marketing Information

The availability of information is commonly assumed in many theoretical management approaches. For example, the real rationality of key market concentration is directly dependent on the availability of adequate information to make the optimum choice of target markets. By implication, in the absence of adequate information, it may be more rational to avoid concentration and to spread risks by dealing with as many markets as are available. Similarly, the common advice to exporters to adopt market-pricing policies is dependent on the availability of information about the market.

In this survey it was found that the vast majority of the firms claimed that they used intelligence data (mainly salesman and agent reports), three-quarters used secondary sources (Government statistics, trade association reports and the like), and some 45 per cent claimed that they used marketing research (although this must be taken as reflecting a very general, non-technical definition of marketing research). While this picture is much as expected, two implications are important. First, for most exporters export marketing information comes largely from qualitative, subjective intelligence sources which are probably restricted to existing markets (where the salesmen and agents providing the data are operating). Secondly, the existence of substantial minorities of firms never using secondary or primary marketing information sources in exporting casts doubts on the general availability of an adequate information base for making export decisions.

The conclusion reached is that there are large differences between firms in their information searching, and that the objectivity of the major source of information may be suspect. Looking back to the market strategy issue discussed above, and forward to the consideration of export pricing which follows later, there are clearly dangers in making assumptions about the widespread availability of marketing information in exporting.

Export Competition
Forms of Competition in Export Marketing
The relative importance of the elements of the marketing mix in gaining and holding export market shares remains a controversial issue. On one hand, it is usually accepted that non-price factors are potent weapons in competing in the home market, while on the other hand it is frequently assumed and asserted that price is the most crucial factor in exporting.

Contemporary analysts argue that price competition is generally an undesirable base for export competition, on the grounds that it leads to the depression of profits [24], that non-price competition is more potent [25,26], and that undue reliance on price competition leads to a "bargain-basement" attitude among buyers [27,28,29,30] with all the marketing dangers inherent in this attitude. On the other hand, many have claimed that price is of central importance in exporting, and that there is no reason for assuming that the competitive base should necessarily be the same in exporting and the home market, since the marketing conditions are so different. It should be recognised that at least part of the emphasis thus placed on price by exporting firms reflects the greater complexity and uncertainty of international pricing [31,32,33].

As a starting point in assessing the competitive base for the exporters in the survey, respondents were asked to rate the importance in export and UK marketing of the various elements of the marketing mix, for their particular companies. The results are shown in Table VI. It can be seen that, predictably, overall product quality was perceived as the most important marketing factor. However, it is of greater significance in this present context, that among the marketing variables price was rated far higher than other instruments like advertising, personal selling and distribution. This was the case for both UK and export marketing. Within this pattern, it can be seen that significantly more firms perceived price as the most important factor in exporting, compared to sales in the UK. Broadly, these findings are compatible with other export studies [34] and more general conclusions on the role of price in competition [35,36].

However, the rating of price may be used further in this present study. The approach used is to take the firm's rating of price as a weapon in exporting as a crude indicator of whether the firm is competing primarily on price or non-price factors in exporting. It was found, at a significant level, that firms placing a high weight on price in exporting, tended to discriminate on price more frequently, to use market rather than cost based pricing methods, and there was some support for the claims that price oriented firms tended to invoice more frequently in customers' currencies and to be those pursuing market spreading rather than concentration. Thus, a pattern emerges of active and passive stances on pricing for exports, which helps to provide a basis for explaining the reasons for the very different pricing policies adopted and the contrast between the prescriptive theories and actual exporter behaviour. No normative judgement is offered as to the relative attractions of price and non-price competition, but the findings noted above suggest the importance of taking a realistic view of the significance of price in exporting from the manager's point of view. In particularly, the interest here is not in the usual question — how can the exporter start to compete on non-price factors? — but rather in the issue — if our stance, for the time being, is to compete on price in exporting, how should export price be managed and are all aspects of export price policy consistent?

Table VI. Ranking of Marketing Mix Elements in UK and Export Marketing

| Ranking | Marketing Mix Elements | | | | | | |
	Product Quality %	Product Design %	Price %	Personal Selling %	Advertising %	Distribution %	Others %
In UK Marketing							
1st	50	25	24	5	1	2	11
2nd	29	28	27	14	0	7	29
3rd or lower	21	47	49	81	99	91	60
	(N = 212)	(N = 187)	(N = 191)	(N = 193)	(N = 165)	(N = 170)	(N = 35)
In Export Marketing							
1st	48	19	30	6	1	2	13
2nd	27	27	27	11	1	10	24
3rd or lower	25	54	43	83	98	88	63
	(N = 228)	(N = 203)	(N = 226)	(N = 203)	(N = 174)	(N = 190)	(N = 37)

Export Price Discrimination

The discriminatory use of price in exporting was assessed crudely by differences between ex-works prices for the UK and export markets, and between ex-works prices for different export markets.

Various opinions suggest that export prices will be the same as UK prices, because of the impact of world prices, and the difficulty of sustaining price discrimination between markets because of arbitrage between markets [37,38,39]. However, the alternative view is that product differentiation increases the scope for price discrimination, since comparability and substitutability are less easy, and that this is particularly so in the absence of perfect market information among buyers [40].

While the survey found that the majority of exporters based their prices for exports on UK ex-works prices, it was more significant that the vast majority charged different prices in export compared to the UK, and charged different prices in different export markets. These findings cast doubts on the accuracy of the view that exporters have to accept world prices, since the finding is of active use of pricing for the most part.

In general terms, active price discrimination was particularly associated with active internationalisation, market concentration strategies, a high emphasis of price competition, and a greater availability of marketing information, thus contributing further to the emerging picture of exporter differentiation in strategy and policy.

Export Pricing Methods

Many views on export pricing methods follow the more general economic debate by emphasising the demand determination of prices. Others, however, have stressed managerial discretion in pricing.

The implication of this second viewpoint is that in many product and market situations, exporters tend to rely on cost-plus pricing [41,42,43]. Naturally, this practice has attracted widespread criticism in exporting as in the home market, particularly on the grounds that it ignores the existence of demand differences between markets, and relies on cost concepts of dubious validity [44,45,46]. Theorists tend to prescribe marginal approaches to export pricing:

> "By adopting this approach the competitiveness of British industry in export markets would be increased. Our competitors have been applying it to the pricing of their exports for many years in a more widespread fashion than ours and this has helped enormously in their ability to outsell us" [47].

However, bearing in mind the limited role of exporting in many firms, the large market numbers competing, and the common lack of information, perhaps it is well to bear in mind Dean's justification of cost-plus pricing as the last resort in conditions of market ignorance [48].

The survey finding was that the largest group of exporters used cost-plus pricing methods (including target and direct cost methods), accounting for 51 per cent of the total, but that this was almost equalled in size by the group of companies pricing primarily to market, customer and competitive requirements. The majority of firms saw no difference between pricing exports and goods for the UK market, although there was some limited evidence that export pricing was less often dominated by cost-plus than was UK pricing. Returning to the main theme pursued by the study, there appeared to be some consistent differences between firms pursuing cost-based pricing (cost-plus formulas, target rate of return and direct cost methods) and those adopting market based methods (pricing to market, customer, or competitive conditions). These patterns are summarised in Table VII. These differences are largely compatible with those already identified, and with the suggestion that different stages in internationalisation and alternative strategies are associated with different operational policies.

Export Invoice Currency Strategy
One of the additional complexities of export pricing, which is of considerable contemporary interest, is the choice of pricing and invoice currency. It is often assumed that little that is new remains to be said on this issue, but the vast gap betweeen theorists' offerings and practical action, and the sheer importance of this question in practical terms justifies renewed attention, particularly using the situational viewpoint adopted in this study.

The currency decision may be structured into the choice between pricing, quoting, and invoicing in sterling, as the exporter's own currency, the customer's currency, or in some third party currency, and a review of the arguments and evidence has been provided elsewhere [49].

Table VII. Export Pricing Methods

	Cost Based Export Pricing Methods	Market Based Export Pricing Methods
Company internationalisation	Reactive	Active
Export price emphasis	Low	High
Export Strategy	Market spreading	Market concentration
Export Objectives	Profit	Volume

Currency Choices
In spite of the many recommendations by export theorists to the contrary, the evidence suggests that exporters prefer to invoice in their own currencies [50,51,52,53].

Department of Trade data suggest that some 75 per cent (by value) of UK exports were invoiced in sterling in the most recent measurement, with the rest being 11 per cent in importers' currencies, 13 per cent in US dollars and one per cent in other currencies. In the entire period of the surveys, the proportion of exports invoiced in sterling has not fallen below 69 per cent [54].

In the survey reported here, a distinction was made between single currency exporters, who made up two thirds of the sample, and multiple-currency exporters. In both groups, almost all firms invoiced in sterling, so no differences emerged between firms in this respect. However, the firms invoicing in some local currencies differed in certain ways from those invoicing only in sterling. Local currency invoicing seemed to be associated more with active than reactive exporters, and more with firms pursuing a market concentration strategy than with those following market spreading. It also seemed that local currency invoicing was commoner among firms with more marketing information and those placing a low emphasis on price competition. In general terms, this fits the thesis developing, that strategy differences have some power in explaining otherwise unreasonable export policies. The existence of a pattern of this kind, and the divergence between the "accepted wisdom" and current practice, leads to some interest in the reasons for sterling invoicing perceived as important by managers, which other studies appear to have overlooked, in their enthusiasm for the financial gains to be made from local currency invoicing.

Reasons for Sterling Invoicing

While accepting that own currency preferences may be part of a more general international pattern, this offers little assistance in solving a paradox: that at different times own currency invoicing may be advantageous or disadvantageous for exporters in a particular country selling to a particular importer. For example, for much of the 1970s, West German exporters gained advantage from invoicing in Deutschmarks (since in most deals the Deutschmark was the stronger of the exporter's and importer's currencies), but on the face of it UK exporters were giving away possible gains by their sterling invoicing preferences (since sterling was weak against most trading partners at this time). Thus, in the one case own currency preferences among exporters made sense, while in the other case they apparently did not.

Table VIII. Reasons for Sterling Invoicing

Reasons for Sterling Invoicing	%
Risk avoidance	41
Administrative ease and economy	37
Customer pressure	22
Tradition	10
Company preference	7
Sterling strategy	5
Local currencies not possible	4
Agent pressure	3
Other reasons	2
	(N = 217)

In the survey, executives were asked to explain their reasons for invoicing in sterling. The answers are summarised in Table VIII and discussed briefly below, since these data cast a new light on this aspect of export behaviour.

It was concluded that the dominance of sterling invoicing was mainly the result of exporters' wishes to avoid the risks they perceive in local currency dealing, and to maintain stability in sterling income and prices. Closely related to this, there was an apparent desire to retain the administrative simplicity of single currency dealing.

After these major issues, which are essentially internal company factors and to some extent controllable, attention must be directed to a number of market factors, which are less controllable from the exporter viewpoint. The market factors leading to sterling invoicing include active pressure from customers and distributors for sterling prices and invoices, the custom and tradition of some markets and a number of more minor factors like the practical barriers to local currency dealing in some areas and the active pursuit of a strategy of exploiting currency floating.

Reactions to Currency Floating
The classical model of devaluation (which is commonly applied to the similar but faster changing downward currency float) shows an improvement in the price competitiveness of exports, leading to increased sales and market shares, although possibly eventually offset by more expensive imports. Naturally, this view makes assumptions about such factors as: the price-elasticity of demand; the availability of capacity for increased export sales; the currency in which the goods are invoiced; the co-operation of the channel of distribution in allowing customers to benefit from devaluation; and the willingness of exporters to allow prices to fall.

The alternative is that prices may be maintained at the pre-devaluation level, leading to an improvement in exporter income and profitability, perhaps ultimately producing improvements in non-price competitiveness [55].

In the survey reported here, respondents were asked to describe their usual reactions to sterling movements in the short-term. While the findings were restricted to short-term adjustments, it was seen quite clearly that the major effect was price *stability* from the *exporter's* viewpoint. For sterling invoicing, this price rigidity has the effect that real importer costs in the local currency fall in a downward sterling float and rise in an upward sterling float, in just the way that the traditional economic model predicts. However, in both types of floating a small, but important minority, did adjust sterling prices to offset the currency movement. In the local currency case, price rigidity was also the dominant feature but, of course, in this situation the rigidity leads to the exporter's income fluctuating with floating currencies (at least in sterling terms). With local currency invoicing, slightly larger minorities adjusted prices to offset the floating effect.

Two conclusions are reached. First, it is clear that in most cases the short-term impact of floating is on importer prices for sterling invoicers and on exporter income for local currency invoicers, as shown on the next page.

However, second, there are substantial minorities of firms acting to avoid the impact of floating, for whom the traditional model does not hold.

	£ Floats Down	£ Floats Up
£ Invoicers	£ price constant (88%) = local currency price is reduced	£ price constant (91%) = local currency price is increased
Local Currency Invoicers	Local currency price held constant (74%) = £ income is increased	Local currency price held constant (74%) = £ income is reduced

Conclusions

It is in the nature of a wide-ranging and exploratory study of this kind that the conclusions reached will be tentative in some places and perhaps speculative in others. This is defended on the ground that there is an urgent need to re-examine the basic issues in export strategy and competition, which appear in many ways to be in danger of remaining in a quicksand of unsubstantiated dogma, semi-valid empiricism, entrenched academic opinion and "accepted wisdom". It is characteristic of the field that a great deal of the written material:

> "has simply been neither empirical nor conceptual. Rather it has tended to be descriptive, anecdotal and sometimes problem-solving in nature . . . it must be remembered that international marketing has only recently outgrown its 'foreign trade' and 'how to export' orientation." [60]

The intention is that by adopting an unconventional (or perhaps rather anti-conventional), and in some cases controversial stance, this study will contribute to a reappraisal of exporting at the company level, and in the academic contribution to export development and training.

The theme introduced at the beginning of the paper and pursued through it, is situational, and challenges the adequacy of the received theories of export marketing and management in the face of the real problems facing companies and the constraints characteristic of the practical setting. The conclusions reached and their implications are outlined below.

Company Internationalisation and Export Objectives

Firstly, it was found empirically that the concept of internationalisation (developed from the extant literature), allowed firms to be divided into active and reactive exporters. It was found that there were significant differences between the exporters in the two groups, in their characteristics and the export policies they adopted.

Perhaps the most important implication of this finding is the futility of viewing exporting firms as an homogeneous entity, since there are measurable differences in export stance and hence methods used. This suggests that the development of useful approaches to export theory can be built only on a foundation that accepts differentiation in the use made by companies of exporting.

Closely related to internationalisation, is the question of objectives in exporting. It was found that profit objectives, primarily of a satisficing type, were given the major emphasis in domestic and UK marketing. While volume objectives were associated more with exporting, the majority of firms pursued the same major objective in the UK and export markets. This casts much doubt on the usefulness of the classical model of domestic business to earn profit and exports to gain volume. In turn, this places under suspicion the general acceptability of the "marginal selling" approaches to exporting, which have often been advocated.

Export Market Strategy
Secondly, there is the central topic of export market strategy. It was found that, for this sample of medium-sized manufacturers, the accusation of spreading efforts over "hundreds of markets" was a gross exaggeration, and that the firms dealt with relatively few markets, at least compared to the criticisms levelled by the advocates of key market concentration. It was concluded that the use of country-market numbers was, at least partly, invalid as a criterion for judging export strategy, performance and control. While the majority of the firms did not limit market numbers, of those selling to large numbers, most concentrated attention and efforts on a small number. It was clear that there were significant differences between market concentrators and market spreaders in company characteristics and export policies.

The most important implication of this finding is the empirical justification of an alternative to the key market concentration strategy, in the form of market spreading. The alternative strategies are associated with different types of exporters and different sets of export policies. It is intended that this addition should facilitate a move from the single-minded recommendation and advocacy of market concentration towards a situational analysis to allow choice between alternatives. As well as identifying the market spreading strategy as a coherent alternative to market concentration with its associated policy set, a rationale was sought for market spreading, based on the perceptions of export managers. A large group of managers pointed out the dual existence of concentration of efforts and large market numbers. These were market concentrators under the definiton developed here.

Further, a group of arguments emerged as a logic for market spreading. The elements of this were: *market factors,* including the existence of specialised product markets, and the cultivation of small markets for the future; *volume factors,* including the practical need to deal with many markets to gain adequate sales volume; *company factors,* including the aim of safety and stability, and the difficulties of control; and *marketing factors,* including the low incremental costs of dealing with additional markets in some cases, and the cheapness of gaining low market shares.

While it may be possible to dispute the general applicability of some of these factors, enough empirical support is thus provided to challenge, and in some cases defeat, the claims of market concentration to be uniquely applicable to all export situations.

Export Marketing Information
Thirdly, and related to the lack of realism of key market concentration, is the ques-

tion of the availability and quality of the information for export managers in the practical setting. Doubts were cast on the quality and objectivity of the main information sources used by exporters, and some generalisations were made about the exporter characteristics and policies associated with the low use and availability of marketing information. The most important implication is that much of the prescriptive theory in exporting falls down because it implicitly assumes the availability of marketing information, and it appears that this assumption is invalid.

Export Competition
The relative power of price and non-price forms of international competition has been debated at great length. In the survey reported here, it was found that exporters rated product quality highest as a competitive weapon, but among the marketing variables price was dominant, pushing advertising, personal selling, distribution and the like to peripheral importance. It was also found that price was rated higher in export than domestic marketing.

These data were used to distinguish between firms emphasising price and those stressing non-price aspects of export competition, and to provide a foundation for examining more detailed aspects of export pricing.

In this instance the suggestion is that, rather than simply dismissing price competition in exporting as sub-optimal and undesirable, we should accept that for some types of exporter it is the dominant form of competition, and the one which requires management in the short-term. It may be that we wish in the longer term to develop guidelines and theories to facilitate the transition from price to non-price strategies of competitiveness, but in this present context attention is directed towards the pressing management problems in export pricing.

Export Price Discrimination
It was found that the majority of companies in the survey based their export prices on the UK price list, but that the vast majority charged different prices in export compared to the UK, and in different export markets. There were found to be differences between firms actively differentiating markets on price, and those not doing so, in support of the recurring theme discussed earlier.

Export Pricing Method
The survey found that exporters were divided almost equally between those using cost-based pricing methods and those using market-centred methods. Cost-based pricing was less common in export marketing than the UK, but in most companies the same approaches were used for export pricing. Returning to the theme of the paper: the alternative pricing approaches were associated with different patterns of export behaviour in a more general way; for example, cost-based pricing was associated with reactive exporting, the pursuit of market spreading, profit objectives and a low emphasis on price competition in exporting.

Export Invoice Currency
Virtually all firms in the survey invoiced exports in sterling to a greater or lesser extent, and the majority invoiced only in sterling. Among the minority of firms invoic-

ing in foreign currencies, it was found that this practice was associated with active exporting and market concentration strategies.

Because of the widespread advocacy of foreign currency invoicing in the literature, some attention was directed towards assessing the reasons for the dominance of sterling invoicing in UK exporting, particularly since the survey was completed at the end of a long period of relatively weak sterling. The measurements are essentially the perceptions of involved practitioners, rather than the assumptions usually offered by theorists. It was found that the choice of sterling as invoice currency was mainly determined by management's wishes to avoid the risks perceived in local currency dealing, and to maintain a stable sterling income and prices, together with the administrative simplicity and convenience of single-currency exporting. After these *internal company factors,* a number of *market factors* were significant. These included active pressure from customers, the custom and tradition of some markets, and the influence of the members of the channel of distribution. Lastly, there were a number of more minor factors varying from companies dealing with markets where local currencies could not be used, to a very small number of firms pursuing a mixed-currency strategy for financial gains.

The implications of these findings is that there are several groups of situational factors significantly influencing export currency choice, which are often overlooked by the existing, mainly prescriptive, literature. It seems that any serious, practical approach to this problem should include situational contraints of the type discussed above.

Price Reactions to Floating Currency Movements
In the majority of cases it was found that the impact of floating sterling in the short term is on importer prices for sterling invoicers and on exporter sterling income for local currency invoicers, as in the classical model. This effect is achieved through price rigidity among exporters in the main. This suggests the existence of a major inconsistency: that those placing the greatest emphasis on export prices are frequently those who price in sterling and thus allow floating to have its impact on importer prices. For firms where the competitive base in exporting is price, there is a clear need to review this particular aspect of policy and to integrate it with the other aspects of export pricing already discussed.

In all, it can be seen that a number of challenges are posed to the "accepted wisdom" of exporting, which provide a platform for reviewing export strategy and the policy mixes asociated with different strategies, and reappraising the usefulness of the established export theories.

Appendix I. Survey Methodology
Data Collection
The main data collection instrument was a postal questionnaire sent to 519 firms, with a reminder to non-respondents after six weeks. The questionnaire had been developed through six depth interviews with export managers and a pilot postal sample of 50 companies.

Response Rate
At the 10 week cut-off point, 250 useable responses had been received giving an effective response rate of 48 per cent.

Timing

The depth interviews were completed in September 1979, the pilot survey in October and the main postal survey in December 1979 and January 1980.

Sample Design

Universe Definition — The universe was defined as all firms meeting the following criteria:

Medium-sized = 100 — 2,000 employees at the operating unit concerned.

Exporting = selling goods to independent overseas buyers.

Manufacturers = producing goods in the UK

Northern = the operating unit concerned being located in an area defined by a combination of the Registrar-General's Standard Regions: Northern, Yorkshire and Humberside and North West.

Selected Industries = the unit being part of one of the industries defined in the Kompass 1979 directory as Clothing and Footwear, Furniture and Fittings, Chemicals and Chemical Products and Scientific and Industrial Instrumentation.

This universe consisted of some 519 companies.

(2) *Respondent Selection* — All identified respondents were contacted.

(3) *Sampling Units* — Senior marketing, export, sales or general managers.

References

1. Tookey, D. A., "International Business and Political Geography", *British Journal of Marketing,* Autumn 1969, pp. 136-51.

2. Piercy, N., "Company Internationalisation: Active and Reactive Exporting", *European Journal of Marketing,* Vol. 15 No. 3, 1981, pp. 26-40.

3. Tookey, D. A., "International Business and Political Geography", *British Journal of Marketing,* 3, 1969, pp. 136-51.

4. Hunt, H. G., Froggatt, J. D. and Hovell, P. J., "The Management of Export Marketing in Engineering Industries", *British Journal of Marketing,* 1, 1967, pp. 10-24.

5. Cooper, R. A., Hartley, K., and Harvey, C. R. H., *Export Performance and the Pressure of Demand,* London, Allen and Unwin, 1970.

6. Tookey, D. A., "Factors Associated with Success in Exporting", *Journal of Management Studies,* 1, March 1964, pp. 48-66.

7. Barnhart, J. R., *Export Profitability: An Analysis Among Indiana Firms,* Indiana University, PhD thesis, 1968.

8. Sinai, C. C., *An Investigation of Selected Characteristics of Export-Participating Manufacturing Firms,* University of Washington. DBA Dissertation, 1970.

9. PEP, *Attitudes in British Management,* London, Penguin, 1966.

10. Bilkey, W. J., "An Attempted Integration of the Literature on the Export Behaviour of Firms", *Journal of International Business Studies,* Vol. 9 No. 1, 1978, pp. 33-46.

11. Simpson, C. L., *The Export Decision: An Interview Study of the Decision Process in Tennessee Manufacturing Firms,* Georgia State University, PhD Thesis, 1973.

12. ITI Research, *Barclays Bank Report on Export Development in France, Germany and the United Kingdom: Factors for International Success,* London, Barclays Bank International Ltd, 1979.

13. Silberston, A., "Price Behaviour of Firms", *The Economic Journal,* Vol. 80 No. 319, 1970, pp. 511-82.

14. Sharman, G. H., *Thinking Managerially About Exports,* London, Institute of Export, 1971.

15. Piercy, N., "Export Strategy: Key Markets vs. Market Spending", *Journal of International Marketing,* Vol. 1 No. 1, 1981, pp. 56-67.

16. ITI Research, *Barclays Bank Report on Export Development in France, Germany and the United Kingdom: Factors for International Success,* London, Barclays Bank International Ltd, 1979 .

17. BETRO Trust Committee, *Concentration on Key Markets,* (2nd ed), London, Royal Society of Arts, 1976.

18. Industrial Market Research, *How British Industry Exports,* London, Industrial Market Research Ltd, 1978.

19. Piercy, N., op cit.

20. Boyd, H. W., "Market Opportunities Across National Boundaries", in Ferber, R. (Ed), *Handbook of Marketing Research,* New York, McGraw-Hill, 1974.

21. Jaffe, E. D., *Grouping: A Strategy for International Marketing,* New York, AMACOM, 1974.

22. Sethi, S. P., "Comparative Cluster Analysis for World Markets", *Journal of Marketing Research,* Vol. 8, August 1971, pp. 348-54.

23. Frank, R., Massy, W. F. and Wind, Y., *Market Segmentation,* Englewood Cliffs, NJ, Prentice-Hall, 1972.

24. Tessler, A., "Alternative Strategies and the Key Market Principle", in *Successful Export Strategy,* London, Graham and Trotman, 1977.

25. National Economic Development Office, *International Price Competitiveness Non-Price Factors and Export Performance,* London, NEDO , 1977.

26. ITI Research, *Barclays Bank Report on Export Development in France, Germany and the United Kingdom: Factors in International Success,* London, Barclays Bank International Ltd, 1979.

27. Christopher, M., *Marketing Below-the-Line,* London, Allen and Unwin, 1972.

28. Livesey, F. *Pricing,* London, Macmillan, 1976.

29. Thorncroft, A., "Pricing Stays in the Dark Ages", *Financial Times* 18 January 1973.

30. Hinkle, C., "The Strategy of Price Deals", in Taylor, B. and Wills, G. (Eds), *Pricing Strategy,* London, Staples, 1969.

31. McAlley, M. I. "Pricing in the International Market", in Moyer, R. (Ed), *Changing Marketing Systems: Consumer, Corporate and Government Interfaces,* Washington, DC, American Marketing Association, 1967.

32. Seakwood, H. J., "Pricing Considerations in the International Markets", in *Pricing: The Critical Decision,* New York, American Management Association, 1961.

33. Business International, *Solving International Pricing Problems,* New York, Business International, 1965.

34. Industrial Market Research, *How British Industry Exports,* London, Industrial Market Research Ltd, 1978.

35. Udell, J. G., "The Role of Price in Competitive Strategy" in Taylor, B. and Wills, G. (Eds), *Pricing Strategy,* London, Staples, 1969.

36. Pass, C., "Pricing Policies and Market Strategy: An Empirical Note", *European Journal of Marketing,* Vol. 5 No. 3, 1971, pp. 94-98.

37. Isard, P., "How Far Can We Push the Law of the Price?", *American Economic Review,* 67, 1977, pp. 942-48.

38. Amano, A., *Export Price Behaviour in Selected Industrial Countries,* Washington, DC, Project Link Conference, 1974.

39. Brown, R. N., *Export Competitiveness and Profitability,* Bank of England, unpublished paper, 24 February 1977.

40. National Economic Development Office, *International Price Competitiveness, Non-Price Factors and Export Performance,* London, NEDO, 1977.

41. Muir, A. W. E., "Pricing Policies in Export Markets", in *Successful Export Strategy,* London, Graham and Trotman, 1977.

42. Hovell, P. J., "Export Pricing Policies", *District Bank Review,* September 1967/68, pp. 34-55.

43. Hunt, H. G., "Export Management in Medium-Sized Engineering Firms", *Journal of Manage-*

ment Studies, Vol 6 No. 1, 1969, pp. 33-44.

44. Kahler, R. and Kramer, R. L., *International Marketing* (4th ed), Cincinatti, Ohio, South Western Publishing, 1977.

45. Business International, *Solving International Pricing Problems*, New York, Business International, 1965.

46. Root, F. R., "Planning Export Pricing Strategy", in Thomas, M. J. (Ed), *International Marketing Management: Readings in Systems and Methods,* Boston, Houghton Mifflin, 1969.

47. Davies, J. R., "Determining the 'Plus' in Cost-Plus Pricing", *Management Accounting,* Vol. 56 No. 5, 1978, pp. 198-200.

48. Dean, J., *Managerial Economics,* Englewood Cliffs, NJ, Prentice-Hall, 1951.

49. Piercy, N., "The Invoice Currency Decisions of UK Exporters", *Management Decision,* (forthcoming).

50. Reid, M., "Exports Priced in Foreign Currencies", *Financial Times,* 18 June 1976.

51. Lethbridge, D. G. and Tylee, I. G., "Pricing in an Era of Shifting Exchange Rates — Removing the Risks", *Management Decision,* Vol. 12 No. 4, 1974, pp. 201-40.

52. Paulden, S., "Foreign Currency Invoicing", *Export Direction,* Vol. 8 No. 7, 1977, (supplement).

53. Wood, G. E. and Carse, S., "Financing Practices in British Foreign Trade", *The Banker,* September 1976, pp. 1025-27.

54. Trade and Industry, "UK Exports Invoiced in Foreign Currencies", *British Business,* 7 March 1980.

55. National Economic Development Office, *International Price Competitiveness, Non-Price Factors and Export Performance,* London, NEDO, 1977.

56. Ryans, J. K. and Woudenberg, H. W., "Marketing's Role in International Business Theory Development", *Foreign Trade Review,* Vol. 12 No. 2, 1977, pp. 208-17.